HOT SUMMER JAMS

POP SONGS THAT BRING OUT THE SUN
1975 THROUGH 2005

JAMES ARENA

ISBN: 978-1-66782-992-0

Dedicated to my wonderful parents, who first introduced me to the beach. To the artists who filled my summers with great pop music. And to Mother Earth, who has given us so many beautiful summery days and places to visit, though I fear her patience with us is wearing thin.

Acknowledgements

Very special thanks to Nick Bunning for his invaluable assistance and to Taco Ockerse for his very kind contributions to this project. Couldn't have made this book without support from August Darnell, Eva Tudor-Jones, Kate Markowitz, Rob Craig, Victoria Ferran, Sher Harper, Hans van Veen, Cory Robbins, Amii Stewart, Sven van Veen, Ray Caviano, Dr. Jonas Ekfeldt, Martin Boer, Warren Schatz, Delroy Rennalls, Joe Cang, Cassandra Wooten, Cheryl Mason-Dorman, Tom Hayden, Debbie Sledge, Sam Harvey, Emanuele Asti, Alf Klimek, Dr. Phil Harding, Mark Reilly, DJ Sammy, Claudja Barry, Mario Aldini, Wessel van Diepen, Roberto Zanetti, Martin Boer, Cheryl Poirier, Audrey Landers, Alfa Anderson, Katrina Leskanich, Kimberley Rew, Terri B!, Bart&Baker, Judy Cheeks, Inaya Day, D.O.N.S. Karl Goedicke, Joy Dorris, Nicki French, Lane McCray, Wardell Piper, Rozalla and Harriette Weels. Thank you to my supportive friends and family.

Alan Coulthard kindly accepted my invitation to contribute commentary for this book, despite pressing health issues. He passed suddenly in the summer of 2021, shortly after we finished our work together. I am very grateful for the opportunity to share his memories here.

Resources (Other sources as noted in text.)

Billboard - *US music industry news, reviews and genre sales/airplay charts*

Cash Box - *US music industry news, reviews and genre sales/airplay charts*

EuroTipSheet - *European music industry news, reviews and pop singles/ album charts*

Melody Maker - *UK music industry/musician news, reviews and entertainment*

Music & Media *(formerly EuroTipSheet) - European music industry/broadcasting/home entertainment news, reviews and genre sales/airplay charts*

Record Mirror - *UK newspaper for pop fans and record collectors*

Record World - *US music, jukebox industry news, reviews and genre sales/ airplay charts*

Billboard's Hot Dance/Disco, 1974-2003 by Joel Whitburn (Record Research, Inc., 2004)

Discogs

Other books by James Arena

Fright Night On Channel 9 - *a look back at vintage late night TV horror movie telecasts.*

First Ladies of Disco - *interviews with Gloria Gaynor, Evelyn "Champagne" King, Martha Wash, Linda Clifford, Carol Douglas, and more.*

Legends of Disco - *interviews with Bonnie Pointer, Sister Sledge, Randy Jones of Village People, Sarah Dash, Denis LePage of Lime, and more.*

Europe's Stars of '80s Dance Pop - *interviews with Mel Brooks, Pete Burns of Dead or Alive, Yazz, Jennifer Rush, Amii Stewart, Hazell Dean, Thomas Anders of Modern Talking, and more.*

Europe's Stars of '80s Dance Pop Vol. 2 - *interviews with Helen Scott of The Three Degrees, Sandy Marton, Ben Liebrand, Engelbert Humperdinck, Precious Wilson, Judy Cheeks, and more.*

Stars of '90s Dance Pop - *interviews with Right Said Fred, Rozalla, CeCe Peniston, Haddaway, Robin S, Lane McCray of La Bouche, and more.*

Stars of 21st Century Dance Pop & EDM - *interviews with Gryffin, Sak Noel, Paul Oakenfold, Inaya Day, Suzanne Palmer, Darude, and more.*

CONTENTS

SUMMER JOYRIDE

Personally, I can't stand temperatures less than my current age, and God knows I've had some nasty winter brushes with Seasonal Affective Disorder. So it's probably no surprise I love long hot summer days, bright sun, the beach, vacations, and getaways to exotic tropical locations. And I'm not alone. They are what a few billion of us live for, and they give us hope and optimism. They represent freedom and fun. They're opportunities to shake off cold weather and the day-to-day grind and are a chance to jump out of the hustle. We spend a lot of time waiting for the summer season and holidays that can create a likeness of it—and even more time working to afford them. But once we get a real taste of the warm sun, soft sand beaches, poolside cocktails and tropical nightlife, we want to indulge in the sensations they give us as often as possible. While it may all be just a temporary reprieve from reality, the impermanence of summer and vacation breaks ensures we will never *ever* tire of them. Likewise, it seems like nothing can keep us from pursuing this bliss, outside of a pandemic. (Even COVID-19 and its variants, at the time of this writing, have proven to be more speed bumps than roadblocks for some travelers and getaway revelers. However, the pandemic appears to be causing every destination to seriously rethink its tourism. Time will tell what comes of this.)

Outside of actually going on these warm climate adventures, there's only one creative expression that really captures and expresses the joy we feel from summer and vacations—music. We love it so much we have to sing about it and create melodies that capture the sensation. It's those summery pop jams and palm tree beats—the music that has celebrated the very essence of the season and our getaways. The sunny side of life. These songs encompass all the emotions we are hoping to feel on 85° F+ days and on our long distance jaunts. It's the hot AM, FM and satellite radio hits, the jams they played on the jukeboxes at bars and patio cafes, the tunes that cover bands couldn't wait to make their own, and the tracks that DJs would spin in the neon light of nightclubs. It's the songs that people bought in stores, heard on American beaches and "American Bandstand," at outdoor summer concerts, picnics, on the shores of the Mediterranean, and at exotic resorts in the Caribbean and around the world—the music that held a mirror up to our passion for sun, pleasure, romance and escape. It's the music that made you feel alive and so perfectly celebrated the art of getting away from it all. Music has always been the most accessible, affordable and dependable means of giving oneself a warm weather high at any time of year, wherever one happens to be—better, perhaps, than nearly any other entertainment or art form. So, basically, nothing says "summer" like a great pop tune!

In *Hot Summer Jams* you'll find a large selection of mostly very upbeat music. Some of the 500+ songs discussed, critiqued and analyzed in this (admittedly wholly biased "fan boy") collection directly reference summer themes, while others suggest tropical or exotic escape in their arrangements and mixes. Still a few more are tracks that were simply so huge in clubs and on the radio during summers past, here in the US and abroad, that they will be forever synonymous with the season and travel. (While putting this book together, I grew increasingly astounded at the variety of approaches artists, songwriters and producers took to capture the spirit of the season. I think you'll be surprised, too.) We'll take a look at pop music released between 1975 and 2005 (a broad, diverse and exciting 30 year span when summer jams were plentiful and memorable), including major American, international and regional hits, a few charming obscurities and a couple of misfires (there's always some rainy days on any vacation). Many of these jams can be heard on YouTube, Pandora, Spotify, SoundCloud, Apple Music and other digital music platforms. I have tried to approach all of these selections—well, most—with love and affection. I believe they deserve a nod because of the remarkably vivid creative visions they evoke and the skill with which their performers delivered a sense of summer and sun. But you'll also find quite a few attempts at humor in many of the critiques. I think you'll agree, it's probably best not to approach "beach music" as if the fate of the world hangs on its beats.

In truth, *Hot Summer Jams* relates to more of a *feeling* than an actual overall music "genre," but even so, you'll find a wide range of popular musical styles in these pages. Naturally, dance music dominates, as one might expect, but there's an abundance of rock, new wave, new age, Latin, flamenco, reggae, reggaeton, jazz, soul, German schlager, Italo-pop, Francophone pop, Brit-pop, easy-listening, calypso, soca, and other sounds in the mix as well. After all, most everyone wants a little variety on a vacation. Each type of music possesses a unique and extraordinary power to convey the delicious sensations of the season and its warmth, to paint pictures of exotic destinations, and to evoke the emotions we all hope to experience in our quest to find that perfect summer day—or night. Each selection is listed alphabetically by song title, followed by artist, primary year of release, key record label or distributor, and a generalized notation of the country or general region of origin or popularity (A - Austria, AU - Australia, BAR - Barbados, B - Belgium, C - Canada, D - Denmark, F - France, G - Germany, I - Italy, J - Jamaica, M - Mexico, NL - the Netherlands, SP - Spain, SW - Sweden, SWZ - Switzerland, UK - United Kingdom, US - United States). A *very* rough "tourist on the street" translation of non-English titles is provided (but please don't think for a minute I am a reliable interpreter) and a note indicating the producer of the track, where known.

Start on any page you want. There are no formalities on this vacation. No matter where you flip, there's some incredibly thoughtful and richly entertaining music discussed. And some of it is just plain fun and silly. (I'd advise you to have access to some kind of music player nearby; you're definitely gonna want one.) I hope you'll get an opportunity to hear these songs for yourself, to sit back and take them in. Or to get on your feet and move to their beats—you do you— this is *your* great escape. Just let these songs take you away from the everyday.

I wrote *Hot Summer Jams* for myself, as an avenue to express my appreciation and love for this music and to document these songs. Thanks for letting me share it with you. If you're into these sounds, I think you'll have a lot of fun with this book. (And if I missed any of your favorite tunes, my apologies.) If you don't have a connection with this music, perhaps you'll discover how wonderful it really is.

Dive deep and may life be an endless, happy and healthy summer for you. Let pop music always be your ticket to the tropics!

PS - On the November 10, 2021, installment of CBS-TV's "The Late Show" starring Stephen Colbert, the host asked guest Bruce Springsteen what song he'd select if he could only listen to one for the rest of his life. The esteemed artist responded, Sinatra's "Summer Wind." Summer, man. Even The Boss can't live without it.

HOT SUMMER PLAYLIST: THE MUSIC

A Bailar Calypso - Elli Medeiros (1987), Barclay (F)
Producers: Elli Medeiros, Ramuntcho Matta

French and Spanish people are said to get along well. If "A Bailar Calypso," a quietly fiery and atmospheric musical blending of their two cultures, is any measure, it's a match as perfect as a blue and white striped beach towel and a poolside lounge chair. Ms. Medeiros was a former member of one of

France's premier punk bands, The Stinky Toys, and here the artist merged some of that influence with jazz, reggae and calypso. The mood is playful in this simple, airy, Latin-style dance tune, accurately described by *Music & Media* on September 5, 1987, as "the ideal summer hit" (and later in 1988 as "irresistible sunny calypso"). From the Uruguayan artist's well-received *Bom Bom* album, which features France's intoxicating song man Etienne Daho on backing vocals—and every breath he takes *surely* feels like a summer breeze.

Ab In Den Süden - Buddy (Vs. DJ The Wave) (2003), WEA (G) *Off to the south*
Producers: Gary B., O-Jay

Fact: Germans make rousing beach music that goes great with a bottle of ice cold Beck's! This particular alliance between a male singer known for a sugary German language pop music style called schlager and an Austrian DJ has lots of testosterone and all the sonic hallmarks a fist-pumping, lager-swigging thumper should. The "Red Stripe Remix" by BKA gives the song a more easy-going reggae vibe. A big hit in Germany and parts of Europe in the late summer of 2003. Let the south go north to your head.

Acapulco Girls - Sol De México (with the participation of The Beach Boys) (1998), EMI Latin (M)
Producer: Not listed

In order to stay relevant and to collect another paycheck (not that there's anything wrong with that), Mike Love and The Beach Boys were known for hooking up with a number of pop artists on remakes of their venerable hits later in their careers. One might expect this curious single to be something *really* bizarre, but actually—not so much. And though this production isn't especially inventive, it's pretty cool (and a bit surreal) hearing "California Girls" sung in Spanish by a Mexican group sporting sombreros and charros. Obviously, the song's been altered a bit with a light mariachi flavor, but it's musically faithful to the original with strong lead vocals by José Hernández. I can't be sure whether or not I hear actual Beach Boys singing in the background of this, but let's assume they took a trip south of the border and are in there having fun, fun, fun.

A Day In The Sun - Rimini Project (2004), ZYX (G)
Producer: Bertelson for Panamericana Music

Brisk EDM beats, simple lyrics and whispery vocals highlight this high-speed electro summer jam that encourages us to leave the cold outside and enter a hot summer world. From the popular Austria-based group, the "Sunburn Mix" packs the most heat. Synth bliss that takes summer back.

A Lover's Holiday - Change (1980), Warner/RFC,
Atlantic/RFC (I/US)
Producer: Jacques Fred Petrus

High-priced dance music, figuratively speaking, and it's worth every penny. The American debut of Italy's Change concept came during a challenging, transitional period for disco music, but also just in time for summer. The ensemble's remarkable debut single, "A Lover's Holiday"—incredibly fluid, intricately structured, and irresistibly melodic—was a stunningly gorgeous and fitting hit for the year's warmer weather. Breaking from the scalding energy of disco's most famous four-on-the-floor successes of the late '70s, this artful track, mixed by Jim Burgess, was noticeably soulful and more modestly paced, yet irresistible both to those drawn to the dance floor and those who sought soulful, radio-friendly pop satisfaction. It was also a well-timed release, initially gaining attention in the spring (when it went to #1 on *Billboard*'s disco chart) and staying strong throughout the summer, along with its companion tracks, "Searching" and "The Glow Of Love."

Change's *The Glow Of Love* LP has been widely hailed by classic disco fans and critics alike as one of the most "artistic" albums ever delivered in the genre. On May 3, 1980, *Cash Box* approached it less loftily but with equal enthusiasm, reviewing, "Anyone who doesn't feel like getting up and shaking their booty to the opening track on this LP ["A Lover's Holiday"] is in serious need of a shot of Vitamin B12." Still, first generation disco music was more or less on the way out (in the US anyway and ever so briefly), and this collection squeaked in just under the wire. However, given the Italo disco wave was heating up Italy in Europe and a more funky sound was gaining momentum in North America, it's quite likely this inspired production would have inevitably found its way forward through any headwinds.

The project was signed and promoted in the US by Ray Caviano, whose dance label RFC, aligned with Warner at this time (Quality and Atlantic Records later in its revered lifespan), oversaw the American release of this production. We owe Mr. Caviano a great deal of thanks for giving us such an elegant and memorable holiday sound.

Commentary from Ray Caviano:

Ray, tell me about the path that led you to discover the first Change record.
"Just to put things into historical context, there was this whole journey that brought me to the point where I brought the Change record forward. Years before, I had joined [pop, disco and soul label] T.K. Records, working for [founder] Henry Stone down in Florida. I had seen this groundswell in the late '70s happening with the clubs. Records were breaking in the New York clubs and on Fire Island, etc. For example, The Hues Corporation sold 60,000 copies of the 'Rock The Boat' single before it even got on the radio. That clued me to the fact that you could break records in the clubs and then cross them over to radio. At T.K., we had K.C. & The Sunshine Band, George McCrae, The Ritchie Family, Boris Midney, Voyage—many artists and many big hits.

"Warner Bros. Records in New York was wondering how T.K. was getting all these hits. We were just a small independent company. I had been extremely successful at promoting the T.K. roster and Warner approached me about doing the same for them. They knew about my relationships with the DJs and how I knew what the dance floor wanted. I basically said, 'I'm gonna give you an offer you can't refuse. If you want me to promote all the Warner Bros. dance product and get it broken in the clubs (they had a good roster—Prince, Chaka Khan, Ashford & Simpson, etc.), then I need my own label.' They came back to me two days later and said we had a deal. So, I started RFC Records with Warner, we remixed Rod Stewart's 'Da Ya Think I'm Sexy,' and it was just hit after hit. And that's a short version of the long road that led to Change."

Would you tell me about your first meeting with Change's Italian producers?

"Knowing the success I was enjoying in the disco/dance field, the executive producer of Change in Italy named [Jacques] Fred Petrus came to me. He was the man who put all the ingredients together—a collaboration of producers, musicians, songwriters and two key creative forces in the project, Mauro Malavasi [executive producer] and Davide Romani [composer, arranger, conductor, and songwriter]. They made the instrumental tracks in Italy and came to the US with the lyrics. They started hiring vocalists, including a young man that wasn't too well known at the time, Luther Vandross. I had a team of 13 promotional people working in major markets at my label, and I hired Vince Aletti (who wrote about disco for the *Village Voice* and was the disco editor at *Record World* magazine). I thought he'd be a good addition as an A&R man to screen product. Vince told me that Fred Petrus had contacted our New York City office and would like to have a meeting. I thought the team that was working with Mr. Petrus sounded great, so we set up a meeting. We sat down, and he played the entire album, *The Glow Of Love.*

"I said to Fred, "This is an absolute smash!" Every cut had potential, the writing, production, the melodies, the singers—all these beautiful colors, these elements. He put them all together like a piece of artwork. It was a masterpiece. We struck a deal in 48 hours, literally. To be honest, not to pat myself on the back, but Fred knew of my success at T.K., and I think he wanted my, dare I say, credible reputation during the disco/dance era, and a major label that could market and promote Change. It was my team that got it going, and when Warner saw it was turning into a hit, they pushed the button and the thing exploded."

It didn't take long for the record to catch on.

"The record came out, I started promoting it that spring—it took about six to eight weeks to get a record moving through the pipeline—and by that summer it was all over New York radio. 'A Lover's Holiday' was *the* summer record. I remember at one point Frankie Crocker at WBLS in New York [a vital urban adult radio station], was playing three cuts off the album. I used a whole formula to test my records. I'd go down to the Paradise Garage club with Frankie Crocker, and we would test our records, 'A Lover's Holiday' being one of them. DJ Larry Levan would throw on my test pressing on a

Friday night and on Monday the record would be on WBLS full time. And look at that title—'A Lover's Holiday.' It almost says, 'summer.' A smooth, melodic beat—it oozed with a celebratory feel, a bright summer sound. Man, it sounded so good coming out of car radios!"

What made you think "A Lover's Holiday" would be a commercial success?

"I listened to this music at face value—as a product that had potential, just good music. Back then, the reason why I liked the album, in general, was that the beats per minute were slower than the hyper, high-energy records that were everywhere. I thought it was a good time to get a little smoother with an R&B sound and to bring the tempo down a notch. 'A Lover's Holiday' also sounded like a good roller skating record to me, which was very big back then. It was my first RFC signing, and guess what? It went gold. A beautiful thing. It almost went platinum. It was about 10,000 units shy of doing a million. It was very exciting to have my first project be so successful."

When you think of summer music, songs that have a sunny vibe, what do they generally have in common?

"We're basically talking about songs that are bright and happy and have a purely uplifting feeling to them. You want something that's going to release all the tension. You're coming out of the darkness of winter, and you want something happy, something that has an emancipating sound. I can't explain it other than to say that you're on the beach and you're listening to music—you're totally free! Pop music, palm trees, summer songs, they're the epitome of being free. You're looking for a song that makes you feel alive. It has a healing quality. It's almost an emotional thing—you made it through the cold and gray. You feel the music in a way that you usually can't at other times of the year or in places, environments, that aren't warm and inviting. It's just not the same. You can't explain that feeling you get when you hear one of these special songs on the beaches, or dancing in a club or at an outdoor venue, or driving with the top down. It's unbelievable! Hot summer jams! Oh my God!"

*[See also: **Paradise - Change, Souvenirs - Voyage.**]*

A Tribute To The Beach Boys '76 - The Sands Of Time (1976), Kirshner (US)
Producers: Tokens, Al Steckler, Ron Frangipane

"Dedicated to The Beach Boys With Love" read a printed message on the label of the 7-inch single version. It's a harmonious medley of retro beach party lyrics made by some of the members of the Tokens ("The Lion Sleeps Tonight") in the style of the legendary surf band.

Alane - Wes (1997), Epic (F)
Producers: Michel Sanchez, Todd Terry

It was the keen ear of co-producer Michel Sanchez (formerly of Deep Forest) that first recognized the potential of this track. And France was one of the first countries to really catch on to the exotic sound of Wes Madiko, whose home village was in Cameroon, located in west-central Africa. Though the pairing of the artist's African chants with a mesmerizing dance beat may have been broadly and routinely classified as "world pop music," Wes delivers a much more layered, adventurously complex track than its categorization would suggest. The song has cultural beauty and authenticity mixed with just the right amount of western mainstream sensibility. Todd Terry provided several house remixes of "Alane," but to my ear it's "Tony Moran's Club Mix" that best captures the essence of the song, accenting its naturally summery sound and pumping it full of addictive house and pop energy. The song made a powerful comeback during the summer of 2020 when Wes was invited by pop/EDM star Robin Schulz to join him for an updated version that became a major world hit.

All Night Holiday - Russ Abbot (1985), Spirit/Teldec (UK)
Producer: Ben Findon

A British drummer, back-up singer, actor, and comedian, Abbot's "All Night Holiday" was one of his most successful tongue-in-cheek pop singles. A simple nod to dancing and having fun on a summer getaway, this light-as-a-feather disco track never wanders into dippy territory, though it may admittedly sound a bit old-fashioned today. The novelty single reached the top 20 on the UK pop chart and spent a handful of weeks on the *EuroTipSheet*

European Top 100 Singles chart. The extended "Summer Party Disco Mix" keeps the festivities jumping for a little longer.

All Night Long (All Night) - Lionel Richie (1983), Motown (US)
Producers: Lionel Richie, James Anthony Carmichael

"Lionel goes Latin…as impressive as it is pleasurable," read the September 17, 1983, review in *Cash Box*. It's an all-nighter you won't regret when the sun comes up. A massively celebratory jam that brings the summer party with warm Caribic influences, Richie's colorful dance/pop classic and its energized video (which capitalized on the growing excitement of breakdancing) are quite irresistible. The track holds an esteemed position on summer playlists worldwide. Its message is simply an invitation to have fun—no more, no less—and the song's enchanting calypso flavor and familial chorus are utterly spiritous.

In the year after this song came out (along with the album which featured it, *Can't Slow Down*), Lionel Richie was widely touted as the #1 top-selling artist in the history of Motown, according to a cover story in the August 18, 1984, edition of *Cash Box*. The artist was chosen to perform the song at the televised closing of the 1984 Summer Olympic games, with an estimated viewing audience of 2.5 billion. Though the elaborate show looked a bit chaotic and unpolished by today's lavish, high-tech standards, it was a prestigious spectacle at the time and a reflection of Mr. Richie's regal standing and the song's mega-hit status. The power of a robust summer jam should never be underestimated. *Cash Box* ranked "All Night Long (All Night)" sixth among its Top 100 Singles of 1983 and gave Richie's long play their nod for the #1 album of 1984.

All On A Summer's Night - Grace Jones (1978), Island (US)
Producer: Tom Moulton

Extracted from Jones' classic disco era LP, *Fame*. With mixmaster veteran Tom Moulton handling the production (the man behind the winning sound of The Andrea True Connection's 1976 summer masterpiece, "More, More, More") and arrangements by another legend of the same period, John Davis ("Ain't That Enough For You" with the Monster Orchestra), it's no surprise this melodic disco track has a polished, breezy and uplifting feel. Summer nights were made for dancing until 6 a.m. And then you'd chill and catch up on sleep at the beach. However, those who embrace Ms. Jones' edgy and more confident sounding '80s material (think "Pull Up To The Bumper," "Nipple To The Bottle") may react to the artist's sweeter, timid-sounding vocal performance here with a...*meh.*

All Summer Long - Chris Rea (2000), EastWest (G)
Producer: Chris Rea

When a gravel-throated man croons *this* earnestly about the season, you better pack some sun protection lotion. This is solar radiation at its highest. If you're a fan of evocative summer sounds (and dare I ask, who isn't), this is possibly one of the British vocalist, songwriter and guitarist's sunniest offerings from his 1985 album, *Shamrock Diaries*. It's impossible *not* to feel like one is sailing along a tropical coast, bright sun overhead, the breeze and ocean current propelling one's soul ever forward. In fact, everything about this lightly danceable track is optimistic, an appealing quality strongly recognized in Germany, where the singer amassed an especially eager following with his beach music. The song was updated on the artist's successful *King Of The Beach* album (a 2000 follow-up of sorts to his evocative 1986 *On The Beach* LP).

Always / Can't Beat The Feeling - Coca-Cola (2002), Land (SWZ)
Producers: Andy Prinz, DJ Tatana

Soda-licious you don't even need to add rum. Two refreshing Swiss productions designed to promote the soft drink during the summer months, these tracks are invigorating house versions of the famously catchy advertising jingles. Fine vocals by Simone Bürkle, reminiscent of Janelle Monáe. Included on a marketing-based CD titled *Summer Dance Mix*, which featured five additional dance/pop tracks ripe for the season. Attention-getting, without sounding thirsty.

Always The Sun - Stranglers, The (1986), Epic (UK)
Producers: The Stranglers, Mike Kemp

The comforting message here may be that no matter what dreadful, negative shit is going on in the world, we will always have the sun. Embedded in a rhythmic synth-pop 'n' rock mix reminiscent of the Pet Shop Boys' sound, the extended "Hot Mix" (credited to the band, rather than a DJ or engineer) and the "Long Hot Sunny Side Up Mix" are the English group's prime contributions to the world of hot summer jams, having initially made an impression during the punk boom. An adventurous production and a hit in France and Ireland. *Music & Media* described The Stranglers' song as "...one of their most commercial singles [in] a long time" and "Lou Reed like" on October 18, 1986.

American Music - Pointer Sisters (1982) Planet (US)
Producer: Richard Perry

There's probably no holiday more warm weather significant in the US than the Fourth of July, and this bouncy single by the Pointer Sisters, released smack in the middle of the summer of '82, just before their high energy breakthrough "I'm So Excited" turned them into a top tier dance act, feels as patriotic as any pop song ever could. The song has a doo-wop/swing style, and its the type of track you'd instinctively turn up loud and sing along with when your favorite AM or FM pop station would play it on a drive down to the beach.

Annie, I'm Not Your Daddy - Kid Creole And The Coconuts (1982), ZE/Island (US)
Producer: August Darnell

No, it's not an episode of "Jerry Springer," but "Annie, I'm Not Your Daddy" *is* a song about a so-called "child" discovering that her mom was, shall we say, a bit loose while enjoying the sun of Saint Tropez a few years back. There's a lyric in there that says mama had a fall or two, but it sounds more like mama had a *ball* or two. It's a bit of clever, highly amusing drama in the often simplified world of safe, summer pop. But Kid Creole And The Coconuts is not a sedate group by any means, nor one that's averse to a little scandal. The track is a wonderfully wry (but cautionary) tale detailing the consequences of having *too* much fun in paradise, bathed in a rambunctious production dripping with tropical atmosphere. And damn if it isn't a scintillating dance jam, too. They must have sensed it had hit potential, as the song was also covered as a single separately by The Coconuts and new wave artist Cristina around the same period.

Truthfully, one could literally pick just about any production from Kid Creole And The Coconuts' vast roster of offbeat, stunningly clever, often risqué, and utterly charming recorded musical adventures and hear a sure-fire, pop song 'n' palm tree winner. Binge-worthy albums such as *Off The Coast Of Me* (1980), *Fresh Fruit In Foreign Places* (1981), *Tropical Gangsters* (known as *Wise Guy* in the US and Canada, 1982), *The Conquest Of You* (1997), and *Too Cool To Conga* (2001), among others, all suggest a kind of music that's uniquely ideal for the season, but far more detailed and observant of life's cracks and twists than one might suspect. Superior storytelling, a hot weather vibe and sly humor abound on tracks and singles that include "Calypso Pan American" (1980), "Stool Pigeon" (1982), "There's Something Wrong In Paradise" (1983), "Midsummer Madness" (1987) and, happily, countless others. The Kid and his Coconuts have been called rowdy, irreverent, and risible purveyors of intoxicating beats—a left-field group with a crowd-pleasing penchant for that Caribic flavor. But even those descriptors fall short of capturing the entire picture, the magic created by visionary founder August Darnell, who's been dependably entertaining folks for decades.

To say the very least, Darnell has some formidable pop and dance music history linked to his name, which came well before the inception of this group. He contributed his songwriting skills to many classic '70s pop nuggets, most often categorized as disco music (though his artistry dabbled in and blended numerous genres), including the landmark "Cher Chez Le Femme/Se Si Bon" (1976) by Dr. Buzzard's Original "Savannah" Band, working with his late brother, composer, arranger and musician Stony Browder Jr. RCA Records took out a full page ad in a music trade publication during the height of Savannah's popularity, calling them "America's new high society band." Darnell also produced Machine's hit "There But For The Grace Of God Go I" (1979) (which Kid Creole covered in a tropical, highly nuanced style in '80), and he produced the quirky club and pop success "Deputy Of Love" (1979) for Don Armando's Second Avenue Rhumba Band.

All of this early material hinted at what was still taking shape in Darnell's extraordinarily creative mind, waiting to be unleashed in the '80s. Soon after the disco boom faded and right in time for the inviting eccentricities of the new wave era, August, along with arranger buddy Andy Hernandez (aka Coati Mundi) and Adriana Kaegi, then his wife (who focused on The Coconuts part of the equation), formed Kid Creole And The Coconuts. In many ways, this was his personal vision of the original Savannah Band concept. Donning the "Kid Creole" moniker (a nod to Elvis Presley's King Creole), his group has been blending rock, pop, R&B, Latin, jazz, disco and the kitchen sink ever since—always with a deliciously mischievous wink and precise, powerful musicianship and showmanship.

"They don't sound like anyone else," observed midwest US radio programmer Bobby Magic, speaking with *Billboard* in a June 12, 1982, commentary on black/urban music. Even in that regard, it's difficult to pinpoint where Kid Creole And The Coconuts' appeal should theoretically lie—they've secured a massive following that's crossed racial boundaries surely as often as their hits have leapt over international borders. The 1982 Ze/Island album *Tropical Gangsters*, one of the group's most popular and accessible sets (the fantasy tale of Kid Creole's Banana Boat crew being shipwrecked off Brindisi Reef and the tongue-in-cheek drama of their ordeal), brought the group fully into the spotlight. Tracks such as "I'm A Wonderful Thing, Baby" hit an irreverent bull's-eye with the record-buying public and clubland, while simultaneously nailing a somewhat unorthodox summer vibe. In the process, these singles became two of the band's most famous songs. In the aforementioned issue of *Billboard*, Brian Chin described the "witty/nasty" (his adjectives) *Wise Guy (Tropical Gangsters)* LP as, "a graceful pastiche of today's dance rhythm and producer/director August Darnell's encyclopedic knowledge of ethnic music and old soul, all of it both strongly commercial and underground." On July 4, 1987, *Music & Media* astutely described Kid Creole And The Coconuts as having "popularized salsa and calypso by mixing it with disco, reggae and jazz."

The group's stylish music has brimmed with a vibrant, edgy, outré summer vibe—"tropical cool" as they refer to it—that has set them apart from the competition, and to be sure, there's been a lot of it over the years. A likely additional explanation for their dominance in the market—Kid Creole And The Coconuts' remarkably entertaining and engaging stage presence, which adds immeasurably to the exotic appeal of this group and their live sound.

Unlike this near-fanatical, long-winded introduction, August Darnell is known for cutting to the chase in his music and his interviews.

Commentary from August Darnell and lead Coconut (for over the past 23 years), Eva Tudor-Jones:

Mr. Darnell, what was the goal of Kid Creole And The Coconuts at its inception?

"The goal, primarily—I was trying to prove to my brother, Stony Browder Jr., that I could do it on my own. He had sort of limited me to being a lyricist, bass player and a background vocalist. When I asked him if I could write some songs for the Savannah Band, he laughed at me. He said the roles were delineated, and they would stay that way forever. He would write the songs and I would write the lyrics. This frustrated me because I was growing in leaps and bounds, so I wanted to jump ship from the Savannah Band and prove to my older brother that I could do it on my own. That was the reason I started Kid Creole And The Coconuts. No other reason but to prove to my brother that I could survive without him. Once I did it, it was pretty damn lonely. Without Stony there, I knew if I failed, he would be laughing at me for the rest of his life. So that's how that happened." *[August laughs.]*

You created a distinctive character with Kid Creole, one who is enveloped in the energy of the swing era. Was he a reflection of August Darnell, or was he a figure created to brand the group?

"Well, not intentionally. Savannah Band did that—they were all into the swing era. Stony was the one who turned me on to Duke Ellington, Count Basie, Cab Calloway and all the great big band leaders. So we dressed like that because we loved the big band style and the old 1940s movies, especially Bogart's, John Garfield, Joan Crawford, Bette Davis. We wanted to look like them. So the whole idea of the swing thing came about because we wanted to find a way to incorporate that feel, that clothing, that mode of dress, into what we were about to create. Kid Creole was just an extension—I wasn't going to change the way I looked in Savannah Band because I loved the way I looked in those clothes, and I thought it was bringing me closer to my heroes.

"You must remember, I only created Kid Creole because, as August Darnell, I was in the Savannah Band, so I needed an alter ego. That alter-ego became Kid Creole. It wasn't that deep. I was a young guy in a band who wanted to create another band and wanted to keep the music styles similar. All that I knew about music came from my older brother. He taught me how to play bass, the guitar, so basically all I did was cop what I learned from the Savannah Band and use it with Kid Creole."

Your music often has a wonderful tropical flair and upbeat feel—that summer vibe. But in truth, Kid Creole's music is nearly unclassifiable in terms of genre. It isn't exclusively disco, dance, pop, Latin, new wave, electronic, jazz, or even exclusively summery or tropical, is it?

"That is correct. That is intentional, because I was influenced by so many different styles growing up in the Bronx. No one style was any better than another in my opinion. I loved everything I heard in the Bronx. So when I created Kid Creole, I wanted to make sure I used all the styles that I loved and not just go for one style. One of my most famous quotes to this day is that I could never be as pure, I could never deliver as pure a sound as, say, Bob Marley and reggae, but I could incorporate some reggae ideas into what I called rainbow music that nobody else could do in the way I could. And that gave me the power to continue, but—once again—this all started with the Savannah Band. Stony was the one who was using all these different styles and it worked, miraculously. It shouldn't have worked, but it did work. And then it was labeled disco because it was the only way record labels thought they could promote it properly. Disco was famous for a short period of time, and, of course, as record companies always do, they try to pigeon-hole [an artist] and make money from it. That's why it was called disco—Savannah Band was never intentionally devised as a band that would be called disco. As a matter of fact, my brother hated that title, that label. But, as for me, the eclectic sound meant everything to me. I could not imagine being anything other than an eclectic songwriter because, as I say, the influences were mighty from all directions."

With Kid Creole, there was always a story, and it was usually dramatic, ironic and humorous at the same time.

"That is correct again—that is me! August Darnell is a very dramatic, ironic and humorous guy, so the songs came out of that lifestyle. Growing up in the Bronx, you better have a sense of humor or you're dead. So that sense of humor came out of a survival instinct. If you didn't want to get into fights every day of your life in the Bronx, you had to have a sense of humor. And drama? Well, I was an English major, so I loved drama. As a matter of fact, my thesis was on William Shakespeare. So talk about drama!"

Your songs are often about awkward social situations, a socially inconvenient dilemma, a kind of "trouble in paradise" theme. But yet the beat, the uplifting arrangements, usually feel lighter than the subject matter, as if you are winking at us.

"I've always wanted to entertain the masses, and I knew this Kid Creole thing was going to be a live entertainment show, much more so than Savannah Band. Savannah Band didn't do that many gigs. Kid Creole was all about gigs, so when you're in the studio writing songs, you're also thinking about the live show. So, I'm thinking people come to the show, they want to dance, hang out, let their hair down, and a lot of the songs did have that uplifting, light feel. However, there was some darkness under the light. I think that's what you're hinting at. I think that comes from being aware of the social injustices in the world, but at the same time not letting them conquer my spirit—thank you very much!"

In the most memorable and infectious of your Kid Creole work, there's that feeling of paradise, that lure of the tropics, the sensation of warm summer air—something so many songs in this book have in common.

"Yeah, I've always been in love with paradise, always been in love with the tropics, even though I was from the Bronx, the furthest thing from the tropics you could imagine. However, I did have a very powerful love affair with the Caribbean. Probably due to my ex-girlfriend, who was Haitian. Going down to Haiti and discovering that lifestyle, which is so completely the opposite of the urban cities, really had a strong influence on me.

"I now live between Sweden, England, New York and Hawaii—I spend a lot of time in Maui these days. My wife and I bought a martini lounge there a couple of years ago called Ambrosia, and we ran it for about four years. What an experience that was. But I should say this about paradise—paradise is not always paradise, is it? And that also excites me—that we have this mythology about paradise that is really, really not completely honest. It's the illusion, and I think that's the same thing that happens with the record business. You sell the illusion to people and that's why so much tourism is built around 'let's go to paradise.' It's not really paradise, but it is a question of, shall I say, is the glass half empty or is it half full? I would always look toward the optimistic outlook of life and say that I would rather go for the positive than the negative. Therefore, everything is relative. It *is* paradise, compared to the Bronx!" *[August lets out a hearty laugh.]*

Twelve-inch remixes were expected to extend the life of songs and make them even more viable for clubs. Was there a risk that an outside DJ/ engineer, hired by a label, might change the direction of your original work and distort your intent?

"Don't get me started on 12-inch remixes. I have a bad relationship with remixers and outside producers coming in and making ridiculous money because they have a name and messing up the music. Some of these guys who remixed had no musical training whatsoever. They didn't even know which chords would go with the vocals, and they'd come in because they had a reputation—they'd make a mess. *[August gives a barely audible grumble.]* So, I'm not a fan of remixes, and also, art is art. When somebody creates something, they create it for a purpose, for a reason. The tempo was that way because that's where the songwriter felt it should be. Along comes some outsider who thinks it should be faster or slower—*arrrggghh*, nah!

"They tried to do this [with my work], but I was very rebellious about it in the early days. A lot of those remixes got through, and I did some remixes myself, but I always tried to stay true in mine, whereas some of these other guys came in—I'm not going to name names, but, no, I'm not a fan."

With success, what was the most challenging part of Kid Creole being noticed?

"*Hmmmm*—what was challenging? Nothing was challenging. We got lucky because we went overseas and conquered Europe. Had we not conquered Europe, Kid Creole probably would have died after the first album. We became heroes over there. We went overseas, we bring this tropical sound, this escapism, to the Europeans. They loved it—it was different that we were combining all these musical styles. And, of course, we looked great! We went overseas with the zoot suit, the two-toned shoes, the fedoras, and the beautiful women, The Coconuts. Scantily clad—The Coconuts—come on! So there was no challenging part of being noticed. Frankly, I was noticed since the day I was born."

The Coconuts – so pivotal in carrying across your story lines and essential to adding that sly, sometimes stinging edge to much of your work.

"As a matter of fact, without Adriana Kaegi, who started the concept of The Coconuts as a—how shall I say—a device in which the Kid could be cut down to size, so-to-speak—I'm not sure what would have happened. Adriana found the other girls, and this was a way, I would say a gimmick. A lot of people came to those early shows just wanting to see the girls. And there was Coati Mundi, my partner from the Savannah Band, and the three of us became the nucleus that made sure this whole thing worked. So, The Coconuts were absolutely pivotal, for more reasons than one.

"There wasn't so much a separate focus and planning effort behind The Coconuts. It was primarily because I was married to Adriana, and she was the way of bringing in the other two girls—the idea was always to have three girls. It was a way to create something visually entertaining that could not be denied. Then they created this personality of their own. Once Adrianna left the band, I was left with this void, and I had to continue to make sure The Coconuts were a part of the band. I could have easily said, you know what, let's drop these girls. They're too expensive, and they're stealing my thunder. But I kept the concept because it worked, and it was a beautiful thing. I got lucky when Miss Eva Tudor-Jones came into my life, because what she did was make sure the quality of that concept remained magnificent."

The Coconuts had a noticeably offbeat sound. Somehow it seemed right in sync with the contrasting musical experiences you were creating.

"Yes, that was intentional. So many bands in those days were using the great voices, the great sisters, in the background—it was overplayed in my opinion. I went the opposite way. I wanted to bring attention to the fact that I didn't need that. I didn't need that gimmick; I didn't need the sound of well-trained voices behind me. As a matter of fact, I got more interest in the music because the voices weren't trained. I always loved that The Coconuts had that untrained sound because, believe it or not, that untrained sound became what many people considered the Kid Creole sound. The minute you hear The Coconuts singing that way, [think 'Annie, I'm Not Y Daddy'] the line about mamma's baby's, papa's maybe—that's fantastic. And it's great because it's done that way. If it was delivered by professional singers, singing in tune, and oh so correctly, it would never have the effect that it does have."

Ms. Tudor-Jones, you're affectionately known as "Mama Coconut," and you've been with The Coconuts for well over two decades. Tell me how you view the trio, this integral ingredient in the Kid Creole experience.

"The Coconuts have always been strong individuals in their own right, but collectively something extraordinary. Putting aside their obvious beauty, dancing and singing skills, the dynamic energy they emit on stage is untouchable. A lot of time and effort is put into the choreography, the costumes, and the vocals ahead of any tour or when rehearsing a new song. The Kid will be present at some point during this process to have his say, of course, but it's the Coconuts and Mama Coconut who ultimately create the magic the audience gets to enjoy. Off stage, the three Coconuts have always had a tight bond, a sisterhood, and it's because of this that when they hit the stage they are a force to be reckoned with!"

Was it ever your intention to create a song with a summer vibe, with a plan for commercial success during the season?

"No, God no. I've never, ever, ever sat down and said I want to create a song just for the summer. Those songs came out of me just loving the escapism of summer and the weather. I'd say it was just luck that they became associated with summer. It says something about my personality though, as well. I'm a summer personality guy, you know what I mean?

(L) Kid Creole/August Darnell with Coconut Eva-Tudor Jones today.

"I'm a summer person, man, I love the summer! When people ask me what's my favorite season, I usually say the summer. As a child growing up, it was—*whoa*! It was get down to Manhattan, to Central Park, go on the lake, boating, bicycling—escapism. So the summer is always a part of my journey, and that is why I ended up in Maui. It's 365 days of summer! I did also like the seasons, though. There was something about when the summer ended and school started when I was a kid. The Autumn and the leaves—I was a seasonal guy, until the weather got too cold. Then I said, you know what, I gotta get outta here!"

If you wanted to experience that summer feeling, that beach vibe, or the energy of the season, what music would you put on your headphones?

"I've got too many artists on my list, but I do still love The Beach Boys, and I still love Caribbean music—the Caribbean vibe of Marley and Burning Spear. Latin jams from Puerto Rico, Tito Puente and Celia Cruz. If I'm in a relaxed mode, I will put on a Frank Sinatra playlist and that does the trick. I still listen to Doris Day, Patti Page, Ella Fitzgerald, The Beatles, Johnny Cash. If we go down that rabbit hole, we'll be having a conversation for 17 and a half hours."

*[See also: **Ticket To The Tropics - The Coconuts**.]*

A Place In The Sun - Pablo Cruise (1977) A&M (US)
Producer: Bill Schnee

The Frisco rockers deliver their tight signature guitar sound in an evocative, upbeat soft pop/rock tune that acknowledges we all need a holiday getaway. From their LP of the same name, which introduced the band to mainstream success. It's a cool, feel good track for a summer drive, lazin' on the beach, or stretching in a hammock by the lake. Very portable.

Are You Ready For The Summer? (from "Meatballs") - Camp Northstar Kids' Chorus (1979), RSO (US)
Producers: Elmer Bernstein, Norman Gimbel

As smile-inducing as the Bill Murray film in which it is featured, this ancillary theme song is a hopelessly upbeat one minute and 47 second jangly piano jam that, if you saw the flick back in the day, has probably stayed lodged in your brain ever since. Oh, and David Naughton's ("American Werewolf In London") disco hit "Makin' It" is on the soundtrack, too.

Arriba (1992) - Francesco Napoli, Electrola/Hansa (G)
Producer: Peter Columbus

"Arriba" was created in much the same style as the artist's massive 1987 international summer hit medley "Balla..Balla - Italian Hit Connection." Francesco's long-time producer, Peter Columbus, again takes familiar evergreens, this time in a Latin vein, and melds them into another summer party anthem. Napoli's enthusiasm and authentic energy, combined with his appealing vocal accent, are a good match for the Spanish material found here, and the artist proves that the possibilities with this type of nonstop medley are virtually endless. It includes, "La Bamba," "Guantanamera," "Cielito Lindo" and more. Give Napoli's earlier single, "Santa Lucia - Ciao" (1990), a listen while you're at it. It has the vibe and familiarity of a danceable "O Sole Mio," a delectable slice of Italian/Mediterranean summer, seasoned to taste with a hint of seaside atmosphere. Francesco should be your go-to for quality Italian and Spanish take-out this summer!

Atlantide - Marina Barone (1992), Duck (I)
Producer: Bruno Barbone

A strong-voiced Italian singer who seems well-suited to breathe life into this dreamy, down-tempo track, a pop representation of the mythical island of Atlantis. The injection of a synth-rock vibe and a dose of electric guitars gives it an edge, but the production never strays too far from the dance sensibilities of the 1985 version recorded by the Italian group Santarosa.

Atlantide - Santarosa (1985), Clever/Carrere (I)
Producer not indicated.

An Italian group formed in the mid-'70s, Santarosa took this evocative synth track in an Italo disco direction, evoking a sultry, oceanic mood. The 1986 French remix by Philippe Renaux (who oversaw France's Clever dance music label) and Jean Phi is the definitive version, with its surf-side sound effects and melody that may remind one of rolling waves on a shoreline. It was a sure bet at the time for airplay in the clubs of southern Italy and Spain.

Away...Isle Del Sol - Kay Franzes (1991), PILZ (G)
Producer: Luis Rodriguez

Kay is a young male German singer who delivered a number of energized dance singles over his relatively short career, and this track about escaping to paradise may have been his last. Fused with Spanish guitars, a strong pulse and a hook-laden chorus, the song is somewhat reminiscent of Madonna's "La Isla Bonita" and contains just a suggestion of Tony Esposito's "Kalimba De Luna," mixing English and Spanish lyrics. Producer Luis Rodriguez was the high-octane engineering fuel behind Germany's legendary '80s hitmakers Modern Talking ("You're My Heart, You're My Soul"). The singer passed in 2000.

Bacardi Feeling (Summer Dreamin') / Summer Dreaming - Kate Yanai (1991), WEA (G)
Producer: Olivier Bloch-Lainé

And, *oh,* what a feeling! Kate Markowitz is an accomplished American singer and songwriter based in California, and she's been a background vocalist for James Taylor since 1990. In addition, she's toured with such luminaries as Carole King, Shawn Colvin and k.d. lang, and provided background vocals on recordings by Billy Joel, Cher and Diana Ross, among other stars. As impressive as her career has been, and continues to be, there's another accomplishment on Kate's resume that deserves close attention. In 1991, performing under the alias of Kate Yanai, she found unexpected success in Germany singing a completely inebriating (wink), surprisingly delicate dance/pop beach song called "Bacardi Feeling (Summer Dreamin')" (and an alternate version, sans the Bacardi references, called "Summer Dreaming"), the foundation of which was the rum manufacturer's popular commercial jingle at the time.

In its full-length form, "Bacardi Feeling (Summer Dreamin')" is a peaceful, breezy, warm and tropical production, with a hint of reggae and a light dance groove, all brought forward by the charming nuances of Ms. Markowitz's voice. It created such a strong sense of bliss because of the singer's ability to capture a laid back summer vibe and the song's highly accessible representation of a free and easy getaway. The track simply washes over the listener as if one is languishing in a warm tropical lagoon. The marketing folks at Bacardi were keenly aware of connecting hip summer melodies like this with their liquor brand, but it's unlikely anyone could have anticipated this jingle would turn into an outright pop chart smash.

After picking up steam in the clubs and on radio in mid-August of 1991, the "Bacardi Feeling (Summer Dreamin')" single reached the top of the airplay charts in Germany and Austria. By late October, the track reached the top five on *Music & Media*'s Eurochart Hot 100 Singles survey. In its final issue of the year, the publication ranked Ms. Yanai's summer classic at

#32 among the continent's top singles, higher even than hits released by the Bee Gees, Cher, Paula Abdul, and Salt-N-Pepa.

Unsurprisingly, a number of "Bacardi" remixes were released in the years that followed, including a 1992 "Hot Summer" mix by Arabella Rodriguez out of London, which added a refreshed undercurrent pulse and some loungy horns, and a 1997 Axel Breitung version that featured a rap by Jamaica's Papa Winnie. At the time of this interview, Ms. Markowitz was planning to record and release her own twenty-first century interpretation of the hit to celebrate the song's popularity and longevity.

Kate recorded one more song with a summer beat a few years after "Bacardi Feeling." "Cry, Cry Louise" (1994), recorded in Los Angeles, had a similar vibe with insightful, poetic lyrics and, again, a pop/reggae dance beat. Though *Music & Media* (June 25, 1994) said this follow-up had a melody line "vaguely reminiscent of 'I Can't Help Falling In Love With You'" by Elvis Presley" and potential as a "radio summer smash," the track failed to gain the traction her previous hit had achieved.

The story behind Kate's recording of "Bacardi Feeling (Summer Dreaming)" is a musical French Cassoulet—it's got everything. All the elements that make pop music so intriguing are in there, including sudden stardom and behind the scenes drama. Ms. Markowitz isn't shy about discussing these points, as well as a few other pros and cons that come with having a hugely popular summer-themed hit.

Commentary from Kate Markowitz:

Ms. Kate, I am keenly aware of your impressive history as an accomplished touring and recording back-up singer for so many esteemed artists, and I appreciate that you're willing to share your fascinating "footnote experience," shall we say, with the 1991 tropical dance/pop single, "Bacardi Feeling (Summer Dreamin')."

"Thanks! It's a really surprising thing that happened to me—and it *has* been really separate from my career as a background singer in the US. I tend to separate the two. I used a different name as well, Kate Yanai, which I kind of regret a little. It's actually a family name. My mother was part Japanese, and I'm a quarter Japanese. It was a name I was going to use when I first started singing—as a professional name. I like the way it sounded. But I started getting work with my real name, Markowitz, and I didn't want to offend my father (his last name was Markowitz). But when the ["Bacardi Feeling (Summer Dreamin')"] song happened, it was such a unique thing, I thought I would just use the name Kate Yanai on it. It did become a bit confusing in the rest of my career. I remember I thought, well maybe I can have this kind of anonymous secret thing happen to me [in Europe], but it eventually got connected to who I really am anyway."

How did you come to be the singer behind this very popular summer hit?
"I was singing back-up for a French artist on tour. Her name was France Gall. I got hired with a couple of Americans, including Cheryl Poirier, a former singer with Kid Creole And The Coconuts, to do this tour with France in the late '80s—late '87 and '88. It was a long tour. I met the drummer (Joe Hammer) on that tour, and he's the one who introduced me to producer Olivier Bloch-Lainé. Olivier did a lot of advertising music, and he was looking for someone to do a jingle for Bacardi. He was based in France, but he did a lot of this advertising jingle music for Germany, Austria, Switzerland and that area. Olivier wrote 100 percent of the music, and he and Joe Hammer had written the lyrics to 'Bacardi Feeling.' So my vocal part, it was what Americans would call a 'buyout.' You get a nice chunk of money, you do the vocal, and you don't see any money after that—it's just the one-time thing. I did the original vocal, which was the 'Bacardi Feeling' lyric, instead of 'what I'm feeling' [from the "Summer Dreaming" track]. Then it became a kind of underground hit as a jingle. So people started bootlegging it in the dance clubs, editing together the one-minute jingle version into a dance-length song. I guess Bacardi, the French producer of the jingle, and WEA Records joined forces and asked me if I wanted to rewrite the lyrics into something about summer love, or something instead of Bacardi, and release it with my name on it. It all happened within a month, or six months, or something—it just felt like it happened really quickly. Everyone reached out to me through Olivier."

Tell me about transforming this brief jingle into a full-on pop song and what happened next.

"Joe (the drummer) had co-written the lyrics and helped arrange the track. Olivier asked me if I wanted to help rewrite the lyrics, so I called my dear friend Christina Trulio, because she is a really good writer. We changed everything that had any reference to rum and made it about love. Shortly after that, Olivier came to Los Angeles, and we recorded the new lead vocal and the back-up vocals. He took the track back to France, where I think he added a few touches, but he didn't change much.

"When Olivier asked me if I wanted to release it under my name, I really didn't think it through. At the time, I just thought it was slightly amusing, and I didn't anticipate anything would happen with it. I'd already been in the music business for a little while, and I'd seen how many things don't, you know, actually work out. I thought, okay, I'll use the Kate Yanai name, since it sounds like a solo artist's name. They didn't ask me for a photo. Then WEA Records slapped it together, released the track, the original version, calling it 'Bacardi Feeling (Summer Dreamin')'. This version didn't have a photo of me on the cover. It was a white cover with pictures of drinks, palm trees and a pineapple. The only face on it was a small inset of a smiling man with dark glasses. So nobody had any idea of who I was or what I looked like.

"Then it just took off like crazy, and they started reaching out to me, having me go over to Germany to do interviews and some promotion. On the next pressing of the single [for "Summer Dreaming"] Olivier took a photo of me during a video shoot in Jamaica, and we used that. At the time, CD singles were sold in actual record stores, and this one had my picture on it. A little bit later, I ended up doing my first TV show.

"I'm not sure if you are familiar with the way they would package television shows [in Germany], especially in the early '90s. It was really a throwback to the way America looked in the '50s. They'd have guys behind me pretending to be a band as I lip-synched. The set would have fake palm trees and boats and beach umbrellas. It was aesthetically kind of an extreme version of, or caricature of, that tiki hut, tropical thing. That's the way it looked to me at the time. It just reminded me of the TV shows in the late '50s that Americans loved."

Cringy and dated? I get it.

"I didn't want to say that—I'm glad you did. Coming from California myself, it was hard for me to relate to how extremely romanticized the beach/tropical thing was. You're right, it was done in a *really* corny way. So that first time I did a television show over there the crazy thing about it was you'd do the rehearsal in jeans, street clothes. Then you go to wardrobe, get changed and do make-up and all that. This was a live taped show. They lead you to the backstage area where you are going to enter from, and it wasn't until literally about 30 seconds before we were going to walk on stage that I saw what they had made the 'band' wear. The costumes. I was—*beyond horrified*! They wore ruffled white shirts and these big straw hats. I knew there wasn't time to change or anything. I took each one of their hats off and threw them on the ground and said to them, 'I am so sorry.' On stage, I had to interact with these guys in these outfits. Now that I look back on it, it was hilarious. But at the time I was really pretty mortified. Also, there was that dry ice fog, literally up to almost my waist. I was wearing this dress and heels. People don't realize this stuff, but when you're a performer, you really *have* to be aware of [these hazards] and you learn as you get older what to be careful of. I'll never forget walking out on that stage in heels and realizing the dry ice was creating this oily, slick surface on the stage. I was going to have to be really careful because I didn't want to fall on live TV. Luckily I didn't."

So, actually two editions of the song were out there, one promoting Bacardi and the other a more traditional pop song for you as a solo artist, without the Bacardi references.

"Yes, the original was called 'Bacardi Feeling (Summer Dreamin').' The second version was simply 'Summer Dreaming.' But many Germans still refer to me as 'The Bacardi Girl.'"

It sounds like you may have had mixed feelings about suddenly becoming a pop star with this song.

"The surreal part of this whole thing was that when I started interviewing, they asked me questions about this one song as if it represented my whole creative life. I never wanted to denigrate the song or not be appreciative of the experience because it *was* a crazy, wild ride, and I was thrilled to be in that position. Not to mention I made a nice chunk of money from it, especially that first year. So it was a really big deal. However, that said, if I was going to choose my first solo statement, creatively, it might not have been that. I can look back on it now and really appreciate how much fun that song was and still is. I'm just saying that the kind of music I was interested in at the time didn't necessarily sound like 'Bacardi Feeling.'

"I ended up getting a job singing with James Taylor right when that was all happening. I was singing with someone who I really admired and who had such musical integrity, a sophisticated lyricist and poet—all the things I really admired in an artist. And then this crazy pop single happened for me. And so at first I was a little bit embarrassed by it just because it wasn't this 'serious work of art.' At the time I was kind of snooty about it in a way. [*Kate laughs.*] I don't look at it that way anymore. Again, I think it was a wild and crazy experience I was lucky to have. I saw the humor in it as I got older."

Tell me about that wonderfully atmospheric video you did for the song, which was a far cry from the TV productions you spoke about.

"Yes, it's on YouTube, but you have to hunt for it under 'Bacardi Feeling/La Frette Studios.' We made it in Jamaica, and that in itself was a whole crazy experience! We shot it at the end of '91, right after the song had gone to #1. They had wanted me to come to Germany to film a video where I'd be a cocktail waitress in a smoky bar, dreaming of a tropical place. Olivier—and I have to give him credit here—said, 'No, we need to shoot this in a *real* tropical place.' He really pushed for that. He got a really amazing French female film director (Domonique Issermann), and Olivier brought them all to Jamaica from France. The video is pretty much me on the beach, under a waterfall, by a lagoon, and it's actually beautifully shot. It was quite the experience. Especially, the handsome guy who played my romantic interest in the video. He was actually the assistant director. After meeting him, I thought it was artistically important to have a kissing scene *with him* in the video, but the director said, no, we want him admiring you from afar. Life is full of disappointments. [*She laughs.*]

"We were there four or five days. They hired a lot of little kids and some locals to be in the film, and it was incredible being with these Jamaican people. I'd never been there before, so it was quite an adventure. I went there by myself, and got picked up by a cab at the airport and got driven for what seemed like two hours through a jungle. I wasn't prepared for how hot and humid it was. In the cab, I was taking off literally every bit of clothing I could because I was so hot. It was hard work shooting the video, because you're up really, really early and working till the light is gone. I had no control over the concept, but I have to say they did a really sweet job with it. I look at it today and say, 'God, I wish I could look like that now!'"

Why do you think "Bacardi Feeling (Summer Dreamin')" resonated so strongly with people, especially in Germany?

"When I did that first TV show in Germany, I had taken my friend Chris, who co-wrote the 'Summer Dreaming' song with me, and we stayed in Berlin for maybe a week. The wall had come down at the end of '89, and the song was released in '91, so not much time had passed. We got a personal tour of the city and saw where part of the wall was still standing. Our driver drove us into East Berlin and we saw some of the ruins from the war. For us, it was a very meaningful overview of what had happened in Germany, the liberation of a big part of it. Chris and I, we thought maybe because the wall had come down so recently, it may have had something to do with the excitement about this song. But in retrospect, I think it may have been simply more about escaping to a beautiful place. I don't know—maybe that had something to do with the song's success. 'Give us a vacation!' By the way, since we were talking about the video a moment ago, I'll never forget going into my hotel room after the tour, turning on the TV and my video was on MTV! I remember screaming and laughing, and Chris and I got a bottle of champagne to celebrate.

(R) Kate Yanai (Kate Markowitz) today, photo by Elena Mitchell.

"Ultimately, I can really see now why songs like 'Summer Dreaming' mean so much, why the perception people have of them is so strong, especially for people that live in areas where they go through long periods of cold, dark weather. They are hard-working people, and vacations are what they live for. I think this music represents that sense of freedom, escape and joy—sun and beach, swaying palm trees and ocean."

Would you share what music gives you that summer vibe?

"I have to say when I think of summer or the tropics, the artists that come to mind first are Bob Marley and Jimmy Cliff. Also, when I was younger, Donna Summer was one of my favorite singers. I loved her voice and some of her disco hits, and 'Hot Stuff' and 'Last Dance' make me think of summer. I really love Stevie Wonder, the groups Earth, Wind & Fire and No Doubt, and I still love Gwen Stefani. I'm a big fan of Lizzo, Adele, and Pink as well."

Back On Holiday - Robbie Nevil (1988), EMI-Manhattan (US)
Producer: Robbie Nevil

Nevil, who hit it big with his 1986 pop single "C'est La Vie," clearly understood the plight of nine to fivers and their pining for long overdue getaways. The song is electronic pop fused with guitars and features some dubby "Ibiza" and "Montego Bay" remixes by Jellybean Benitez that would sound quite riveting in a club setting. When the boss asks how you can be reached on your next vacation, the correct response is, "I can't."

Back To The Islands - Janis Siegel (1982), Atlantic (US)
Producer: Joel Dorn

A member of Manhattan Transfer, Ms. Siegel peppers this unhurried, jazz-fused tale of a woman letting her lover know that she's returning to the tropics but she'll be thinking of him (she coveys all this with a heavy dose of Streisand-like seasoning). Lyrically, casting aside relationship issues for a far away island sounds like a reasonable enough plan, but ultimately the song's a bit theatrical rather than liberating, and the arrangement forgetfully bypasses any equatorial feeling. So something tells me not to worry, she probably booked a roundtrip ticket.

Bahia - Véronique Sanson (1994), WEA (F)
Producer: Bernard Saint-Paul

A spunky, heated electronic dance-the-house-down update of the French singer/songwriter's 1972 pop ballad about the wild waters of Bahia, Brazil. Vigorously energized and thoroughly absorbing. The singer's more mature voice in this recording perfectly complements the track's powerful new arrangement. A summer song when you're feeling *on!*

Baila El Limon - Bacardi Limon (release date unknown), Bacardi (G)
Producer: Howard Ave

A extra-summery, danced-up, promotion-only cover of Tito Puente's "Oye Como Va" composition (recorded by Santana back in 1970) that offers scant few production details other than being a German production. No doubt a marketing tool used in conjunction with Bacardi's active participation in beach, travel, sports and club culture events during the '90s and early 2000s, this catchy, well-produced Latin/pop number seems ideal for making holiday revelers very thirsty. At which time they all become Bacardiologists.

Bailando - Paradisio (1995), Dance Development (B)
Producer: The Unity Mixers

A hugely popular Belgian summer eurohouse production sung in Spanish, featuring three female performers. High energy, sensual nights, dancing with friends, parties, and dreaming of paradise—it all comes together in a fun video that pumps away in a tropical beach party setting. Reportedly, the single sold millions, and its thumping beach beats no doubt shook the bodies of lots of spry, young European holiday travelers. You'll know what a blender drink feels like after hearing this one.

Baja - Baja (1996), Alabianca (NL)
Producer: Alan Michael

Punchy Dutch eurohouse with a modest touch of Latin influence, this production concept attempted to also be a "brand" of summer dance/pop for the party circuit, taking cues from Bacardi and others. A long running series of *Baja Beach Club* compilation albums, sort of like *Now That's What I Call Music* for the tropical nightlife set, followed. Fun, no-calorie stuff that may evoke that Mexican beach resort feeling.

Balearic Blue - Blank & Jones (2005), Sony/BMG (G)
Producers: Blank & Jones

This German production duo out of Cologne (Piet Blank and René Runge, aka Jaspa Jones) didn't settle for simply releasing evocative singles with a beach vibe. They created an entire series of popular compilation CDs emphasizing the theme beginning around 2003, much along the lines of the very popular *Café del Mar* albums. Their collections gathered together often obscure singles and a few Blank & Jones productions, all with a summer deep chill flavor. Blank & Jones' ongoing *Relax* and *Milchbar* compilations are essential listening, featuring an eclectic mix of ambient, lounge, trance and light dance/pop sounds. "Balearic Blue" is a fine example of the production partners' brand of new-age-basted, seaside beats. Unlike their popular club-targeted, full-on house and electronic jams, "Blue" and other tracks composed for their album series set their sights on a softer mood, relying on gentle rhythms, soft vocals and a casual atmosphere to generate their tranquil but generally rhythmic vibe. You need to put your feet up sometimes, and this is the music that'll get you in your happy zone—and you won't need a pill.

Bamboléo - Gipsy Kings (1987) P.E.M./CBS/Elektra (F)
Producer not indicated.

Breaking out in France in the autumn of '87, this exuberant, fiery song was almost immediately followed on the charts by the single "Djobi, Djoba" and still yet another edition that combined the two songs. With that kind of power play, there was no stopping these conquering music royals, who mixed the Spanish language with French dialect to great commercial success. Danceable Latin pop was all the rage (Los Lobos also had the flame on high at the time with "La Bamba"), and "Bamboléo" had just the right mix of authentic gipsy passion and frenetic rumba beats to make it a huge international hit. The seven-plus minute Arthur Baker remix was extremely popular in US clubs. The hit was later covered by dozens of artists. The song title refers to the body movements it inspires—its swing sensation—which helped make it a summer playlist favorite. Stretch before you listen!

Bamboleo Time - Fruit De La Passion (1998),
Aureus Records (US)
Producers: Paul Galati, Michael A.

Predictable female vocal dance/pop melds lyrics about partying on the beach with friends while incorporating a knockoff of Gipsy Kings' "Bamboléo" in the chorus hook. Simplistic, but it gets the job done.

Banana Boat (Day-O) - Claudja Barry (1980), Lollipop (G)
Producer: Jürgen Korduletsch

(L) Claudja Barry today.

There's nothing like a classic—be it singer or song. Which brings us to Ms. Barry, who has an esteemed history in dance music and is truly one of the first ladies of disco. Her high-energy beats were a staple of dance floors in the US and Europe in the '70s, with "Sweet Dynamite" (1976) and "(Boogie Woogie) Dancin' Shoes" (1978) among her most popular disco hits. She continued to make her presence known in the '80s with floor-filling tracks such as "Work Me Over" (1982) and the pop crossover hit "Down And Counting" (1986). "Banana Boat" is, of course, a remake of the traditional Jamaican folk song made so famous by calypso king Harry Belafonte. Here the singer is able to channel her Jamaican roots confidently and delivers an especially natural vocal performance over a lightly disco-fied pop arrangement that might be pleasing to both island music traditionalists and dance fans.

Commentary from Claudja Barry:

"'Banana Boat' is a song that invokes joy and happiness and lighter times. I was born in Jamaica, and I remember hearing that song by Harry Belafonte, a wonderful philanthropist, a lot in my life. I just thought it would be something that would bring a little bit of joy to my fans and to myself. I loved the lyrics about working all night and drinking rum, even though I don't like rum. For some reason it reminds me personally of all those times in my life of working really hard and performing. I don't know why I asked to record the song, but I really believed it held a magical feeling for me. It reminded me of my roots, of what island life is all about. It was just something I wanted to do. The two major songs I did before this track, '(Boogie Woogie) Dancin' Shoes' and the rock song 'You Make Me Feel The Fire,' were so totally different. I felt I was doing a whole lot of dance music, the disco diva thing, and there must have been a deeper reason why I wanted to do the 'Banana Boat' song. But it might just have been that it was a fun song. I just wanted to give it my take, my feeling, and put my direction and talent to it, and see what I could do to make it an up-to-date sounding song. I think it worked.

"I'd like to add that Jamaica's a beautiful place to be. But I also have to say, heat doesn't impress me, especially when I'm on stage and perspiring and glowing. In the heat of a tropical country, it's wonderful for a month. Then I want to get back to a nice cool climate like New York, or Toronto, or Munich. You know, I sort of don't know anymore where I'm really from, but when you're in a place like Jamaica, you have to get vibes that are great, that are fun. The people, the food, the foliage, the madness of the driving there, the craziness of the music—it makes you feel happy and joyful, that you're part of something special. You don't get that same vibe on 42nd Street, in Regent's Park, London, from the colder climates.

"I am grateful that I'm in Jamaica often enough to experience and enjoy the warmth. But I also really do appreciate the changing of the seasons, the changing of the foliage. But, you know what? If everything's in place, you really don't miss anything—you're happy with what you've got. When it's really hot, you're okay because you know there's somebody in Norway who is saying, 'I want to go to Las Palmas or the Canary Islands.' And there's plenty of people in Jamaica who say, 'I want to go to New York and get some cool air.'"

*[See also: **Love Is An Island - Claudja Barry**.]*

Bandiera La Playa Del Sol - Del Faro (1987), ZYX (I/G)
Flag of the beach of sun
Producer: Mino Siciliano

Del Faro was an artist alias used by the producer of this production, a drifting, mid-tempo Italo disco track with vocals that at times seem to be channeling the '80s sound of "People From Ibiza" singer Sandy Marton. The production has a flowing Italian-Spanish style that suits its beach party vibe.

Barbados - Party Pa Ti (1999), Toi,Toi,Toi (G)
Producer: Gino D'oro

This five-person mixed race group doesn't take the oft-covered 1975 song by Typically Tropical in an especially new direction, but the polished production and rich harmonies make it sound as sunny as the venerable composition ever will. The "Long Edit" opts to lose the tropical feel in favor of an awkward, busy eurodance style, so that feels like a miss. But the radio version definitely gets a check in the "yes, please" column. The maxi-single also contains a festive original song that completely channels holiday fever called "No Dinero," not to be overlooked.

Barbados - Typically Tropical (1975), Gull (UK)
Producers: Jeffrey Calvert, Max West

Arguably one of the most pointed pop songs ever made to capture the euphoria of getting on a plane and heading down to the Caribbean. The atmospheric and colorful intro featuring Captain Tobias Wilcox of Coconut Airways' Flight 372, taking us to Bridgetown, Barbados, instantly generates a palpable sense of ease—even though this may be one of those bumpy twin engine commuter flights for island hoppers. But it's okay. Exhale knowing you've left the gray and the cold behind at last, and you're on your way to paradise!

The identity of the song's creators, English duo Jeffrey Calvert and Max West, was initially a mystery, a ploy by their label to enhance sales. It may have worked. They were interviewed by *Record Mirror*'s Ray Fox-Cumming, published on July 26, 1975, as the song climbed to #2 on the British pop chart. By August 9th it reached #1 on *Record Mirror*'s singles survey. "I just thought it was a nice little reggae song," said Jeffrey. Max simply noted that,

"It fell together much more easily and more quickly than anything else we'd ever written." This casually bouncy track, their first commercial release, turned out to be a one-hit-wonder for Typically Tropical. However, the song has been covered numerous times by other acts, including Wild Banana in 1994 and, most notably, Vengaboys in 1999, who traded Barbados for a Mediterranean hot spot with "We're Going To Ibiza," returning the song to the pop chart in a very big way.

Barcelona Rumba Medley - Various Artists (1992), Ariola (SP)
Producers: Manuel Cubedo, Los Manolos

Cram 15 rumba and flamenco songs by Los Amaya, Los Manolos and Peret into one summery Europop medley (that's over a whopping 12 minutes long) and things get a bit tediocre. Yes, one is reminded of just how influential the Gipsy Kings' sound was in the early '90s, but this may be considered over-kill. The lengthy medley doesn't change pace, and the songs soon become indistinguishable from each other—and it simply goes on way too long. As your mood grows a bit salty or your hips give out, don't let this well-intentioned but monotonous track sway you from further exploring the capital of Catalonia and its legendary music.

BC Feeling Song, The - Summer Hit '91 (1991), Ohrwurm (G)
No producer indicated.

An alluring maxi-single jacket sleeve image showing a gorgeous tropical beach safeguards a mysterious German 12-inch vinyl record, a remake of Kate Yanai's "Bacardi Feeling (Summer Dreamin')" hit. The production, stickered as "Dance Version," incorporates steel drums and a more pronounced beat. It's actually pretty solid. The single may have been, in part, a charity effort, as indicated by a one-line jacket banner claiming that a .50 DM donation for each unit sold would be made to support a Bangladesh relief effort after the region had been devastated by a cyclone in April of '91.

Beach, The - Afrika & The Zulu Kings (1986), Posse (US)
Producers: Afrika Islam, Melle Mele

A hard slammin', '80s-style, electro-rap track featuring Afrika Islam, Grandmaster Melle Mele, Ice T and Bx Style Bob that pays tribute to hitting the beach and literally everything that goes along with it. Think: getting there at 2 P.M., fly girls, volleyball, cooling off in the ocean, chowing down lunch, lounging under shady umbrellas, and even falling in lust. Good clean fun, with an undercurrent that recalls Afrika Bambaataa & The Soulsonic Force's '82 hip-hop monster, "Planet Rock."

Beach, The - New Order (1983), Factory (UK)
Producer: New Order

This track is a kind of "dub" instrumental work, an alternate version of the kinetic electronic milestone, "Blue Monday." However, it stands on its own merits. One could argue its almost James Bond theme-like quality and driving aura of determination certainly might reflect the urgency with which one would, say, drive down to the beach on a hot day. But really any interpretation of this production and its sensations, the tingling it delivers, would be valid.

Beachball - Beachball Ft. Theresa Burnette (1997), CNR (NL)
Producers: Frank Loncar, Nata Cumerfield

A remake of Nalin & Kane's "Beachball" trance hit (which follows). It has a vibrant, bouncy production, but it would be largely indistinguishable from the original were it not for Burnette's ballsy delivery.

Beachball - Nalin & Kane (1997), Motor (G)
Producers: Andry Nalin, Harry Cane

Jumpy, high flying energy hit trance track with a strong female vocal that really has the power to soar. It's all about freedom, which you'll find plenty of at the beach. The track has been remixed and reinvented dozens of times. Seems like a good lead in for our next artists, who know a thing or two about the beach.

Beach Boys Medley, The - The Beach Boys (1981), Capitol (US)
Producer: Capitol Records

Wouldn't it be nice…to have snippets of the guys' original and immortal '60s surf rock music hits edited together into a super groovy mash-up by Capitol Records' esteemed producer and sound engineering wizard, John Palladino? Yes, it would, and Capitol thought it might generate a few simoleons, too. It did. It's a fun, smoothly sequenced seven-inch single that hit the US charts in July of '81 and garnered enough airplay and sales to send it all the way up to #8 on *Cash Box*'s pop singles chart by late September. This surprisingly effective and irresistible hit mix (not unlike the barebones "Diana Ross And The Supremes Medley Of Hits" released by Motown in 1979) includes "Surfin' USA," "I Get Around," "Barbara Ann," "Good Vibrations" "Help Me Rhonda," and more. Additional production by The Blade Runners was incorporated into a 1990 remix version for Europe, and a hard-to-find "The Beach Boys Collection II Medley" was released there in 1991.

The Beach Boys of the '60s (L-R, as shown, Carl Wilson, Dennis Wilson, Mike Love, Al Jardine, Brian Wilson), Capitol Records (press still).

Beach Bump - Baby Ford (1989), Rhythm King (UK)
Producers: Conning, Ford, Healy

A full-on cluster funk! This highly addictive, electro-new wave summer jam from London-based house music DJ and producer Peter Ford (aka Peter Frank Adshead) has tons of energy to spare. It's a noisy, enthusiastic synth jumper with sparky keyboards and, oh—hit me again with that perfect beat! Tailor-made for summer nights in the clubs at the dawn of a new decade. Top 10 on *Billboard*'s dance chart in 1990. Bump me, baby!

Beach La Playa, The - Rosabel (1999), AM (US)
Producers: Rosabel (Ralphie Rosario, Abel Aguilera)

Pulsating tribal electronica with a house touch, plus lots of moaning and whispery vocals suggesting a very sexy late night trip to the beach. At least I *think* that's what they're suggesting. You'll definitely want to know more.

Beach Love - Rofo (1987), Infinity (B)
Producers: Michiel V.D. Kuy, Rob Van Eijk

There's more than a hint of Kano's '80s Italo disco classic "Queen Of Witches" in this Belgian production, which capitalizes on the synthesizer-laden sound so popular at the time. It's all about falling in love with a lovely lady on the beach, hitting the clubs, and then returning to that very same beach to tap in again. The circle of life? Sounds like an episode of "Bachelor In Paradise!"

Beach Of The War Goddess - Caron Wheeler (1992), EMI (UK)
Producer: Derek Johnson

A soulful, downtempo jam that stirs in some rap and reggae beats in a complex production from the British singer, songwriter, producer and former member of Soul II Soul ("Back To Life (However Do You Want Me)"). It's a song about empowerment (no more bowing to the man, for example), and the title track from Ms. Wheeler's second solo album. The track possesses a multi-cultural vibe and groove well-suited to the summer. It's also in synch with today's movement for a feminist future based on equality and empowerment.

Belen / Islas Baleares / Andalucia - El Capitan (1991), Polydor (G)
Producer: Jean Garcia

Maravilloso! Three-track sampler maxi-single in support of the flamenco group's 1991 album, *Porque Si...*, bursting with upbeat rumba energy and the type of Spanish flavor that makes this fluidly musical and multi-layered summer sub-genre so irresistible. If you're down with Los Reyes and Gipsy Kings as a heat source for your August holidays, you won't be disappointed with this tribute to beautiful Spanish regions.

Bella d'Estate - Mango (1987), Fonit Cetra (I) *Summer beauty*
Producers: Alberto Salerno, Mauro Malavasi

Written by veteran Italian singer/songwriter Lucia Dalla and the dreamy crooner Giuseppe Mango, this ballad about a summer romance gone wrong (wrapped in a cutting, mid-tempo Italo disco mix) has a melancholy yet surprisingly edgy feel. It was appropriately paired with the downtempo dance track "Stella Del Nord" (*Star of the north*) on the 12-inch maxi-single B-side.

Bermuda Nights - Gerald Albright (1988), Atlantic (US)
Producer: Gerald Albright

Jazz and quiet storm aficionados will revel in the Los Angeles native and accomplished saxophonist and bassist's bright, funky, layered tribute to dreamy evenings in the tropics. In a 2006 live performance YouTube video posted by JavaJazzFest, the artist says, "This tune was inspired by my wonderful experience on an island called Bermuda." It must have been. And really, if a sub-tropical wonderland with pink sand beaches in the Saragosso Sea doesn't rouse creativity, nothing will.

Bermuda Triangle - Bionic Steve (1980), Crystal D (J)
Producer not indicated.

Spacey, groovy Kingston reggae has both an amusing and mesmerizing effect, but be careful—don't get too lost in it. You're likely to fly high as a kite and mysteriously disappear off the radar.

Best Mix Of Our Lives - Modern Romance (1985), WEA (UK)
Producer: Les "The Mix Doctor" Adams

It's no wonder so many people (including me) say the '80s produced the best music of their lives. An especially popular and fashionable group from that decade, chiefly during their early years, Modern Romance (which started off with members Geoffrey Deane, David Jaymes, Robbie Jaymes, Paul Gendler, John Du Prez and Andy Kyriacou) found their niche in a style that favored British funk crossed with a kinky, punchy Latin/disco vibe. Here they get the megamix treatment by UK DJ Les Adams in a fast-moving production that gathers some of their best hits into a non-stop mash-up, perfect for the summer. It includes "Everybody Salsa," "Best Years Of Our Lives" (the jewel of the group's repertoire), "High Life," "Don't Stop That Crazy Rhythm," and a few others. It's nearly eight minutes of rump-shaking bliss, a full-on pool party laced with a festive tropical atmosphere. Shake it!

Blue Night Of Hawaii - Curocas (1988), Hansa (G)
Producers: E. Stein, G. Grabowski

A one-time recording effort with vocalist Wolfgang Schwalm (Die Wildecker Herzbuben). Pure and pleasant English-language schlager-pop in the vein of Jack White's popular German productions of the period, this song is all about leaving one's job for the pleasures of, you guessed it, the Islands of Aloha. The song was also covered by Goombay Dance Band.

Boogie All Summer - Dan Hartman (1979), Blue Sky (US)
Producer: Dan Hartman

Hartman broke the high fever he had registered with the frantic tempo of his disco and pop classic "Instant Replay" thanks to this, I'm sorry to say, uninventive phone-in. An accomplished singer, songwriter and producer, he must have been having an off day, for this song has none of the distinctiveness or engaging originality of his previous hit. This off-the rack disco shuffler sounds like it could have been a background track for a goofy '70s teen movie comedy. Apparently, it was briefly promoted by the record label in the US and then mysteriously withdrawn, perhaps when it quickly went nowhere. In July of 1979, *Cash Box* said it was "well-produced and mixed, with bright instrumentation and chirpy vocals. This sounds like a Top 40 winner." *Record World* agreed, saying, "destined for hit status." Alas, it most definitely wasn't. I'm not entirely sure these publications actually listened to all the music they reviewed. Hartman more than made up for this faux pas with subsequent releases, including the brilliant hits "Relight My Fire" and "I Can Dream About You." The artist passed in 1994.

Bomb The Beach - Bomb The Beach (1988), Skyhigh (G)
Producers: Axel Breitung, Marc Wanko

A whirlwind of electronics, vocal sampling, a vicious eurohouse beat, and even a touch of that Stock Aitken Waterman pop sound in this slick German production. Ultimately we're encouraged not to be shy about bombing this beach party—so don't be. Breitung was known for his work with Germany's Silent Circle trio and Swiss megastar DJ Bobo.

Bossa Da Batida - Batida (2002), DDG Wien (A)
Producers: Volker Kretschmer, Ramon Kramer

Following the blueprint laid out by Bacardi, this promotional song, heard on European TV spots and produced in Austria, was utilized by the Mangaroca company to draw attention to its tropical Batida De Coco brand of liqueur. It's a slinky bossa nova concoction with appealing male vocals, offered in various dance mixes. Smooth. Go on, have a shot, cuz you'll need to man up for our next star.

Boys (Summertime Love) - Sabrina (1987), Five (I)
Producer: Claudio Cecchetto

A voluptuous figure has launched many a female one-hit wonder in the annals of pop music. But don't you dare call Italy's bomb diggity Sabrina Salerno a flash in the pan. The singer had several hits across her music career in the late '80s and into the '90s ("Sexy Girl," "All Of Me," "My Chico"), and "Boys" is the bubbly high-energy Italo disco pinnacle that will be forever and affectionately attached to her name and the summer season. It's a high-energy romp that unapologetically celebrates a determined, empowered, teasingly gorgeous brunette sex kitten on the hunt for some sun-kissed boys. This sizzling song not so subtly embraced everything that European party-goers were looking for during that hot holiday season and lasted well beyond it.

(L) Sabrina Salerno in 1987, Five Records (press still).

In a 1987 issue of *Music & Media*, Sabrina was described as "Italy's hottest disco diva of the moment...taking Europe by storm." In a January 1,1989, article titled "The Hottest Stars of 1988," the publication awarded the singer with a #1 ranking on their Pan-European Awards countdown. As much as this track became, and remains, a sticks-in-your-brain seasonal standard, it was was the red hot music video for "Boys (Summertime Love)" (filmed poolside in which the buxom singer experienced multiple Janet Jackson-like wardrobe malfunctions with her bikini top) that made her a star across Europe. In this case, one could say the project actually *did* go bust. Sabrina brings all the boys to the yard!

Boys Of Summer - Don Henley (1984), Geffen (US)
Producers: Don Henley, Danny Kortchmar, Greg Ladanyi, Mike Campbell

Former Eagles founding member Don Henley scored a sweet handful of prizes (Grammy, Best Male Rock Vocal Performance and MTV Video of the Year, for example) with this heated, passionate synth-rocker and ode to a summer love (figuratively viewed, lost in the rear view mirror). According to Dave Lifton (VCR Classic Rock & Culture/ultimateclassicrock.com,

November 2, 2020), it was Tom Petty's rejection of a demo track made by Heartbreakers' guitarist Mike Campbell that led to Henley's recording of one of his biggest solo hits. Campbell offered it to Henley, who listened to "Boys Of Summer" and reportedly said, "Okay, maybe I can do something with that." The rest is hot summer jams history. In 2021 *Rolling Stone* ranked the song 209 in their list of "500 Greatest Songs of All Time."

Boys Of Summer / Sunlight - DJ Sammy (2002), Robbins Entertainment/Urban (US/Europe)
Producer: DJ Sammy

Sammy says, "Put your glasses on!" Sound advice, as this song will blind you with its brilliance. Don Henley's electric-pop hit translates perfectly into a brisk and exhilarating, but at the same time surprisingly gentle, EDM-pop jam. Vocals by Dutch performers Loona and Mel make it real, and dancing to "Boys Of Summer" ends up being an emotional experience skillfully fashioned by DJ Sammy (Sofiane Bouriah Neiama—"My friends have called me Sammy since I was a little child."). The track was featured on DJ Sammy's extremely well-crafted album *Heaven*, which includes the Spanish hitmaker's take on "California Dreaming" and the set's uplifting title track (a remake of the Bryan Adams pop smash and a hugely popular #1 *Billboard* US dance chart success for the artist). "Sunlight" is another track from the LP deserving of special note, a brilliantly soaring piece of inspiring electronica that has a contagious, distinctly uplifting energy, and, like "Boys Of Summer," possesses an equally powerful sense of warm weather serenity.

(R) DJ Sammy today.

Commentary from DJ Sammy:

You come from an especially scenic, very summery place.

"Yes, I am from Palma de Mallorca, Spain. It's a beautiful island in the Mediterranean Sea. It's the place most people come to visit, the capital of the Balearic Islands—Ibiza, Menorca, Formentera, and so on."

How did you come to transform "Boys Of Summer" into such an appealing trance experience?

"To be honest, after the huge success of the single 'Heaven,' which reached #1 around the world, I was very confident about remaking the Don Henley song. The idea came to me when I heard it on the radio driving the high road in Germany. Somehow I got a special feeling. I said, 'That's it! I have the second single!' Right away we did a demo version to see if it would work, and booooom—bingo! After playing the chords, I thought, 'yeah, here we go again!' It fit perfectly with the vision I had in my mind. [To this day] I still think this cover was really well done. It is my favorite tune simply because of that summer feeling I put into it and the very nice, positive energy it has, which fits with the way I see life."

The song has energy and power, yet there is a softness, peacefulness and gentleness in its sound. It must have been challenging to achieve this balance.

"It represents me, like a profile of how I am. [*Sammy laughs.*] If you listen to my songs you will find out nearly all of them are based on high-energy and a positive message. I think somehow it's like an 'island feeling'—from where I am and where I had been raised. Yes, I agree with you—a summer flow with energy, peacefulness and gentleness. Spot on!"

It's interesting that you chose to center on the female vocals of Loona (Marie-José van der Kolk), as opposed to a male vocalist. Loona's voice matched the track vibe perfectly. Tell me about this decision.

"I chose Loona's voice on the song simply because she represented sweetness and greatness and she understood exactly what I wanted. We have worked together for over 17 years on all the Loona projects in Europe ["Hijo De La Luna," "Bailando," "Mamboleo," etc.], which have been very successful. So I asked her to go inside the [recording] booth and sing the original Don Henley version. I put the playback on and the rest is history. She is amazing!"

The video had a great summer beach vibe.

"All of my videos are made in my hometown, Palma de Mallorca, because that's the feeling I want to bring to my songs. Blue sky, ocean, nature, love, fun and, of course, a lovely cocktail to put a smile on your face. We already have so much bad energy around the world. I prefer to inspire people with happiness."

I'm curious, did you ever receive any feedback from Don Henley about your production?

"No, I never did. That would have been very nice. But I did get great feedback from Bryan Adams! We had wine in his home in London, and he did congratulate me for the remake I had done with 'Heaven.' He's a nice guy."

It's clear to me you recognize both the beauty and fun of summer music. Is there a formula that separates music intended for the summer season from music created and released at any other time of year?

"No, there is no formula for this kind of work. It just comes from inspiration. I am always influenced by the positive side of life. Summer represents fun and, just to be clear with you, life goes by so fast. It's not worth it to be unhappy. Everything I do, I do it with a smile on my face just because I choose to be that way."

I think I already know the answer, but what's your favorite summer getaway place?
"My summer destination is Ibiza and Palma de Mallorca because I have all I need there to be me! With such great places I have freedom, music, love and blue sky! *Yeahhhhhh!*"

Brazil - The Ritchie Family (1975), 20th Century Records (US)
Producer: Jacques Morali

This vibrant, exotic staple from the Xavier Cugat catalog translated perfectly into the disco sound, then a genre relatively in its infancy. Produced by future Village People mastermind Jacques Morali and recorded in Philadelphia, the first Ritchie Family line-up (the uncredited voices of "Brazil") were actually a studio ensemble. Shortly after the big success of the "Brazil" single and album, a trio consisting of Cassandra Wooten, Gwendolyn (Oliver) Wesley (who passed in 2020) and Cheryl Mason-Jacks (later Dorman) was quickly assembled to perform and record as the group onward through 1977.

"Brazil" proved to be an actively played discotheque title as early as July of 1975, if club surveys reported to *Record World*, especially from Florida and New York, were any gauge. By late August the song was #1 on the publication's Disco File Top 20 chart. With its feverish beat, clean strings and excitable horns, the title also reached #1 on the *Billboard* disco chart and stayed there for several weeks. The Ritchie Family recycled "Brazil" the following year by including it in their hugely popular medley, "The Best Disco In Town." A 1997 remix of The Ritchie Family version of "Brazil" was released by Italian producers in a dubby house style, and, over the years, the song itself has been re-recorded numerous times by a plethora of dance music acts, including Batida Do Brazil and Bellini. Sure makes you want to immediately hit the Avenida Nossa Senhora de Copacabana!

Commentary from Cassandra Wooten:

"We usually open our show with 'Brazil,' and that sets the tone for the rest of our performance. There's a sexy, classy feel to it that immediately brings the audience in. 'Brazil' is one of those songs that makes me think of a street carnival. I envision riding on a float in the late summer, intoxicated by the mood of the revelers. The air is fragrant, and all around there are happy people enjoying life."

Cassandra's favorite summertime song:

"In my teens, Martha And The Vandellas recorded 'Dancing In The Street.' I can hear it now! We had great block parties back then, and when this jam was played, the party went into high gear. It named all the major cities, including my hometown, Philadelphia, PA."

Brighter Than Sunshine - Aqualung (2003), B-Unique Records (UK)
Producer: Matt Hales

The only thing better than summer is falling in love during the summer, and I can't think of a finer way to express that joy than English singer/song-writer Matt Hales' brilliantly earnest pop/rock ballad fused with evocative piano playing. It's a fair comparison, in this case, to compare such positive emotions to the brightness of the sun. This equal opportunity composition was featured in the 2005 Ashton Kutcher straight romcom "A Lot Like Love" and in the 2019 fifth season of the hit TV comedy "Schitt's Creek," played during a moving gay wedding scene.

Brown Eyed Girl - Jimmy Buffett (1983) MCA (US)
Producers: Jimmy Buffett, Michael Utley

This Mississippi-born singer/songwriter and proud leader of the "beach bum" movement has been inspiring that getaway feeling in millions for decades, sending his disciples to Key West, all in search of a slice of paradise. Here, his remake of the 1967 Van Morrison song infuses an understated, but never-the-less irresistible, tropical feeling into the mix. Upbeat and addictive pop/rock from the album *One Particular Harbour*. *Billboard* had a rather cautionary impression of the LP, advising on September 24, 1983, that, "... the most taxing part about this album—as with his others—is resisting the lures or melody and rhythm steadfastly enough to glimpse his often less-than-sunny visions of how things really are." If anyone noticed that, it didn't seem to bother them.

Brown Eyed Girl - Steel Pulse (1997), Edel (G)
Producer: Graham Dickson

The British reggae champs cover the nostalgic Van Morrison hit in a sweet, breezy, upbeat and distinctly summery fashion. Uncomplicated and agree-able. It's high-calorie sugar, but go ahead and treat yourself. You've been through it and you deserve it!

Café del Mar (Compilations) - Various (1994), Café del Mar Music (SP) *(Sea café)*
Producers - Various

This extensive series of compilation albums became world famous for their tracks that offered ambient beats by a wide range of artists proficient at projecting a chillout music beach vibe. The concept was originally inspired by a bar found in Saint Antoni de Portmany, Ibiza. DJ José Padilla, producer of evocative ambient music mixes that melded perfectly with the island's stunning sunsets, created the first few editions of the series. (He passed in

2020.) The concept inspired a brand, recording label, live streaming service, and YouTube channel that continue to present a wide variety of mood-generating electronic sounds in a host of genres, including new age music, deep house, flamenco and more.

California Sun - Frankie Avalon (1987), Columbia (US)
Producer: Gary Usher

The former beach bum teen heartthrob ("Beach Blanket Bingo" from 1965 comes to mind) delivers a semi-new wave version of The Rivieras' 1964 surf rock tune (also covered by the Ramones in 1976) with that reverb tang. Featured in the 1987 movie, "Back To The Beach," and on its soundtrack. It may remind you of your dad embarrassingly cutting loose after one too many Married Man Mules at a wedding reception, but I think you can give Frankie a pass. Shallow waters and tongue-in-cheek fun, so no lifeguards needed. Check out Annette Funicello's "Jamaica Ska" from the same movie a bit later in this book.

Calypso - John Denver (1975), RCA Victor (US)
Producer: Milton Okun

Like Christopher Cross' "Sailing," "Calypso" creates the sensation of taking to open waters, though here the feeling is more majestic, an adventure on the high seas quite fitting for this tribute to legendary explorer Jacques Cousteau. Its simple folk rock melody briskly rises and falls as if the song itself were the vessel named in the title. Mr. Denver gently sings with an agreeable sense of enthusiasm and makes the creative connection between Cousteau's conservationist goals and the beauty of the sea. *National Geographic* would no doubt approve. I'll add that this #2 *Billboard* US pop hit feels damn summery, too.

Calypso Crazy (1988) - Billy Ocean, Jive (UK)
Producer: Robert John "Mutt" Lang

"Calypso Crazy," recorded a few years after his hit "Caribbean Queen," has an appealing Caribic charm but with a harder beat than the former (more reminiscent of his "Get Outta My Dreams, Get Into My Car" hit). The track never reached the level of worldwide popularity that the breakthrough

"Queen" enjoyed, but it's still an inviting jam comparable in vibe and style to Lionel Richie's "All Night Long (All Night)." Billy Ocean, a truly great singer, might very easily have been pigeonholed into singing this type of holiday beach music endlessly, so it's interesting that his contributions to the world of pop and palm tree music are pretty much limited to two singles.

Calypsonacht - Jeannine (1997), Sound-Around (G) *Calypso night*
Producers: Tony O'Melley, Howard O'Melley, Thorsten Schotten

The youthful voice of this pretty blonde German schlager singer is a pleasant match for the irresistibly catchy, uptempo dance/pop songs she sang through-out the mid-late '90s. Her singles frequently celebrated romantic summer themes with ocean sound effects, including "Hey Mr. Sommer "(1995) (*Hey mister summer*), "Insel Im Wind" (1996) (*Island in the wind*), and "Ein Verrückter Sommertag" (1996) (*A crazy summer day*). "Calypsonacht," recalling the hook of "In The Summertime" by Mungo Jerry in its chorus, is a fine example of the artist's work with its danceable beat and incidental use of steel drums.

Capitaine Abandonne (Sail Away) - Gold (1985), WEA (F)
Captain Abandon (Sail Away)
Producers: Gold, Jacques Cardona

With its trademark masculine chorus and rich synth-pop sound that gives the impression of it possibly having been a shelved "Pirates of the Caribbean" theme song, this record of spirited adventure had plenty of that summer vibe. It was also the 67th biggest hit of 1986 in Europe, as ranked in a year-end survey by *Music & Media*. The France-based group Gold was composed of lead singer and guitarist Émile Wandelmer, Lucien Crémadès (vocals and guitar), Bernard Mazauric (keyboards), Etienne Salvador (drums) and Alain Llorca (vocals and bass).

"'Capitaine Abandonné' was born of a merger between a song com-posed by Bernard and the music of another song composed by Émile," says Alain Llorca. "It was the brilliant idea of Cardona to bring these two songs together. I remember that we had to re-record the vocals for the chorus dozens of times to get that big sound of unison we were after. It was very hard, because the key was very high on this melody. We spent a lot of time working on it. The recording took place in Toulouse at the Condorcet Studio. The lyrics were inspired by sports enthusiasts who go on explorations of the land or sea, then disappear, die or are never found. The subject of the text deals with adventurers who were known worldwide—sailors (Alain Colas), sportsmen (Arnaud de Rosnay), adventurers and journalists like Philippe de Dieuleveult. I think that appealed to listeners of many countries. And no matter where a person is from, a good universal chorus (the 'Ohé Ohé' sound, as heard in our song) is irresistible." *[From the book: Europe's Stars of '80s Dance Pop, Vol. 2, Arena, Bookbaby, 2018.]*

Capital Tropical - Two Man Sound (1981), TSR (B/US)
Producer: Lou Deprijck

This is one spicy Margarita! Two Man Sound was actually a *three*-man Belgian act consisting of composer, producer, performer Francis Deprijck—aka Lou Deprijack (Lou And The Hollywood Bananas, "Kingston Kingston"), Yves Lacomblez and Sylvaine Vanholme. They had enjoyed some success in the eurodisco pop market since the mid-'70s with hits that included "Disco Charlie Brown" (1976) and the medleys "Disco Samba" (1978) and "Latin Waves (Disco Cha Cha)" (1981). The group had a modest US dance hit in the clubs with "Que Tal America" in 1979, prior to "Capital Tropical" making its way to America's west coast. There, Tom Hayden, founder of California's TSR Records, released the song for the US market. A vivid, infectious, and far more authentic sounding song and production than the group's previous ventures, "Capital Tropical" is a breathtaking dive into jubilant holiday escape, especially in its Lou Lacoste disco remix. Frankly, the extended version can make one feel airborne, with nothing but the music and its infectious vibe giving you wings. The track spent 19 weeks on the *Billboard* dance/disco chart in '81, indicating a lot of club-goers had that very same feeling of elevation, though party favors may have explained some of that dance floor lift. The album *Capital Tropical* was released in the US the following year. See where it takes you.

Commentary from Tom Hayden:

"'Capital Tropical' was very near and dear to me as it was the first release on TSR. A good friend of mine from Belgium, producer Roland Kluger, for whom I had promoted a few projects, sent me a test pressing of the record and asked if I knew a company that might be interested in licensing and releasing it in the US. I said that I would start a label and release it and could get the record out within a couple weeks. It went top 10 on many disco charts and was played at some of the biggest stations nationwide."

Caribbean Blue - Big Mountain (1995), Giant (US)
Producer: Handel Tucker

The Big Mountain reggae band broke beyond their Californian roots and became an international sensation with their version of Peter Frampton's "Baby, I Love Your Way" off the "Reality Bites" movie soundtrack in '94. In this follow-up, a simple, easy-going reggae rhythm makes a rather sad song about a man facing the sunshine alone in paradise (without the girl he loves) feel almost happy. Released in Spanish and English versions.

Caribbean Blue - Enya (1991), WEA (UK)
Producer: Nicky Ryan

The queen of Celtic-inspired music has an instantly recognizable, heavenly sound, and this dreamy, meditative single oozes with the same ethereal essence found in her smash hit "Orinoco Flow" (which was included on many cd maxi-single pressings of "Caribbean")—though this one is, incredibly, even more soothing. You'll feel the sun shimmering off tranquil waters and quickly get caught up in this airy song's inviting current, as exotic islands beckon.

Caribbean Disco Show (1981) / Soca Calypso Party - Lobo (1982), Mercury (NL)
Producers: Eric Boom, Roy Beltman

Two medleys done Stars on 45 style from the Netherlands. Breezy recognizable highlights of the hit "Show" include "Day-O (Banana Boat)," "Island In The Sun" and (gasp) "Judy Drowned." The term "soca" is said to have come from a decades old news publication's misquoted abbreviation of "Soul of Calypso," which happened to catch on in the' 70s—sort of like celebrity couple hybrid names. In the "Soca Calypso Party" follow-up, the syncopated rhythms of the genre, which includes many sub-genres and pulsates with the Indian and East African rhythm influences that melded in Trinidad and Tobago, are so immediately jumpy, bright and cheerful that the second you hear the evocative drums and that calypso undercurrent, one's mind and body are transported to paradise. Here we get vintage Caribic joy with "The Big Bamboo," "Shame And Scandal In The Family," "Rum And Coca Cola" and other standards. Both tracks set the mood for our next entry, perhaps the ultimate pop music salute to the Caribbean.

Caribbean Queen (No More Love On The Run) - Billy Ocean (1984), Jive (UK/US)
Producer: Keith Diamond

Back in the days when information about less familiar names on the pop chart took some time to circulate, Ocean was beginning to garner world attention with the #1 *Billboard* dance and pop chart hit, "Caribbean Queen." He'd been around for a while, but this song was getting him noticed in a big way. There was debate as to whether he came from the African or American music scenes, but soon everyone knew the deal with this distinctive, soulful, British-Trinidadian vocalist and his scintillating and stylish mix of pop, R&B, dance, reggae and Caribic sounds. "Caribbean Queen" earned Ocean a 1985 Grammy award for Best Male R&B Vocal Performance. The track was released in Europe as "European Queen" and in other territories with slightly modified lyrics to have greater appeal in particular regions. This incredibly catchy song remains a model of the summer, sun and tropical dance/pop sound.

Studio 10 from Australia posted a video interview with Ocean on YouTube, June 13, 2019. In it, program interviewer Angela Bishop noted that Ocean's songs were predominantly "happy," and asked why this was so. "Because I'm a happy person," said Ocean matter-of-factly. "Why be self-indulgent and sing about problematic things?" That's the very foundation of hot summer jams.

Caribbean Sea - Etienne Daho (1989), Virgin (F)
Producers: Ben Rogan, Etienne Daho

Seas the day! This bloody brilliant, ethereal Francophone production may remind one of Enya's better known "Caribbean Blue," but actually predates that track by over two years. It's a downtempo and haunting synth-pop song expressing seemingly riled sentiments about a break-up. But you wouldn't know it from the atmosphere. The dichotomy of this dark premise versus what musically sounds like a romantic journey to tropical islands bathed in warm blue light is fascinating. Whatever was intended, Daho, who co-produced, co-arranged, co-wrote and remixed this track, shows he is a master of mood, impressively delivering mature lyrics, a sophisticated, relaxed arrangement, and a vocal rendition that is extremely tranquilizing and very much island spirited. At the time of this release, the artist was something of a megastar in France, but hadn't quite reached the rest of the continent, perhaps causing this single to go relatively unnoticed beyond his home base. That's a pity. Take the deep dive into the maxi-single's "Longue Plage Version"—the water's fine. And if you're not in love with this singer by the end of your swim, see a doctor.

Caribic Dream - Salida Del Sol (1998), Beatz Only (G)
Producer not indicated.

Attractively orchestrated trance/EDM track with a strong hand-clap beat and a tweaked steel drum-like sound that effortlessly propels the melody and breathy vocals. A feisty, breathy creation from Germany said to be the work of electronic music artist Michael Schidlo.

Catch A Ride - Eddie Money (1987), Columbia (US)
Producer: David Kahne

Head for the coast, we're advised. I'm already there! The Brooklyn-born rocker ("Take Me Home Tonight") contributed this spirited electric guitar jam with a lightweight California surf vibe to support the opening credits of the film "Back To The Beach" at a time when his pop career was on fire. Retro-minded and more than just fun—it's an amusement park, as Connie Stevens says in the flick. Eddie caught his last wave in 2019.

Celebrate Lambada - Combo (1989), BCM (G)
Producer: Detlef Petersen

Catchy, upbeat, Latin-enriched dance/pop that weaves in the summery Brazilian sound without trying too hard. Nicely done with a festive, filling vibe in its "Beach Club Version," so digest it a bit before you hit the surf.

Christmas In The Caribbean - Jimmy Buffett (1985), MCA (US)
Producer: Tony Brown

Buffett would have us believe the Caribbean has everything the winter holiday requires—and it checks out. However, the only ice you'll find here is in your drink. I think he's on to something, and if you ask me, steel drums sound every bit as inviting as sleigh bells. The proof is in this upbeat, beachy, atmospheric tribute to December 25th. Tis the sea-sun!

Circle In The Sand - Belinda Carlisle (1988), MCA (US)
Producer: Rick Nowels

Former Go-Go Miss Belinda, sounding a bit like Stevie Nicks, really hits her stride with this dreamy, rhythmic dance ballad and its richly melodic chorus, all draped in a lush, appealing pop production. Love endures beyond the end of summer, she assures us. The William Orbit "Beach Party Mix" adds some more Latin influence, with guitars and bongos evoking a deeper seaside feel. But if it's full-on summer heat you're looking for, his "Sandblast Multi-Mix" is the ticket, blending in the singer's equally powerful hits "Heaven Is A Place On Earth" and "I Get Weak" in a breathtaking dubby mashup.

Club Tropicana - Wham! (1983), Innervision/Epic (UK)
Producers: Steve Brown, George Michael

At face value, it might not register that "Club Tropicana," a songwriting effort by George Michael and Andrew Ridgeley from Wham!'s earliest days, was possibly intended to be a snarky dig at a vacation package company whose marketing targeted young adults. Regardless of the boys' objective, they created a deliciously uplifting, worry-free beach party song. The ingredients in this tasty cocktail include a modest disco vibe with effervescent Latin-style percussion mixed in and a kind of loungy piano sound twirling around to make it go down smoothly. Seeing the model-fit duo perform on the UK's "Top Of The Pops" wearing board shorts and open Hawaiian shirts, dancing among kitschy glittering palm trees, one can almost smell the sweet scent of Bain de Soleil orange tanning gel (which, sadly, is no longer being manufactured as of July, 2021).

Club Tropicana - Vinylshakerz (2005), Kontor (G)
Producer: Vinylshakerz

Credited vocalist Leroy Daniels does a terrific job of sounding like George Michael on this remake of the Wham! hit, which is turned into an electro-house throbber. The video features an island paradise, a posh mansion and pool, lots of liquor, and a bevy of scantily clad women, adding a ballin' new dimension to the mix and suitably transforming the song into the Ibiza or Ayia Napa anthem it always felt like it could be. It's difficult to watch a video like this and not feel a sense of missing out, even if what we're viewing is all just an illusion.

Coco Jamboo - Mr. President (1996), Club Culture/WEA (G)
Producer: Kai Matthiesen

I voted for this president. Like splitting open a ripe coconut and drinking the sweet water inside, "Jamboo" is a fortifying mid-tempo breezer, one of the world's most popular dance/pop summer jams, is really about nothing specific at all—just the good feeling that easy sing-along lyrics and the suggestion of tropical rhythms can generate. Its mid-tempo rhythm is brilliant, and its irresistible melodic charm undeniable. The song debuted on *Music &*

Media's European Top Singles chart on May 4, 1996, and about two months later it was top five. The publication's July 6, 1996, review of the group's second album, *We See The Same Sun* (which included the single and was produced by Kai Matthiesen), said, "It doesn't happen often that eurodance acts deliver strong albums, but this hard-touring German trio pulled it off." Mr. President delivered other summer-themed executive orders over the years with varying levels of success, including "I'll Follow The Sun," "Where The Sun Goes Down,""Love, Sex And Sunshine," and "Jojo Action," each delivering some of the sunshine element found in "Coco Jamboo." Delroy Rennalls held the office of "President" (beside a changing line-up of two female vocalists) beginning in 1994 until the group disbanded in the early 2000s, and he still performs their hits today. In recent days, he's performed under the moniker LayZee.

Commentary from Delroy Rennalls:

Would you tell me where the name Mr. President came from?

"It's a long story, but before I joined the group, there was another person performing as Mr. President. [The producers said] the name meant something like, 'Music and rhythm to the highest level.' The highest level a person can reach as a private person is 'president.' That's the reason they gave. That's what they wanted out there, so I played along with that."

How did you come to join the group?

"I was a DJ and rapping in northern Germany. I did some rapping because I wasn't as good at mixing at the time, and the rapping went over well. But I got better and better at both over time. I knew a lot of people at the time, the early '90s, such as DJ Bobo and Tony [Dawson-Harrison] (Captain Hollywood). We shared a lot of ideas, but we hadn't made a real impact on dance music at this point. My brother and I also worked for a small label called SPV [Schallplatten, Produktion & Vertrieb], and we learned about marketing and A&R and all the things it took to make a hit. I got a phone call from someone in a group whose rapper had left, and he wanted me to come in and help them out for a couple of months. The project was Mr. President. I had heard of it, but I didn't really know what it was all about. I figured I'd work with them for a couple of months until they found a new rapper—after that I'm out.

"I was doing a European promotional tour with them, and I kind of liked it. It kind of gelled. Because I knew a lot of people in the record business, these contacts helped get the Mr. President record deal extended. The producers asked me to stay for a year. We promoted the hell out of our first album. It didn't do that well, but we reached #12 in Germany with the single 'Up'n Away,' which went gold. It was one of the first records that didn't get into the top 10, but managed to achieve gold certification. I thought that was kind of cool!"

What were the origins of "Coco Jamboo" from the We See The Same Sun *album?*

"I agreed to help with the writing of the second album. There were some really good songs on it. There was a song on the set that really stood out, way above the others. But I didn't like the title: 'Coco Jamboo.' I liked the music, but I kept asking the producers to change the title. It was cool singing it in the studio, but, you know, that was it. For me, it just wasn't a hit. Keep in mind, at that time the beats were going up—it was techno time. We were touching on 142-150 beats per minute. I thought we should do something more like that. They thought, nah, everyone is going faster, but we gotta be cool. No, I thought, this is *not* cool. How wrong was I?"

(R) Former "Mr. President" Delroy Rennalls today.

Are you able to identify the magic element of this song that so many fans identified with worldwide?

"Exactly that point—that it wasn't like everybody else's music. The music was very laid back, very cool, and nobody was doing that kind of reggae fusion, reggae-calypso with a laid back dance beat. There were a few attempts by others, but they usually went way over the top and made it really Caribbean, and we kept the European flair with the Caribbean feeling. Everyone could identify something in that track.

"I didn't want to write a rap for it; I just wanted the girls to sing it, but the producers thought then it wouldn't be different. I had that De La Soul kind of rhythm in my head , and I had about 15 minutes to write the rap. When I went to record it, the first take, everyone stopped talking and moving in the studio. I thought, are they pissed off, did I do something wrong? The producers played it back, over and over, then told me they thought it was—absolutely brilliant! It wasn't a one-take, I had to record it a couple of times, but it was one of the quickest tracks we had done."

Tell me about that delightful tropical video for "Coco Jamboo" filmed in Venezuela.

"I still had my doubts about the record when we made the video. The producers were saying it was going to be massive—yeah, yeah, yeah. We went to a small island off the coast of Carúpano in Venezuela. We filmed on the beach there, and we were supposed to do a scene in the village square. They had just finished a big festival, and it was kind of empty. We got permission to use the square and started filming. The people had just finished a siesta and started coming back into the square. A lot of people started gathering. Then the lord mayor came out and started talking to the video director.

"The mayor wanted the people in the square to be a part of the video. They offered to do their festival over again for us! That whole party scene, the guys walking on stilts, the little girls in party dresses, that wasn't planned. The people were loving it—it was amazing! Then it clicked with me—that's when I fell in love with 'Coco Jamboo.' It was no longer what this song can do for me, it's what I can do for this song!"

You seemed to enjoy taking off your shirt a lot during live performances.

[*Delroy laughs.*] "I don't know what it was about the '90s—as soon as the music went on, as soon as we started moving, bang, the shirt was off! I don't know what it was—it was the first couple of years! 'Oh, I gotta get the shirt off! The girls are screaming, gotta get the shirt off!' Well, I *thought* they were screaming anyway."

When you think back to this time, Delroy, what feelings come up for you?

"There were a lot of great lessons to be learned. It molded me. I never really changed—but it kind of made me *not* change, if you understand what I mean. Today, we're still in the middle of this '90s/'Coco Jamboo' hype still going on, and I love that. I guess it signals to me that I didn't do anything wrong, and everything I did at that time was the right thing to do. To tell you the truth, I've haven't done anything else. After Mr. President, I took some time out to do songwriting and producing, learning those ropes—that was the only thing I didn't really get to do—so I took some time off to do that. But then I got right back on stage!"

Coconut Groove - Rice And Beans Orchestra (1977), T.K. Disco (US)
Producer: Pepe Luis Soto

Instrumental piece (and B-side of the single "You've Got Magic") from a studio disco group assembled by Puerto Rico-born Soto. Best served when the mood calls for vintage, easy going, string-heavy background disco music. Typical of the style released by T.K. Records and other dance labels during this period. High carb beats.

Coconut Grove - David Lee Roth (1985), Warner (US)
Producer: Ted Templeman

Diamond Dave had no problem venturing out on his own after his stint as lead singer for Van Halen (though he returned to the band in 2006), but those expecting that hyper hard rockin' sound he so vigorously forged with the band were in for a surprise. A track from his "Crazy From The Heat" sampler 12-inch single, it's an unexpectedly soft, gentle tune in praise of a beachside getaway that is calming and inviting. The track has a very personal sincerity about it (it's amazing how well Roth expresses his appreciation for a laid back lifestyle), and it instantly generates a feeling of tranquility.

Coconut Medley - Saragossa Band (1993), Polydor (G)
Producer: Anthony Monn

A popular German cover band that enjoyed many hit albums on their country's pop charts, Saragossa Band feverishly made their way through medleys of easily recognized mainstream hits. This one is a fun trip to the tropics, with competent cover renditions of the tropically oriented "Annie, I'm Not Your Daddy," "Cuba," "Ritmo De La Noche," "Gimme Hope Jo'Anna" and more. Cover bands like this often do a great job of cutting to the quick, quickly.

Coconut Tree - King Kurlee (1993), RCA (G)
Producers: Ramond, Hansing

Give it a listen and I'm pretty sure you will go coco-nuts over this song. What a great, wonderfully carefree pop/rap/reggae/dance track this is—the kind of fun, escapist storytelling that instantly transports you to a cool place under swaying palm trees while lifting your spirit with its warm, infectious melody. King Kurlee was an alias used by singer/songwriter/composer Joe Barone, who studied his art in New Orleans, according to an RCA artist fact sheet that was included with promotional copies of the single. He released just a handful of rhythmic, Caribic hip-hop/pop jams during the mid-'90s ("Banana Manana," a version of Deep Purple's "Smoke On The Water," "Red River"). It wouldn't exactly be precise to call his music "soulful," but he earns plenty of props for creating a near perfect island atmosphere and for the spirit of his agreeable vocals and cleverly rapped/sung lyrics. "Coconut Tree" somehow languished under the radar, but it's a wonderful salute to late summer in the tropics—and, sadly—heading back north to the cold and snow, as the singer laments. Because, let's agree, it kinda sucks when you're not at the beach.

Come To My Island - KC And The Sunshine Band (1979), T.K. Records (US)
Producers: Harry Wayne Casey, Richard Finch

It would be unthinkable that possibly the most famous of upbeat summer music pop bands to ever come out of Miami would *not* have a song in their catalog with that palm tree getaway feeling. Though it may have been relegated to the B-side of their hit single "Do You Wanna Go Party," "Come To My Island" is an A-list effort. Love in the air, freedom, and dancing and singing all day and all night are just a few of this musical real estate's selling points, promoted in an exceptionally smooth pop/disco entry that follows the same formula as "That's The Way (I Like It)" and "(Shake, Shake Shake) Shake Your Booty."

Conga - Miami Sound Machine (1985), Epic (US)
Producer: Emilio Estefan, Jr.

"We played at . . . Kuala Lumpur in Malaysia," Cuban-born singer/songwriter Gloria Estefan told Diana Montane of the *Los Angeles Times* on January 18, 1990, "and we were warned, 'These people are very quiet.' Well, after 'Conga,' I said, 'Quiet, my foot.'" "Conga" had just that kind of stimulating effect on people. It's a restless samba monster with riveting percussion. Ms. Estefan's colorful vocals certainly ginger up the production's summer flavor. Her distinctive voice was a major reason the group (founded by her husband, Emilio Estefan, Jr., 10 years earlier as the Miami Latin Boys) came to the fore and found pop star status in the English speaking world. After receiving much acclaim on the international and US Latin circuits, the group finally began to get noticed by the general American record-buying public with the release of the 1985 *Primitive Love* album, a set rife with cross-culture club and pop sounds, including "Conga," "Bad Boy" and "Falling In Love (Uh-Oh)." The single "Conga," and its fiery extended dance mix by Pablo Flores, placed the passionate voice of Gloria front and center so much so that the ensemble would become known as Gloria Estefan and The Miami Sound Machine a short time later.

Copacabana (At The Copa) - Barry Manilow (1978), Arista (US)
Producers: Ron Dante, Barry Manilow

Arguably the most famous pop song about a nightclub ever recorded, this hot spot was located north of Havana. Manilow's top 10 *Billboard* disco and pop hit from the summer of '78 has a palpably exciting feel. Its ebullient arrangement and movie-like storytelling are tremendously appealing and memorable, which may explain why so many people can still recite the song's lyrics effortlessly. For sure, they at least know it's about a showgirl named Lola (and her admirers, Rico and Tony). The best *Cash Box* could say about the track in a June 10, 1978, review (coordinated by Peter Hartz) was, "A Latin beat, congas and added percussion, strings and horns make it unusual." *Ummm*…in retrospect, it was a bit more than just that, ultimately becoming one of Manilow's all-time biggest signature hits. Best lyric in the song: the cute but snarky observation that the Copa, once a posh show palace, was now (it is implied) a lowly disco. Lola may have had a bad night, but disco certainly wasn't to blame.

Costa Mykonos - Helena (2002), Robbyland Records (G)
Mykonos coast
Producers: Helena, Ivo Moiser, Robert Jung

This actually *is* unusual, even for this book—mid-tempo German schlager dance/pop with a traditional Greek feel. You'll either feel like you're on Crete's Elafonisi Beach, dancing the kalamatiano, or listening to a German-dubbed episode of "The Lawrence Welk Show." Whatever floats your boat.

Crazy English Summer - Faithless (2001), Cheeky (UK)
Producers: Rollo, Sister Bliss

Blistering, trippy electronica-house in its gorgeous DJ Aloe extended remix form, it elicits a melancholy feeling that reflects the power of the season to bring back thoughts of summer loves we may have left behind in the past. Far less melancholy sounding than some of the duo's other work.

Cruel Summer - Ace Of Base (1998), Mega (SW)
Producers: Stephen Hague, Joker, Buddha

Ace Of Base was a Swedish eurodance group consisting of founding members and siblings Jonas "Joker" Berggren, Linn Berggren, Jenny Berggren, plus Ulf Ekberg. They debuted on the world pop music scene in the early '90s and were often likened to a modern-day ABBA with their hip, bright and appealing female vocal style (and, of course, because they shared the same homeland). Ace Of Base melded europop dance beats with the suggestion of something warm and tropical-ish into many of their hits, notably "All That She Wants" and "The Sign." By 1998, the group was still going strong, so, while taking a familiar, reliable song like Bananarama's "Cruel Summer" and giving it a reboot was less bold than one might have hoped for at the time, it was undeniably a pleasing safe bet. The song peaked at #10 on the *Billboard* dance chart and was popular throughout Europe. Steffi Thierstein, head of music at Radio 105 in Basel, Switzerland, commented to *Music & Media* on July 25, 1998, "Although 'Cruel Summer' is nothing sensational, Ace Of Base know their strength lies in producing good radio records. It's surprisingly close to the original, and I should know, because I used to scare my parents by wearing my hair in a messy Bananarama cut!"

Cruel Summer - Bananarama (1983), London (UK)
Producers: Tony Swain, Steve Jolley

While it's true summer can sometimes be bittersweet, "cruel" seems a bit of a stretch. Ironically, ask anyone what songs generate warm weather *good feelings* and you're likely to see "Cruel Summer" near or at the top of the list. But this jam departs from the usually upbeat nature of summer-themed productions, despite its clubby sound, and looks at how lonely the season can be when your love is gone. Bananarama (original members Sara Dallin, Keren Woodward and Siobhan Fahey) effortlessly blend smooth vocals with a slightly tropical mid-tempo dance pulse, creating a unique vibe in this synth-pop history milestone, which peaked at #11 on the *Billboard* dance chart. On July 2, 1983, Paul Sexton of *Record Mirror* claimed the song "thuds unconvincingly away with a variety of some five notes to choose from and if they were singing for their lives they'd never have been around to make the pesky record." He was, no doubt, overdue for a holiday. In a July 21, 1984, review of the single, *Billboard* said a, "Piquant disco beat supports the hippest unison vocals in the business."

The trio appeared on BBC One's "The Graham Norton Show" in 2017, where original group member Sara recalled, "The first time we thought we maybe actually made it was in L.A. because we were coming from breakfast, about to go to the beach, Santa Monica, on the bus, and we saw Mike Tyson sitting in front of his limo, and he started singing 'Cruel Summer' at us. We just went, 'Wow!'" Perhaps that was the inspiration for the title of their fourth album.

Cuba - El Mariachi (1996), Strictly Rhythm (US)
Producer: Roger Sanchez

It's surprising US travel restrictions to Cuba weren't lifted immediately after the release of this scorching track. This version of the song made popular by the Gibson Brothers makes you want to jump on the next flight to José Martí International. Brenda K. Starr lends her powerful vocals to this fiery, rollicking house rocker, featuring live bass, guitar and horns that give the oft-covered song some extra dimension. "The Havana Club Mix" is unstoppable and burns the joint to the ground! *Wepa!*

Cuba - Gibson Brothers (1979), Zagora/Mango (F)
Producer: Daniel Vangarde

The first time I heard it, I knew it was love! With their homage to the island known for more than just a missile crisis (its architecture, rich culture, cigars, rum, and over 3500 miles of legendary beaches, for example) the Gibson Brothers trio (Chris Francfort, Patrick Francfort and Alex Francfort, who originally hailed from Martinique) mixed a stomping, red hot dance rhythm with Latin percussion to great effect (understatement). It's like getting hit by a rogue wave. With it, they scored themselves a vibrant, instantly recognizable pop and club hit moments before the so-called "end" of the disco era, just as a modest backlash against the genre was taking a short-lived hold. This pounding French production, sung with a distinctive, bravado-filled, gravelly voiced sense of urgency and powerful chorus bursts, was a success in the

US clubs, where it earned the boys a *Billboard* top 10 disco chart ranking. Nigel Wright remixed the track in 1988, giving it a slightly lighter, electronic spin. "Cuba" was originally included on the group's 1979 album of the same name and on the US version of their follow-up set, *On The Riviera*. It was also featured in an updated version on their most recent album in 2005, *Blue Island*. Group member Patrick Francfort passed in 2020.

Cuba - Dein Rhythmus Ist Der Salsa - Gino D'oro (1998), Toi, Toi, Toi (G) *Cuba - your rhythm is salsa*
Producer: Peter Sebastian

Brisk, polished, infectious German language remake of the Gibson Brothers hit, injecting a less gruff, more youthful sounding male vocal than found in the 1979 original. Good news—it's just as appealing. The maxi-single also contains a festive "Gute-Laune-Medley" (*Good mood medley*) sung in German and Italian versions.

D

Dancing In The Summertime - Sunshine Hit Collection - À La Carte & Mungo Jerry (1989), Coconut (G)
Producer: Hazel Stoner

An attempt to bring this seasoned German female trio (who enjoyed success beginning in the '70s with a regularly changing line-up) back into the limelight. However, the gimmick of bringing raspy-voiced Ray Dorset of Mungo Jerry into the mix and splitting vocal duties with him in a medley of mainly '80s eurodisco and Italo disco summer hits doesn't quite jell. Stick to a table d'hôte.

Dancing On The Beach (Bailando En La Playa) - Kasso (1984), Banana (I)
Producer: Giancarlo Meo

If this luxurious instrumental mid-tempo Italo disco piece written by Mario Flores and mixed in Rimini was referring to an actual waterfront real estate hot spot, it would probably be owned by Richard Branson. It's an exceptionally expensive and enchanting piece of music that takes a wonderful Balearic melody and adds the zest of old skool disco. Music like this goes straight for the heart and doesn't let go. The B-side of the act's "I Love The Piano" hit single.

Dancing On The Beach - Phil Sun (1985), Gala International (I)
Producer: Dino Marcato

I love the ice cold rain, sleet and snow of sun-starved winter stinging my face—said nobody ever! Lots of synths and talk of dancing away those winter blues in this track. Arranged by Italo disco specialist Marco Tansini, this track has all the catchy hallmarks of an '80s Italian summer holiday hit.

Dancing On The Beach (1997) / Holiday (1998) - Sandman, Muve/ZYX (SWZ)
Producers: Andreas Nager, Mark Wyss

With "Dancing" we have a song about being far from home on a beach where everyone's grooving to the radio. And suddenly one doesn't feel so lonely anymore. You've been in this spot before, and you'll stick around to ensure those blues stay away. Nothing extraordinary, but a pleasant enough, toe-tapping electro-pop diversion. The song was remade with a high-energy twist in 2008 by Robb Cole, with vocals by '80s hitmaker Spagna. Sandman's similar themed "Holiday" incorporates the famous Madonna melody into a eurodance arrangement reminiscent of Mr. President's "Coco Jamboo," plus plenty of tropical location name-drops. Both tracks were recorded in Switzerland. Between the two, you'll be shaking a lot of sand out of your shorts.

Der Sommer Ging So Schnell Vorbei (1993) / Eine Reise Mit Dir (1994) - Salto, Polydor (G)

The summer passed by so fast / A trip with you

Producer: Peter Wesselmecking

With their perfect teeth, bright smiles and blond hair, you should be able to appreciate that Salto is a clean-cut German boy band specializing in schlager dance music. And, boy, do they have that polished Euro-unison sound down to a science. They sing about summer, vacations and romance, which is just what they should be daydreaming about at their age. Latin guitars, bright keyboards and a feel-good mood accompany the sugary dance beat of both tracks as the lads whisk us away to fantasy destinations.

Der Sommer Ist Vorbei - G.G. Anderson (1998), Hansa

Summer is over

Producer: Engelbert Simons

An initially cloudy, downtempo, melancholic power synth ballad quickly changes course and saves the day with enough joyful energy to bring out the sun, thanks to a anthemic, highly infectious and singable chorus. Performed by one of the all-time champs of German schlager music, also known as Gerd Grabowski. Despite the bittersweet mood it initially evokes, the song ultimately insists summer never really ends. Anderson is no stranger to tropical holiday themes and settings in his music, scoring hits in German language territories with "Sommernacht In Rom" *(Summer night in Rome)* (1985), "Die Sonne Von St. Helena" *(The sun of St. Helena)* (1986), "Jamaica" (1987), "Sommer Sonne Cabrio" *(Summer sun convertible)* (1989), "San Valentino" (2013) and "Wenn In Santa Maria" *(When in Santa Maria)* (2021).

Destination Sunshine - Balearic Bill (1999), Xtravaganza Recordings (B/UK)

Producers: J. Gielen, S. Maes

After being advised that it's the last call for our flight to Barcelona, the beats kick in, this track's landing gear goes up, and this instrumental trance experience becomes airborne, cruising at a dizzying 40,000 feet. The song's melody is a rallying call to young people who are ready to party, and good luck keeping up with them. A terrific video featuring a jaunt in a Jeep across the bumpy terrain of Ibiza is enticing.

Deux Minutes De Soleil En Plus - Enzo Enzo (1990), Ariola (F)
Two minutes of sun and more
Producers: J.P. Bucolo, G. Augier

A world-weary chanteuse (stylistically and vocally reminiscent of France's Patricia Kaas) speaks of the concept of time, having just two more minutes of sun left in which to live in the moment. A "Vodka Version" offers a crisper, poppier mix, while the "Rhum Version" has a melodic warmth about it that really suits the summer season. The singer was a priority artist for a time on the BMG label roster.

Die Rote Sonne Von Barbados - Die Flippers (1986), Bellaphon (G) *The red sun of Barbados*
Producers: Karlheinz Rupprich, Uwe Busse

Though Germany isn't known for great beaches or resorts (it actually *does* have a number of pleasant hot spots and island resort areas, such as Rügen), its songwriters and artists sure know how to create a solid getaway vibe. Here's a mid-tempo, atmospheric and very popular German schlager song distinguished by the group's smooth trademark vocals as the trio celebrates warm sunsets in the Caribbean. Die Flippers have recorded literally dozens of songs in the same vein since as far back as the 1970s, including "Mexico," "Summer-Lady," "St. Tropez," "Acapulco," and "Mitternacht In Trinidad" (*Midnight in Trinidad*).

Disco Calypso - Beckett (1977), Casablanca (US)
Producer: Buddy Scott

Featured on the soundtrack to the 1977 Caribbean thriller movie "The Deep," directed by Peter Yates, soca singer Alston "Beckett" Cyrus' party jam is a busy production vaguely reminiscent of Salsoul hits popular at the time, but lacking in their signature heartfelt enthusiasm. The disco beat washes out a good deal of the Caribic flavor, making this feel like a missed opportunity to merge the uplifting power of both those music styles in what was then a high profile film vehicle.

Disco Calypso - Oscar Harris (1980), Ariola (B/NL)
Producer: A. Holten

Disco music, rum and Cokes, beaches, and mangos under the Jamaican sun—need I say more? Harris, a Dutch singer originally from Suriname with a strong, soulful voice, delivers what easily could have been an early Boney M. single. No connection to the previous Beckett track.

Do The Limbo Dance - David Hasselhoff (1991), White (G)
Producer: Jack White

A song about everyone's favorite resort activity (at least the "in public" kind). The Hoff's role on the TV series "Knight Rider" was the source of much of his popularity in Germany at this time, especially among children. *Music & Media* reported he was able to sell out venues with a capacity of "8000 - 10,000 shouting school kids" (October 18, 1991). I'm not convinced that kiddies were really the bulk of his audience (nor am I sure who actually was), but just the same "Do The Limbo Dance" is, indeed, a family friendly affair. This calypso-livened pop song was released just as his "Baywatch" series was hitting the TV airwaves there. For all the criticism and putdowns Hasselhoff receives, much of his music is, inarguably, cheesy but still quite likable. And his voice, as demonstrated in this made-for-summer hit, is more than capable. Why did David Hasselhoff change his name to "The Hoff?" He wanted to live hassle-free. One of those concert-going brats must have told me that one.

Dolce Vita - Ryan Paris (1983), Discomagic/Carrere (I) *Sweet life.*
Producer: John Bini (Pierluigi Giombini)

Life is short—make it sweet. One of the Italo disco genre's golden classics, this English language track resonated broadly across Europe in the summer of '83. It definitively captured the flavor of European holidays with its distinctly Italian charm. The song's uncomplicated, hypnotic melody and meticulous production by Pierluigi Giombini, bright lyrics by Paolo Mazzolini (also known as Gazebo, another early Italian dance music pioneer who hit it big with "I Like Chopin"), and the everyday man vocal stylings of Ryan Paris (Fabio Roscioli) came together brilliantly. It generated nearly the same romantic atmosphere as the classic Fellini movies that indirectly inspired the song's creation. Surprisingly, the track was a monster hit in the UK, which almost never saw Italian productions in the top five of its pop surveys.

"It's interesting because in Italy, 'Dolce Vita' was not quite as powerful on the pop chart as it was in other countries, but it was a very big hit in the Italian discothèques," says Fabio Roscioli (Ryan Paris). "All the people of Europe would come down to Spain and Italy in the summer—men looking for girls, girls looking for men, and everything in between. They would remember the song from the parties and nightclubs, and when they returned to their countries, they would ask for the song. Carrere Records bought the song from [the publisher] Severo Lombardoni, and BBC1 filmed the video for the song in Paris [for the British release]. The song just went up, up, up. The record was an amazing success in Spain. I have heard that it is the biggest selling record in Spain—*ever*—750,000 maxi-singles sold." *[From the book: Europe's Stars of '80s Dance Pop, Arena, 2017, McFarland.]*

Don Quichotte - Magazine 60 (1984), Baja (F/US)
Producer: D.J.L.

Like Two Man Sound's "Capital Tropical" earlier in the decade, this summery, unorthodox electro-synth classic with a Spanish flair (but made in France) eventually made its way to the US via Euro-licensor Roland Kluger and Tom Hayden's Baja Records label in 1985. The track spent 16 weeks on *Billboard's* dance/disco chart and was remixed for the clubs by Martin Rodriguez. It also (eventually) crossed onto the *Cash Box* pop singles chart in June of '86.

"It was our first release on our Baja Records label," says Hayden, "and it was a huge club hit. We also got airplay for it on every format of radio, including dance, pop, R&B, rock and Latin here in L.A. and across the country." Lifted from Magazine 60's 1985 album *Costa Del Sol*, a set which proved the group had a few more beachy electronic disco tricks up their sleeve, including "Rendez-Vous Sur La Costa Del Sol" (*Meet on the Costa Del Sol*), "Playa Del Amor" (*Love beach*) and "Hasta Luego Trinidad" (*See you later Trinidad*).

Don't Blame It On That Girl* / Good Times - Matt Bianco (1988), WEA/Atlantic (UK)
Producers: *Emilio Estefan, Jr., *George Casas, *Clay Ostwald / Mark Reilly, Mark Fisher

I blame it on the boogie. The British group Matt Bianco, formed in 1983 by vocalist Mark Reilly and fellow musicians from another pop band of which he previously was a member (Blue Rondo À La Turk), came into the spotlight in the mid-'80s. Polish singer Basia was featured in the Matt Bianco ensemble for a time, leaving the group around 1985 to pursue a solo career. Mr. Reilly's ensemble developed a sophisticated, jazzy, highly contagious Latin/pop/dance style with an abundance of panache, a sophisticated alternative to, say, the flamboyance and quirkiness of Kid Creole And The Coconuts. But to be sure, Matt Bianco was no less alluring than the Kid on the dance floor. Released throughout the '80s and '90s, singles such as "Yeh Yeh," "Half A Minute," "Dancing In The Street" and the fabulous house blaster "Sunshine Day" are fun and spirited hits with plenty of hooks, solid grooves, smooth harmonies and a warmly inviting, airy vibe (a sound that was also popularized at the time by Swing Out Sister, though more sedately).

(R) Mark Reilly of Matt Bianco, circa 1986, WEA (press still).

Of special note is Matt Bianco's third album, Indigo (1988), which *Music & Media* called "an absolutely crucial record full of potential hits" (July 30, 1988). With this project, the group had honed an upbeat, festive sound that surely defines summer. While the first single from that set, "Don't Blame It On That Girl," didn't specifically reference the season, the track'a precision vocals, vibrant horns and rousing, electronics-fused rhythm perfectly captured the energy and excitement of a hot summer night and quickly became one of their signature classics. And good release timing didn't hurt either. The song, remixed by Phil Harding, debuted on *Music & Media*'s Eurochart Hot 100 Singles chart in late June of '88 and quickly became a hot weather top 40 hit across the continent, especially popular in the UK. In the same review, the publication described the track quite simply as "excellent." Meanwhile, in the US, "Don't Blame It On That Girl" climbed to #10 on *Billboard*'s dance chart during the fall season, in combination with the track "Wap Bam Boogie." On September 10, 1988, *Cash Box* said, "A nice Latin feel elevates this wonderfully ignited track. Bianco sounds like a spruced-up Joe Jackson. If you like Miami Sound Machine, you'll love this." A week later, the publication commented on the *Indigo* album, saying, "Matt Bianco doesn't exist but the band that bears the name is a long cool tropical cocktail of dance pop, sprinkled with horns and a liberal dose of fun."

No relation to the Chic classic, but serving it up just as playfully, "Good Times" was also extracted from the band's *Indigo* set and is a "deliciously festive" (*Music & Media*, September 3, 1988) blender mix of the elements Matt Bianco so perfectly and consistently combined. Two prime remix choices here: a pumping disco version enhanced by Mixmaster Phil Harding for PWL and a more radio-slanted pop-style Miami Mix by Eric Schilling.

Four years before this track was released, Matt Bianco vocalist Mark Reilly revealed to Jeremy Lewis (of the UK's *Melody Maker*, September 15, 1984) the essence of the group's appealing sound, a thread found in "Don't Blame It On That Girl" and "Good Times" and common to most of Matt Bianco's recordings. "It's dance oriented," Reilly said. "We like to use a lot of percussion, and it has a Latin feel—samba and Brazilian mixed up with jazz. We like the atmospherics; we like each record to have its own character. We throw all these influences together and mix them up." Sounds like a Batida!

If the music of Matt Bianco ever made your heart race on a hot summer night, you can leave a healthy tip at the bar for Mark Reilly.

Commentary from Mark Reilly:

At the beginning of the Matt Bianco story, where did you see the group finding its place in the musical spectrum?

"When we started Matt Bianco, we were unsure where our niche would be, as the group we had just left (Blue Rondo À La Turk) hadn't been deemed successful. Although we were taking a jazzier bossa nova direction, it was still a Latin/jazz/pop fusion, and the current trend in the market place was heavily electro-pop. Only one label was interested in us for a two-single deal. The first single ('Get Out Of Your Lazy Bed') was a big hit!"

Eventually, the group became strongly connected with a stylish, rhythmic, danceable, summer sound in Europe. Did you go into the studio intentionally working to create music with summer appeal, or was this a pleasant by-product of your creative process?

"Myself, along with other members of Blue Rondo, were keen dance club attendees, from Northern soul to funk/soul underground. Mix those influences with Latin rhythms and most people associate that sound with the summer. I normally had a sense of what would work in the clubs up until "Wap Bam Boogie" which went massive in the clubs."

"Yeh Yeh" was among your first hits to have that holiday sound with its lively, fun, Latin club feel, and, from the same album, Matt Bianco (1986), "Summer Song" was a standout with its dreamy, gentle connection to the season.

"I really liked Georgie Fame's [version of] 'Yeh Yeh' and thought we could put our own stamp on it. 'Summer Song' was supposed to be a full-on lyric song, but we preferred the vibe with less vocals as an instrumental."

Two years later you created a powerful eurohouse track with a truly vibrant tropical vibe, "Don't Blame It On That Girl." Thoughts about it?

"We were happy with our [original] version of 'Don't Blame It On That Girl,' but when Emilio and Miami Sound Machine added their Latin recording

[vibe] to the track, it took it to another level. We then took it back to London where Phil Harding did a great mix."

Were you ever concerned your original vision of a song might be compromised by dance remixes?

"It is a bit of a lottery having dance remixes done of your music, and, to be honest, I have only liked about 20 percent of them (that other people have made for us)."

Being that Matt Bianco was strongly connected with a summer holiday sound, was there an expectation that you must always deliver that type of music?

"Matt Bianco have never deliberately followed a formula to repeat what was done before (if it was a big hit), but our musical influences have been pretty constant within the Latin, jazz, R&B, and pop genres."

Are you able to recall a stand out performance in your history with Matt Bianco that perhaps took place in a tropical setting where you felt your music was in perfect sync with the environment?

"We recorded an album in Rio, Brazil, in the early '90s [*Samba In Your Casa* (1991/EastWest)] where the place, the people and musicians were a great inspiration!"

If you personally wanted to create a hot summer getaway playlist, what would be on it?

"Probably greatest hits albums from people like The Isley Brothers, Bob Marley, Al Green."

Don't Worry, Be Happy - Bobby McFerrin (1988), EMI/ Manhattan (US)
Producer: Linda Goldstein

Don't worry, be beachy is more like it. This record presumes everything will be alright, and rightly so. It's a priceless easy listening pop gem with a light reggae vibe (composed by the artist) that is so simple and is such a feel good experience that it has summer written all over it. On September 18, 1988, *Music & Media* said, "…stripped down to the basics, but missing absolutely nothing." Featured in the movie "Cocktail."

Down, Deep Inside (Theme from "The Deep") - Donna Summer (1977), Casablanca (US)
Producer: John Barry

"On the surface of the ocean, men wage war and destroy each other…just a few feet beneath the surface, there is a calm and peace, unmolested by man." So said Jules Verne in his 1896 novel, "Facing the Flag," but then again he hadn't seen "The Deep." "Down" is an unjustly neglected sonic pleasure that wrapped up the first phase of Donna's disco career (riding on the coattails of the cutting edge "I Feel Love" to #3 on *Billboard*'s disco chart). This sensual track and Golden Globe nominee for Best Original Song is as tempting as the aqua colored waters off the coast of Bermuda, the setting of the adventure movie "The Deep" (based on the book by Peter Benchley) for which it served as a theme song. The singer is emoting at her breathy and sexy best, in sharp contrast to the song's admittedly mechanical and chugging pulse, which almost sounds like the engine of The Orca vessel from "Jaws." Still, John Barry's undulating arrangement conjures up sensuality, lusty passion and adventure, the kind of sensations that we often dream await us on our trips to the sultry tropics. The film may be best remembered for Jacqueline Bisset's striking ability to fill out a very wet white T-shirt, but Ms. Summer's hypnotic theme, some menacing sharks, and Lou Gossett, Jr.'s sinister character, Henri 'Cloche' Bondurant, were also engaging highlights of the movie.

Dreadlock Holiday - 10cc (1987), Mercury (UK)
Producers: 10cc

10cc was an eclectic English rock band that never hesitated to be experimental with their music. There's enough of a popping beat in this reggae-glazed track to get one's groove on, despite somewhat nervous lyrics about an outsider's troubles assimilating into Jamaican culture. Lifted from their perfectly titled *Bloody Tourists* album, the song was a modest pop hit in the US but fared better overseas. It's been featured in the films "Snatch" (2000), "The Social Network" (2010) and "Life Of Crime" (2013).

Dream In Paradise - Joy Salinas (1997), One Thousand Records (I)
Producers: Alex Neri, Marco Baroni

Ms. Salinas, from the Philippines, had a lot of success in Italy, most notably with "Rockin' Romance" in 1990. She's got a smooth-as-silk voice that goes down easy, and she's equally capable of shaking the walls with power and positivity. The artist gives a fine performance on this bright, uplifting, piano-accented house track. The "Moonlight Mix" shines even brighter than the "Sunlight Mix." Either way, you'll discover paradise within the first 60 seconds.

E - F

Easy When The Sun Go Down - James Adams (2001), 5000records (UK)
Producer: S. Panknin

Dry as dust. The song evokes an arid environment something akin to the middle of the hot Arizona desert in July, and with his weather-beaten voice, one might half expect the singer to look like the dusty hero of a spaghetti western. (Actually, I don't know what James Adams looks like.) Acoustic guitar work juxtaposed with some hammering percussion and the singer's indifferent, weary vocals makes for a diverting, unusual downtempo electronic pop/rock thumper, perfect for any heat wave. From the maxi-single, the "easy sundown mix" is the oasis in this scorched musical landscape.

Echo Beach - Martha And The Muffins (1980), Dindisc/Virgin (UK)
Producer: Mike Howlett

There's a reason why way-out tracks from the early '80s like this (and those of The B-52's, Haircut One Hundred and other new wave artists) connected so well with sun and sand. They often recall that killer shakin' and shimmyin' beach party vibe of the '60s. In that respect, "Echo Beach" is a full-on surf shindig drenched in avant-garde, synth-pop simplicity. The song dares to lift the curse of office work drudgery, suggesting the remedy to that affliction lies in the pleasure of daydreaming about the beach. On August 9, 1980, *Cash Box* said, "Sandy-haired singer Martha Ladly may draw some comparisons to Blondie's [Debbie] Harry stylistically, but the band cooks with poppy passion."

A few years back, Leonard Nevarez interviewed the principal players of Martha and The Muffins, which he called "Toronto's greatest band." In a video interview posted on YouTube (July 10, 2015), Muffin band member Mark Gane, who wrote "Echo Beach," discussed the origins of the song. The singer/songwriter, sitting in a park, pointed to a body of fuzzy gray water partially obscured by large trees, saying he and his friend drove to that location one night on a motorbike around 1977 or '78. The area became the inspiration for the verse of "Echo Beach" about a silent summer evening. "This is where it happened," said Gane. "I think we probably smoked a bit of dope and looked out, and it became a surrealistic sight." An earlier verse in the song was inspired by working in a wallpaper factory, he added. Should be easy to spot. Find your Echo Beach!

Echo Beach - Toyah (1987), EG Records (UK)
Producer: Mike Hedges

Feisty English actor and singer Toyah (Willcox) doesn't try to radically mess with the punky perfection of Martha And The Muffins' hit, but she does put some high octane fuel in its tank. On May 2, 1987, *Music & Media* noticed, "the rendition has an unmistakable compelling drive but leaves out the chorus after the first verse which decreases the magic of the song." Like the seagull snitching grapes off my beach blanket, I didn't notice it.

Ecuador - Sash! (1997), ByteBlue (G)
Producers: Sash!, Tokapi

Escuchame! Move over Pasillo, there's a new beat in town. Something about the way "Ecuador" is heralded in this electrifying trace/house track gets the heart racing and the blood pumping. This pulsating production crushes so hard, Ecuador ought to consider licensing the song for summer tourism ads, and, who knows, maybe they did back then. Sash!, a German dance music act overseen by DJ Sascha Lappessen, were no strangers to the hit chart, with "Ecuador" closely following their previous monster success, "Encore Une Fois," in August of '97. The track's throbbing beats made their way to *Music & Media*'s top five of the European Hot 100 Singles chart, and the publication ranked "Ecuador" #29 for all of 1997. As lit as they get!

Electric Avenue - Eddy Grant (1982), Portrait/ICE (BAR/US/UK)
Producer: Eddy Grant

Born in Guyana, Grant moved with his family to Britain in 1960 and later enjoyed some commercial recording success as a guitarist and songwriter for the group The Equals. He relocated to Barbados in the early '80s, where he built the Blue Wave Recording Studios in St. Phillip. There he created a series of international electronic reggae/pop hits, including "I Don't Wanna Dance," "Gimme Hope Jo'anna," "Romancing The Stone" and perhaps his most popular track, "Electric Avenue." Like most of his works, "Electric Avenue" has a point to make under those wonderfully distracting beats, this one reflecting Grant's discontent with conditions in an area of London with a large Caribbean population, the scene of riots, racism and violence. While "Electric Avenue" gives off a summer vibe by means of its electronics-fused reggae-dance vibe and the cultural appeal of Grant's invitingly gruff voice, it can't be ignored that the song is, more meaningfully, the artist's creative reaction to witnessing the district's injustice and poverty.

"Career-wise, moving to Barbados turned out to be the best thing I could have done," Grant said in an interview credited to Pete Lewis/*Blues & Soul* (retrieved from: bluesandsoul.com, Issue 1098). "Because musically all those experiments I was able to do in my studio over there would soon translate and explode into meaningful, globally-acclaimed recordings." An October 13, 1979, review in *Record World* of the artist's album, *Walking On Sunshine*, seemed to predict that outcome, saying, "[If] reggae will be the movement of 1980, Eddy Grant will likely be at the top of the field." "Electric Avenue" was Grammy-nominated for Best R&B single, peaked at #6 on the *Billboard* dance/disco chart, climbed to #2 on its pop chart, and the video was a monster hit on MTV. A "Ringbang Remix" by Peter Black released in time for the summer of 2001 was also a pop smash in the UK.

Elegy For A Lost Summer - Anne Clark (1994), SPV (G)
Producer: Anne Clark

I politely disagree—all is far from lost! A gorgeous mid-tempo synthesizer production provides the musical backdrop for some powerful vocal poetry about a break-up that is tough, dramatic, introspective, and, come what may, utterly encouraging. In its original and "606 Mix" versions, Ms. Clark reveals she hasn't actually lost summer, but rather found it with deep blue depth and bright clarity. An exceptional combination of music, message, voice and atmosphere. Yes, please!

En La Playa - Los Fieras (1988), Ariola (B) *On The Beach*
Producer: Sylvain Vanholme

An enthusiastic six-member flamenco group takes a Spanish guitar to the beach and the fun begins. A spiritous joy jam in the style of Gipsy Kings, but more simplistic in its production and possessing a leaner, exceptionally authentic sound. Listening to this track can conjure up a fantasy scene in one's mind where a fun group of people are gathered on a Spanish beach as the sun goes down, a lively melody is being spun on a Latin guitar, and you stumble upon them while walking off an enchanting seaside dinner. Perhaps that's not so far-fetched on a holiday jaunt, where summer really brings out the sociability in people.

Endless Summer - Scooter (1995), Edel (G)
Producer: The Loop!

Scooter vocalist H.P. Baxxter shouts, 'Can you smell the summer?' Oh, yeah, I'd recognize that scent anywhere! More happy hardcore from the band that knows how to make eurodance and rave *really* fast and *really* loud! Uplifting chants about the joys of summer and dreamy female vocal bridges make for an extra hot techno experience that sizzles—but stays oh so cool! You've gotta get in on this!

Endless Summer Nights - Richard Marx (1988), EMI (US)
Producer: Humberto Gatica

Marx turned the thermostat way up during the last gasps of winter with his soothing voice, a steady beat and lyrics that lament a love who left with the summer. You may wish you hadn't complained so much about the cold, cuz this is 90 degrees in the shade hot. The song is said to have been originally inspired by a trip the artist took to Hawaii. This caressing (though your skin may feel clammy) soft rock single, the third from his self-titled debut album, reached #2 in late March of '88 on *Billboard*'s Hot 100.

Eté Super - Kristal (1983), Monkey Productions/Full Time (I)
Great summer
Producer: Al Festa

Italian disco, sung in French and English (with an odd American style rap that still sounds very European). That's a lot to digest. This track tries hard to emulate the funky soul dance beats that were coming out of America's Solar Records at the time, as a loungy male-female act alternately sing, rhyme and whisper about hot fun in the summertime (and Saint Tropez, specifically). Something gets lost in the translation.

European Summer - President (1987), Rekords (UK)
Producer: Will Birch

A trendy looking English boy band delivers a one-shot anthem, a slightly cornball (though genuinely enthusiastic and undeniably catchy) electro-pop dance effort. Lead vocals by Tony Wright spin a hope that summer will never end. Put it out in the universe, boys. Fun fact: the group was reportedly a supporting act for a Rod Stewart tour of the UK, though that seems like an odd pairing.

Everybody Loves The Sunshine - Roy Ayers Ubiquity (1976), Polydor (US)
Producers: Roy Ayers, Maurice Green

Anyone who doesn't is probably out of an Anne Rice novel. As their name suggests, the Roy Ayers Ubiquity band may have set out to evoke a feeling of being everywhere at the same time, but with this track the soul/jazz frontman clearly wants to place you directly in the sunlight. The song is an emotional snippet, a blissful moment in time enveloped in peace, harmony and contentment, best appreciated lying on your back, watching the clouds drift by. What's not to love?

Everybody Sunshine- Stevie Woods (1994), White/BMG (G)
Producer: Jack White

A Virginia-born singer with a few US R&B hits to his credit ("Steal The Night," "Just Can't Win 'Em All," "Ain't That Peculiar"), Woods tried to build his following in Germany with this entry, a track also covered by US actor David Hasselhoff. While Hasselhoff went the more alkaline pop/rock route, Woods takes a lighter Caribic approach that works much better with what lyrically seems like an airy, upbeat beach song. His smooth, friendly, pop-ready vocals are a fine fit as well. Woods dipped his toe in equally warm tropical waters the year before with a featured vocal on Paradise Project's dance cover of the Amen Corner hit, "If Paradise Is Half As Nice." The singer passed in 2014.

Fantasy Island - Tight Fit (1982), Jive (UK)
Producer: Tim Friese-Greene

No, it's not ABBA, but an incredible simulation. Rich female session-singer voices, crisp pianos, a slapping mid-tempo disco beat, and love on an island. Do you really need anything else for a getaway? The song was also performed by a Dutch group called The Millionaires the same year. You probably won't get much of a "tropical" vibe from the track, but you'll surely want to watch "Mamma Mia!" again.

Farewell My Summer Love - Michael Jackson (1984), Motown (US)
Producers: Freddie Perren, Fonce Mizell

Originally recorded in 1973 but not released until 1984, Motown pulled this one out of the vaults in the wake of the artist's stunningly successful *Thriller* album, electronically enhancing and mixing the track to give it more of an '80s vibe. It's that seemingly untroubled young Michael sound we all loved so much with a pleasurable, easy going groove and catchy, gentle, clean-cut lyrics about a love that drifts away with the last days of summer. It may have been a cash-in, but it was strong enough to crack the top 30 in Europe and nearly did the same in the US.

Feeling Free (Caribbean Sea) - Happiness Ft. Tania Dee (1994), RCA (G)
Producers: Teddy Delight, M., Selitzch, Petersmann & Stan

Happiness is the word for it! The melody is extremely inviting and upbeat with a simple, shuffling rhythm and some added beach sound effects. The lyrics about liberation under the sun are appropriately positive and singer Tania Dee has the perfect tone for the track—soulful without indulging in over the top gusto. Has a tiny bit of a Chic vibe. There's a lot to love about this tasty pop track, and it perfectly reflects the serene pleasure of an uncomplicated sunny day in the Caribbean. Best all day excursion: The Trance Trip Mix.

Fiesta De La Noche - Beach Bumpers United (2001), Dance Street (G)
Producer: Apres Beach Entertainment

The "Summer Radio Version" opens with a radio DJ letting us know that the sun is shining and it's sweltering hot! Are you in? It's off to Mallorca for a Latin-tinged dance/pop thumper with bright harmonies and an inviting electro-synth melody. Another song appears on the CD-maxi-single in two alternately titled versions, "Summer Feeling" / "Cala Guya"—both just as sultry and festive as "Fiesta." Easy-going, feel-good dance music, highly recommended.

Fiesta De Los Tamborileros - The Sunclub (1996), Sony Dance Pool (NL)
Producers: Jaydee, Typar, Atbe

A plucky Dutch electronic (and mostly instrumental) work considered by some to be a diamond of progressive eurohouse music, with a faint Latin scent. For those who were young and clubbing around town on hot summer nights back in the mid-'90s, this was the type of jam that would really stick with you. The vibe and sonic hook fused especially well with any fun times one might have been having.

Fire Island - Village People (1977), Casablanca (US)
Producer: Jacques Morali

It's difficult to know if producer Jacques Morali and executive producer Henri Belolo could have fully anticipated the impact the release of the *Village People* debut album (from which the song "Fire Island" is a key track) would have, not just on pop culture and disco music, but specifically on gay empower-ment. Whether that outcome was planned or not, it was a rare media event the gay community (long before its expansion into the LGBTQ community - lesbian, gay, bisexual, transgender, and questioning or queer) could rally around at the time. There was a sense of significance that surrounded this production as the album received a fair amount of mainstream attention. This all seemed like a major step forward for the gay movement, albeit in a kind of understated way, by covertly slipping gay-themed disco songs into the establishment. Casually sat this big gay underground album on record store shelves in "everyday" America, just eight years after the Stonewall riots and as disco fever began to spread.

The cover photo on the vinyl's jacket, featuring a distant suggestion of the iconic Village People characters yet to come, was unquestionably a bit fuzzy but still quietly bold in its visual of underground gay nightlife. And there's Felipe Rose, the Native American in full headdress, looking on knowingly in the background. It may seem somewhat innocuous today, but it was a breakthrough at the time. The musical production itself uniquely celebrated important gay community hubs (though steering clear of being too "in your face" about it—after all, this wasn't the "we're here, we're queer, get over it" era just yet). Classic tracks such as "San Francisco (You've Got Me)," "Village People" (cheering the Mecca of gay NYC, Greenwich Village), "In Hollywood (Everybody Is A Star)" (the gay porn capital of the world) and "Fire Island" (on the south shore of Long Island, New York) all paid tribute to the handful of places where American gay people had a foothold and a relatively significant sense of limited safety, freedom and belonging.

Of course, "Fire Island" is just like any other song that celebrates a happy summer place, only this one's, well, gayer. Fire Island's buzz zones, The Pines and Cherry Grove, were well-established beach destinations for gay people at the time, and they remain that way to this day. ("Provincetown" might not have sounded quite glamorous enough for a song title.) Lead singer Victor Willis, said to be the only straight member of the original Village People group that would eventually form, delivers an urgent, heated vocal performance that proclaims it's a great place for a hot, funky summer weekend, and he entices the listener with the prospect that you never know who you're going to meet there. Sounds innocent enough, but many can attest to what an understatement the song's lyrics were, especially if "The Meat Rack" means anything to you.

As the Village People became more and more popular and commercially successful in the mainstream, their connection to gay empowerment became increasingly diluted by the dawn of the '80s. Eventually the group itself, more comic book characters than rebels, dried up from overexposure, despite vigorous efforts to reinvent themselves. In 1989, they managed to enjoy a pop chart revival with a popular mega-hit-mix fashioned by DJ Alan Coulthard that took hold in France, and they eventually began touring again as a vintage disco/pop nostalgia act with some new cast members. A modified form of Village People is still stompin' around in the twenty-first century.

While it may never have the mainstream stature of "Y.M.C.A," "Fire Island" remains, perhaps, the ultimate old skool gay summer anthem. And appropriately marketing-smart at the time, the inside record sleeve of the *Village People* album featured cross promotion for the then hot summer Casablanca film soundtrack, *The Deep*.

Flames Of Paradise - Jennifer Rush (Duet with Elton John) 1987, CBS/Epic (G/US)
Producers: Andy Goldmark, Bruce Roberts

An American singer born in Astoria (Queens), New York, who's been described in the media as vocally powerful, confident and even melodramatic, Ms. Rush was looking to break out beyond the borders of her huge success ("The Power Of Love") in Germany and the UK at the time. "Flames Of Paradise" seemed like a sure bet single to get her noticed in the US. Alas, this blazing duet with Elton John, though infectiously catchy and relentlessly energetic, fell short of giving her that top-charting stateside hit many anticipated. "The timing…wasn't right," explained Ms. Rush in a 2015 interview with me for the book *Europe's Stars of '80s Dance Pop* (McFarland), adding it was, "of course disappointing." Still, the song absolutely gives off summer sparks and its two stars exude the vitality of a couple of teenagers on jet skis!

Following The Sun - Enigma (2003), EMI (G)
Producer: Michael Cretu

By this time, the Enigma project, which had broken ground in 1990 with ethereal, Gregorian chant-based ambient dance music (think "Sadeness, Part I," originally created by Frank Peterson and Michael Cretu), was past its peak popularity. However, Cretu was still managing to turn out abstract, inventive and appealing concept productions in a new age electronica style over a decade later. Evoking a warm emotional reaction similar to the sensation his Enigma track "Out From The Deep" elicited in 1994, "Following The Sun" is at once stunningly understated, compellingly mysterious and exotically celebratory, in perfect harmony with summer. One for the gods! Arguably among the producer's best efforts, "Following The Sun" is a just over five-minute solar flare.

Forever - Gipsy Kings (1995) Columbia (F)
Producers: Claude Martinez, Gérard Prévost

Hidden away on the album *Estrellas* (*Stars*) and the maxi-single "A Ti A Ti" (*To you to you*), this stunningly expressive instrumental combines emotional Spanish guitar strumming and a bright piano melody that soars high above the swaying palms and gentle ocean waves. It envelopes you in a feeling of summer serenity, yet it has that uplifting rhythm and a special kind of positivity that flamenco music is able to uniquely convey in any season. A truly beautiful musical painting, this composition lives and breathes and renews. A must when you're in need of a mood change on a warm summer evening.

Fun Fun Fun - Status Quo With The Beach Boys (1996), Polygram (UK)
Producer: Pip Williams

Good, good, good vibrations as these titans of rock 'n' roll, who, as we all know, got their starts in the '60s, become a lively twofer, serving up a fairly traditional but zesty surf rock cover party. The Boys handle the back-ups mostly, and Francis Rossi of Status Quo takes the lead vocal. The track was a modest hit in the UK. Enjoy it—just for the *shell* of it!

Fun Fun Mega Hit Mix - Fun Fun (1987), High Fashion (N/I)
Producers: Dario Raimondi, Alvaro Ugolini

So much fun they had to say it twice! Of the many studio groups that emerged from the '80s Italo disco scene, few had the broad success of the act Fun Fun, initially brought to recording life with the studio vocals of future pop superstar Ivana Spagna ("Call Me"), Antonelle Pepe and Angela Parisi. With their breakout 1983 hit "Happy Station" (remixed by Dutch DJ Ben Liebrand) a sizable commercial success beyond Italy, there arose an incentive to take the concept further. Models were hired to perform live as Fun Fun, and Ivana eventually left to pursue a multi-national solo career. Producers Raimondi and Ugolini were ultimately the driving force behind the project, and they consistently fashioned irresistible, hook-laden hits for the Fun Fun entity, including the near perfect summer dance/pop jewel, "Colour My Love" in 1984 (a top 10 *Billboard* dance chart hit in the US) and the equally bouncy "Baila Bolero" in 1986.

Megamixes were the mashups of the '80s (going all the way back to the Stars on 45 concept in '81), culling together an artist or group's most popular hits in a fast-paced dance medley, ideal for club DJs looking to create breezy high-energy trips down memory lane (or to take a cigarette break).

"The Fun Fun Mega Hit Mix" is arguably one of the best-suited for summer dance floors, with every track having that brilliant, danceable holiday cheer feel. On March 28, 1988, *Music & Media* described the hits contained in the "Mega Hit Mix" as, "inventively joined together to a thumping electro beat with plenty of scra-scra-scratching." The engineering of this project was handled by a Netherlands DJ named Martin Boer, who would later go on with his brother Bobby to create the international hit dance act 2 Brothers On The 4th Floor.

Commentary from Martin Boer:

"One of the first singles I bought when I was a 13-year-old kid was 'Happy Station' by Fun Fun. It was the 'Scratch Mix' made by famous Dutch DJ/producer Ben Liebrand. I was very impressed by the freaky edits Liebrand did in this track. Also, Liebrand had a mix radio show on Dutch national radio, and I wanted to find out how he created those smooth transitions from one record to the other. That was the moment I began studying editing and mixing every day. A few years later I made the first version of the Fun Fun Mix with loads of edits and sent it to Frits van Swoll, the A&R manager of High Fashion Music. He liked the mix and asked me to remove some of the edits and make it a little bit more smooth and danceable.

"Frits expected to sell about 500 copies on 12-inch vinyl, but in a short time it became very popular in the clubs and radio stations were asking for a short edit for airplay. After that we sold over 75,000 copies in the Netherlands, and it was released in all of Europe and the US. I don't know exactly how many copies were sold worldwide, but it must have been a few million. The record company only paid me a flat fee of 600 Dutch guilders (about $300 US dollars at that time). This mix didn't make me rich, but it was the start of a successful career as a DJ/remixer and producer."

Fun In The Sun - Fun Cruiser (1997), CDL (G)
Producers: Achim Oppermann, Achim Sobotta

A group clearly fashioned to emulate the group Mr. President ("Coco Jamboo"), two female singers joined by a male reggaeton-style vocalist. You know the drill. The song is a sugary euro-popper aimed expressly at the summer market. That's not to say it isn't catchy—if one has been enduring a long, cold winter, it's gonna feel mighty good to hear this track playing poolside at your hotel in Málaga, Santorini or Lagos. Producer Opperman also helmed Heath Hunter & The Pleasure Company's hit "Revolution In Paradise."

Funkin' For Jamaica - Tom Browne (1980), GRP/Arista (US)
Producers: Dave Grusin, Larry Rosen

Also released as "Funkin' For Jamaica (N.Y.)," just to clarify that this is indeed the noted jazz trumpeter's earthy, soulful tribute to the real estate where he was born and raised, not the Caribbean island. His goal was to get us totally funked up. That's perfectly fine, for this street-ready slide, with its retro-disco feel and urban party background chatter, has a tremendously warm vibe that absolutely feels like a hot summer day in the Queens neighborhood of NYC. The song has been sampled numerous times in works by artists such as Mariah Carey and Quad City DJ's.

Funkin' For Jamaica - Towa Tei (2001), EastWest (UK)
Producer: Towa Tei

Crisp remake of Tom Browne's 1980 jam by a former Deee-Lite group member. This single saw a 1999 release in the artist's native Japan and was re-marketed for Europe in 2001. The track keeps much of the Browne version's original vibe, adding some spice by mixing a fertile arrangement with deep house beats and jazzy flairs. The production also features contributions from Les Nubians, Wizdom Life and Mr. Browne himself. Among the boat load of remixers enlisted to support the single, Boris Dlugosch's & Michi Lange's popular club mix maintains a real retro-disco feel, once again a throwback to the original's enduring charm.

Funky Nassau - Infinito Ft. Mandel Turner (2000), BMG (G)
Producers: Corrado DJ, Marco Dalle Luche

The original flavor of The Beginning Of The End's vintage soul hit is revived with a hard, thumping pulse here, and the stomping electronic house arrangement and retro-disco nuances give the track a big party sound. Turner sings with conviction, and the effect is quite rousing.

Funky Nassau - Ray Munnings (1979), Tammi/EMI (UK)
Producer: Don Taylor

Ray Munnings, a former member of The Beginning Of The End, who had a hit with the song back in '71, takes care of business with this old skool disco jam reinvention. It's got the same soulful grind as the earlier version, but the beats are '70s club-ready, even sounding a bit like an Italo disco production at times. A rather mundane drum break, however, seems unnecessarily long-winded, but the song still reminds us that the Bahamas hot spot's got plenty of sunshine.

G - H

Garden Party - Herb Alpert (1983), A&M (US)
Producer: Herb Alpert

Well past his Grammy-winning disco era success with "Rise" but ahead of his ambitious work with one Miss Janet Jackson on "Diamonds," the musician, songwriter, philanthropist, and founder of A&M Records kept busy with some diverting and highly entertaining pop projects, not the least of which was his single "Garden Party." This instrumental piece of course benefits from the ambience generated by Alpert's dynamic trumpet playing, but the touch of Latin warmth and background party voices heard throughout the track elevate the atmosphere of this Sunday afternoon get-together into an engaging, sunny and very expensive sounding outdoor affair. Don't confuse this soiree with the Boris Johnson debacle.

Gibson Brothers Megamix - Gibson Brothers (1990), Zagora/ Carrere/BCM (F)
Producer: Zagora Productions

Individually, almost all of the Gibson Brothers' hits positively shout summer! Put a bunch of them together on one record and we are at risk of serious heatstroke. This 1990 mashup serves as an exciting hit resumé for the boys and consists of a seamless melding of "Ooh What A Life," "Cuba," "Mariana," "Non Stop Dance," and "Que Sera Mi Vida," remixed and culled together by the UK's Alan Coulthard with a pulsating house groove.

Commentary from Alan Coulthard:

"I still remember hearing 'Cuba' for the first time on Radio Luxembourg in 1978, when Tony Prince introduced a 'disco playlist,' which meant that all the DJs played disco tracks. I had never heard of the Gibson Brothers, but I thought it was the perfect summer track, with its calypso rhythms and partially Spanish lyrics, although I subsequently discovered that the brothers were French (originally from Martinique). Following my #1 with the 'Boney M. Megamix' (1988), Boney M.'s manager at the time, Simon Napier-Bell, made contact with me. We had a meeting and he told me that he also managed the Gibson Brothers and asked if I would like to do a Gibson Brothers Megamix. We did a deal, and I completed the megamix in a recording studio in East London, the name of which I cannot now recall.

"This megamix is completely unique amongst all the megamixes I have ever done. Since I had the multi-track tapes, I was able to remix all the tracks before megamixing them together. I had done this for my 'Village People Megamix' (1989), although for the 'Boney M. Megamix' (1988), PWL's Pete Hammond had remixed the tracks first for a remixed album, and I megamixed those remixed versions. However, I took this one a stage further. With the 'Gibson Brothers Megamix,' each track was perfectly synchronized to a beat and the bass line changed key as the mix progressed through each track. This made the mix one of the smoothest I have ever done, particularly as the tracks had been recorded with a live drummer in the late '70s and early '80s. In fact, it was rather like a 'medley' (albeit using the original recordings) and, perhaps for that reason, it didn't do as well as I thought it might have done. But I am still very proud of it from a technical perspective.

"Since I had had access to the multi-track, I also decided to do a remix of my favorite Gibson Brothers track, 'Ooh What A Life', for the Music Factory subscription service. I am very proud of this remix, which is a 'summer classic.'"

Alan Coulthard left our world in the summer of 2021.

*[See also: **Megarama '89 - Bananarama, Knock On Wood / Light My Fire / Megamix - Amii Stewart.**]*

Gimme The Sunshine - Curiosity (1993), BMG (UK)
Producers: Mark Taylor, Terry Adams

Formerly known as Curiosity Killed The Cat (of the hit single "Down To Earth"), this British band (reduced to a three-man outfit at the time of this recording) was adept at delivering jazzy pop confections that were instantly likable with solid grooves and appealing hooks. "Gimme The Sunshine" has all those elements plus an uplifting party feel that's funky, danceable and delectably summery. Lead singer Ben Volpeliere-Pierrot, still wearing his distinctive beret, offers a cool, swagger-filled interpretation of the song that emits a hip '90s vibe, in contrast with the mellow two-step R&B leanings of the Leo Sunshipp version from back in 1980. *Music & Media* offered a curious (and awkwardly worded) review of the single on November 6, 1993, saying, "At the beginning of the autumn, craving for sunshine sounds a bit pointless, but not if you do it on such a hot funky beat as patented by Level 42."

Give A Little Love / Red Red Wine - Shari Belafonte (1989), Metronome (G)
Producer: Jakko M. Jakszyk

The daughter of the legendary singer, actor and humanitarian/activist Harry Belafonte, Shari enjoyed a successful modeling and acting career (TV's "Hotel" and "Love Boat"—and, much later, in the twenty-first century show, "Sistas") before turning to international singing. I'm sure she must have felt some pressure to live up to her esteemed father's musical legacy and was therefore somewhat obliged to try her hand at tropical pop. She doesn't sound highly polished as a singer (shades of Princess Stephanie of Monaco), but Miss Shari does a competent job with these reggae-fused singles from her second album, 1989's *Shari*. "Give A Little Love," the Diane Warren/Albert Hammond song made popular by Ziggy Marley And The Melody Makers, among others, is punctuated by steel drums in a quality calypso/dance-oriented production. She sounds a bit more comfortable in her understated, UB40-fashioned take (no surprise) on "Red Red Wine." There's nothing hugely venturesome here, but it's likable, pleasantly engaging pop music, and there's something to be said for delivering just a "nice" record. Regrettably, these endeavors were the swan songs of her mainstream recording career.

Girl From Ipanéma, The / Guess Who's The Girl From Ipanéma - Lio (1990), Polydor (F)
Producer: Etienne Daho

From France, a stunningly evocative, casually shuffling electronic house version of Antônio Carlos Jobim's Brazilian summer music masterpiece. Though the refreshed beat gives the bossa nova track a secure club vibe, not an ounce of the warmth or the exotic liquidity of the original is lost. Belgian-Portuguese singer Lio ("Banana Split") had been popular in France since the early '80s. In this rendition, her dreamy vocal is reminiscent of the haunting songbird behind the 1962/Stan Getz international hit version, Astrud Gilberto, though Miss Lio is unquestionably stylish in her own right. The long version and "Gota Remix" features producer Etienne Daho sharing the mic with Lio, and their joint effort has a way of seeping into every particle of your being. Too perfect for this world!

Going To Havana - Tony Christie (1991), White/Ariola (G)
Producer: Jack White

The British singer best known for his early '70s hit "Is This The Way to Amarillo" enjoyed a great deal of popularity in Germany in the early to mid-'90s. Teaming with producer Jack White, who had a penchant for sharing the same songs with a multitude of vocalists, the two dusted off and retitled a tropical disco track from the vaults (recorded earlier by Audrey Landers as "Hideaway Havana"). A revitalized arrangement by The Gardeners and Uve Schikora livens up the sound, which is brimming with equatorial atmosphere and an enhanced dance beat. Christie sings with an old skool bravado that sounds a bit extra today, but it works well with a cornball song like this, and the track is really a lot of fun. The striking and colorful maxi-single jacket graphics (a commuter plane whisking low over gorgeous blue-green waters on its way to the island, presumably) put you right in the mood. Christie recorded a number of songs with Jack in this vein ("Come With Me To Paradise," "Down In Mexico" and "Island In The Sun" are good examples) but "Going To Havana" pulled out all the stops and is one of the most "beachy" in his catalog, especially in its extended version. Book your trip now!

Good Times - Chic (1979), Atlantic/WEA (US)
Producers: Nile Rodgers, Bernard Edwards

Are they ever! Coming off "Le Freak," which at the time was being widely celebrated as the biggest selling single in the Atlantic label's US history, it would seem a nearly impossible task to wrangle up something that could bring the house down yet again. With "Good Times," I'd argue producers Rodgers and Edwards succeeded. Check that—surpassed, for this song is, frankly, much easier to dance or roller skate to. As a paragon of the classic disco era, the track powerfully conjures up elements of care-free summer-time with its potent, pulsing bass line, clear, crisp piano, and blissed up talk of clams on the half shell, the sporting life, roller skates—yeah, I could go on all day. If you were lucky enough to be in a club when the "Good Times" groove blew across the dance floor like an electric paraglider skims the ocean surface on a hot beach day, it was as if the track infiltrated your soul, possessing your body and guiding every fluid movement you made with its rhythm. It also elicited loud cheers. Further enhancing the experience were the track's vocalists, Alfa Anderson, Luci Martin, Michelle Cobbs, Fonzi Thornton and Ullanda McCullough, who elegantly delivered the song's sublime lyrics with grace and distinction. Their brilliantly cohesive chant of the song title could not have been a more unifying force.

Surprisingly, the original version of "Good Times" only peaked at #3 on *Billboard*'s disco chart, but it went on to top the publication's US pop singles survey in August of 1979, cementing its unshakable ranking as an eternal summer anthem. Its instantly recognizable groove was sampled or emulated on an astonishing number of records, perhaps most famously (and initially without proper crediting of Rodgers and Edwards, later rectified) within "Rapper's Delight" (1979) by The Sugarhill Gang. In the twenty-first century, Michelle Gayle borrowed the "Good Times" bass line in her 1995 release, "Happy Just To Be With You," and Janet Jackson's hit "All For You" famously incorporated the gorgeous piano melody of the song. Each inventively illustrated the endless creative possibilities inherently built into the DNA of Chic's landmark production. The song ranked #68 on *Rolling Stone*'s 2021 list of "500 Greatest Songs of All Time."

In an August 29, 1981, interview titled "The Men of Chic on Making Hits" by Nelson George for *Record World*, Bernard Edwards commented on the enticing groove of "Good Times," saying, "It's so funny about that record. Nile came in one day with some chord changes, and [drummer] Tony [Thompson] and Nile just started playing away. I came in late, picked up the bass and just started walking with them, saying, 'yeah, this is great.' So we built a record around it." He added, "…we kept saying, 'Damn, that 'Good Times' is a hot track.' The bass line took the tune from where it was right up to another level. It was something that took only two or three minutes to come up with."

Billboard gave "Good Times" a positive, but rather unremarkable review on June 16, 1979, saying the track "is another classy effort from this consistent pop/disco group. A steady but driving beat is complemented by perky vocals." Perky seems far to mundane an adjective.

"Good Times" was re-released in a more electric sounding house style remix by Jolley, Harris, Jolley in 1988, and again in 2001 with an amped-up remix targeting the EDM crowd by Stonebridge. I'm all for updating tracks and approaching them with a new spin, but it's doubtful anything will ever top the original, which I expect will sound untouchably hip, euphoric and summery 50 years from now—if summer as we know it still exists by then.

"A Warm Summer Night," the B-side of most original pressings of the "Good Times" single, is a gently danceable, warm and dreamy composition that evokes the sensations of breezy, romantic late evenings in August. The King Britt Scuba Remix, released in 2005, injected a brisk beat and a Spanish guitar, changing the pulse, but not the atmosphere, of this otherwise tranquil track.

Commentary from Alfa Anderson:

Ms. Anderson, would you share your take on the connection "Good Times" holds with summer and a few of your memories of recording this classic?

"I have always loved the sights, sounds, tastes, smells and activities of summer. If truth be told, I also adore the music associated with summer. As one of the original lead singers of the group Chic, I recorded two iconic songs that are associated with my favorite time of year.

"When I walked into the studio to record *Risque*, our third album, I had no idea what to expect. Writer/producers Bernard Edwards and Nile Rodgers never let me hear the songs prior to the studio session. We had just had a mega hit with 'Le Freak' on which I duetted with Diva Gray. I was so excited to hear what they had in store this time and if the new music could rival the successes of 'Le Freak!' I needn't have worried because the moment we heard the track for 'Good Times,' which features Bernard's classic bass solo and Nile's signature guitar licks, I knew that 'Good Times' was a clear winner and the perfect follow up to 'Le Freak.' Luci Martin, Michelle Cobbs, Fonzi Thornton and Ullanda McCullough quickly found the pocket and the vibe. With smiles on our faces and joy in our hearts, we settled into the vocal groove of a sound that would become the penultimate summer anthem for decades to come."

Any flashbacks of recording "A Warm Summer Night?"
"Everybody that knows me knows that I love a good, sexy, smooth ballad. I loved the track but had a real embarrassing studio moment. Part of the lyric includes these words in Spanish: papi, te quiero. Now I had taken Spanish in junior high school in my hometown of Augusta, Georgia, but I forgot one incident. One of my classmates turned to me in the middle of a Spanish lesson and said, 'Alfa, I have never heard authentic Spanish, but I am quite sure it doesn't sound like this. This pronunciation can't possibly be right.' [While recording "A Warm Summer Night"], instead of taking a moment to remember her words or asking how to pronounce the phrase, I bolted ahead and whispered, 'Tay Key err o' in my flawed Spanish.

"When Nile, Bernard and Luci finished a huge belly laugh and picked themselves up off the floor, they had Luci whisper the line in authentic sexy Spanish. It's one of those times when I had to laugh at myself. So, I only joined in on the English background parts. This is still one of my favorite instrumentals that features Nile's great guitar work supported by Bernard's sexy bass playing and our (now corrected) sultry background parts."

What records do you drop the needle on when the weather outside gets warm?

"Some of my favorite summer songs include 'Dancing In The Street' by Martha and the Vandellas, 'Summer Breeze' by the Isley Brothers, and anything by The Beach Boys. I think I will include 'Good Times' and 'A Warm Summer Night' on my summer playlist, too, along with 'Hot Fun In The Summertime' by Sly Stone, 'Let's Go On Vacation' by Sister Sledge, Luther Vandross' 'The Night I Fell In Love,' 'The First Time Ever I Saw Your Face' by Roberta Flack, Chic's 'São Paulo', 'Upside Down' by Diana Ross, 'Saturday In The Park,' by Chicago, and `Donna Summer's 'Hot Stuff.'"

Good Times - Sister Sledge (1993), New Music International (I) Producer: Pippo Landro

In the early '90s, Italian producer Pippo Landro had the idea of recording veteran US disco artists such as Gloria Gaynor and Sister Sledge in modest but up-to-date house style renditions of their original hits. The results were pleasing and fairly successful in Europe. In this effort, Sister Sledge (in 1993, a trio consisting of Kim, Debbie and Joni, without the participation of Kathy) is given a unique opportunity to record the Chic classic. Of course, Landro doesn't give the production quite the same artistic nuances that Chic producers Bernard Edwards and Nile Rodgers originally had, but it's still a carefully balanced, thoughtful and appealing dance formulation. The Sledge sisters, singing in strong, confident unison, show they, like their Chic counterparts, most certainly would have had a massive hit with the track had it originally been offered to them back in 1979. The ladies' capable voices are polished, crisp, vibrant, and abundantly summery, and the track is a refreshing reinvention that is respectful of the original. Lifted from Sister Sledge's excellent 1992 album *And Now...Sledge...Again.*

Good Times - Blaxone (1996), CDL (G)
Producers: Bernd Waldstädt, Uwe Dreissigacker

Injected with rap by Chicago's A.K.-S.W.I.F.T., this eurohouse/pop vision of the Chic hit has a spacey vibe that's both ethereal and intriguing. As remakes go, it's damn good take on an old classic, adding an elevating electronic dimension to the song and giving it a left field vibe.

Good Vibrations - Marky Mark And The Funky Bunch (1991), EastWest (US)
Producer: Donnie Wahlberg

Though it became surrounded in legal complications thanks to some dicey sampling of the legendary Miss Loleatta Holloway's powerful vocals from Dan Hartman's production of "Love Sensation" (1980), there's no denying this fusion of disco, hip-hop and house was brilliantly executed and hopelessly addictive. Coupled with visions of Marky Mark's (Mark Wahlberg) washboard abs and his Calvin Klein underwear waistband, it was no surprise this summer anthem was a #1 *Billboard* pop chart hit and reached the top 10 of the publication's dance chart. Ultimately, Mr. Wahlberg traded pop music stardom for fame on the big screen. At a London press conference in July of 2013 (post by Russell Nelson, YouTube share by Red Carpet News TV), the actor/singer commented on his two careers. "Music always kind of promoted this attitude of being able to do whatever I wanted," he said. "I show up late, don't show up at all, go in an hour late…there was no discipline with music. And when I found movies, I became very disciplined." *Eh*, discipline seems overrated. Give me an unpunctual dude who's sparky as hell, singing hot summer jams like this, anytime!

Gran Canaria - Paveier (1987), Papagayo (G)
Producers: Paveier, Hans Knipp

One of this Cologne-based band's most popular singles, it became something of a standard within the German schlager genre (along with "Sommer, Sonne, Sand & Meer" [Summer, sun sand and sea] from '91). The track celebrates a "whatever will be, will be" mindset on the heavenly white and golden sand beaches of Spain's Canary Islands. Tranquil and blissful though the islands may be, the archipelago is not immune to the forces of nature. On the last days of the summer of 2021, a volcano erupted on La Palma island, a popular tourist destination in the northwest region and said to be one of the best places on earth to observe the night sky. The eruption brought with it unstoppable rivers of lava, forcing thousands to evacuate, and it actually expanded the perimeter of the island. At the time of this writing, the hot stuff was still flowing.

Gran Canaria - Roxy Rose (not specified, possibly mid-late 1990s), Strehl-Music Records (G)
Producer: Torsten Kamps

A German schlager singer who brings a romantic feel and the twang of country strings to her light, fun pop music ("Frankfurt International Airport," for example) celebrates the beauty and escape that can be found in Las Palmas, capital of the Canary Islands and a major cruise ship port. It's a pleasant, soft, inviting melody in its radio edit, and the track is given a brisk electronic pulse with Spanish overtones in its party mix. Either way, the up to roughly 14 million people who are inclined to visit Gran Canaria each year are likely to appreciate this musical tribute to the popular summer destination. But please, when visiting, be respectful of the protected coastal dune field at Maspalomas and maybe think about staying out of it. Scantily clad (code for naked) pleasure-seekers are reportedly creating a hot mess, trampling the dunes and leaving discarded condoms, trash and, um, shall we say a "variety of waste products" behind. Environmentalists say the activity of these horny tourists can potentially cause as much deterioration of the area as off road driving! Blame it on the sun, the horny goat weed of the sky.

Guajira Guantanamera - Vieja Trova Santiaguera (1997), Intuition (S/G)
Producer: Manuel Dominguez

Vieja Trova Santiaguera is an authentic and vintage male Cuban group, highly seasoned, who effortlessly transport the listener to the hot streets of Havana with their pleasantly rhythmic five-minute rendition of the much loved José Martí composition. It's absolutely genuine, antiquely danceable, and evocatively earthy in a way no modern day electronic production could ever hope to achieve.

Guantanamera - Luis Calvo (1990), ZYX (G)
Producer: Luis Calvo

As a pop song, "Guantanamera" is remarkably flexible in that it translates so well to a variety of arrangements despite its traditional structure and instantly identifiable melody. Luis Calvo pushes the Cuban ballad in a noticeably Italo disco style direction, maintaining the original feel but giving it a fun dance vibe. Pulsating electronics and Calvo's whispery spoken/sung vocals make the production sound both hokey and delightfully bubbly. Remember, you never have to apologize for liking any kind of music, including a zesty, so-called "guilty pleasure" like this. But wait, check out the next dudes' rendition.

Guantanamera '96 - Los Paraguayos (1996), CMC (D)
Producer: Los Paraguayos

By the time this single was released, this diverse group of Paraguayans (their musician and singer line-up constantly changed) had been making delightful music reflective of their culture for nearly four decades. Yes, Los Paraguayos covered this Cuban evergreen as a ballad in the past. Oh, but *they never done it like this*—with a hotly contemporary, scaldingly powerful, tight-like-spandex dance arrangement. The "Latin Boyz Samba Mix" is hotter than the noon sun, mixing old world vocals with a blistering beat that absolutely won't quit. Relentless! On June 22, 1996, *Music & Media* called it "a potential smash especially with the summer season coming up." The single jacket, featuring a tropical beach shoreline image, boasts that the track is "100% Summer Proof." It probably should have read, "100% Summer Approved!"

Havana - Kenny G (1997), Arista (US)
Producers: Kenny G, Walter Afanasieff

With "Havana," the Seattle-born saxophonist is far from the "Songbird" brand of romantic, lilting melodies that helped make him so popular, instead moving his sound clearly into the heart of sweltering South Beach. Tony Moran's powerful mix effectively takes this largely instrumental piece (save for female

"Havana" chants) into hot Latin club territory. Still, Kenny G's admittedly highly skilled sax work, though not entirely inappropriate, feels a wee bit awkward and floaty at times in such a robust, energized mix. Trumpeter Herb Alpert often tried the same thing to greater effect with his instrument. But what do I know? The song was still a #1 hit on *Billboard*'s dance chart.

Havana Club - Ottmar Liebert + Luna Negra (1994), Epic (G)
Producer: Ottmar Liebert

Grammy nominee Liebert's marvelous nouveau flamenco guitar work grabs your soul and squeezes it like a sponge. In "The Latin Mix" opus, the pulse is pumped up and the undercurrent carries you for six minutes of summery bliss (eight an a half in Rosabel's 1997 remix) that defies the clock. It is impossible to resist the hypnotic charm of this production.

Havana Club - Pépé Le Mokò (1997), DFC (I/G)
Producer unknown.

Fiery, high energy samba-meets-house version of the Ottmar Liebert composition. Sweat inducing! I suppose the artist was inspired to take his stage name from the 1937 French gangster movie. Cute!

(Havin' A) Beach Party - Caribic Girls Ft. Tam (1991), ZYX (G)
Producers: T.G.Pfanz, Recordia Music, J.E. Wildhack

With a 12-inch version sub-titled the "Happy Soft Drink Mix," one might rightfully anticipate a sugary pop track, and that's precisely what you get. But wait, there actually *is* something modestly exceptional about this song. Clearly it is "inspired" by Kate Yanai's "Bacardi Feeling (Summer Dreamin')," nearly, but not quite, to the point of copyright infringement, yet it manages to have just enough originality to break through on its own. A heavily accented female vocalist invites us over for a mid-tempo beach party where there are steel drums, palm trees and a breezy Caribbean atmosphere. This invitation assures us we'll beach more and worry less.

Heat Is On, The - Agnetha Fältskog (1983), Polydor (SW)
Producer: Mike Chapman

From the singer's first solo album while with ABBA, *Wrap Your Arms Around Me*, Agnetha clearly felt the lure of the tropics. It's a simple pop/rock shuffler that celebrates the uncomplicated yet transformative appeal of rising temperatures. The tune has a theatrical flair and, at times, a jazzy vibe with its sultry horns, strings and party feel, especially in its extended maxi-single version. A lot of fun. On October 1, 1983, *Record World* quoted the singer, who was reflecting on the popularity of her summery solo venture. "In a way," she said, "it's even more exciting than having a success with ABBA. There, it's four people, and you can take just one-quarter of the credit." ABBA's 2021 reunion served as a great opportunity the revisit the group member's tangent projects, like this hot number.

Heat Is On, The - Glenn Frey (1984), MCA (US)
Producers: Keith Forsey, Harold Faltermeyer

It's on and it's up high. Providing a big boost to the "Beverly Hills Cop" movie soundtrack with a tune that's as hot as a slice Nevada asphalt in July, Glenn Frey, one of the founding members of the Eagles, finds that synth-pop sweet spot between dance music and rock. Remixer and engineer Brian Reeves takes all the hook-laden elements of the song—that crisp drum beat, the flailing guitars, the fiery sax, and Frey's infectious "Ohh-uh-oh" rally—and stirs them into a vividly exciting, get-on-the-floor shoulder-shaker that reminds us how electrifying the mid-'80s were and how much fun summer pop music can really be. Glenn Frey passed far too early at the age of 67 in 2016.

Heatwave - Peacock Palace (1993), Columbia (G)
Producer: Nhoah

You'll be hard-pressed to find a pluckier (literally), summer stompin', banjo bumpin' jam than this catchy, infectiously folksy and contagiously upbeat dance/rock/country hybrid about love catchin' you in a heatwave. The "Mardi Gras Megamix" keeps your feet kicking longer, while the "Swelter In The Delta Version" rides mostly on the fire and energy of the group's feisty female lead vocalist, Petra Jansen. When the forecast is this hot, even the ice in your margarita glass doesn't stand a chance.

Helene - Julien Clerc (1987), Virgin (F)
Producer: 'Sir' Michael Howlett

It's time to kick off your sandals. With perfect timing, Clerc's hypnotic summer hit "Helene" made its debut on the *Music & Media* European Hot 100 Singles chart on July 18, 1987, enveloping one's senses with a feeling of euphoria. Clouds part, colors brighten and the air becomes charged with positivity. The song itself is a humorous love letter to a beautiful woman, referencing San Francisco Bay rather than an exotic Caribbean port and such, but no doubt a lot gets lost in my English translation. Clerc, a French chansonnier who found a great deal of success in the '70s, spent just shy of six months on the singles survey with this song, finding, unsurprisingly, an enthusiastic reception from his fans in France and the Benelux territories. "Helene" is like a cool drink of coconut water, a nourishing hybrid of dance/pop, reggae, calypso and merengue that sways and rocks the listener with its irresistible hook. The song is pure summer escapism from an artist some called "The Elton John of France." I don't fully grasp all the Francophone nuances of Clerc's "Helene," a top 20 pan-European hit and the 69th biggest song of 1987 in *Music & Media*'s year-end singles chart, but I'm buying into ('n' loving) every note of them!

Here Comes The Sun - R'n'G (1997), Motor (G)
Producers: Alex Christensen, Tom Civic

A gnashing beat and gritty rapping set a dark tone for a song that's lyrically actually a relatively upbeat celebration of a sunny day. Well produced, but it still comes across a bit cold-hearted and somber. Producer Christensen was the former frontman of U96 ("Das Boot") and in the twenty-first century developed a series of popular albums celebrating '90s dance music in a classical meets EDM style working with The Berlin Orchestra.

Holiday - Kool & The Gang (1987), Mercury (US)
Producers: Khalis Bayyan (Ronald Bell), I.B.M.C., Kool & The Gang

Attempting to channel some of the energy they generated at the beginning of the decade with "Celebration," the group delivers another funky pop jam that cheers the joys of a summer holiday—rocking under the sun, on a beach, or at a private getaway spot with a very big pool. It's got that party vibe alright, but it doesn't quite have the exuberance or catchiness of their signature hit. On August 8, 1987, *Music & Media* concurred, saying the track was "not very innovative" and advised listening to the Jam Mix on the B-side, which they believed had "far more sparkle." Group co-founder Dennis Thomas passed in 2021.

Holiday - Madonna (1983), Sire (US)
Producer: John "Jellybean" Benitez

Madonna Louise Ciccone was arguably the hottest star on the planet beginning in the mid-'80s, and she burned bright throughout the decade that followed—arguably, even beyond. The single "Holiday" (a standout track from her self-titled debut album) was appropriately released on a warm July day in the US. By the fall of 1983, the song (in combination with the track "Lucky Star") was fighting off challengers to the top spot on *Billboard*'s dance chart for over a month.

(L) Madonna, circa 1983, photography by Gary Heery, Sire (press still).

Although many doubted Madonna's musical credibility during these early days, the artist had the last laugh. While she may not have been one of the best singers of the era, she was certainly its most intriguing and electrifying performer and her hits were often irresistible. In this early example, her flashy, trendsetting style (ever changing, often imitated) and "Holiday"'s pleasing brand of '80s synth-pop dance beats fit together like pieces of a brilliant puzzle, creating an irresistible testament to the joy of sunshine escape. It was also the artist's first major pop hit. On August 27, 1983, *Billboard* somewhat apathetically reviewed Madonna's self-titled debut album, calling the set's major singles "Everybody" and "Holiday" "pretty standard dance tunes, but Madonna has the pipes and presence to make them a bit special." The singer delivered another warm weather musical getaway anthem in time for the summer of 1987, "La Isla Bonita.

Holiday - Mad'house (2002), Universal (NL)
Producers: Groeneveld, van der Zwan, Voermans, Verrips

So many, many producers have pulled a Madonna out of their collective pockets over the past few decades. The singer's hit "Holiday," a popular knock-off target, is an uncomplicated song, instantly recognizable, and it easily lends itself to virtually any rework or sub-genre within the world of dance music. Feels like they took advantage of that with this rather lackluster trance-house remake. But the track does sport an agreeable video with lots of appealing summer scenery as a luxury cruiser ferries the fashionable Mad'house crew around the Mediterranean.

Holiday - The Other Ones (1987), Virgin (G)
Producer: Christopher Neil

The Other Ones, consisting of Australian siblings Alf, Jayney and Johnny Klimek and German musicians Stephan Gottwald, Andreas Schwarz-Ruszczynski and Uwe Hoffmann, was an edgy, super cool group who hit it big in Germany for a time. Their smile-inducing, new wave-spiked, sing-song-ish synth-pop track "Holiday" (in some mixes alternately titled "Another Holiday" and featured on their self-titled 1986 debut album) zeroed in on the all-consuming need of Northern Europeans to escape the ordinary and the grip of winter and relish the delights of summer in the south. (In all fairness, that genetic programming is found in people nearly *everywhere* in the northern hemisphere.)

"Holiday" has a bright, slightly satirical feel, with perhaps a bit of a textural nod to The Manhattan Transfer. The track was a top five hit in Germany and was a fixture on the *Music & Media* European Hot 100 Singles chart during the backend weeks of the summer of '87. On March 7, 1987, the publication said the sextet "specializes in well-crafted, driving pop songs in a transparent production of Christopher Neil (Mike & The Mechanics, Sheena Easton). This band is gonna be big, no doubt about that." *Music & Media* reinforced that notion by voting The Other Ones as "Most Promising Act Of The Year National" (Germany) in their December 26, 1987, year-end edition. You should have no reservations about booking this holiday trip.

(L) The Other Ones, circa 1987, Virgin Records (press still), (R) group member Alf Klimek today, photo by Michael O'Ryan.

Commentary from Alf Klimek:

How did you come to sign with major label Virgin for your debut?

"We sent demos out to some companies but really wanted to sign with Virgin, as they were considered 'cool,' and we heard that the boss, Udo Lange, was a passionate guy about music. So we spent a few days making a package that was the size of an LP record, made it look like it was made of marble (airgun sprayed). It had a trapdoor big enough to fit a demo cassette in it and a blinking, green LED arrow pointing to a little red tab attached to some ribbon. When you pulled on the tab the trapdoor opened up and a cassette popped out. The cassette had a black and white photo of my face on it and the eyes were where the cassette spindles were. Udo later said that when he got that he had to put the cassette on immediately, and, if I remember correctly, it was the song 'Holiday' that played first. He came to Berlin from Munich the next day and said, 'I don't need to know details yet. I just want to know that you'll sign with Virgin.' We said yes. That was it."

Was your disdain for European winters (per Wikipedia) a contributing factor for your third single, "Holiday?" I'd love to know how this song came about.

"Definitely! We had already signed with the management of the group Alphaville ('Forever Young'). Johnny and Jayney had to fly back to Australia in order to get a legal stamp on their passports so that they could stay in Germany. I got married (we're still together), so I didn't need to go. We were all penniless, but their flights were paid for by management. Johnny wrote the music and said it reminded him of a holiday. I wrote the parts about walking straight ahead but you're looking to your right, etc. Hating my job, no car, and my aching feet won't take me far, as I was stuck in Berlin and because my lousy siblings got to have a holiday in Australia." [*Alf winks.*] "Jayney, who got to go home, meanwhile wrote about the beach, sun and sand dunes taking one far away, as well as the chorus lyrics. The track reflected how we were all feeling at the time. The rest is history."

The song was a huge hit in Europe. Why do you feel it caught on in so many countries?

"European winter is gray and cold. So when an appropriate 'Holiday' themed song comes about, I guess people like to hear it. 'Holiday' was written from genuine emotions of wanting to escape European winter and also [the joy of] having escaped the winter. It was also fun to listen to and to perform."

You had significant pop success in the US as well, reaching #29—which, for an unknown group out of Germany, was an accomplishment. Did you get to perform here?

"We only did five shows in the US. The first was, if I remember correctly, in Boston. Our gear got stuck at New York customs and only arrived at the gig 20 minutes before we were supposed to perform. The audience helped us load the stage, and we started like 20 minutes late—not our best gig, but the audience was great. In New York we played some cool club where even the bartenders were too cool to talk to a Euro band. However, after our set we were the hit of the night (three bands played) and that cool staff [ended up being] really nice and gave us free drinks!"

There was a remix of "Another Holiday" released in 1991. Was this single a possible attempt to revive interest in the group?

"Yes, because the group had split up by then. I went to live in Australia (returned to Berlin in '92) because I became a dad and wanted a bit of sunshine. Johnny, Blacky [Andreas] and Stephan worked on that to get some attention and maybe [with the idea] we could get back to gigging. We always, all of us, remained, and still remain, friends. It didn't pan out. Jayney and Blacky started a new project, Johnny got into techno and then (and still) film music. I got back into acting and then children's music and story productions. Hoffmann became a music producer and Stephan performed and produced music for various bands."

Is there a standout memory from your days on "Holiday?"

"The video for the US single. It was made by Alex Proyas, who went on to make *Dark City*, *I Robot*, *Knowing*, and other classic movies. He totally embraced the holiday theme and created all these different 'postcard' scenarios, with postcards floating horizontally across the screen. We had as much freedom as we wanted—to be as crazy as we wanted. Joking on set, Johnny demanded to know who this director Alex Proyas was. Alex answered that he's just doing the job the 'real' Alex Proyas wanted and that he was on the payphone issuing his directives. From that moment on and for two days Alex went to that payphone (on set) and pretended to 'talk' to Alex Proyas before he directed every single shot, saying, 'Alex wants you to do this now...' It was a blast! We laughed so much, and we remain friends to this day."

Nearly 35 years later, I was wondering how you feel about the song and if you appreciate the summer energy you captured with "Holiday."

"I don't know if I or the others feel we accomplished something great. We just came up with a song and wanted to perform our whole repertoire. There were other songs we loved—and still do. I'm grateful for the time and the fun we had. But, in the end, you move on to other things, as we all did. We recently got together and performed the song, with the dance moves and all, for a friend's birthday. We rehearsed twice for about two hours. Stephan couldn't get a keyboard onstage so he played the keyboard parts on his iPhone. Really! He did. It was really good and we didn't 'stuff' it up. But we have no plans to reunite."

What tunes do you reach for when you want to feel a summer vibe?

"Believe it or not, the first song that comes to mind is 'Summer Holiday' by Cliff Richard. I'm trying to think of something more 'cool'—perhaps from my childhood—but no, that's it."

And when you want a warm weather getaway, where would you head?

"I like to go to Melbourne, Australia, because that's where I'm from. Beautiful country, and I have some great family and friends there. Also, Gran Canaria because it's always warm, great beaches, it's in Europe and the people are friendly. And Italy, cuz of the food, culture and beauty, both in the countryside and in the cities."

Holiday! - Captain Jack And The Revolution Club (1997), Beatdisaster Records/EMI (G)
Producer: Beatdisaster Records, Udo Niebergall, Richard Witte

Female vocalist Liza Da Costa dominates this rework of the Madonna classic, with the Captain taking a noticeably diminished role (compared to the artist's previous work) as a supporting rapper. The jam still pumps. Captain Jack continues to sing and rap about warm weather fun today, recently teaming with LayZee (Delroy Rennalls of Mr. President) on the single "Summersun" in 2021.

Holiday-In - Geoff Deane & The Tropical Fish (1985), Record Shack (UK)
Producer: Geoffrey Deane

No connection to "the world's innkeeper." Deane, a former member of the UK group Modern Romance ("Can You Move"), brings the same kind of Latin flourishes, male swagger and playful energy to this track about—no surprise—going into vacay-cay mode, packing your bags and flying away. This time it's off to Marbella, on the Costa Del Sol. Strapless metallic mini dresses, messy rock star hair, shoulder pads, white sneakers and acid washed jeans, please step forward.

Holiday Am Ballermann - Holiday (1996), Herz Klang/Sony (G)
Holiday at Ballerman
Producer: Günter Würfel

Okay, hang in there with me on this one. In contrast to the American slang term "baller" or "balla" (a person who had nothing but makes it to the top anyway), "Ballermann" is a German term, which, according to a friend of mine in Hamburg, roughly translates in English to, at least in part, the act of *banging* someone. It's also got a variation of Spain's Balearic Islands name fused in there somewhere. And it's partially derived from the moniker "Balneario," the name of a beach resort hot spot with a hardy party reputation, and which, according to my friend again, is "very popular with some Germans and those who love XXL buckets of sangria and lots of straws to share with random friends, and who are looking for sex on the beach." If all that's true, it's probably not exactly the vibe this song was trying to convey with its sweet vocals and schlager disco beat, but it's nice the region's penchant for seasonal sun, sex and summer fun gets its own tribute tune. You'll find "Ballermann" tacked onto the titles of on an endless supply of festive schlager dance/pop albums and songs, just like this one.

Holiday Rap - M.C. Miker "G" & Deejay Sven (1986), Dureco (NL)
Producer: Ben Liebrand

Combining suggestions of Cliff Richard's '60s oldie "Summer Holiday" and Madonna's '80s club classic "Holiday" and infusing them with a rap about heading to summer season hotspots was a creative stroke of genius on the part of this duo. The credit goes to two Dutch rapper/DJs, Lucien Witteveen and Sven van Veen, as well as producer Ben Liebrand, who polished up their original concept in the studio. The track really began to heat up across Europe in July of 1986 after tourists and holiday-makers dancing at French and Italian discotheques heard the song repeatedly. It turned out to be the 17th biggest hit single of that year according to *Music & Media*'s annual ranking. The record was eventually picked up by indie label JDC in the US, but failed to make an impression there. America's loss.

Commentary from Sven van Veen:

Sven, how potentially powerful could the direct connection between a song and the summer season be for pop success in Europe? Seems like your hit, "Holiday Rap," caught that wave perfectly.

"I had a discussion of this topic a couple of years ago on the BBC. I was there with Cliff Richard, Lulu, The Beach Boys, and some other artists. Why are some songs a summer hit and others are not? Nobody really knows the real answer to that. It has to be, one, perfect timing. It needs to be released or on the radio by the time everyone starts to get that summer feeling, when they are getting ready to travel and go on a holiday. So, a summer hit is always a guess. Nobody can make one [deliberately]. You make a record, and it takes off at the right time. But nobody can plan that. If one were able to do that, then why didn't Michael Jackson have one every summer, and all the other artists? Most summer hits are accidental, if you know what I mean."

So "Holiday Rap" was an accidental summer hit?

"Our song, 'Holiday Rap,' was never meant to be a summer hit because I was working on the idea of using Madonna's song 'Holiday' a year before, maybe two years before, in the winter time. I was just fooling around with the intro of her hit. So, we had been playing it for about a year on pirate radio in our sets—Miker and I were DJs at different stations. I was also playing it on a cassette in discos during my sets. It was just a demo then; we didn't have an actual record. A year later it was picked up by Frits Van Swoll, an A&R manager for the Dureco record label. Frits had heard the song on the pirate radio stations, but he didn't know what it was. He started calling Italy, Spain, all the labels he was connected to. He told them he heard a rap version of Madonna's 'Holiday' and wanted to know if they had released it. Of course, they said no. I had a talent night at the club I worked at, and we had a panel judging the acts. Frits was on the panel. During a break I started playing the 'Holiday Rap' song, and Frits ran up to me saying, 'Who is this? What label is this on?' I told him it was me and Miker. 'It's fucking you?' [*Sven laughs.*] He couldn't believe it, after chasing this song for weeks.

"Frits sent our demo tape to remixer Ben Liebrand to re-record the music (because we had used Madonna's actual music in our demo). Three weeks later, the end of May, Ben called me and said he would be ready in about two weeks for Miker and I to come in and do the raps. However, Miker G was going to Italy for four weeks (his first vacation ever), so Ben agreed we needed to come in right away. We hopped in the car and drove to Ben's house. In the car we rewrote the lyrics to make them more about a summer holiday, since [the season] was almost here. This is how it all went down. It was never meant to be a big summer hit, or a hit at all—it was just fun to do it. So, in regard to having a hit in the summer season, it's all about luck. That's really it."

Do you recall an especially good time performing the track in any tropical or summery locations, perhaps a beach setting or holiday resort?

"In that first summer, the song was a hit all over, including, of course, sunny countries like Spain and Italy. We got our first summer booking in the Canary Islands, off the west part of Africa and belonging to Spain. A lot of Europeans spend their summer holidays there. We flew there (it was my second time in a plane and Miker's first), and we did some shows on the beach and at the resorts, in plazas, things like that. We also traveled to Mallorca and places off the coast of Spain, so we were performing in a lot of really beautiful summer settings."

Did you feel pressure to have another summer hit to keep things going?

"The record company was pushing us to make a follow-up. 'We need some more ideas,' Frits said. So, we already knew that whatever we came up with, it wouldn't come out in the summer—this was during the winter. We thought we needed two hits, two floor-fillers to meld in a mash-up again. Again, we'd need a rap part and a singing part. I came up with the idea to use Kool & The Gang's 'Celebration,' which was definitely a floor-filler, and [Sister Sledge's] 'We Are Family.' Frits called Ben Liebrand again to help, but he was too busy. So Frits called the people from Shakatak in the UK (I love their music). We were flown to London and recorded 'Celebration Rap' there. We didn't capitalize on the summer theme this time; we intentionally did something else."

Sven's favorite summer and holiday getaway song:

"I think it's got to be 'Funkytown' by Lipps, Inc. I always spent my summers back then, 1980, those years in Spain with my current wife—she was my girlfriend back then. At that time, if you were in Spain, you could not miss that song, from one side of the country to the other. Everyone was playing it. I think that's my best memory of a summer hit."

Honeymoon (In Puerto Rico) - Paul Jabara (1979), Casablanca (US)
Producer: Paul Jabara

Bachelors in paradise take note. Brooklyn-born Jabara's cheesy tongue-in-cheek disco salute to Puerto Rico serves as the perfect companion track to the A-side of his single, "Disco Wedding." The 12-inch mix by Bob Stone is cued more to the bump-thump, horns and string sound of the era rather than a Latin tang, ultimately making the song sound a bit like an alternate "Love Boat" theme. But it's all in fun, and if the track doesn't make you smile, the record sleeve photos featuring Jabara playing both groom and drag bride surely will. Paul's *The Third Album* features "Disco Wedding," "Honeymoon (In Puerto Rico)," and "Disco Divorce" if you're looking for the full relationship/break-up experience! Paul Jabara passed in 1992.

Honeymoon In Trinidad - Audrey Landers (1984), Ariola (G)
Producer: Jack White

Audrey is best known for her role as Afton Cooper on the long-running prime-time TV soap opera, "Dallas." At the peak of the show's popularity, the actor began pursuing a music career in Germany with Laura Branigan's ("Gloria") producer, Jack White. "Honeymoon In Trinidad" was from the artist's second album for Ariola, *Wo der Südwind Weht* (roughly, *Where the trade winds blow*), and like the set's other tracks ("Santa California," "Santo Domingo," etc.) this song capitalizes on the successful summer beach theme of her previous hit single, "Playa Blanca" (1983/84). Feel free to assume that "Honeymoon" was lyrically about exactly that—newlyweds in tropical paradise—but don't underestimate the appeal of its liveliness or good spirit. German schlager music characteristically embraces very old-fashioned romantic themes (especially evident in Audrey's spoken word interlude midway through "Honeymoon") that may feel a bit dated and saccharine today, but they can also be highly addictive and entertaining—so-called "guilty pleasures." In addition to singing these sugary German tunes, Ms. Landers was often tasked with writing English lyrics for the songs she recorded, including this one.

Hooray! Hooray! (Caribbean Night Fever) - Boney M. 2000 (1999), MCI/BMG (G)
Producer: Frank Farian

Seventies disco purveyors Boney M. often brought a calypso/tropical flair to their music, and at the dawn of the twenty-first century, their music still remained reliably marketable in Germany and across Europe, provided their chart hits were given current sound trend remixes or the megamix treatment. Tacking a hip "2000" onto their name, the group takes some of their most summery successes ("Hooray! Hooray," "Brown Girl In The Ring," "No Woman No Cry," and "Calendar Song") and blends them with a crisp beat and polished production. The well may have run a bit dry by this point, however, for the track wasn't a big hit. But not for lack of trying.

Hot Bodies On The Beach - P.M. Sampson (1991), Sony Dance Pool (G)
Producer: Peter Columbus

The premise here is that there's more to the beach than just white sand and palm trees. Alright, I sea where this is going, and I'm in! With "Hot Bodies On The Beach," an enthusiastic American rapper (Phillip-Mychal Sampson) lays down clever, colorful rhymes about some of the "other" surf side sights to enjoy, such as suntan oil slathered girls who don't wear very much. Completely danceable with a percolating pulse and bright horn stabs in its "Nasty Beach Mix," the track has a sly but harmless old skool feel. The artist enjoyed most of his success in Germany, where his single the year before, "We Love To Love," was a pop/rap hit.

Hot Fun In The Summertime - Dayton (1982), Liberty/EMI (US)
Producer: Rahni P. Harris, Jr.

This Ohio-based group delivers a classy electronic funk jam with that smooth, early '80s vibe, vocoder effects and an Earth, Wind & Fire/Emotions type of disco groove to liven up their cover of the Sly And The Family Stone classic. A modest *Cash Box* US pop crossover hit in the summer of '82, it also reached #15 on the publication's Top 100 Black Singles Contemporary Singles chart. It's the kind of music that feels so right just drivin' 'round on an 85° F afternoon or partying poolside with your crew.

Hot Fun In The Summertime / Island Fever / Summer Of Love - The Beach Boys (1992), Brother Entertainment (US)
Producer: Terry Melcher

From the Boys' often maligned *Summer In Paradise* album (presumably, in part, because it featured Mike Love rapping), these tracks actually feel like solid beach beats. I can hear the jeers, but had they been recorded by anyone other than The Beach Boys, they'd likely be viewed as fun summer surf rock with a retro-pop vibe, and totally appropriate for 1992. Everything seems a bit "Kokomo" here, which is understandable given the success of that single a few years earlier. The tick-tock rhythm and spare arrangement of "Island Fever" is kind of avant-garde and almost has a new wave feel, while "Hot Fun" is a jazzy, synth-rock and even somewhat soulful update of the Sly And The Family Stone hit. "Summer Of Love" gets all the attention thanks to that cringe-worthy rapping, already (and reluctantly) mentioned, and its "Baywatch" parody video. But remember, summer should never be taken too seriously. Just as its perfectly fine to sing, dance and soak up the summer sun, it's also okay to get a little goofy when it comes to pop music and palm trees. Eccentric, but I'll allow it.

Hot Hot Hot - Arrow (1982), CNR (US/J/BAR)
Producer: Alphonsus 'Phonsie' Cassell (Arrow)

Arrow (Alphonsus Celestine Edmund Cassell), the late soca-calypso artist from the island of Montserrat (he passed in 2010), was the first to score an international hit with this energetic, ridiculously irresistible pop song, literally about people rocking to a Jamaican party jam. Steve Harvey's "Hotter Mix '84" really kicks. One should be required to have a Passion Fruit martini nearby when this song comes on. It has been covered by numerous artists, most famously in the summer of '87 by Buster Poindexter, who's up next.

Hot Hot Hot - Buster Poindexter And His Banshees Of Blue (1987), RCA Victor (US)
Producer: Hank Medress

Unrestrained vivacity! Party people everywhere loved this celebratory anthem (add it to the wedding reception playlists), a remake of the Arrow song and a monster hit on MTV. Buster (David Johansen of the New York Dolls) and his nine-piece band peaked at #11 on the *Billboard* dance chart with a house-fused "New Club Mix" version of the soca smash, engineered by John Morales and Sergio Munzibai, which is a little over five minutes of pure hip-shaking fun. On October 31, 1987, *Billboard* reviewed the 12-inch single, saying, "Poindexter will cause many to burn a hole in the sole of their dancing shoes…Salsa inferno!"

Hot Hot Summer Day - Sugarhill Gang (1980) Sugar Hill Records (US)
Producer: Sylvia Inc.

With winter dead, summer moves full steam ahead as the venerable "Rapper's Delight" trio rhymes about bikini short-shorts, beach balls, beaded hair, and skates on your feet. Light and fun with a kind of vintage Kool & The Gang spirit.

Hot In The City - Billy Idol (1982), Chrysalis (UK)
Producer: Keith Forsey

It was always cool (but safe) to dig snarling rebel Billy Idol. He exuded just enough leather clad punk edge and bad boy sexiness to make you feel a bit anti-social listening to his music, but his appeal on a pop/rock/new wave-dance level was reassuring and fun. "Hot In The City" is, as expected, a jangly synth-pop/rocker, snappy and melodic, and it throws in a little friction with a tight "Bette Davis Eyes" hand clap. Idol reminds us not to forget what it's like to have youth on our side during a hot summer night. For me, that memory is locked in tight. "…catchy enough to be a hit. God help us!" reviewed *Record Mirror*'s Simon Hills with a frown on August 7, 1982.

Hot Nights In Ibiza -Angie St. John (1987), ZYX (G)
Producers: Frantz, Jaspers

Released at a time when Italo disco and German dance music sounds had effectively merged, the song celebrates the "international flair" of the party island, its excitement, romance and how difficult it is to leave the place (not because you can't book a flight, but because it's so lovely there and you wouldn't want to). Is there a worse feeling than ending a vacation like this? It became a signature hit for the artist, but was covered by several dance acts, including Vanilla and Casablanca.

Hot Sand - Coco Beach (1985), Fellow Music (G)
Producers: W. Quintus, J. Rasmussen

Hot sand and even hotter love in Ibiza take center stage in a crisp synth-pop eurodisco number with edgy female vocals. Exceedingly catchy ear candy that you might expect to be playing on beach radios in Capri, Sardinia or Rimini back in the day.

Hot Stuff - Donna Summer (1979), Casablanca (US)
Producers: Giorgio Moroder, Pete Bellotte

Let's just say it: Donna *is summer*! Prior to the release of "Hot Stuff," the highly anticipated track was being touted by the tabloids as the singer's big chance to finally record the "rock" music she always wanted. It's true the song was a unique hybrid of disco and electric guitar rock, but the overwhelming feeling it generated transcended both genres. Imagine hearing the opening thunderous beats of this song booming over club speakers for the first time. It was so powerful that the dance floor and sound system literally shook. In the discos, dancers cheered as that massive pounding thump felt like Godzilla marching towards Tokyo. The mammoth depth of this track grew heavier and came roaring ever closer toward eager dancers. It was intimidating and arousing at the same time! The only song that one can really compare it to is Amii Stewart's "Knock On Wood," another flammable, out-of the park hit that arrived around the same time. It's doubtful we will ever see a year in dance music as explosive as 1979.

"Hot Stuff" exceeded most anyone's expectations, a boiling sea of slamming energy. Ferocious in power, this booming single was among Ms. Summer's greatest achievements, second only to perhaps the enormously influential "I Feel Love" in '77. By 1979, her vocal style had been honed away from the coy, girlie sex-kitten image she originally projected to one of confident female power, and anything her producers wanted to try at this point was almost guaranteed to be successful. This one took off just in time for the summer season. Donna is fire—with wailing vocals that burned through the happy medium between disco and rock (not long before the anti-disco movement reached its anti-climactic peak), and the roar of this guitar-fused production still leaves one breathless and sweaty today. It's difficult to fully describe how insanely ferocious this song felt playing on a hot summer night decades ago, but I think you get the idea.

On June 16, 1979, *Billboard*'s Dick Nusser critiqued Miss Summer's 1979 *Bad Girls* album and described the "Hot Stuff" track as probably the "catchiest" of the set. "Kicked off with a rock intro," he said, "it's a perfect disco song that Summer delivers in a sexy vocal style that takes in Mae West and Ma Rainey as well as her own breathy, little girl persona…" I'd argue again there was nothing "little girl" about Ms. Summer at this point. *Record World* called the album "exquisite." In a 1982 flashback, *Cash Box* ranked the *Bad Girls* set as the #2 album of 1979 (second only to Supertramp's *Breakfast In America*). Funnily enough, I only remember one song off the Supertramp album, but Donna's hits seemed to drop at a breakneck pace, each distinctive and unforgettable. Now that's what I call an endless summer!

In 2020, EDM artist Kygo revived "Hot Stuff" in his extremely successful, though somewhat less forceful, electronic reinvention of the song featuring Donna's vocals. Miss Donna said goodbye to us in 2012, and the loss still feels fresh.

Hot Summer Night - The Three Degrees (1979), Ariola (G)
Producers: Giorgio Moroder, Harold Faltermeyer

Written and composed by Chris Bennett and Giorgio Moroder, the same team who gave us the "Midnight Express" theme. This track served as the B-side of the ladies' single "My Simple Heart," apparently an "extra" recording not included on their 1979 album, *3D*. The song is typical of the electronic disco beat, bass rhythm and syndrums 'n' strings sound coming out of Moroder and Faltermeyer's production camps at the time, though comparably less ambitious than the producer and songwriter's work with Donna Summer. Still, the contrast between the song's popish, slightly funky and upbeat groove and The Three Degrees' ("When Will I See You Again") sophisticated and soulful vocals is agreeable. It's a hot summer night *whenever* these ladies are working. And while we're longing for the heat of a hot summer night, let's head over to New York City with Miss Vicki Sue.

Hot Summer Night - Vicki Sue Robinson (1981), Prelude (US) Producer: Warren Schatz

You bet it is! Vicki Sue Robinson, born in Harlem, New York, will forever be associated with classic disco music thanks to her unforgettable rendition of the 1976 RCA Records pop hit "Turn The Beat Around," produced and arranged by Warren Schatz. By the early '80s, Warren was working independently and came up with a scorching, throbbing instrumental track that eventually became the foundation of "Hot Summer Night." It's a pulsating jam with a distinctly New York feel—listening to it, one instantly gets the sensation of a humid, 90° F Friday night in the city. It was an ideal vehicle for Schatz's longtime friend and dependable vocal collaborator, and the song reached #24 on *Billboard*'s dance chart, just as the days began to get shorter in the late summer of '81.

Commentary from Warren Schatz:

"At the end of my stint running Ariola America over at Arista, when we closed the company, I was freaking out. I didn't know what to do. I had an Atari eight-track recorder at home that I played around with, and at one point later I had gone down to a place called Secret Sound Studio. I had gone there and recorded just rhythm tracks, just drums and percussion and mixed it down—just to have. I don't know why. So, I had about 20 minutes of this whole thing, which started to sound like a dance track, and I decided to put it on one track of the Atari recording. Then I started playing around with it some more, then playing with the synthesizer, and I started writing the song. It was December, I think, so it was totally *not* a conscious thing to go and create a summer song. It was just that the music made me say, 'hot-hot-hot summer night,' and I came up with this hook. I called Vicki Sue Robinson and said I had this idea, why don't you come in and we'll mess around with it?

"So she came in, and we wrote the hook. And she wrote the little semi-rap part, and we put it all together. Vicki and I had the kind of relationship where she trusted me so much and we had fun making music. So she never really commented too much on this record or anything we did. Except that she wanted to do more jazz stuff, and I wanted her to do dance music.

"In the middle section of 'Hot Summer Night,' there's this breakdown. When I was working for RCA, I had all these people go into the studio, [and I recorded them] making noise, orgasmic noises. One woman was moaning 'Harder! Harder!,' and I just thought it was so funny. I ended up putting all that in the middle of 'Hot Summer Night.' I brought the song over to Stan Hoffman [Executive Vice President] and [producer and DJ] François Kevorkian at Prelude Records. Prelude was literally right around the corner from where I live, and they loved it! Right that day, they signed the record. But when I got the contract, there was something on it I didn't like, so I never signed it. But by the next week, they already had begun pressing it, and the track just started climbing up the dance chart. Coming after [my departure from] Ariola, when I was very depressed, it was a very uplifting thing to have happened. I thought it went higher than #24, but that's okay, I'll take it!"

Hot Summer Nights - Love Club (1983), West End (US)
Producer: Jay Dixon

Sweet female vocals and a funky electronic beat reminiscent of D-Train's "Keep On" managed to keep DJs and dancers occupied long enough for this old skool jam with a New York groove to hit the *Billboard* dance chart in the late summer of '83.

Hot Summer Nights - Miami Sound Machine (1986), Columbia (US)
Producers: Emilio Estefan, Jr., Giorgio Moroder

Instead, there's a chill in the air. The cold, synth-heavy electric dance influence here really obliterates any of the earthy warmth one might expect of the Miami Sound Machine, making this sort of an obligatory effort to pair Ms. Gloria with the frosty pop production signature of '70s/'80s hitmaker Moroder. That said, the song is right for the movie "Top Gun" (it's featured on the soundtrack) and fitting for the era; it's just not especially memorable or an ideal design for Miss Gloria. It might have been a better fit for Bonnie Tyler.

Hot Summer Salsa - Jive Bunny And The Mastermixers (1991), Music Factory Music (UK)
Producers: Andy Pickles, Ian Morgan

If Bugs Bunny and Fred Flintstone did some shots and hosted a four minute salsa pop party, it might sound something like this. Tepid interpretations of "Everybody Salsa," "La Bamba," "Hot Hot Hot" and one or two others in medley form interspersed with cartoon character soundbites. A goofy soundtrack for a very low budget staycation.

(I've Had) The Time Of My Life - Bill Medley & Jennifer Warnes (1987), RCA (US)
Producer: Michael Lloyd

A surprising hit duet from the left field "Dirty Dancing" movie soundtrack, which went to #1 on the *Billboard* pop albums chart, catching the industry off guard. The album had no superstar music artists on board, but managed to leapfrog over the recordings of Michael Jackson and Bruce Springsteen, who also had albums vying for the top spot at the time. The song reached #1 on *Cash Box*'s and *Billboard*'s pop singles surveys in late November of 1987, and won an Oscar for Best Original Song. According to Tom Eames of Smoothradio.com, "The Story of... '(I've Had) The Time of My Life' from Dirty Dancing," posted February 21, 2020, the song was originally intended as a duet for Donna Summer and Joe Esposito, but Ms. Summer turned it down, not liking the title of the movie. With the romantic drama 'n' dance film set at a vacation resort in the summer of 1963 and the song's lyrics as immensely uplifting as the screen images that accompanied them, "(I've Had) The Time of My Life" became synonymous with the season. But if you're in the mood for something with a little more get-up-and-go from the soundtrack, don't miss Merry Clayton's fiery single, "Yes."

I Feel So Good - Mr. Freeman (2002), Polydor (G)
Producer: Toni Cottura

Do you? Tongue-in-cheek pop rap that, in the video, features (Anthony) Freeman playing a guy who informs us he has no money in the bank (but he's not concerned) as he cavorts around an insanely picturesque Caribbean resort (where he appears to be sketchily employed). He flirts with an attractive female guest there, but, in the end, we discover it was all just a dream. An unbothered Mr. Freeman shrugs it off saying, "it was a good one!" There's a lot of mixed messaging going on here, and I'll let you adjudicate whether you think this is a "feel good" song or not. I wanted him to succeed, and when it all turned out to be a fantasy, I felt somehow disheartened by it. Maybe he should try his luck in Rio.

I Go To Rio - Pablo Cruise (1978), A&M Records (US)
Producer: Bill Schnee

A completely respectable, lively entry by the San Francisco rock band with faint disco flourishes and a kind of honky tonk piano sound. It moves in the right direction and is certainly animated enough, but like Peter Allen's version, it's a recording that, by today's standards, yearns for a more ambitious production. As a time piece, however, it's primo.

I Go To Rio - Peter Allen (1976), A&M Records (US)
Producer: Brooks Arthur

A signature hit for Mr. Allen that energetically salutes the allure of the legendary Brazilian city, it has the type of showman bravado and exceptionally theatrical sound for which the entertainer was famous. But somehow, as with Pablo Cruise, one wishes Allen had pushed the envelope, the energy, a little further, perhaps more towards the style of his "Bi-Coastal" hit from 1980.

I Go To Rio - T.C. Circus (1990), RCA (G)
Producer: T.C. Productions

This is the little record that could! Not much is known about this recording released by the German branch of RCA around June of 1990, but one might guess that "T.C." represents the lyricist of the delirious B-side track, "This Boy Is Too Much," someone named "Tom Coocoo." There's definitely a little cray-cray in "Rio," but in a good way, with its relentless energy, infectious beats and breathy breaks. A rousing disco arrangement battles it out with a highly competent and appropriately enthusiastic male vocal, and joining forces they take the Peter Allen/Pablo Cruise gem to the thrilling heights where it belongs. The track could almost pass for a PWL '80s disco/pop production (think Kylie, Big Fun). T.C. turns the party with his super high energy!

I Wanna Be A Lifeguard - Blotto (1979), Blotto Records (US)
Producer: Farnsworth Blotto

The Albany band with a Jersey Shore sense of humor salutes the empowerment of ditching a mall job and pursuing the joys of a whistle around the
neck and zinc oxide (um…that's what that white stuff on the nose is, right?).
It's a jumpy punk wave rocker that mixes well with "Rock Lobster" and that
type of shaker jam. Blotto sing about summer blondes, tan lines and making
"moves"—comparing themselves to Allied Van Lines. Now that's funny!
Sergeant Blotto (aka "Sarge,"and the band's main vocalist) passed in 2019.

I Won't Let The Sun Go Down - Nik Kershaw (1984),
MCA/WEA (UK)
Producer: Peter Collins

When focusing on this new generation British pop singer/songwriter, the
'80s media often centered on his photogenic good looks. However, Kershaw's
artistry, and many of his songs, were deserving of closer attention. This track,
from the LP *Human Racing*, became an evergreen of European synth-pop,
and its warm weather, sing-along magnetism quickly began exploding across
Europe in July of '84. Though the song had nothing to do with the summery
theme its title suggested, it nevertheless captured a seasonal sensation with

its catchy hook. The track peaked at #8 on the *EuroTipSheet* Top 100 Singles chart in mid-August. In subsequent years, remixes and updates of Kershaw's recording were released, and a number of other artists took a swing at the track as well, including Robin Cook, Kiriman, Sunshine Ft. Pato Banton, and Najette, all of whom interpreted the composition in a reggae/pop style.

I Won't Let The Sun Go Down - Robin Cook (1996), Stockholm Records (SW)
Producer: Jonas Ekfeldt

Though his work may not be globally known, this Swedish artist's remake of Nik Kershaw's synth-pop classic "I Won't Let The Sun Go Down," and many of the supporting tracks from his debut album, *Land Of Sunshine*, proved Jonas Ekfeldt (alias Robin Cook) understood the pop song and palm tree sound—and how to deliver it. *Music & Media*'s Raúl Cairo was full of accolades when commenting on the "Sun" single back in his August 31, 1996, "On The Road" column, saying, "With its upbeat reggae foundation, the track is perfect summertime fun, while Cook's warm voice gives the song a most romantic feel." The single entered high on *Music & Media*'s Border Breakers chart at #16 on August 31, 1996, but peaked at a modest #55 around the same time on the publication's European Top 100 singles chart. Ekfeldt's music, which sounds remarkably polished for a then youthful newcomer to the professional music scene, possesses a confidence and spirit that he truly "gets" the lure of summer and the tropics, and his artistic charisma is felt throughout all of it. There's a pretty interesting backstory baking in all this sunshine, too.

Commentary from Dr. Jonas Ekfeldt:

Dr. Ekfeldt, how did your version of 'I Won't Let The Sun Go Down' take shape?

"In order to answer that, I have to tell you a bit about my background and what brought me to that point. I started at a young age. I was 13 when I had my first DJ gig at a local youth center. I got that job from working at a church, where I cut grass, and with the money I earned I bought a stereo and as many records as I could afford. I was a DJ for something like 10 years every weekend, and I also played the keyboards and had a sampler. At 22 years of age, I was an unproven producer. I hadn't gotten to my first studio yet, but I knew I wanted to become successful. That was the main goal—I wanted to make hits. At that point, I didn't really make a distinction between covering someone else's songs or producing my own songs—just as long as they became hits. I made a list of about 25 songs that I wanted to produce—covers, my own material, all kinds of ideas. I then started to make demos of these songs at home with a small tape recorder. I was just singing, and with my sampler I was able to have some kind of background. Among those songs I recorded was 'I Won't Let The Sun Go Down.'

"So this was back in 1993, and that summer I went to Italy. I'd wondered why there were so many great songs coming out of this country. You'd look at these dance records, and they all said, 'Made In Italy.' They sounded great, and I just had to go there. I took the demos I made with me. In 1994 I got a deal with this Italian record label—they made records, did publishing deals and handled everything themselves. I started to work there and brought all my ideas to them. They heard my version of the song 'I Won't Let The Sun Go Down,' and they wanted me to sing it. I had just used my voice to create the demo—I hadn't actually considered being a singer before. But that's what they wanted. So we began our collaboration. We started recording the vocals in Rome in 1994, but at some point I had to go back to Sweden, and the entire production got put on hold. I had begged them to finish it, but they had other priorities, and the project just fell apart.

"I played the demo for a friend back in Sweden at his home. I left the cassette at his home, and after a while he called me. He was a bit irritated, saying, 'My girlfriend is listening over and over to that demo you made.' Somehow, she got addicted to my recording. That made me decide that if I could hook one 18 or 19 year old girl, I could probably hook a couple of hundred thousand more. In a new studio in Sweden, I decided to start all over again, all by myself. That meant making new recordings and arrangements that were different from the Italian ones, obviously."

The original version by Nik Kershaw was already a well known track. What new elements did you believe you could inject into it?

"It was very clear to me that I had to try to improve it. It's very hard with covers—they often don't add anything to the song. It was very important to me that I make some sort of addition, my contribution, to the song. It had to be really good and fit with that song. I don't have anything bad to say about Nik's original version—it's wonderful. But I felt the original arrangement—making a distinction between the melody, the song and the actual arrangements, guitars, drums—they had become so dated. Also, I felt if I was going to do this, I needed to bring into it something along the lines of a reggae vibe. We're talking about the sun, a summery vibe, without becoming a ragga genre song. I really wanted to avoid that. (I've seen some pathetic tries to get there from white artists.) I also wasn't concerned about comparisons of my work to Nik Kershaw's. I was making this song for a younger generation—the older one had already enjoyed it. The younger generation probably had never heard it."

What inspired you to take the stage name, Robin Cook?

"Oh, yes, that's a good question. It's not this big story with a lot of philosophy behind it, though. It was very simple. When I was younger, during my time in Italy, they had these magazine stands out there on the street. They also had books that they were selling. I remember passing this magazine stand, and they had this massive wall of books with this huge author name on it—Robin Cook. It made an impression on me. I thought that would make a good artist name someday. A few years later, I needed an artistic name for my music project, so it was kind of easy to choose that one. That's the whole story; it just came to me—boom!"

"I Won't Let The Sun Go Down" was a summer and pop chart hit in Europe, which is quite extraordinary considering you were a relatively inexperienced and unknown artist who literally made the track himself. That's not unheard of today, but back then it was unusual. The single didn't quite go the full distance on the charts, but were you still happy with your achievement?

"This was my first experience, so this must be how it works, I naively thought. I had no references. I now know that many people had to work for decades to have *any* chart success. This may sound ungrateful, but I was aiming for the top 10. I believe it should have gotten a lot more promotion that it actually got. I think the label wasn't very interested in promoting this track. The song was released in Sweden first, then Scandinavia, and then, on my 25th birthday, it reached #1 in Sweden. That's when I asked the label what they were doing to promote it internationally, but they said it was holiday time and people [were taking time off]. I said no, if this is going to happen this year, we need promotions in other countries. Now! They had no ideas, there was no real promotion plan going on, so I asked them to give me their promotional records and cds, and I would go to Italy, and I'd try to make it happen there.

"I tried Polygram in Milan, and the guy there said, 'It's a cover. I'll think about it.' Okay, yeah, you think about it. I ended up releasing it with a small label that actually specialized in folk music, Musica Solare. They liked the track. The guys at that label actually brought me to a record store somewhere in Milan, and I gave the store owner a few promo copies of my single, who also had connections in radio. He played the record in the store, and we noticed a line forming at the counter. They were all like, 'What is this song?' The next day my song was on Radio DeeJay, a major national station! Once that happened, the guy at Polygram Italy was suddenly interested, but I said no, it was already signed. So, again, this is how things work. We reached the sales charts in Sweden, Poland and now Italy. With three countries, it was policy that it gets released across Europe. And so my label in Sweden finally got it out. And I did have some success, and, yes, I was happy about that.

"My intention, without a doubt, was to have a summer hit. Absolutely. But in order to have a hit, there are a lot of factors involved. It's about timing, competition, many things you can't control. Now, unfortunately, this other track was also released just a few months prior to the release of my 'I Won't Let The Sun Go Down.' 'Macarena' [by Los Del Rio, the 1996 global smash, Bayside Boys remix]. I felt it screwed things up royally for me—it was catchier, and it had a cultural influence, which my song lacked. (Julio Ferrarin, the man I originally started collaborating with on this track in Italy, gave me this piece of advice. If you put some cultural element in a track, you'll have success somewhere, anywhere. It was a good lesson.) It sounded better, and it came out full force. They had full promotion, MTV was playing it on high rotation from day one. As soon as I saw that crazy video, the jumping around, the dance, I said, 'shit, we're done.' Anything else will be second to 'Macarena.' We won't make #1, which is what I was hoping for. I was aiming for that. That's what can happen when you set out to have not only a summer hit, but a summer #1."

Why did you step out of music production afterward?

"There was a lot going on, as happens in the music industry, where I as a creator had different views than the record companies I was working with. I completely lost interest and faith in doing this work for a couple of years. I had an artist crisis, I guess you'd say. I felt my surroundings in Sweden were horrible, and the people were so close-minded—that's how I felt at the time. I closed my studio down in Sweden and flew parts of it to Italy and set up there. I moved to Italy and lived there for many years and sort of rediscovered my love of dance music. I tried to go in different directions with music. If I had stayed in the same type of sound, I would have that stamp forever, and I didn't want that. I made the record 'Susanna' as Robin Cook in 2002, and that was my last production. You'll notice my face is on the cover of that single. I realized this is my act, my project, my vocals, so why not put my face on it? By this point, I wanted to be the artist on stage. I did hundreds of performances as the artist, although nobody probably noticed the difference. Maybe they did, but nobody told me."

And then you became a lawyer. That's a twist! "I Won't Let The Sun Go Down" contributed to that, correct?

"Ah, yes! After my 'Susanna' production, I returned to Sweden and started thinking about what to do with my life. Music production wasn't something solid; I couldn't count on it to support myself. I was a little over 30 by then, and I thought, why not give being a lawyer a shot? Also, there was a sample infringement case with my version of 'I Won't Let The Sun Go Down' that played a big part in that decision.

"A national, government-owned radio network in Sweden had a show where they did satirical covers of famous songs. They made these parodies and amongst them was a cover of 'I Won't Let The Sun Go Down,' in which they used my production and put their own lyrics over it. They started putting this and other tracks out on records and selling thousands of copies of them. So, I thought, where are my sampling royalties? My label investigated and said the radio station claimed they didn't use my track—they made their own to sound like mine. That pissed me off for a good ten years. That was in 1997, but initially I said screw it all, and moved to Italy. When I came back, I had grown angrier because they had now sold hundreds of thousands of records. And this radio network refused to acknowledge it was based on the recording I had created. They had taken some of the instrumental parts of my original extended version, looped them together, and created their parody version. That would have been fine if they had stopped there, but they started actually selling records and started making a lot of money from them. That was the trigger for me.

"So, I again asked the record company to do something, but they wouldn't risk having their records banned from the station. They gave me a release to handle it myself. It's now 2006, and I went to several intellectual property lawyers, but nobody knew how to handle it. The radio network also had unlimited resources, which I didn't have, obviously. I can't go to court because I don't have the money. I can't make a deal with a lawyer because they don't know what the outcome will be and won't risk it. Nice, huh?

"I heard about work done by a forensic laboratory in Sweden, and thought maybe that's the direction to take. Get a forensic examination of their track and mine and do a comparison. I contacted the National Laboratory of Forensic Science [now known as the Swedish National Forensic Centre] in Sweden. They never performed such an investigation before, but they felt it would be interesting to conduct one of this nature. It ended up costing me about $1,500. This was a major discount, since a forensic investigation like that normally would cost along the lines of $25,000 – $50,000. I'd have to wait in line, so to speak, as there were other projects ahead of my investigation. Three months later they were ready with a method of comparing audio files. I sent them my original recording and the one in question. Three weeks later they sent me a 10-page report. It included a scale that went from minus four (highest degree of certainty that my recording was *not* being copied) up to plus four (the opposite, that they were certain my recording *was* indeed being copied). My results were—*plus four*. Obviously, the radio network was using elements of my original recording in their parody. I faxed this information to the network, and within two hours I got a call from them saying we needed to have a meeting.

"The negotiations took place in my lawyer's office and lasted for about an hour. The radio network admitted only to 'technical issues.' They were behaving like assholes. But at the same time they knew they were completely screwed with that piece of forensic evidence that I now had. I'm bound today by a confidentiality agreement, and I can't say anything about the amount [we settled on]. But I can say in the following years I went to law school!"

What does the hot summer jams sound mean to you? How would you describe this kind of music?

"It could be what I would call the *Balearic* sound that I tie to the Balearic Islands off the coast of eastern Spain where Europeans have been traveling for decades, mainly Mallorca and Ibiza. Those islands are connected with the summer hit philosophy in Europe. If your song made it there during the summer, or in Italy or France, in the nightclubs or on the radio, rest assured the people will party to those songs and will go back to their home countries after their holiday, and they will start demanding those tracks. If you want to be a bit cynical, within the dance music culture, summer dance music is really a commercially sought after commodity. It's still true today, but the distribution methods have changed. Today, with the internet, the process works much, much faster. Before, you had to wait, perhaps a couple of months—you'd see the results in September or October. That's when a lot of the records that had been hits in the summer started selling. Today, it happens much faster. And, of course, today artists are making money off deejaying and concerts, rather than selling files.

"In order to describe that Balearic sound, the hot summer jams sound as you described it, we must agree on a definition. I don't have one. I just put it on like a label. Whatever the song may be, you associate it with summer—for the rest of your life. I wanted to make an impression on people with my music for the rest of their lives, not just one summer. I wanted to make an impact. Back then, the '90s, there were a couple of formulas that seemed to work. I don't really like the idea of formulas, but the drum, the 909 hi-hat open, a female singer, a guy rapping—that's it. There's your hit. But for me, the Balearic sound can be any genre, any kind of production that appeals to some part of almost everyone. I'll put it another way. So, if you look at a sunset anywhere in the world, not even the most insane person would say, 'Oh, I have to close my eyes; this view is so horrible.' You simply can't deny the true universal beauty of a sunset. That feeling when you hear or experience something that is in harmony with the universe—*that* is the Balearic sound, the beach sound, the summer sound. Something that people take with them the rest of their lives—the summer hits."

How wonderful it must be to create music that captures those emotions.

"That was always my goal. I think I may have managed to capture just a little tiny bit of that universal beauty in 'I Won't Let The Sun Go Down.' I think—I'm not sure yet."

*[See also: **Summer Of Love - Ondina**.]*

Ibiza - Amnesia (1988), BCM (B)
Producer: DISCO SMASH/Bruno Van Garsse

A blistering Belgian production that feels like it should have handle with care warning label! Whatever is in this concoction, it furthered the acid-house movement of the late '80s. Well-structured and almost menacing in tone, it was ideal for late night clubbing. You'll need to hear this at maximum volume to appreciate the full impact of this trendsetting hit. Van Garsse followed it up with an equally robust track, "Hysteria." "Ibiza" has that timeless and distinctly "underground summer" feel, so naturally it's been covered by others, notably El Loco in 2002.

Ibiza - Ibo (1985), Bellaphon (G)
Producers: Walter Gerke, Mick Hannes

A German schlager classic about living the good life in Ibiza, where breakfast is served at noon and the sun warms your body all year round. Stop it—you're killing me. Remixed and re-recorded many times by the artist, who was born in a region once part of Yugoslavia. A summery follow-up track in 1987, "Bungalow In Santa Nirgendwo," was also extremely popular. Ibo (the stage name of Ibrahim Bekirović) passed in 2000.

Ibiza Party (Compilation LP) - Various (1986), Ibiza (I)
Producer: Claudio Cecchetto

Cecchetto cornered the market on commercial pop/Italo disco during the mid-late '80s thanks to his then newly formed recording company, Ibiza Records, his European pop culture-savvy music productions, and the promotional power of his Italian radio and TV empire (Deejay Television). On this LP, essentially a greatest hits 12-inch single with tracks mixed non-stop on each side, he brings together his family of artists, including Sandy Marton ("White Storm In The Jungle"), Tracy Spencer ("Run To Me"), Taffy ("Once More"), Sabrina ("Sexy Girl") and more. Some of the versions presented were exclusive remix versions heard only on this set. The Ibiza record label logo appropriately features a beach umbrella perched in the sand, and this music ideally captured the magic of '80s summer disco music, southern Italy shoreline style. The label took out a colorful full page ad in *Music & Media* to promote the record in November of '86.

Ice In The Sunshine - Beagle Music Ltd. (1985), RCA (G)
Producer: Beagle Music

Originally a commercial jingle seen in movie houses, the song, much like Kate Yanai's "Bacardi Feeling (Summer Dreamin')" a few years later, quickly caught the public's attention and was released as a successful pop single. In its original form, it's classic '80s synth-pop with an agreeable horn break and an electrified new wave quirkiness, frosted with shared male-female vocals. Lyrically, it's pure summer and everything a pop song should be, with the accent on young romance, walks on the beach with ice cream in hand, and laying out in the sun. A 1995 remix picks the pace way up and turns it into a frantic eurodance rave, while a more traditional "Caribbean Mix" offers a much more laid back vibe, steel drum accents, and ocean surf sound effects. The song has been covered by numerous artists, including No Angels, Lacuna Project and Carlos Ceya, often with the word "Like" tacked on to the beginning of title.

Ice In The Sunshine - Carlos Ceya (1992), RCA (G)
Producers: A. Kassel, M. Rick, L. Rodriguez

A breezy (and inevitably) reggae/pop styled reinvention of Beagle Music Ltd.'s favored electro-pop hit. Well-produced and the arrangement adds a very tropical atmosphere to the song, released at a time when the dancehall sound was big on the pop charts.

Iko - Unique II (1992), Sony Music (A)
Producer: Unique 2

The venerable standard "Iko, Iko" is given a stomping synth-drenched euro-pop/house arrangement mixed with some lightweight rap. The song "Iko Iko" easily lends itself to jumpy dance mixes like this, so it's really hard to mess it up.

Iko, Iko - Natasha (1982), Towerbell (UK)
Producer: Tom Newman

Besides being the first artist to have a major hit with the song in the UK (nearly at the same time as The Belle Stars' original run with it), Natasha's lean, sax driven rhythm fest is truly an example of less is more. Deliciously uncomplicated, the artist has an edgy, rock styled vocal that cuts right through the simple beat, taking the song in a stimulating new wave direction, as opposed to the island flavor The Belle Stars gave it, who are up next.

Iko, Iko* (1982) / Indian Summer (1983) / Sun Sun Sun (1983) - The Belle Stars, *Capitol/ Stiff (UK)
Producer: Brian Tench

Wild women do…and it's a trip! This densely populated all-girl band out of London was a lovin' machine with a powerful, bold sound that benefited from a resonate unanimity that favored an unconventional edge. Stated more simply, it's a Bananarama meets Tom Tom Club hybrid. The septet's cover of The Dixie Cups' 1965 hit "Iko, Iko" cooks with a highly infectious, fly boy-ready tribal pulse draped in an exotic tropical atmosphere. Add in a vibrant horn section and you get that untamed party feel. The song seems to activate the adrenaline response inside one's body, which feverishly makes its way straight to the hips and feet. Long after "Iko" had run its breakout course in 1982, the track enjoyed a second wave of popularity following its appearance in the 1988 movie "Rain Man," which finally earned The Belle Stars a well-deserved US pop hit. Sounds good to me!

For their dual-sided 12-inch maxi single, "Indian Summer" and "Sun Sun Sun," the ladies continued to explore warm weather themes. "Indian" is a mid-tempo ska jam with a shuffling melody, evocative electric guitars and a dreamy atmosphere. "Sun" is a decidedly offbeat synth-popper shaking about heat waves and that summer sound with nervous electronic energy.

While all of these tracks dive delightfully deep into a summertime groove, it's still that awesome Belle Stars' 1983 signature hit, "Sign Of The Times," that burns the brightest, any time of year.

In The Summer Sun Of Greece - À La Carte (1982), Coconut (G)
Producers: Karin van Haaren, Michael Cretu

Wasn't this an ABBA hit? I guess not, but the three-girl group effectively channels the Swedish quartet in this sentimental song about living a carefree life in the land of the setting sun. No yassification going on here. Pure as fresh ocean air, it's just a really pleasant and romantic song with a positive attitude—and there's a lot to love in all that simplicity. The song's German producers have more sophisticated records to their credits, including lionized '80s dance hits by Bad Boys Blue and Sandra, but they prove here they were just as adept at creating a breezy, satisfying pop song. Check out the B-side of the single, "Cubatão," which also has an appealing warm summer vibe. From the album *Viva A La Carte*.

In The Summertime* - Mungo Jerry & Brothers Grimm (1987)
(UK) / In The Summertime (Dance Rave Medley) - Mungo Jerry
(1990), Ilegal (UK)/ZYX (G)
Producers: *Ray Dorset, *The Brothers Grimm / Ray Dorset

Here we have two versions of the famous 1970 Ray Dorset (and his Mungo Jerry band) song, which was a US #1 rock hit. The first is an extremely bizarre—I'd even say wack—reggae/electronica remix from 1987 that was hugely popular in the UK, though with its paper thin (we're talking Tenjugo) arcade video game sound, how it managed that feat is perplexing. The other is a 1990 remix out of Germany that fares much better, giving the song a secure dance beat with a bit of a "Macarena" shuffle, and mixing in other hits by the band, including "Lady Rose" and the Matthew McConaughey favorite, "Alright, Alright, Alright." The Merenberg-based ZYX label that released this version called it "a package no summer should be without" on the CD maxi-single jacket. But there are literally dozens of other remixes and reinventions of the song out there, so take your pick. Over the decades, the evergreen's vice-like grip on the warm weather season overcame its somewhat dark, sketchy lyrics about drinking, driving and hunting for women (which, admittedly, seem positively Disney-like by today's songwriting standards). *Record World* reviewed a reissue of the original single on May 31, 1975, calling it "an undeniable classic pop song in all senses of the word."

In The Summertime - Shaggy Ft. Rayvon (1995), MCA (US)
Producers: Robert Livingston, Shaun "Sting Int'l" Pizzonia

The one-time US Marine, who took up music after returning from the Gulf War, made a name for himself with the reggae/pop hit "Oh Carolina" in 1992. Originally appearing on the artist's *Boombastic* album in 1995, "In The Summertime" was an extremely popular remake of British band Mungo Jerry's 1970 smash, and Shaggy's version was listed among the top five Eurochart Dancehall Hits of that year by *Music & Media*. The track was refreshed and re-recorded for the 1996 *Flipper* movie soundtrack, bypassing references to having sex on one's mind in favor of a lighter, friendship-themed message. Either way, this "Summertime" hip-hop-dancehall-pop jam pumps up super cool ragga dubs while seamless rhymes bounce about effortlessly. It's a remarkably on-point, fluidly natural and beguiling reinvention, prompting *Music & Media* to comment in a 1996 review, "Having a good time was never so easy." The "In The Summertime '96 Version" maxi-single also features Crosby, Stills and Nash performing the "Flipper Main Title" theme with the London Symphony Orchestra as a bonus.

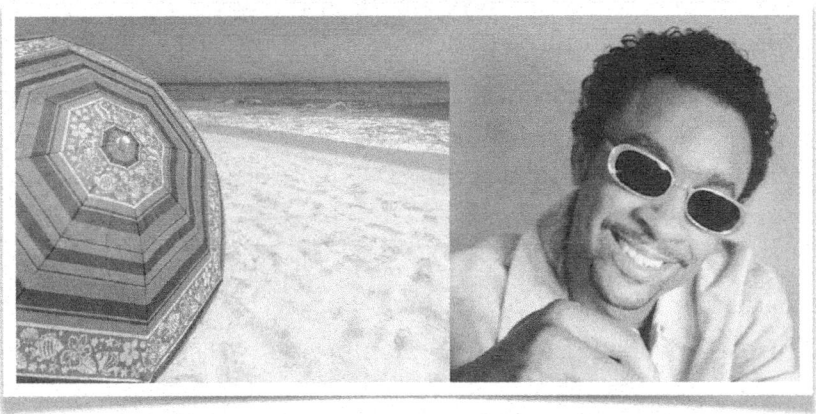

(R) Shaggy, circa 1999, photo by Thomas Zolin, MCA Records (press still).

"I'm not here to send no big messages," said Shaggy in an August 3, 1997, spotlight for *Music & Media*, "my songs are here to put smiles on people's faces. I make songs to perform songs. Give me an hour, let me transform [an audience who doesn't really know what reggae is], and let them leave, if not a reggae lover, a Shaggy lover." Truth! They sure loved his collaboration with Rik Rok, "It Wasn't Me," a few years later.

In The Sun - Blondie (1977), Private Stock/Chrysalis (US)
Producer: Richard Gottehrer

Debbie Harry and her New York underground crew emerge from that dark, smokey, beat up CBGB punk scene of their early days to soak up some sun in this zippy, terrifically cool shoulder-shaker from their self-titled debut album. One can see the influence of this band in the similarly fun, vibe-conscious efforts of The GoGo's and The B-52's a bit later on. Debbie asks, where is her wave? But with this surf music spin-off it feels like we're already in the barrel catching a tube ride.

Into The Sea - CJ Stone (2001), Kontor (G)
Producers: CJ Stone, Henning Reith

A techie trance concoction that dives deep into hard beats with a whispery, ethereal undercurrent, inviting one to take the plunge into what can best be described as euphoric, booming tranquility. An epic EDM production.

Into The Sun - Weekend Players (2003), Warner (UK)
Producer: Andy Cato

Rachel Foster's diamond vocals and a fortifying electro-house production by Andy Cato add up to an absolutely beguiling track that chases the sun in search of happiness—and finds it. On your worst day, this song turns everything completely around.

Into The Sun (Come To St. Tropez)- Poperetta (2000), Flower Records/Universal (F)
Producer: Greg Perry

One of several delightful tracks from the concept act's *Poperetta @ Saint Tropez* album. An enchanting bossa nova rhythm is sprinkled with wispy French female vocals. It projects an airy sensation that has all the atmosphere and elegance of the sunny French Riviera tanning town. A total pleasure.

Isla Blanca - DJ Carlos (1997), Sony Dance Pool (F)
Producers: Aldo Verbeek, Steve Watteeuw

Somehow, DJ Carlos and his producers manage to give this unusual party track, which appears to salute Ibiza, a haunting, gothic feel, broken only by club whistles and the occasional shout outs of a Spanish-speaking male vocalist. But it's hard to deny it has a weirdly fascinating, almost ghostly sound. It stirs what I can best describe as medieval emotion that rises out of nowhere. Perhaps I've been out in the sun too long. Maybe sunstroke also explains our next track.

Island Girl - Elton John (1975), MCA (US)
Producer: Gus Dudgeon

I don't know, perhaps this is some kind of dark sequel to "Jamaica Jerk-Off" from the artist's earlier *Goodbye Yellow Brick Road* LP. Musically, it's classic, catchy Elton, but lyrically it's embarrassingly insensitive, though to be fair, if this song is any sort of measure, being woke clearly wasn't much of a thing in 1975. A honky tonk piano, rock and roll pop rhythm and a diminutive hint of calypso chimes create a deceptively upbeat atmosphere that starkly contrasts with Sir Elton's rather—er—stony hearted story-telling, which focuses on a woman of color drumming up trade on the streets of New York City. Told in a completely tone-deaf manner by twenty-first century standards, I guess all you can say is—(hopefully) they don't make 'em like this anymore. Had the lyrics taken a different tack, there'd surely have been high fives all around.

Island In The Sun - Harry Belafonte (1998), Island (G)
Producer: David Belafonte

Taken from the album *An Evening With Harry Belafonte & Friends,* this promotional single features the (then) 71 year old performer smoothly, gently getting his island on for a live audience. The production of this signature classic has that mature, theatrical polish to it, softening the enchanting calypso atmosphere of the original 1957 tune. Even so, Mr. Belafonte's voice is a magical experience in any setting, and the spirit of the composition (written by Harry Belafonte and Irving Burgie) proves again to be timelessly tropical.

Island In The Sun - Weezer (2001), Geffen (US)
Producer: Ric Ocasek

Plan on having fun with this semi-chill alternative rocker that sports a lilting California vibe and neat electric guitar breaks. It has a real floating in a pool on an inner tube with the drink of your choice in hand feeling—the very essence of summer laziness.

Island Of Desire - Antonella Versace (1985), Cruisin' Records (I)
Producer: Cruisin' Records

I'm pretty sure the name "Versace" was designed to cash in on the clout of Mr. Gianni's esteemed fashion label, so esteemed in the '80s. This is an Italo disco production about a magical island in the sunlight and love under the moonlight, and if the place actually existed as a resort, it'd probably run you about thirty grand US a night. The track also served as a theme song for the '80s Italian TV show "L'Estate E' Un' Avventura." Gianni Salvatori's mix gives the production a flowing and pleasantly exotic sound that feels throughly European.

Island Of Lost Souls - Blondie (1982), Chrysalis (US)
Producer: Mike Chapman

You won't find actor Charles Laughton ominously asking "What is the law?" here. (Sorry, that's an ancient movie reference to the original "Island Of Lost Souls" movie that no one under 60 is likely to get.) Instead we're treated to Debbie Harry's unusual, horn-heavy calypso jam, a production which has an appealing sort of punk quality to ponder. On the other side of the island, they're filming the video for the track, which plays more like a fever dream left over from the aforementioned 1932 flick. One isn't sure where Blondie was going with this musical effort, but keeping us guessing and throwing us curve balls is what they did best, and we love them for it.

Island Of The Sun, The (Turutu'-Tutu) - Iudy (1983), Hole Records/Topflight (I)
Producer: Discomagic

One of the few early '80s Italo disco records to get a US release, indicating this was something special. Piercing through a brilliant electronic arrangement with an unusually crisp, pop-ready vocal (reportedly sung by Milan-born songwriter and guitarist Giorgio Vanni or possibly singer Jimmy McFoy— who knows?), the track is a spirit-raising account of finding love on an island. It gets under your skin, in a very good way.

Island Woman - Pablo Cruise (1975), A&M (US)
Producer: Michael (James) Jackson

Upbeat, danceable guitar rock number from the Bay Area crew, a pop ode to the title character. The track has just enough tropical splashes to cool its broiling guitar work, qualifying it as a true pop music and coconuts gem. *Record World*'s June 7, 1975, review said, "Blue-eyed jungle saga creates its own unique tropical paradise." Meanwhile, Jo Cang's about to take us into uncharted territory.

Islands - Jo Cang (1991), Arista (UK)
Producer: Jo Cang

A standout composition from his 1991 Arista debut album, *Navigator*, Joe (aka Jo) Cang's ode to the refuge of a symbolic island rolls along fluidly, subtly pulsating with a rockish, yet loungy Caribic groove and a solidly earnest vocal. It's got something to say as its intricate, flowing rhythm somehow both revives and relaxes the soul, and Mr. Cang is the best tour guide to explain it.

Commentary from Joe Cang:

"'Islands' is one of the first songs I wrote, and it expresses the longing to leave the senseless hamster wheel existence of urban life and find a place of peace and inner tranquility. It was recorded [during] illegal all night sessions at a London studio (where my friend was an engineer) so we could record after everyone had gone for the night and leave before the cleaners came in the morning. All done on tape in the days before the computer ruled the airwaves. This song was one of the main reasons that Clive Davis signed me to Arista, and it still has a special place in my heart."

Joe's music picks for that summer feeling:

"I'm struggling between Aretha Franklin's 'Day Dreaming' and Stevie Wonder's 'Don't You Worry 'Bout A Thing.' Both fill me with a sense of movement and travel into a dreamlike space with no edges. A sense of overview, distance and a letting go of stresses, whilst understanding the pointlessness of worrying and the acceptance of others in the world around us."

It Feels Like Summer - Aquarius (1994), MCA (G)
Producers: Alexander Hawking, DJ Stevie Steve

If it smells, sounds and looks like summer—it sure ain't winter. That means it's time to pump it up with simple harmonies, Euro-rapping, Spanish guitars and a frisky beat. Get this—some pressings of the 12-inch single were packaged in spongy plastic jackets containing water and sand, in case you didn't get the message. Subtle. Squeeze the day!

It's Better In The Bahamas - Unknown (early 1980s)
Producer unknown.

Anyone watching TV in the US during the '80s will no doubt recall the enticing ad campaign that was designed to encourage us to get our tropical on. It featured stunning beaches, young couples enjoying romantic embraces in the warm sunshine, aqua blue ocean waters, and a lilting melody that ends with the catchphrase, "It's better in the Bahamas"—one of the most enduring commercial tag lines ever. Or a variation of the theme, where simply a fluidly whispered "Oooh Bahamas" was all that was needed to get one packing. Those magical words and images, enhanced by the inviting melodies that enveloped them, made these ad spots among the most successful tourism boosters (for the West Indies or anywhere else) of all time. Though no commercial release of this music seems to exist, I can't help but think what mad bands it could have earned its creators. There's a seven-man group called Madbox who released a European synth-pop single in 1986 called "It's Better In The Bahamas," released through Polydor Germany, but whether this is another variation of the theme or not couldn't be verified in time for this writing.

It's Gonna Be A Lovely Day - The S.O.U.L. S.y.s.t.e.m.
Introducing Michelle Visage (1992), Arista (US)
Producers: Robert Clivillés and David Cole

From *The Bodyguard* soundtrack, Bill Withers' seminal summer pop hit was turned into a #1 house music smash on *Billboard*'s dance music chart by the boys from C + C Music Factory. Ms. Visage, looking lovely, sleek and blonde here, currently shares (some of) RuPaul's spotlight on the ongoing hit TV show "Drag Race." Back in 1992, the artist sounded as glossy, breathy and seductive as some of the queens she critiques on the show today, while posing poolside through shimmering, filtered lenses on the track's video, which also features some hot and hunky young muscle dudes. The production is highly enjoyable and updates the song with a heated elegance that doesn't mess with the genteel essence of the original composition. Back in the day, this track definitely did its part to bolster the massive appeal of Whitney Houston's album.

Itsy Bitsy Teeny Weeny Yellow Polka Dot Bikini - Bombalurina (1990), Polydor (UK)
Producer: Nigel Wright

The story of a *very little material* girl was a big US hit for Brian Hyland in 1960. British entertainer and TV presenter Timmy Mallett decided to give the song an update, formed Bombalurina (named after a character from the "Cats" musical) and had a #1 pop chart smash with the song in the UK. Andrew Lloyd Webber was one of the track's executive producers, remarkably or perhaps unsurprisingly. It's a zippy disco house novelty number that emulates the Stock Aitken Waterman production style. A mock beach party video filmed on a soundstage with plenty of coquettish young men and women accentuates this track's playful groove. Minimalism is always in style.

J - K - L

Jamaica - Bobby Caldwell (1982), Polydor (US)
Producer: Bobby Caldwell

A combination of smooth jazz, blue-eyed soul and lots of heart in which Caldwell turns to the island of Jamaica when the world gets to be too much. The singer's vocal channels Stevie Wonder, and the sincerity of his musings feels quite palpable. Caldwell's voice glides over sensuous strings and a patient, deep bass groove that eventually fades us out of this summery vision. "Jamaica" is about the mood and sensation of the island, rather than a precise musical reflection of it.

Jamaica - Doris D And The Pins (1982), Utopia (NL)
Producer: Piet Souer

New wave disco from a five-girl Dutch group with a kind of snapping "Bette Davis Eyes" electric beat, very much in The Belle Stars vein, but a lot sweeter. Not especially tropical, but there's a lot of bubbly energy to enjoy.

Jamaica Ska - Annette Funicello & Fishbone (1987), Columbia (US)
Producer: David Kahne

From the soundtrack to the 1987 film musical "Back To The Beach," a smile-inducing movie the late critic Roger Ebert described back in the day as, "….the most entertaining comedy on [Paramount's] summer schedule, a quirky little gem filled with good music, a lot of laughs a proof that Annette still knows how to make a polka-dot dress seem ageless." There was a lot to love about this affectionately goofy movie tribute, which was less a parody of the FrankieAvalon/Annette Funicello beach party flicks of the '60s as it was an evolution of their story. There's even more to embrace with its soundtrack and Annette's team-up with ska/soul/punk band Fishbone on "Jamaica Ska." It's a deliriously catchy pop/dance tune that brings the proverbial movie beach dance breakout cliche into the modern era with a charming sense of fun and humor. This whole thing right here—outta sight!

(L) Annette Funicello and Frankie Avalon in the 1987 film "Back To The Beach," photo by Bonnie Schiffman, Paramount (press still).

Jammin' En Brazil (1981) / Sun Is Here (1978) - Sun, Capitol (US)
Producers: Beau Ray Fleming, Byron Byrd

Horns are blaring, people are partying, and the thick bass line and kicking backbeats are raising the roof as this Ohio-based funk group celebrates the lure of the South American hot spot. The group may remind you of Kool & The Gang on the slimmer but equally jammin' splurge, "Sun Is Here." There's a nicely familiar, sweaty, old skool cookout feel in these vintage jams, the kind of groove that sounded so awesome on good old boom boxes—you can have your buds.

Jibaro - Electra (1988), ffrr (UK)
Producers: Phil Harding, Ian Curnow

A modest hit on the UK pop charts, this infectious track melds festive horns and a simple "Jibaro" chant into a lean but pumping electro-pop house jam dipped in industrial sauce. A video for the track featuring scenes from a hot summer day in Spain just adds to the mood. Produced by Phil Harding, Ian Curnow and Paul Oakenfold, there's a Spanish and English version.

Commentary from Dr. Phil Harding:

"This was another track we made specifically for that Ibiza movement of the time and was requested by the influential British DJ, Pete Tong. Although its name doesn't sound particularly summery, it definitely has that groove of the season—all that percussion, the driving fours kick. It's definitely a reflection of the Balearic sound from Ibiza. It wasn't a big pop hit, but it was massive in the clubs. Because once people knew that influential British DJ Pete Tong and Paul Oakenfold were behind it, once you're a part of that DJ mafia, everyone gets behind you!"

Juegalo - Candela Azul (1998), EMI (G) *Play it*
Producers: Ralf Kemper, Marco Losso, Sameh Mina

More Latin-seasoned dance music sponsored by the Bacardi folks, a sweet tasting, infectiously energetic number with a TV commercial feel. Three gals named Bethina, Yanin and Barbie comprised the group and they released a few singles during their short-lived collective career as Candela Azul, but nothing as lively and titillating as this cha-cha fire starter. The video features the girls dancing and partying in a festive tropical setting, and you'll want to be jammin' with them *sooooo* badly! *La vida es un juego, juégalo!*

June Afternoon - Roxette (1996), EMI (SW)
Producer: Per Gessle

With Roxette celebrating a bright summer afternoon, this very upbeat, extremely colorful rocker never lets the sun go down. The song was just a modest hit in Europe, but it should have fared better with its gleaming jump-in-the-air spirit, reminiscent of Katrina And The Waves' "Walking On Sunshine." A new recording at the time, lifted from their 1995 album *Don't Bore Us - Get To The Chorus! (Roxette's Greatest Hits),* which put a spotlight on the formidable pop chart presence Sweden's Marie Fredriksson and Per Gessle enjoyed over the years. Ms. Fredriksson passed in 2019.

Jungle Music - Rico and The Special A.K.A. (1982) 2Tone Records/Chrysalis (UK)
Producer: Jerry Dammers

You'd have to be crazy not to like this jungle beat, as the artist insists in this recording. That's the simple message delivered by "Rico" Rodriguez, born in Havana and a noted ska/reggae artist, and he's spot on. The artist was thinking out of the box when he teamed up with The Specials band for this trombone fest and the end result is something insanely infectious. It grooves along at a lazy pace then suddenly turns into a total slammin' party, all the while basting us with its tropical juices. Rico's "Jungle Music" is one big musical reason to smile. The artist passed in 2015.

Kalimba De Luna - Tony Esposito (1984), Bubble/Hansa (I)
Producers: Mauro Malavasi, Willy David

"Kalimba De Luna," sung by Gianluigi Di Franco, is more than just an exquisite summer dance song. With its exotic instrumentation and soothing, almost tribal beat, it seems to have its own healing powers. It's an exceptionally restorative creation for world-weary souls. One of the tools Tony Esposito, the song's creator and an extraordinarily talented drummer, used to fashion the single was the kalimba, a hand-held musical instrument he played for the first time on a trip to Nigeria in 1984. He also created an instrument used on the track called a "tamborder," which creates a kind of bass sound. The track was enormously popular across Europe and a top 30 hit in several countries. It was also reinterpreted by a number of other artists, including Boney M. (who scored a US *Billboard* top 50 dance chart hit with it and stormed the European pop charts at the same time as Esposito), Garcia, Pepe Goes To Cuba, Dalida, Robin Cook, and others. The track's German "Sevilla Remix" and "Italian Tamborder Club Mix" out of Italy, respectively mixed by The Wild Boys and Max 'N' Frank Minoia in 1992, add Latin and club tones that make Esposito's hit pulsate with even more exotic energy, taking us deeper into the land of the sunshine.

"I think the simple reason this song was so successful was the infectious beat and the unique sound these instruments created," says Mr. Esposito. "To be honest, I was very confused and surprised by the popularity of the song. I was very young at the time it became a hit, and I had all these famous artists offering me their congratulations. At such a young age, I was amazed how I was in a position to actually understand what it meant to have a world hit. If it hadn't been for 'Kalimba De Luna,' I might not have been able to play the many stages of the world I have performed on since then. Italo disco was very popular at the time, but it was not so hot as far as I was concerned. I liked some of it, and I was influenced by it to some degree, but I was more interested in getting my personal style across—a Mediterranean/tropical fusion." *[From the book Europe's Stars of '80s Dance Pop, Vol. 2, Arena, Bookbaby, 2018.]*

*[See also: **Papa Chico - Tony Esposito**.]*

Kingston Kingston - Lou And The Hollywood Bananas (1979), Hansa (G)
Producer: Lou Deprijck

Lead singer Francis Deprijck (aka Lou Deprijck), dressed in ship captain's garb, bears more than a casual resemblance to Daryl Dragon (Captain & Tennille), but you'll never confuse the two musically. This Belgian novelty record is a strange little one-note reggae-esque effort that seems to just endlessly repeat the title over loud horns and a basic drum beat. Recorded in Jamaica, it became a decent-sized hit at the time. I guess seasonal miracles do happen! Am I likely to play this record again? No. No, I am not.

Knock On Wood (Remix) / Light My Fire (Remix) / Megamix - Amii Stewart (1985), Sedition/PRT (UK)
Producer: Barry Leng

When women go big and and invest their voices, hearts and souls into a song, as Amii Stewart did with "Knock On Wood" back in 1978, it can be as if a force of nature is unleashed on an unsuspecting world. Amii's ferocious vocal rendition and the song's blazing hi-tech disco arrangement resulted in a #1 position on the US *Billboard* pop singles chart during the late spring and early summer of 1979. "Light My Fire," the follow-up single that Ms. Stewart had a hit with on the disco circuit at the end of the '70s, stirred things up again. With European and American interest renewed in the vocal prowess of Amii following yet another hit for the singer, the 1984 Italian production of "Friends," Britain's Barry Leng perhaps saw an opportunity to revive Amii's disco classics, which he had co-produced with Simon May and originally recorded in London. Sedition Records in the UK managed these new versions in 1985 and enlisted British DJ and engineer Alan Coulthard to join the project. Coulthard worked closely with Leng (who he describes as very "hands on") to create the blistering individual remixes of "Wood" and "Fire," and later Alan merged those new versions into a megamix. Thunderous in their impact, Coulthard and Leng infused the classic tracks with a tremendous sense of power—no small accomplishment considering how formidable they already were in their original disco versions. "Wood," "Fire" and their megamix were top hits on the UK singles chart once again, and beginning in August of 1985, they conjured up a red hot heat wave for Europe's summer season.

Commentary from Alan Coulthard:

Mr. Coulthard, before we look at your work with Amii Stewart's hits, would you share how you first became involved with dance music and how that led you to become a central figure in creating popular megamixes in the mid-late '80s?

"I am based in South Wales, and I became interested in dance music towards the end of the 1970s. I used to buy records from a shop called 'Flashback Records' in Newport. A guy who worked there, Dave Bumford, was also a DJ, and he was one of the earliest DJs to mix tracks together, and I became fascinated by the concept. I used to follow him around to the clubs he worked at, even though I was only 16 years old at the time! I then bought a DJ console for my home around 1980 and taught myself to mix, although the console didn't have variable speed turntables and it wasn't easy. I also got to know some local DJs, in particular, one named Steve Wiggins, and I used to be his 'roadie' for some of his gigs! (I helped him set up his equipment.) I used to send charts and letters to the dance music journalist, James Hamilton, and he was impressed by my writing style and helped to secure me a job writing articles on a freelance basis, which led to me interviewing heroes of mine, such as Shalamar and Stephanie Mills for the music magazine, *Record Mirror*. James also helped me secure a job DJing at one of the leading London clubs, Le Beat Route, which I did whilst studying for the first year of my law degree in 1981.

"In the summer of 1981, a record called 'Stars on 45' by Starsound [the studio act was known in the US as Stars On 45] was huge, particularly its segment of Beatles hits. This was a medley of cover versions, it did not use the original recordings. Toward the end of 1981, I invented the 'megamix', which has the hallmarks of a medley but was made with the original recordings. The summer seems to be a very popular time for megamixes and medleys. I am not entirely sure why, but perhaps it was due to their suitability for outdoor parties and barbecues.

"I sent a tape of my megamixes to Tony Prince, then at Radio Luxembourg, in March 1982 and he invited me to present a weekly mix on his Friday night show. This commenced in July 1982. Later in the summer, I completed one of my favorite megamixes, using the tracks of Kid Creole And The Coconuts. This megamix was perfect for summer but, although many of my Radio Luxembourg megamixes were reproduced as DMC mixes, Kid Creole never was, and the tape of the mix I have in my garage is the only one in existence! Due to the popularity of my mixes, DMC was set up and commenced in February 1983. My first commercially released megamix was Wham!'s 'Club Fantastic Megamix' in December 1983, which reached #15 in the UK pop charts.

In addition to Wham!, you've created many hugely successful megamixes for top dance and pop stars over the years.

"Yes, I completed many megamixes and remixes for DMC and for commercial release by the artists' record companies, but, to my surprise, my megamixes became a 'craze' in Europe (particularly in France) in 1989. The megamix craze was due to my 'Boney M. Megamix,' which I completed in 1988 for a flat modest fee, thinking it would only be used in a limited way by the record company. I then discovered in the summer of 1989 that it was #1 in the French pop charts as an 'A side' and had been for six weeks! A lot of money must have been generated by this release, but sadly, I didn't receive any of it! I was, however, commissioned to do a Village People megamix which did lead to me receiving royalties. It reached #4 in the French charts. I was also commissioned to do megamixes for Mel and Kim and the Gibson Brothers, and these had some success in Europe."

(L inset) UK press ad for Coulthard's 1985 remixes of Amii Stewart's disco hits, Sedition/PRT Records, (R) Alan Coulthard, circa 2020.

One of your most impressive megamixes was for Amii Stewart, who had enormous success in the disco era with "Knock On Wood" and "Light My Fire." How did this 1985 production develop?

"This remains one of my favorite projects and was one of my most successful in the UK. I was fully familiar with Amii's two massive disco hits from 1979, 'Knock On Wood' and 'Light My Fire,' as they were played to death on Radio Luxembourg at that time. By 1985, I was starting to make a name for myself as a remixer, having completed remixes of Dayton 'The Sound of Music', Whitney Houston 'Someone For Me' and Gloria Gaynor 'I Will Survive.' However, the Amii Stewart project gave me the opportunity to work with the original producer, Barry Leng, and a number of excellent session musicians in creating what were essentially reproductions. The project was commissioned by Sedition Records and we completed the remixes at Genetic Studios in Oxfordshire, which was owned by superstar producer, Martin Rushent of Human League ('Dare') fame.

"[Amii's] original 'Light My Fire' was actually released as a combination of two tracks, 'Light My Fire/137 Disco Heaven'. I later discovered that this was commonly done with a 'cover' as the producer could claim publishing royalties in the 'new' composition (i.e. '137 Disco Heaven') even though this was not really a song in its own right, but a continuation of the 'Light My Fire' theme. It was similar to the idea that you should write an original 'B' side when you released an 'A' side which was a cover. With 'Knock on Wood', we decided to add an instrumental section which was called 'Ash 48', containing some excellent keyboard work using an emulator (played by a session musician). This was a rather spectacular conclusion to the track and some parts of 'Ash 48' also appeared in the seven inch version of the release. However, I wasn't credited as a co-writer of 'Ash 48', although I was paid a fee for doing the remixes. The new remixes reached #7 in the UK pop charts, although it didn't seem to get much radio play and it might have done even better if it had received more.

"Another notable feature of the remixes was that I used 'stuttery' vocal effects on 'Light My Fire', using a sampler. I 'triggered' these samples manually, so it wasn't easy to get them in time. As the '80s progressed, I would use a computer sequencer to 'trigger' the samples so as to make them perfectly in time, but I did not have the equipment to do this in 1985."

And then came the megamix?

"Yes, I also completed a two-track megamix of the remixes of 'Knock on Wood' and 'Light My Fire', which wasn't easy to do as the tracks were very different and even had a different time signature. I am not sure how well this would have worked on the dance floor as a result, but I did get some positive reaction to it."

*[See also: **Gibson Brothers Megamix - Gibson Brothers, Megarama '89 - Bananarama**.]*

Kokomo - The Beach Boys (1988), Elektra (US)
Producer: Terry Melcher

"A snappy little throw-back of a tune from the Boys. Has a real islands-vibe and hooky chorus," said *Cash Box* on July 9, 1988. An anchor selection from the *Cocktail* movie soundtrack, this hugely popular track about a fictitious island off the Florida Keys gave the group a #1 pop hit in the US, some 18 years after they last occupied the top spot with "Good Vibrations." Though it never received a commercial extended remix, the track occasionally found its way onto club dance floors, ironically or simply for the fun of it, until, like Kool & The Gang's "Celebration," it became a wedding reception staple. Somehow, it seems to compel people to sing (or recite) its mesmerizing lyrics whether one really wants to or not. But I'm guessing you want to…I sure do.

L'Amour A La Plage - Niagara (1986), Polydor (F) *Love at the beach*
Producers: Daniel Chenevez, Daniel Pabœuf

New wave electronics meld with a '60s vibe in this popular French song about dancing the chacha, making love on the beach, and everyone's favorite summer souvenirs—seashells and kisses. Performed by Muriel Laporte and Daniel Chenevez, who were very much in vogue in France during the '80s and early '90s. The track has a reckless "out-all-night" Parisian feel.

L'Estate Sta Finendo - Righeira (1985), CGD (I) *Summer is ending*
Producers: La Bionda

With two hugely popular international summer anthems already under their belts, "No Tengo Dinero" and "Vamos A La Playa," it gradually became increasingly challenging for Italian group members Stefano Righi and Stefano Rota to keep the momentum going. Interestingly, and perhaps with a touch of foreshadowing, the theme of this song centers on the fading summer and how, loosely translated, the singers "don't like it."

La Bamba - Los Lobos (1987), Slash/Warner (US)
To dance (or shake) [indirect meaning]
Producer: Mitchell Froom

I probably shouldn't call this song a drug, but it's so addictive a prescription should be required to hear it! Los Lobos, a Los Angeles group with Mexican folk roots, was a cult act for years, but this overpoweringly upbeat track, a folksong said to have originated in Veracruz, was their international break-through ticket. From the Ritchie Valens bio pic soundtrack of the same name, this fiery, soulful version of the 1959 classic fueled a surge in pop-crossover Latin music and became an instant summer pop staple. Ironically, the band had been playing the song for years before they recorded it, back when they were known as The Wolves of East LA. A big chunk of the sales for the "La Bamba" single actually came before the majority of record-buyers had even seen the film. "…Los Lobos were not merely [the film's director, Taylor Hackford's] first choice to recreate Valen's music, they were the ONLY choice…," said the *Observer*'s Charles Shaar Murray, according to Warner, who used this information as a bragging point in a full page ad for the *La Bamba* soundtrack in the 1987 year-end issue of *Music & Media*.

"La Bamba" has been covered by countless other artists. The 1987 French dance version by Los Portos (with Lio) is a major standout, along with Antonia Rodriguez's 1978 disco mix and Monkey Circus' hyper 2002 version. Can't leave out Valen's original Del-Fi Records vocal masterpiece, club mixed in 1987 by Taavi Mote and Bob Keane. It's no surprise everyone in the bar, club or venue cheers wildly when any live music act strums the first delicious guitar licks of this flammable, crowd-pleasing jam.

La Bamba - Marco Da Silva (2000) Mercury (G)
Producers: Jeo, Jan-Eric Kohrs, Carsten Heusmann

Faithful to the Valens/Los Lobos versions, but it's also an especially inventive interpretation by tossing in a reggae rap, heightening the summer vibe. Da Silva's charisma, strong vocal and infectious energy bring the heat. "West Side Story" meets "Grease" in the fun video, as rival groups engage in a colorfully choreographed and edited soccer game on a sunny playa dotted with palm trees. This German-Portuguese hot shot's take on "La Bamba" is a total beach party blast. A modest hit in Europe during the summer of 2000. Da Silva became a model, dancer and DJ in the years that followed.

La Cumbia - Sailor (1991), RCA (G)
Producers: Georg Kajanus, Alan Scott

A celebration of the then highly popular Columbian dance craze. In the June 8, 1991, edition of *Music & Media,* a reviewer said, "In the previous decade [the group] enjoyed great success with 'Sailor' and 'Girls Girls Girls.' With this single, they set sail for the Caribbean doing the 'Lambada.'" The track was quite popular in Holland, though it hadn't a prayer of competing with the actual powerhouse "Lambada" by Kaoma and its irresistible sensuality.

La Fiesta (Party Mix) - Los Hijos Del Sol (not specified, late '80s), Music Plus/ZYX (F) *The party*
Producer: Manuel Ramon

This cover medley was produced sometime in the late '80s, but not pressed until the early '90s (under different names in various countries). It was even released as a "New Years Party Mix," illustrating the "good for any occasion" versatility of its high energy remake countdown, including "Rivers Of Babylon," "Brazil," "Vamos A La Playa," "Bamboléo," "Cuba" and other familiar summer hits. It was arranged, mixed and executive produced by Mario Aldini. Aldini went on to create numerous summer and holiday hit mix albums for ZYX Records in Germany, especially popular in the '90s. He was also creator of a series of maxi-singles utilizing the moniker Los Hijos Del Sol (*Children of the sun*), which offered non-stop mixes of the most popular dance hits of the time.

Commentary from Mario Aldini:

"The 'La Fiesta' medley was made in Germany following a proposal made by acquaintances who were also customers of mine when I had a record store in 1979. They introduced me to a group which was doing covers at that time, and the idea was to make a medley of commercial holiday tracks. It was [initially] a 12-inch and was released in France, Spain, Italy, Holland (possibly a 1998 re-release there), and, of course, by ZYX Music. This was my very first 'summer medley.'"

La Isla Bonita - Lucia (1986), Did Records (I) *The beautiful island*
Producers: Elio Crociani, Elvio Pieri

A remake of Madonna's hit. Nothing radical here, but it's got a lean, solid production and a few jungle effects thrown in for good measure. Arranged by Italy's Davide Romani, whose expertise helped make the group Change ("A Lover's Holiday") a household name in the US. The "Liverpool Rap" version recalls MC Miker "G" & Deejay Sven's "Holiday Rap." Lucia recorded a handful of Italo disco records during the first half of the '80s.

La Isla Bonita - Madonna (1987), Sire (US) *The beautiful island*
Producers: Madonna, Patrick Leonard

Long, long before less glamorous recent days that find Ms. Ciccone crawling up on Jimmy Fallon's host desk to wow "The Tonight Show" audience with her ample posterior (*ahem*), she was globe trotting like the consummate "Queen of Pop" she was. Madame X kindly took all of us on an exotic, first class vacation. You can bet reservations for a holiday in San Pedro, a town on the island of Ambergris Caye, Belize, were hard to come by after the release of this single from her *True Blue* album. That's the location some believe was the inspiration for the song. (Madonna reportedly told *Rolling Stone* she didn't know where San Pedro was.) It really doesn't matter—one is free to imagine it's anywhere far away from the day-to-day. Americans made it a top five *Billboard* US pop chart single. Europeans jumped on its appealing Latin flavor, Spanish guitars and references to wanting to be where the sun warms the sky, and they turned it into the #1 single of 1987, according to *Music & Media's* year-end ranking of Europe's top hits. The publication thought it was the best track off *True Blue,* though they modestly described Madge's hit as simply, "...a wonderful Mexican-tinged pop tune" on October 18, 1986. The irreplaceable Madonna gave the people what they wanted—another "Holiday"—and they devoured it.

La Isla Bonita - Micaela (1986), Disco Magic (I)
The beautiful island
Producer not indicated.

"Indeed, if Madonna waits long enough to release this track (probably the best from her *True Blue* album), others will have the credit," said a *Music & Media* critic in a December 27, 1986, review of the Micaela version. Still, Madonna didn't actually release her version from the 1986 *True Blue* album as a single until later the following year. Meanwhile, Micaela, a saucy looking brunette, took her Italian production further than most knock-offs (appearing on "Top Of The Pops" and garnering a lot of club attention and airplay, especially in Holland). However, the effort feels lightweight and less sincere than The Material Girl's definitive rendition. Still, Micaela's 12-inch single contained an inventive medley combining "Bonita" with the Gary Low Italo disco hit "La Colegiala." Micaela? I hardly know her!

La Plage De Saint Tropez - Army Of Lovers (1993), Stockholm
(F) *Saint Tropez Beach*
Producers: Alexander Bard, Anders Wollbeck, Per Adebratt

Much lighter than the group's punishing hit "Crucified," "La Plage De Saint Tropez" has a brisk semi-swing/disco vibe that is irresistible, especially in its "Cancanpourbonbondepapa Mix" (a name that flows trippingly off the tongue). There's some wry wit in its blithe storytelling as a dirty love affair unfolds in Saint Tropez, the chablis runs dry, and the air is filled with music (not to mention the sound of Hitchcock's seagulls mulling about). Everything about that seems spot on. You'll wish every summer day could be this carefree.

Lambada - Kaoma (1989), CBS/Epic (F)
Producer: Jean-Claude Bonaventure

While some English translations of Kaoma's song reference dance, sun and sea, it's actually a melancholy ode, as far as I can tell, to a lost lover who will one day regret not treating a romance more respectfully. But this song, with music and lyrics credited to Chico de Oliveira, always had an air of sketchiness about it. Seems the unauthorized translation of the original music and lyrics (by another group that served as the foundation of the newly created Kaoma version) was the subject of a lawsuit against producer Jean-Claude Bonaventure, settled in 1990. Eventually, licensing credits for the song (on compilation albums, for example) read: "Lambada comes from Saya, a Bolivian folk music. Ulysse and Gonzalo Hermosa and Olivier Lorsac contributed to its realization." That seems like a lot of knots to untie on a hot summer day, so maybe we'll shift our beach umbrella in another direction.

Why did everyone start doing "the forbidden dance," as it was called, that summer? The Lambada craze owes its popularity to the enormous success of the song recording, which was the result of a joint media effort begun in 1989 by a soft drink maker (Orangina), radio and TV stations, and the CBS record company based in France. Together, their massive marketing campaign to promote the sensual Lambada dance and this track led to a surprisingly big surge in interest for the project worldwide. In late August of that year, CBS France took out a full page color cover ad in *Music & Media*, proclaiming the song to be a "massive summer hit," and reporting sales of 1.5 million singles in France alone. The seven-piece French-Brazilian Kaoma band toured the continent (and the US), and when the year came to a close, "Lambada" was Europe's top-selling single of the year, according to the publication's year end survey on December 23rd, where they called it "without doubt *the* sensation of 1989," outpacing Madonna's "Like A Prayer." Ultimately, "Lambada" reportedly sold upwards of anywhere from three to five million copies worldwide. But Kaoma only took a fraction of those sales from the US, where the song proved a bit too exotic for American tastes and never cracked the pop top 40. The tune only reached #21 on *Billboard*'s US dance chart.

(L) Publicity photo featuring passionate dancers, widely distributed to promote the "Lambada" single by Kaoma, Epic (press still).

The worldwide Lambada craze was relatively short-lived, despite the group releasing several derivative singles, none of which had quite the traction of the original Kaoma hit. In 1991, they unveiled a new single and dance,

"Danca Tago Mago," a mix of African rhythms and the lively dances of Northern Brazil. However, by then a significant backlash had taken root against Kaoma, which group spokesperson Jean Karakos (who formed the group with Olivier Lorsac) made reference to in *Music & Media* (July 6, 1991). "Our success was so big that it had a negative effect on the band's credibility—as a band. Everyone thought it was a one-off concept…" Karakos added, "Our ambition is to be a pop band, playing different styles of ethnic music from all over the world."

Kaoma and its entourage continued to follow their ambitions well into the twenty-first century, but were never able to recapture the magic of their spectacular debut. The BBC reported the death of "Lambada" lead vocalist Loalwa Braz online on January 19, 2017.

Lambada Festival - Sand Party (1990), RCA/HOT Productions (G/US)
Producers: Davis, Stone, Klein

"The hottest dance craze is here in this Lambada medley" reads the record jacket of this cash-grab, which, for the most part, feels a wee bit disingenuous, simply capitalizing on the then trending Brazilian dance and hit single name rather than the actual exotic sound of the music. Instead, it's more of a tacky disco mix, something you're likely to hear any bar cover band do adequately, consisting of mostly '80s beach hits, including "Kalimba De Luna," "La Isla Bonita," "Conga," "Bamboléo," and, wait for it, "Lambada." The campy beach party scene photographed for the jacket screams it's summertime and the livin' is cheesy. Rumor has it that's a young Jon Secada out of Miami honing his vocal skills on the recording, but for sure that's not him on the cover. I'm about 51% on board with this one, but—I have to agree—on the coldest, rawest of winter days, even lukewarm temps can still melt ice. And sand is way better than snow!

Last Days Of Summer - Imagination (1985), R&B Records (UK)
Producer: Derek Bramble

A funky and melodic jam about the frustrating impossibility of going back in time to summer's prime and finding a lost romance. Leee John's silky smooth lead vocals and a strong, crisp pulse highlight a wonderful mood-inducing production that fits nicely with the group's career beacons, "Music And Lights" and "Just An Illusion."

Latin America 2000 - Gibson Brothers (2000), ZYX (G)
Producers: Lisa Alison, Ultrashockpeople, DJ Disco King

The gentlemen attempt to recreate some of the excitement of their vintage disco hit "Cuba" and succeed in this high energy house pumper. Latin America is paradise, claims the trio, name-dropping Trinidad, Puerto Rico and Cuba as evidence. Though there's not much in the way of lyrics (a jam like this doesn't really need them), the beat is fierce in both the "L.A. & Zela House" version and the leaner "Ultrashockpeople" Mix.

Latin Summer - Thomas Battenstein (1996), Tomte (G)
Producer: Thomas Battenstein

German guitarist delivers a warm, upbeat, easy listening rhythm and melody with the magic touch of congas to keep the beach always in sight. A highlight of the instrumental *Rain In Spain* album, which includes the similarly themed and quite wonderful track, "Hotel Voyager." Evocative music like this allows your mind come up with its own lyrics.

Laurel & Hardy Song, The / Honolulu Baby - Silverscreen
Starring Laurel & Hardy (1995), RCA (G)
Producer: The Crazy People for K&L Music Production

If you happen to be familiar with the brilliant and utterly timeless Hal Roach-produced 1933 MGM comedy film "Sons Of The Desert," starring Stanley Laurel and Oliver Hardy and directed by William A. Seiter, you'll no doubt recognize the name of the movie's "theme song," "Honolulu Baby." Ollie happily sings the tune with Stan beside him upon returning home from a trip to Hawaii, away from their duck hunting and occasionally violent wives, so that Ollie could recover from a (faux) nervous "shakedown." But they *haven't* actually been soaking up the spirit of Aloha in sunny Honolulu at all—twist—they've secretly been attending a rowdy fraternal lodge convention in Chicago, a party absolutely forbidden by the wives—or at least Oliver's. And unbeknownst to the boys, the cruise ship they should have been on is making headlines after sinking in a Pacific typhoon. Ninety years later, the vintage film still delivers nonstop (and relevant) laughs, mostly about the tortures of marriage and lying to survive it ("honesty is the best policy" is the moral here). This reinvention of the "Honolulu" tune mimics the rendition given by campy actor/singer Ty Parvis in the film (performed during a convention scene with the entertainer surrounded by tacky 1930s female dancers) and injects it with an electronic eurodance/house beat and rave vibe. An electro-swing style interpretation might have delivered a more appropriate dance floor sound, but the effort here is definitely appreciated. *I'm sorry Mrs. Hardy, but a voyage to Honolulu is the only cure for your husband."*

Le Sega Mauricien - Stephanie (1986) Carrere/Julisa (F)
[Do] The Mauritian sega [dance]
Producer: Yves Roze

A romantic musical escapade that finds the Monaco-born princess singing about dancing all summer on the Indian Ocean island of Mauritius, in its picturesque towns (such as Mahébourg) and on one of its isle extensions, Île aux Bénitiers, providing all the diversion she needs to forget a cavalier lover. The track comes from the celebrity and vocalist's 1986 self-titled, French/English-language debut album (also known as *Besoin [Need]*), and it's a major standout of the set. Arranged by Thierry Durbet and the song's co-writer, Gérard Blanc, and remixed by J. Philippe, the gentlemen give the production a throughly charming calypso dance vibe, and, in turn, provide the artist with an opportunity to sing in a very natural, relaxed manner. Here she sounds more invigorated and noticeably warmer than on the major international pop hits from the LP, "Irresistible" and "Flash/One Love To Give," as if perhaps she's actually been to this island and quite possibly had a blast there. You don't have to appreciate Francophone pop to feel the sparkle of this refreshing summer excursion.

Les Sunlights Des Tropiques - Gilbert Montagne (1984), Carrere
(F) *The tropic sunlight*
Producer: Dario Farina

Retro-sounding Italian disco/pop that broke out in France in the spring of '85. Montagne (a blind artist from that country) peaked with the track at #31 in late June on the *EuroTipSheet* Top 100 and spent 14 weeks in all on the survey, establishing himself as a sure fire summer hitmaker. He sings about living in love in the southern hemisphere, feeling the sun on his skin, and having a bongo in his heart. Add those images to your vision board under the heading "life's a beach."

Let The Sun In - Atlantic Starr (1987), Warner (US)
Producers: David Lewis, Wayne Lewis

Remixer Bruce Forrest gave this positive-minded, though rather undistinguished (at least in its original version) soul number by the New York-based R&B/dance group, a powerful beat upgrade and a hipper feel. Throwing in some cool, unexpected chant effects, the track is transformed into a summer-ready club jam. The mix, which followed shortly after the group had a #1 US pop hit with "Always," reached #28 on *Billboard*'s dance chart. On April 9, 1988, *Cash Box* described the song as, "A spirited dance tune that bumps and skips along with a lighthearted feel...representative of their best dance work."

Let The Sun Shine In - Milk & Sugar (2002), Universal (G)
Producers: Mike Milk, Steven Sugar

A stellar reinvention of the *Hair* musical hit, randomly released with "Sun Shine" as one word and ending it there on some version titles. But such details are inconsequential. Trust and believe, under any name it's a feast. What matters here is the distinctively sumptuous, enveloping sonic atmosphere that Milk & Sugar (Steven 'Sugar' Harding & Michael 'Milk' Kronenberger) deliver so effortlessly across their production work and most famously on this gospel-like, twenty-first century classic. The gentlemen also created successful remix editions of this spiritual gem in 2009, 2012 and 2017.

Harding describes how he and Michael achieved the powerful vocal sound found in "Let The Sun Shine In." "We ended up in a studio in Munich with a big recording room to get that choir sound," he says. "Five microphones, two pre-amplifiers, Sony eight-track recording machines. I ended up recording I don't know how many tracks—we ended up with something like 10 mono tracks in all to get that choir sound. This is the only record that people in *every* city come to us and ask us to play." *[Excerpt from an extended interview with Milk & Sugar, edited in the book: Stars of 21st Century Dance Pop & EDM (McFarland, 2017).]*

Let's Go On Vacation - Sister Sledge (1980), Cotillion (US)
Producers: Bernard Edwards, Nile Rodgers

Yes, let's do just that! Third single from the *Love Somebody Today* album, which was the sister act's follow-up to their categorically perfect *We Are Family* LP. At first listen, the song may perhaps be taken as a simple homage to California, but lead vocalist Debbie Sledge convincingly sells the track's broader underlying spirit of determination, convincing us that a holiday at the shore might just be able to solve any relationship problem. When it' all too much, just take a vacation. (However, there is a detectable current of low spiritedness deep within the track, a reflection of the relationship troubles that motivate the getaway in the first place.) A sophisticated arrangement and signature Chic strings shine pleasantly and for a bit longer on the extended album version. The track was also included on the *Soup For One* movie soundtrack. On June 14, 1980, *Cash Box* reviewed the single, saying it was, "…a timely cut for the summer season."

(R) Debbie Sledge today, photo by Chris Loomis.

Commentary from Debbie Sledge:

"At the time we were in the studio with Nile and Bernard from Chic, producer and artist were learning of each others' gifts, talents and way of working. Because Sister Sledge is a multi-lead vocal group, the producers wanted to explore each person's vocal personality to decide which person should lead which songs. The Chic production style did not allow the artist to learn the songs beforehand. So I was pleasantly surprised when they presented 'Lets Go On Vacation' to me to record. I believe Nile's words were something to the effect of, "This song has a jazz feel, so I want you to bounce some jazzy riffs." Nile wanted me to especially note the beautiful, playful, jazzy work of the piano in the track."

Debbie's playlist for a summer getaway:

"I love all of the following because they promote summer feelings of freedom and fun, and I believe there is something to the love that is in the performances. 'Summer Madness' by Kool & the Gang, 'Summer Breeze' by Isley Brothers, Sly And The Family Stone's 'Hot Fun In The Summertime,' 'Don't

You Worry 'Bout A Thing' by Stevie Wonder, and Martha And The Vandellas' 'Heat Wave.' (I just notice that many of these choices are from family groups!)"

Like Ice In The Sunshine - Faithless (2003), BMG (UK/G)
Producers: Rollo, Sister Bliss

The electronic band's ethereal musings seem very far removed from the ice cream synth-pop hit by Beagle Music Ltd., which it is somehow distantly connected with. It's downbeat, kind of dark, progressive, somewhat sad, and yet somehow still completely hopeful. Musically, it's dreamy electronica with a hip-hop vibe. But is it summery? Maxi Jazz's voice literally gives off heat as he raps about an island in the Indian Sea (among other thoughts), perhaps one of the 26 atolls of Maldives (just a guess). Sister Bliss' music seems to glisten like beads of perspiration, gently rolling off one's skin—so I'll say, damn straight it is! Go on, give it a lick.

Like Ice In The Sunshine - Lacuna Project (1995), Dance Street (G)
Producer not indicated.

You'll have to have a taste for that super hyper-speed, euphoric style of rave/club/eurodance music that was popular for a few years in the late '90s to get into this version of the hit Beagle Music Ltd. song. Sometimes when a producer isn't listed on a recording, um, there's a reason. This is dance music on crack. It's a hard no for me, dawg, but if it's your groove, do your thang!

Like Ice In The Sunshine - No Angels (2002), Universal (G)
Producers: Nik Hafemann, Syndicate Music

This remake of Beagle Music Ltd.'s hit, on the other hand, feels like a bull's eye, showing how perfectly suited the song is to the unison of this tremendously popular five-girl group, formed from a German music reality TV series, and backed by a hip, eurohouse production. Fierce!

Little Island / Jammin' At Barbados / Jackimo / Soca Dance - Batida De Soca (1990), Teldec (G)
Producers: Franz Plasa, Peter Hoffman

Unfairly lost in the shuffle of soca and Lambada pop hybrids so popular in Europe at the time, these musical efforts by a male-female vocal duo are super fun dance/pop ditties that aren't pretending to be anything more than ear candy. The calypso vibe is smoothed out to a more conventional dance sound in these four highlights off their self-titled debut (and only) album, but that doesn't lessen the inviting tropical atmosphere or delicious cheerfulness of this production. Just a fun record, start to finish. But if you want your fun spiced up, like, say, Mad Dog 357 No. 9 Plutonium, our next entry might do the trick.

Livin' La Vida Loca - Ricky Martin (1999), Columbia (US)
Livin' the crazy life
Producer: Desmond Child

Once blindingly sexy Puerto Rican Ricky Martin (aka Enrique José Martín Morales) performed the hell out of his hit "La Copa De La Vida" (*The cup of life*) at the 1999 Grammys (performed is an understatement, by the way), he instantly became the CEO of Latin pop. As fiery as that track was, he managed to step up his game with an astonishing follow-up that introduced him to the US English language pop market. Released in the spring of '99, "Livin' La Vida Loca" is so thrilling it can still give one goosebumps over two decades later. Back then, it topped the *Billboard* chart and became one of the biggest selling singles of all time. The publication described it as "terrifically filled with life" on April 10, 1999. On May 8, 1999, critic Christian Lorenz, over at *Music & Media*, seemed a bit less impressed, calling "Loca," "a Salsa-tinged, sweaty party tune." I'd like to offer another view—the combination of its high energy Latin rumba pulse, a groovy Dick Dale and the Del-Tones-like electric guitar reverb pulsating with "Surf Beat" energy, and Martin's unstoppably infectious vocal and visual charisma make this one of the most explosive songs in a generation. And best of all, he radiates likability. The song is unconditionally a summer blast, but "Loca" is truly a heat seeking missile for all seasons (I sense the phallic symbolism in that analogy). In a press bio issued by Columbia Records, Ricky said "Vida Loca" was the single with which he wanted to say, "Hey! Boom! I'm here!" We noticed.

(L) **Ricky Martin circa 1999, photo by Diego Uchitel, Columbia (press still).**

What a way to wrap up the century! I suppose we should have seen this coming all the way back in Martin's Menudo days, or when he was intriguing us with his role on ABC-TV's venerable daytime soap opera, "General Hospital." I tried reaching Ricky for an interview while visiting Puerto Rico, but, alas, he didn't take the call. No worries—I consoled myself with a visit to the Castillo San Felipe del Morro instead, and got a great shot of a cruise ship for "The Love Boat" entry coming up shortly. (Ricky Martin, by the way, actually made an appearance on "The Love Boat" TV show back in 1985.)

Living In The Sunshine - Tom Hooker (1990), Baby Records (I)
Producer: Baby Records

This American singer (also known as Thomas Barbey) hit it big as an '80s Italo disco star in his own right ("Looking For Love," "Feeling Okay") while also recording as the primary secret real voice behind europop superstar act Den Harrow (another Milli Vanilli debacle from back in the day). Here the artist emulates Robert Palmer with a "Simply Irresistible"-like dance/rock track, unexpectedly harder-edged than some of his previous pop material. In truth, Tom's voice seems truly at home in this slammin' guitar setting, and I suspect he was having a lot of fun with this break from the norm.

Lo Mejor De Los Reyes - Los Reyes (1994), Activ Music (G)
The best of Los Reyes
Producer: Sven von Strauch

Though a bit less prolific (in terms of separate recording output) but musically interchangeable with the Gipsy Kings (the Gipsy Kings were once known as Los Reyes, if I've got their rather complex history right), the effect on the casual listener is still the same. *Latin sizzle!* This French group was most active in the club-minded summery rhumba/flamenco/dance/pop arena from the late '80s through the early '90s. Here they briskly run down some of their hottest efforts in a dance medley mix of "Volare," "Bamboléo," "Bem Bem Maria," "Lola Si Si," "La Quiero," "Bailara" and "Baila Me." Their music recalls where the group came from and at the same time pushes their cultural richness forward. Absolutely impossible to resist, so don't even try!

Loca Noche (All Night Long) - Spanish Energy (1990), Bounce (NL) *Crazy night (all night long)*
Producer: Pino Toma

Reimagining Lionel Richie's summer classic "All Night Long (All Night)" in Spanish and trading his Technicolor calypso flavor for some simple but tangy Latin seasoning really got me together. It's exceptionally atmospheric with its wonderfully effervescent festival vibe percolating in the background. *Cálido, emocionante y de primera clase!*

Loco In Acapulco - The Four Tops (1988), Arista (US)
Producers: Lamont Dozier, Phil Collins

At face value, one might expect this track to be a silly summer cash-grab, but the venerable R&B group, together for 34 years at this point in time, actually spares us an overdose of kitsch and serves up a well-orchestrated story of romantic escape in paradise with a touch of class. The production is a bright mix of soulful, old-skool beats with an injection of electro-pop energy. Basically, soul food for the beach. Two stylistically different versions were released: a super smooth, pop framed and Motown flavored LP version (Body Mix), slightly longer than the radio cut, and a livelier, extended UK ("pH Balance") mix by PWL's Phil Harding & Ian Curnow, who reimagine the track with a stronger tropical flavor fused with festive Latin-style keyboards. *Music & Media* took an overall dim view of the song and the album, however, calling them (collectively) "uninspired" in an October 1, 1988, review of the group's *Indestructible* LP. They added, "There is scarcely anything on here that one could label as 'spellbinding' or 'exciting.'" Seems harsh. Jeez, can't music just be—*entertaining*? The Four Tops advise us not to stay too long in Acapulco for fear of going crazy over a girl, but that's not really much of a deterrent.

Commentary from Dr. Phil Harding:

Before we discuss "Loco In Acapulco," this song came out when the island of Ibiza was emerging as Europe's #1 summer party destination. You were able to witness, and very much be a part of, some of those wild Ibiza summer nights in the late '80s. Tell me a little about that.

"Everything about the Balearic sound of '87 and '88, was summer—beach, Ibiza, sun, the islands. I went there a few times during that summer club season. You start off in a must-go club called Pacha, 7 o'clock, then you'd head to a huge one, the KU Club I believe it was called, like a stadium in the middle of the island that you'd need a car to get to—a fantastic scene with celebrities and models! Then, let's say two or three in the morning, you'd go to yet another club called Amnesia straight through to dawn. We never got through to the one that took you to dawn, but we certainly enjoyed the other two.

"I remember being at the Pacha bar and a song we did at PWL by Mel & Kim came on. To hear something that you've just finished mixing in London, and—bam—it comes on in the club, was amazing! Ian Curnow and I would often go to New York in the mid-late '80s for a Tommy Boy label dance conference (called New Music Seminar), and we'd check out some of the gay clubs and hear all the PWL records played there, too. I remember hearing Dead or Alive going right into Bananarama, Pepsi & Shirlie—incredible!"

In an effort to have a hit during the summer season, was there any marketing advantage to directly referencing the summer, sun and beach in a dance/ pop song title or within its lyrics? What about a desirable destination, such as Acapulco?

"I suppose there could be, but—dare I say it—referencing the beach and summer would have been the cornier side of pop. You know what I mean? If you were aiming for that real European summer club culture, you wouldn't reference those themes directly in the '80s and '90s. It would be considered too corny to be played in the really big clubs. However, it would be fine for the places on the beach and the radio stations. You'd go to Spain and Portugal, for example, and there'd be British DJs on Spanish radio stations catering to the British crowds. And that was a big thing to get onto that sort of radio.

"I did a lot of work with Matt Bianco—they were a very popular, summery, Latin/pop-based group. A couple of their dance tracks very much had that 'yeah, this will be a summer track' feel. That sound we put into The Four Tops' 'Loco In Acapulco' is not a million miles away from the sound of Matt Bianco's 'Don't Blame It On That Girl' (1988) or 'Summersong' (1986), or even 'Tequila' by No Way José (1985). As for the title, 'Loco In Acapulco,' to us over here in Europe, that sounds kind of exotic; it's cool. It's not saying the word beach or the word summer. There's a difference in perception. I don't know if it was [co-producer and co-writer] Phil Collins who came up with that little phrase, 'Loco In Acapulco,' but referencing a tropical place might have more impact than referencing the summer or the beach directly. Absolutely. 'Loco' was a very house-driven song, wasn't it? So hopefully it was played in the cooler clubs as well as the cornier ones. Same with the famous Wham! song and video, 'Club Tropicana' (1983), which is associated with summer and being in the Balearic islands, jumping in the pool, and such, without referencing those concepts specifically."

Let's take a look at your work on "Loco In Acapulco."

"The main record, the seven-inch single, the basic song, doesn't sound Latin, but I think we took it much further by adding it in our extended version. I am sure I would have driven [my production partner] Ian Curnow toward that. That wasn't on the original record—that's us. That Latin/house sound, the drums, bass and piano, only comes in the breaks for club DJs, and it seemed to work. Our remix had a slightly strange name, the 'pH Balance Mix.' 'pH' is me, but I don't think that's what it means. I'm not sure that was the name Ian and I gave it; it may have been a joke. Can't figure that one out.

"The thing with that Four Tops record and 'Indestructible' (we also worked an extended version of that song from the same album), and as you might have heard in remixes that Ian and I did at that time, we always did a radio edit version, and I would always send that to the label, whether they wanted it or not. Some labels did want both an extended version and a European radio edit for the tracks they gave us. I would have made one for 'Loco In Acapulco,' but it never got released, and no one has ever heard it. I am sure I was a little bit disappointed that it wasn't considered."

Anything else we might be interested to know about this track?

"There's a tiny bit of history with 'Loco In Acapulco.' I had worked with [the song's co-writer and co-producer] Lamont Dozier earlier in the '80s. British producer Pete Waterman brought Lamont over to London for a six-month period. Somewhere around '82 or '83. That six months was mostly spent at the Marquee Studios, where I was an engineer, and we became friends. We are still friends to this day. Something with 'Loco In Acapulco' must have been done in the UK, maybe the original mix, I don't know, and Lamont got in touch with me to remix the record. Phil Collins was okay with that. But I would have to go to Phil Collins' studio, which, of course, was probably the Genesis studio.

"In the discussion of that with Pete Waterman—he was very protective of PWL studios and our production work—he insisted that the work be done at PWL He felt they couldn't be promoting PWL engineers to be working at other studios, unless there was some urgent need for it. We had one of those moments [Harding laughs] where I would have been happy to do that—go over to Genesis studios and mix it with Phil Collins and Lamont—and then I might have been involved in the seven-inch version as well. So, in the end, we compromised and were able to get the label to send us over the tapes, and we did some extended versions. That's how it came about and how it led to my—let's just say—slight disappointment at not being able to be involved in the radio edit. At that time, PWL was all over UK and European radio.

But there's never anything you can do about those decisions—it's happened to me many times."

Long Hot Summer 89 - The Style Council (1989), Polydor (UK)
Producers: Peter Wilson, Paul Weller

With this summer sojourn, the livin' is breezy, despite somewhat sad lyrics about relationship trouble. Released shortly before the English group disbanded, this record ironically makes their split-up feel all the more heartbreaking. Smooth vocals ride the rhythm of the ocean, rising and falling with passionate emotion, as a percolating mid-tempo beat keeps this retro soul-synth-pop hybrid simmering steadily. Just the right temperature.

Long Hot Summer Nights - Wendy Waldman (1978), Warner (US)
Producer: Mike Flicker

The songwriter behind Vanessa Williams' Grammy-winning 1991 hit "Save The Best For Last" delivers an unshrinking, rather poignant nod to summers past spent with her best girlfriend, when cruising the streets and switching hook-up partners was the stuff. The song works well in its pop/ rock and churning guitar setting (upbeat pop and dance aren't the only genres that can convey the magic of the season), and it's easy to relate to the hot nights and cool attitudes she sings about so affectionately.

Love Boat (Theme From TV Series) - Jack Jones (1979) MGM (US)
Producer: Ken Barnes

Welcome aboard! "The Love Boat" and "Fantasy Island" were staples of ABC-TV's Saturday night prime-time US line-up for many years and both projected that getaway feeling rather splendidly, if farcically. Though most everyone is familiar with the general melody of the kitschy "Love Boat" theme song (written/composed by Paul Williams and Charles Fox), it may be interesting to revisit this recording and hear just how deeply entrenched it is in a vintage '70s disco funk vibe. Jack Jones, a pop singer whose records date back to the late '50s, infused the vocal with a loungy muzak approach that couldn't possibly have conveyed the schmaltzy nature of the show's weekly romantic comedy episodes any better. Latin hot shot Charo covered the song in a cheesy disco style in 1978, while European songstress Amanda Lear gave it a eurodisco/Latin/French spin in 2001. Likely no surprise to anyone, there aren't too many other songs out there that focus on the rather limited subject of cruise ships (let's skip that Celine Dion theme song from "Titanic" for now), though it's been one of the most popular means of enjoying a vacation getaway on the planet. (Carnival Corporation, one of the biggest cruise companies in the world, had revenue in excess of $20B in 2019, pre-COVID-19 pandemic of course, according to Tanner Callais of Cruzely.com, April 21, 2021.)

Love Is An Island - Claudja Barry (1991), RCA (US)
Producers: Jurgen Korduletsch, N. Vorkapich

Though the song was recorded in New Jersey, "Love Is An Island" has a wonderfully sweeping and far away feel, precisely tuned with the pulsating, energized house and electro sound so popular at the time. It feels like an advance agent for Madonna's "Ray Of Light" if you delve deeply enough into its texture. "Love Is An Island" is one of the most unusual productions to which Ms. Barry ever lent her voice—and she's got a remarkably diverse discography to her credit—so that's saying something. In its "Tropical Heat" version, the track is both hypnotic and dreamlike as it weaves otherworldly background vocals into a driving rhythm that feels exactly like the swirling sea. On June 15, 1991, *Cash Box* called it "a hypnotic, soulful number." Somehow, the song failed to make a chart impression, but it gets an A+ for capturing a highly spiritual summer vibe.

Commentary from Claudja Barry:

"'Love is An Island' was written by my producer and a member of the group Frequency X [Nicolai Vorkapich]. I loved it. People may say it was sort of a 'Love To Love You, Baby' sound, but I believe it was a Bulgarian choir used on the background of the track that gave it a very different sound—it takes you somewhere. They weren't harmonizing in a western style. A whole different kind of singing. It gave the song sort of an eerie feeling. The instrumentation underneath, that bass and synthesizer, it's unbelievable. You can put every kind of thought or meaning you want to that song. It doesn't have to mean a literal island. It doesn't have to mean love is Ibiza, Jamaica or Barbados. Love should really be your island of comfort. RCA wasn't as active as they should have been with it, and I really wish it would get a re-release or remix."

(Love Is Like A) Heatwave - The Jam (1979), Polydor (UK)
Producer: Vic Coppersmith-Heaven

Well, duh! Covering the Martha And The Vandellas hit, the punky UK band turns the classic song into a compressed, high speed, spunky, guitar-flaring ass-kicker. There's still that R&B undercurrent in there that often adds considerable dimension to rock 'n' roll, so this reinvention isn't quite as radical as it might seem on paper, but it will definitely make you break a sweat. From the album *Setting Sons*.

Love Plus One - Haircut One Hundred (1982), Arista (UK/US)
Producer: Bob Sargeant

On May 15, 1982, after a live show in New York City, the *New York Times* wordily declared, "Haircut One Hundred has found a way to combat the danger of becoming last month's model by making eclectic pop that blends rap, funk, Beatlesque nostalgia, salsa and Talking Heads-style yelping into an all-inclusive international style not tied to a single sound." Meanwhile, Brian Chin over at *Record World* more concisely said their album, *Pelican West*, was "just right for mellow dance floors…sophisticated…lots of fun and cool, man, cool." "Love Plus One" is a superior example of light, under-stated, rhythmic dance/pop with a tropical undercurrent, and it's perfect for the summer season. The song asks where it goes from here. I'd say directly to the shore.

Lovely Day (Sunshine Mix) - Bill Withers (1988), CBS (N/G)
Producers: Bill Withers, Clarence McDonald

Withers' immortal 1977 soul hit (Rolling Stone ranked it 402 in their 2021 list of "500 Greatest Songs of All Time") was given a stellar update eleven years later by remixer Ben Liebrand that *Music & Media* called "sunny and hi-tech." That it surely is, but Liebrand's exquisitely finessed remix is so much more. It has all the warmth of a Saturday afternoon in July, and this transformative masterpiece, I'd argue, was responsible for reintroducing this soul classic to a new generation. Withers' original version was already a seasonal standard, and Liebrand's fluid remix made this song a fresh, hip and affecting musical journey, ideally suited for the '80s, and, as it turns out, well beyond. It hasn't lost an ounce of that power in the years since.

"It was one of my favorite tracks," recalls Ben Liebrand. "By the time this remix came out in 1988, I was also working for Dutch radio. It was a weekly one-hour mix show called 'In The Mix,' plus a short section called the 'Minimix'. I had been working on a remix for The Four Seasons ('Oh, What A Night'), which was taking up my time and most of my available channels at the mixing desk. I had my sequencers, drum machines and bass lines lined up for their track. I didn't want to mess that all up, so I decided to use these elements and an edit of the original track from a Bill

Withers CD. I was able to add elements I had in my studio, and they'd be in sequence with the original track edit. I started at 10 in the morning on a Friday, finished it by eight in the evening, mastered it to tape, raced to the radio studio—and I featured it as my weekly Minimix. 'Lovely Day' found its way to the CBS record company, who I worked for (and the connection was very easily made), and it turned into a huge hit." *[From the book Europe's Stars of '80s Dance Pop, Vol. 2, Arena, Bookbaby, 2018.]*

M - N - O

Macarena (Bayside Boys Remix) - Los Del Rio (1996) BMG (SP/US)
Producers: Jesus Bola, Manuel Soler, Remix producers:
The Bayside Boys

One either gets a kick out of this commandingly addictive pop song about a woman who lures men on with her dancing charms or you flat out hate it. I was working for the Bertelsmann Music Group in New York City at the time it broke out and recall numerous occasions where office mates would greet me with the "Macarena" melody, singing, "Hey, Jim Arena," so I both loathed and loved the song. Arguably the most recognizable Spanish (mixed with English) song of all time, it was the Miami-based Bayside Boys' (Carlos A. De Yarza and Mike Triay) hypnotic 1996 remix (based on an earlier "River-Fe" mix by Fangoria/Big Toxic) that helped make this track a huge summer hit the world over. Originally released in 1993 by Los Del Rio (Antonio Romero Monge and Rafael Ruiz, who were already well established in Latin music), the rumba flamenco song was the left field smash of the summer of '96, and only the fourth hit from Spain to ever reach the top 10 of *Billboard*'s US pop singles chart at the time, as reported by the publication's Fred Bronson on

June 29, 1996. Europe, meanwhile, had caught on to the song's magic a bit earlier, with airplay and sales building there in the spring.

On *Music & Media*'s year end European pop singles sales chart that year, "Macarena" was ranked #2, second only to Robert Miles' "Children." In the US, *Billboard* ranked it at #1 for the year. The track was also covered very successfully, though not quite as broadly, by the group Los Del Mar. Like "Lambada" a few years earlier, "Macarena" was bolstered by a popular dance (much simpler than the former) that involved a series of Village People-like "Y.M.C.A." hand and arm movements more than anything else. Good news for those of us with two left feet. Don't even get me started on "The Ketchup Song (Aserejé)" by Las Ketchup.

Magena - Taco (1991), Polydor (G)
Producers: G. Peacey, M. Kahler

Playful, warm weather europop, enhanced by Taco Ockerse's breezy vocal charisma, this was the B-side of the artist's "Tico Tico" single, itself an upbeat, fair weather Brazilian reliable.

Commentary from Taco Ockerse:

"The song was picked for me by the producer or the record company—we artists weren't always given a choice. I was inspired to rewrite some of the lyrics of this song, elaborated on the story, and tried to capture that summer feeling. We incorporated steel drums, and it really gave it that Caribbean flavor. It was a shame it wasn't a bigger hit because I thought it was a fun song."

Taco's summer playlist favorites:

"'Bacardi Feeling (Summer Dreamin')' by Kate Yanai—you hear it and immediately you are in a good summer mood. 'Close To You' by The Carpenters, which I heard for the very first time on the beach, and so I automatically associate it with summer. 'Good Times' by Chic. And, of course, "Lovely Day" by Bill Withers. I still love singing that song—that track was truly my summer jam."

*[See also: **Singing In The Rain - Taco.**]*

Main Title (Theme From "JAWS") - John Williams (Composer/Conductor) (1975), MCA (US)
Producer: Not indicated. ("Jaws" film producers - Richard Zanuck, David Brown)

The movie event of the summer of '75 was also a huge buzz-kill for beach lovers, causing even the most hardy of us to start freaking out every time we dipped our collective toes in ocean water. John Williams' ferociously ominous theme for the movie "Jaws" both captured the unstoppable threat unseen beneath the water's surface and the final seconds that precede what will be—*gulp*—a really, *really* bad ending to a beautiful beach day. Released as a 45 rpm single and included on the *Jaws* soundtrack album, it is two minutes and twelve seconds of pure summer terror essentially built around the alternating pattern of two notes played on a tuba. It's perhaps the most horrifying piece of music since Bernard Herrmann's scoring of the shower scene in Hitchcock's "Psycho." "It is as if God created the devil and gave him...*JAWS!*"

Margaritaville - Jimmy Buffett (1977), ABC (US)
Producer: Norbert Putnam

Timeless in its popularity, "Margaritaville" was inducted into the Grammy Hall of Fame in 2016 as, essentially, a major cultural moment in pop music. A homage to a carefree tropical lifestyle, which may serve as a refuge from, perhaps, the pain of a lost woman. Indirectly, it may also salute the drink that can dull life's sharper edges. The song paints a vivid picture of a man giving into the futility of his existence, but he does so in such an appealing, sun-baked way that you can't help but want to follow him down that path to oblivion (which leads directly to Key West). Hopelessly catchy and equatorial, it's easy to picture a wasted and sunburned Sam Elliott character sitting on the stoop of a beaten up beach shack, tequila bottle in hand (barely), staring out at the jade colored ocean. Top 10 on *Billboard*'s pop chart that year.

Marina - Chico & The Gypsies (1996), EMI (F)
Producers: Agent Smith, Walter Ripley, Marc Stabel

Led by "Chico" Bouchikhi, a founding member of the Gipsy Kings, "Marina" is electronic rumba and flamenco at its most inventive. It's buoyant, hip, accessible and mostly just great *fun*! Ridiculously uplifting, especially in its original "Salsa" mix and "Marina's Amor Mix," the song is a hand-clapping jam about a man who desperately wants to marry his darling, written by (and a late '50s hit for) Italian Rocco Granata. The song is one big summer fiesta that will make you want to immediately invest in castanets.

Mar Y Sol - Luisa Fernandez & Peter Kent (1995), Polydor (G)
Sea and sun
Producer: Peter Kent

Luisa and Peter, a wife and husband musical team, collaborated on Latin-fused dance tracks for many years, most famously scoring a huge hit in Germany and across Europe with "Solo Por Ti" (1986), though each has had a successful musical career individually. Together, they've sung numerous songs that evoke sun and tropical themes, including "Fiesta Del Sol" and "Manana." Kicking things off with a "Guantanamera"-like rhythm, "Mar Y Sol," recorded and mixed in Ibiza, is perhaps their most refreshing ocean dip, a delightful, sparkling summer holiday track that is romantic and spirit-boosting. A vibrant horn section carries the melody sky high and the track seamlessly blends the singers' contrasting but well-paired voices to great effect. Luisa and Peter are photographed on the single jacket posed in front of what looks like a beguiling hideaway on that famous island off the coast of Spain—Ibiza—where the project was recorded. Makes you wish you were there, too.

Master Blaster (Jammin') - Stevie Wonder (1980), Motown (US)
Producer: Stevie Wonder

In an unspecified live performance YouTube clip of the artist delivering "Master Blaster" in concert, Mr. Wonder exclaims to his audience, "Are you ready? *Raaastaaa!*" Naturally, the crowd cheers wildly. From there, that oh so memorable shuffling percussion kicks in, and we are soon witness to an ebullient display of rock, funk, soul, disco, and reggae coming together in one flame broiled pop jam. Its highly infectious and celebratory lyrics pay tribute to Bob Marley (and include a reference to Mr. Wonder's hugely popular album, *Hotter Than July*, which features this single), while the momentum sails blissfully forward, building upon the song's unstoppable pulse and potent bass line. Like the universe itself, this classic's energy is virtually limitless. The December 6, 1980, issue of *Cash Box* saw "Master Blaster (Jammin')" reach the #1 spot on their Top 100 Singles chart, although in the publication's year-end survey of 1980's top singles the song pulled in at just #38. But those are simply numbers—the song's legacy is far greater. It's now an undeniably cherished summer fest classic around the world, year after year. You know how every summer we often do the same things? We hit the same beaches, go on the same trips, and somehow never get tired of it? Well, same thing here.

Megarama '89 - Bananarama (1989), FFRR/London (UK)
Producers: Swain + Jolley, Stock Aitken Waterman, DMC (UK)

There's something utterly fascinating about Bananarama hits mixed together in a brisk, exciting mash-up. It has the effect of making one truly appreciate just how dynamic this girl group was in the '80s and how they seemed to have an unlimited supply of summer energy fused into their spirited pop catalog. Tony King put a mix together in '88 for the ladies' album *Wow!*, and Alan Coulthard handled "Megarama '89," which, in its full length version, included not only the group's Stock Aitken Waterman produced eurodisco smashes (such as "Venus" and "Love In The First Degree"), but some of their funky warm weather killer cuts as well (the brilliant "Robert De Niro's Waiting," "Cruel Summer," and more).

Commentary from Alan Coulthard:

"I did, in fact, do two Banarama megamixes. The first was one for DMC in 1988 which concentrated on their Stock Aitken Waterman-produced catalog. This was, as you might expect, a very smooth mix and worked very well. This impressed Pete Tong, Bananarama's record company executive at the time, and he released the mix for promotional purposes in the UK and also commissioned me to do a remix of 'Na Na Hey Hey.' This is another mix of which I am proud, as I made a pop track into an acid house track by using the popular TB-303 sequencer, which generates the 'squidgy' acid bass which you heard on several tracks at this time. The mix also contains some interesting sequenced vocal sample effects using the 'Na Na' vocal. I would imagine that Bananarama were pretty surprised when they heard this mix, but I was very pleased to hear that Pete Tong was happy with it, as his positive reaction is important for any remixer.

"A little later on, following the success in Europe of my megamixes, I was asked to do another Bananarama megamix, which they called 'Megarama '89.' They were much more specific about the tracks I could use, as it was going to be released for the summer market and needed songs like 'Cruel Summer' in it. As a result, it was a much more difficult megamix to do. Also, I wasn't able to remix all the tracks, as I had done with Village People and Gibson Brothers, and some of the tracks were very difficult to mix (e.g. 'Help', which was extremely fast). Even so, I did the best I could, and it worked well I think. This is a good example of a mix which contains 'the hits,' even though they are not the 'most mixable' hits. This is a tension I often had to cope with when doing megamixes. Do I include a track which is very popular even though it doesn't fit very well with the other tracks? And do I include an album track which has never been released as a single as it works very well in the context of the mix?"

*[See also: **Gibson Brothers Megamix - Gibson Brothers, Knock On Wood / Light My Fire / Megamix - Amii Stewart.**]*

Mi Curaçao - Bell Carinya (1994), Brunswick (G)
Producers: J. Zwart, M. Rick

A production sponsored by Bols Blue Curaçao, a popular orange flavored liqueur, this tempting europop song drifts along with the same relaxed vibe found on the Dutch Caribbean island off the coast of Venezuela. Bell's powerfully soulful and joyful vocals invite us to pack our bags and visit Curaçao's white sand beaches and crystal clear waters, see its beautiful sunsets, and immerse ourselves in its rich southern Caribbean culture. I wonder if they played the "Long Drink Version" of "Mi Curaçao" at the Tu Tu Tango or Mambo Beach clubs. The patient groove of the "Curaçao Mix" will have you booking a flight long before the song fades out.

Miami - Boca (2001), Alphabet City (G)
Producer: Stephan Bodzin

Ladies and gentlemen, the captain has turned on the fasten seatbelt sign! Wow—this South Beach musical tempest is quite brilliant in its EDM class, dialed up to 11. It's a stripped down, raw techno thumper that hits you in your gut, and just when you think you can't take it anymore, around the midpoint of the track, it takes an unexpectedly sharp tempo turn that slams you with an even more intensified beat. It's somewhere on the borderline between "woohoo!" and WTF. It's like an EDM version of Disney World's Space Mountain. Or maybe it feels like you're shooting down one of those giant twisting water park pool slides that will send you hurtling into a watery bliss. Either way, you're in for a serious trip. The "Biscayne Mix" is treacherous, the "South Beach Mix," though more musical, sounds a little threatening, but I think you've got this. Just keep repeating: It's only a trance record… only a trance record…only a trance record!

Miami - Will Smith (1997), Columbia (US)
Producers: L.E.S., Poke, Tone

From the album *Big Willie Style* comes the type of song Mr. Smith does so well: catchy dance/pop/rap with a clean cut, relatable theme and fun atmosphere, glazed with a whiff of urban swag. This one turns the heat up with the bonus of some Latin grind that's hot as the devil's ass. Blending in a sample of The Whispers' vintage soul jam hit "And The Beat Goes On" was a smart move, too, considering how popular was Smith's #1 US hit "Gettin' Jiggy Wit It" (which famously whisked in Sister Sledge's "He's The Greatest Dancer") just a few months before. The video for "Miami" brilliantly serves as a send up for the Florida party mecca as Will and his crew long to leave the winter insanity of the Northeast and, in a flash, they're flying in a private jet over South Beach. Do I wish I could be with them? Claro que si! Throughout the clip, Smith is promoting this hot spot so damn cleverly and *squeeeeezing* so much glamour and excitement out of the Latin party scene down there, you'd think he had a stake in The Ritz-Carlton. All that's missing is Alfonso Ribeiro. Jason Nevin's "Live on South Beach Dub" is an infectious tribal jam all on its own.

(L) **Will Smith circa 1997, photo by Michael Lavine, Columbia (press still).**

In "An Oral History Of Will Smith's Miami" by Alex Siquig for *GQ* (online, March 24, 2016), Smith said, "When the Climate Change comes and Miami is destroyed, this video will teach our descendants the importance of carbon footprints and how to treat our 'beautiful fever-dream of a world' as Wayne [Isham, the video's director] calls it."

Miami Vice Theme - Jan Hammer (1985), MCA (US)
Producer: Jan Hammer

The track that made Jan Hammer "vice" president. At the time, this was considered a *very* hip piece of instrumental electronica by the Grammy winning Czech-American composer, musician and producer, and it still stands up today. Its crisp beats evoke all the stylishness and allure of the city and the hit NBC-TV show which featured it so prominently. Both the *Miami Vice* soundtrack album and this hugely popular single debuted in the late summer and both topped the *Cash Box* US pop album and singles charts by November 9, 1985. Earlier, on September 7th, the publication had described the single as, "…full of techno-tension with an underlying dance pulse…" A hard-hitting remix by Francois Kevorkian and Ron St. Germain ensured massive club play, capturing the excitement and energy of the Florida buzz zone's '80s mystique and placing it firmly in the spotlight on the dance floor.

Milk From The Coconut (1983) / I Eat Cannibals (1982) - Toto Coelo, Radialchoice (UK)
Producer: Barry Blue

The natives are restless! It could be their diet. A British collective of five female singers (originally Ros Holness, Lindsey Danvers, Lacey Bond, Anita Mahadevan and Sheen Doran) serve up infectious, synthesizer drenched new-wave with a sly, exotic undercurrent. Their vocal strength, pounding beats and tongue-in-cheek lyrics proved to be irresistible worldwide, but UK's *Record Mirror* didn't much care for "Cannibals," likening it on July 17, 1982, to "…a terrible song from one of those awful musicals just off and just off and just off Broadway. Yuk!"

Montego Bay - Amazulu (1986), Mango/Island (UK)
Producer: Andy Hill

This self-assured female group takes you on a trip firmly into *glamazon* territory! A remake of Bobby Bloom's vintage Caribbean classic, Amazulu (Lesley Beach, Ann-Marie Ruddock and Sharon Bailey, at this point in the group's history) were wonderfully adept at mixing a calypso vibe with dance floor-ready pop sensibility. The track got as high as #55 on *Music & Media*'s European Hot 100 Singles chart as the summer season drew to a close in '86. "Montego" has a real sing-along Caribic energy, much like their other hits, "Too Good To Be Forgotten" and "Excitable," from their eponymous debut album. Also worth noting is a track off Amazulu's (then reduced to a duo, Ann-Marie and Sharon) second album, *Spellbound* (1989)—the sultry "Paradise Island." These ladies are virtuosos at creating richly colored tropical tapestries.

Montego Bay - Sugar Cane (1978), Ariola (G)
Producer: Pete Bellotte

This five-member group, produced by Donna Summer's famous collaborator, chooses a Boney M. flavor to reimagine their version of the 1970 jam by Bobby Bloom. The track was promoted on the 12-inch vinyl jacket artwork as "The Disco Version."

Moonlight On Water (Sex On The Beach) - Laura Branigan (1990), Atlantic (US)
Producer: Richard Perry

Just call her "Branigan" if she's got you feeling randy! In the '80s, soprano Laura Branigan was a fixture on the pop and dance charts singing powerful songs with passionate lyrics, insanely addictive hooks, and highly infectious beats ("Self Control" and "Solitaire" to name a couple). As her smash single "Gloria" was poised to enter the top 10 of *Cash Box*'s pop chart on November 13, 1982, the publication made her their cover artist and quoted the vocalist as saying, "When I sing a song, it's like pouring it out of my heart." That edginess, ardor and earthiness made her one of the most distinctive singers of her time, even as Laura's popularity began to ebb in the '90s. Her prowess, however, is undiminished on "Moonlight On Water," and its erotic overtones have a truly seductive edge. That adds up to an erotic summer boilermaker and a cool change of pace for Ms. Branigan, though the song was only a minor US pop hit. Laura left this world in 2004, but her voice remains an unstoppable force.

More, More, More - The Andrea True Connection (1976), Buddha (US/J)
Producer: Gregg Diamond

Speaking of erotica—despite Ms. True being a porn movie showgirl at the time and unabashedly singing to the world about it on the hit single "More, More, More" (admittedly, rather tamely and with an oddly appealing, slightly off-key luster), Donna Summer's take on Barry Manilow's "Could It Be Magic," making the rounds at the same time, had a far more graphic "adults only" vibe (re: Donna's lusty urging of her partner to "come, come"). Ms.

Summer got a lot more attention. *Cash Box* described "Could It Be Magic" as "sexy and volatile" in May of 1976, but largely ignored Andrea, the queen of New York City's (and Mayor Abe Beame's) XXX playground, 42nd Street. While the media spotlight was focused elsewhere, ever-determined Ms. True went to *werk* with her dirty movie disco/pop track and future classic, strapped to her back with its infectious (not the STD kind) drums and piano work (Gregg Diamond), pulsating bass (Jim Gregory) and bright, summery sax and trumpet work (Enrique Moore, James Smart), on a steady climb up the mountainous pop, dance and R&B charts. Her trek didn't end until she reached the #3 spot on *Cash Box*'s Top 100 Singles survey on July 10, 1976. The publication ranked the song #29 in their year-end survey of the Top 100 Singles of '76.

Many veteran New Yorkers will recall the true blue movie star's "More, More, More" being played on the radio constantly on the 4th of July weekend that year, and it became one of the most identifiable songs of *any* summer season spanning that entire decade. Perhaps the track culled some of its sunny warmth by being recorded in Kingston, Jamaica, but most of the credit must be given to DJ and engineer Tom Moulton, who remixed Diamond's rather flat and flawed original recording into a thing of beauty, giving it that rich, dynamic sound heard all season long in the clubs and on the radio. It wasn't until the singer's second single was released, "Party Line," that *Cash Box* finally gave the hardest working girl in the saucy side of show business some decent press, saying on July 24, 1976, "A very strong single...her vocals have been accentuated in the studio and it sounds great...although the melody isn't as strong as the previous outing." Ms. True left the pleasures of this world behind in 2011.

More, More, More - Diorr (1989), Stylus Music (UK)
Producer: Not listed, though possibly Steve Rowland.

Said to be the voice of singer/actor Yvette Rowland, this obscure remake of the Andrea True gem was released on British label Stylus Music's neat little compilation album, *Hot Summer Nights*. This percolating electronic version adds a modest steel drum percussion effect, drawing attention to the possibility that Miss Andrea's original might have been made even more exotic had some reggae influences been brought into her 1976 mix. "More,

More, More" has been covered by several other artists, each taking the song in a new direction, including Bananarama, Rachel Stevens, Dayl, and Len, who famously incorporated the song into their hit, "Steal My Sunshine," covered later in this book.

My Sweet Summer Suite - Love Unlimited Orchestra (1976), 20th Century (US)
Producer: Barry White

#1 for nearly a month on *Billboard*'s disco chart, this soulful studio orchestra, under the direction of conductor Barry White, became purveyors of several legendary early disco evergreens. Strings meet funk and energy for over seven minutes here, with seasonally dreamy arrangements by White and Gene Page giving it a bit of a jazz feel. Mr. White, the composer of the track, had an uncanny sense of groove, and it's on full display here.

Never Been To Spain - Smyth (1999), White/BMG (G)
Producer: Wildmax

An early '70s rock number written and sung by Hoyt Axton and, shortly afterward, popularized by Three Dog Night. Here, the female storyteller contemplates the exotic places she *hasn't* been, comparing them to those local spots she *has*. It's a lean electronic reinvention with kind of folk sound and hip-hop background vibe, but it's driven by a soul-searching, smoldering pulse in its "Miami Mix" that registers at least 103° F in the shade. Some artists can do a lot with a little.

New York-Rio-Tokyo - Trio Rio (1986), Metronome (G)
Producer: Mike Herting

Trio Rio were a Cologne-based five-piece band who hit it big in Germany with this breezy, electro-funk, summer-touched jam that peppers in a touch of bossa nova. All about groovin' and movin' in international hot spots, it has an unusual vibe that doesn't seem to initially make sense, but then you hear it a couple of times and you wouldn't have it any other way. Though the band's electro-pop mix of various musical styles was a commercially novel and appealing formula, this was pretty much the band's only big hit. But it proved to be a festive and enduring one.

No Credit Card - Amanda Lear (1985), Merak (I)
Producer: Roberto Gasparini

Never leave home without it. The French model, singer, TV show presenter, and muse of Salvador Dalí is best known for her German-made 1978 deep-throated eurodisco hit, "Follow Me." Oh, and also decades of speculation about her original sexual identity. Here, Ms. Lear trades dark, smokey clubs and the shadows of Chinatown for a hot 'n' campy equatorial jungle, where there are no credit cards and her only friend is a monkey! One might expect "Tarzan Boy" to swing into the picture at any moment. This Italo disco song has an exotic feel much like the kind found on her 1983 jungle beat-fused LP, *Tam Tam*, also recorded in Italy. Beyond her distinctively baritone voice, there's an eccentricity about Amanda's Italian work that is compelling, mysterious and very appealing. And for more summer-suggestive fun from La Lear, check out her 1982 rendition of the Peggy Lee scorcher, "Fever."

No Limit (On The Beach) (2003) / Magic Summer Night* (2004)
- Klubbingman, Epic (G)
Producers: T. Schleh, R. P. Shah / *T. Schleh

Sounding much like something from Scooter, this is hard trance music with a eurodance flair, especially when Klubbingman (Thomas Schleh, formerly with Masterboy) shares the vocal duties with female songstress Sabine. The contrast is very effective. Both are big, unwieldy club action tracks: "No Limit" is impact-structured and a major fist pumper, while "Magic" takes some quick, jolting turns that swoop in and grab you (thank you, Cascada). *Shakalaka boom* sums it up perfectly!

No Tengo Dinero - Los Umbrellos (1997), Flex Records/Virgin
(D) *I have no money*
Producers: K. Bager, M. Pfundheller, J. Elhöj

You'd have to be of a certain age to recognize that the melody of this Latin-spiked dance/pop grinder is the tune "Never On A Sunday" (popularized by singer Nana Mouskouri) cleverly disguised with a new title (that may also inspire summer flashbacks to Righeira's unrelated 1983 hit of the same name). A review of this three-member Scandinavian group's project in *Music & Media* on June 7, 1997, said "No Tengo Dinero," "won't win any cultural awards but it will probably shift significant numbers of units." It did—sell a whole bunch of units, that is. It did *not* win any cultural awards.

Nobody's Perfect - Tuxedo (1991), Welcome (F)
Producer (Artistic Realization): Jean-Marc Pessin

Imperfection is a part of life, as they say, but this song may actually be pretty close to the pinnacle of pop purity. In my original notes about this single, I wrote, "Probably one the most agreeable beach songs you'll *never* get to hear." I stand by that statement as this record is a real obscurity, but well worth the hunt to find. A thoroughly enchanting electronic French dance/pop arrangement with underlying acoustic guitars gives a breathy and handsome young male duo the ideal setting to show off their silky voices. Beachy vibes build steadily to an uplifting sonic crest. The boys' cheerful unison, some nicely placed horns, and the general ease of the hook-laden chorus place the listener squarely in the sunshine. The "Island" mixes were the early work of superstar David Guetta.

O.T.B. (On The Beach) - York (1999), Adrenaline (G)
Producer: T. Stenzel

No connection to Off Track Betting. But you can place a wager that it's a high-energy trance-house cover of Chris Rea's sensual 1986 hit "On The Beach," with the infectious melody intact and the electricity amped way up. Magic Marc's Mix is dreamy and hypnotic and the CRW Mix is thrilling. Solid EDM summer sounds. It was a top 20 hit on *Music & Media*'s Eurochart Hot 100 Singles chart in the summer of 2000.

One Of Those Summers - P-Funk All Stars (1982), Hump (US)
Producers: George Clinton, Walter "Junie" Morrison

Alumni from Parliament and Funkadelic (I just bowed my head) jammin' together on a meaty mid-tempo bump and grind dance number that has the power to melt the listener faster than ice cream fallen on to hot pavement. Yet it's retro-Detroit vibe is as refreshing as the cool spray from a fire hydrant sprinkler cap. Vocalist Hugh Boynton beams with vintage soulfulness.

On The Beach (1986) / On The Beach Summer '88* (1988) - Chris Rea, Magnet* / WEA (G)
Producers: Chris Rea, Dave Richards / Chris Rea*, Jon Kelly*

Mr. Rea cast his line out and caught us with "All Summer Long" in 1985 and then reels us in with "On The Beach," from his 1986 album of the same name. Perhaps one of the most literal tracks in this book, the song creates a beach mood that is amazingly authentic and nearly manifests the actual sensations of a day spent in the sun and on the sand. With this song, we come one with our sunny surroundings. Warner acquired the Magnet label in 1988, where most of Chris Rea's music was housed, and gave his monster summer classic a refreshed re-recording, though it's not radically different from the original. It's the type of song you expect to hear playing at an open air bar in Key West—lightly jazzy with a pop/rock feel and a hypnotic, 7 PM sunset on the beach" vibe. In fact, speaking of Duval Street, some may feel a Jimmy Buffett vibe bubbling in this track. Carl Wiser interviewed Rea for *Songfacts.com* (September 19, 2017), asking about inspirations for his *On The Beach* album. "That was Formentera, a little island off Ibiza in Spain," said the artist. "That's where me and my wife became me and my wife. That's what it's about….it's a lovely island if ever you're in Europe."

On The Beach / Surf's Up - The Flirts (1982), "O" Records/Rams Horn Records (US)
Producer: Bobby Orlando

When three feisty, punky gals sing about checking out a man's beach balls (which are four different colors, no less), you know you're in for a good time, '80s new wave style. "Surf's Up" (from the European release) is the instrumental version. Noticeably emulating The B-52's, The Flirts' slapping guitar, drum and synthesizer beats scream "Surf Party, USA!" Various formations of the girl group had hits with "Passion," "Calling All Boys," "Jukebox (Don't Put Another Dime)," "Danger" and "New Toy."

Our Last Summer - ABBA (1980), Polar (SW)
Producers: Björn Ulvaeus & Benny Andersson

What kind of unearthly power made the sound of ABBA so heavenly that nearly everything they sang about was a magical, nearly religious experience? This rhythmic, mid-tempo sentimental ballad that takes one to the Élysées for one summer night of romantic misfortune will either make you cry your heart out or carry your soul to a higher plane—likely both. Frida's (Anni-Frid Lyngstad) voice is exceptionally enchanting. From the glorious album *Super Trouper*. It may be necessary to immediately shake this song off with a party jam, as no one wants to feel *this* melancholy during the summer. Maybe try our next selection.

Our Summer Love - Fun In The Box (1997), RCA (G)
Producers: Hanno Harders, Mark Wills

Pure electronic eurodance with a bright melody, minimal female vocals and a healthy nod to the sounds of Haddaway, La Bouche and Dr. Alban. The track fares best in its ethereal "Booya Mix" by Papa Bear. It's not the only chip in the bag, but it's still a good beach snack.

P - Q - R

Palma De Mallorca - Chris Wolff (1988), Koch (G)
Palms of Mallorca
Producer: Altera Pars

Chris provides a lot of valuable tourist tips in this upbeat, hand-clapping German schlager summer fest, such as where to find the most beautiful girls, where to book a cheap, sunny holiday, and the best spots to dream peacefully in a scenic cove. Spoiler—it's Palma de Mallorca off the coast of Valencia, of course! The singer frequently visited tropical themes with his genre hits that included "Am Strand Von Maspalomas" (*On Maspalomas Beach*) and his greatest beach hits medley "Summerparty-Nonstop-Mix" (which naturally includes "Palma De Mallorca").

Papa Chico - Tony Esposito (1985), Bubble (I)
Producers: Tony Esposito, Mauro Malavasi

Just as evocative as his previous Italo disco hit, "Kalimba De Luna," Tony Esposito's follow-up flows gently with a bongo beat and poetic lyrics that have a summer warmth, but also an underlying, if a bit camouflaged, message of peace (with an unexpected reference to children who don't want guns in their lives). The song, like "Kalimba," was sung by vocalist Gianluigi Di Franco and followed nearly the same flight plan as its predecessor, becoming a pan-European hit and serving as another opportunity for multiple cover versions by other artists. Boney M. Ft. Liz Mitchell took on the track (though much later, in 1994, infusing some rap). Electronic studio act O.N.B. moved it into calypso/reggae territory in 1997. Jamalak recorded "Papa Chico" with a bit of a Spanish flair, quite faithful to Esposito's original, and reached the top 50 of *Music & Media*'s pop singles chart in the waning days of the summer of 1999. Also in '99, C-Bra, a girl group, in case that isn't obvious, gave the track a breakbeat hip-hop vibe. If imitation is the sincerest form of flattery, Tony must be flush from all the adulation!

"'Papa Chico' was dedicated to an African (Senegal) man who was a master of percussion and a very wise person," Esposito recalls. "He always said that musicians are soldiers of peace. In this track...I took the African sound and combined it with a tropical style. It was a very unusual type of song, different from what they were playing on the radio at the time. I really didn't think it would succeed, but, instead, it became a very big hit across Europe. *[From the book: "Europe's Stars of '80s Dance Pop, Vol. 2, Arena, Bookbaby, 2018.]*

[See also: "Kalimba De Luna" - Tony Esposito.]

Paradise - Change (1981), RFC/Atlantic (I/US)
Producers: Jacques Fred Petrus, Mauro Malavasi

Somewhat eclipsed by a number of hits off the group's first album, *The Glow of Love*, including "Searching" and "A Lover's Holiday," "Paradise" (from their sophomore LP, *Miracles*) has a powerful rhythm of its own and an undeniable connection to summer. The track was released in the US on Ray Caviano's RFC label, once associated with Warner Bros., this time distributed through Atlantic Records. A *Record World* review of the *Miracles* album (April 18, 1981) described the group's sound as "a winning combination of tasty European tracks and urgent vocals." In the April 11, 1981, installment of his "Disco File" column for the publication, Brian Chin said, "Last year's Change album was such a success commercially and artistically that one might have expected it to be impossible to follow, but *Miracles* stands up to it, with its own very coherent viewpoint and style." The track was #1 on the publication's Disco File Top 20 chart a few weeks later. A brief June 27, 1981, commentary in Britain's *Record Mirror* described "Paradise" as a "fabulous, creamily chugging…subtle throbber…widely considered the one that got away," a reference to the song failing to make much of an impression in the UK.

Commentary from Ray Caviano:

"There's some background history to explain while discussing 'Paradise.' I only stayed with Warner Bros. for a year and a half. There was the disco backlash; disco is dead. Warner started to get cold feet about disco and dance music. The majors were late into disco to begin with. Warner was more of a white rock 'n' roll company. Even though I did very well with their product, I left Warner, took my label and artists with me, and went independent. I also did independent promotion (Yoko Ono's 'Walking On Thin Ice,' for example). I did that for about a year and a half, and then Atlantic Records' president, Doug Morris, contacted me and asked if I wanted to handle promotion for their dance music. So I moved my RFC label over with them, and took Change with me, and we released 'Paradise.'

"It was a whole new feel, a fresh start with Atlantic. 'Paradise' did go to #1 on the dance charts and did very well. I didn't really feel any pressure or worry about comparisons to 'A Lover's Holiday' and other hits [from Change's first album]. I'm the type of guy who works very intuitively. I move very, very quickly when I think I have a hit—I'm like a thief in the night! 'Paradise' certainly stood on its own legs. Change had solidified its name. My ear had been fine-tuned to find the right product, and this was one of them.

"Like 'A Lover's Holiday,' 'Paradise' definitely had that summer feeling. If you go to that bass line in 'Paradise,' it was unbelievable. They had a block party on King Street in New York City a few years ago celebrating the late Larry Levan and the club Paradise Garage, which was once located there. It was summer, and thousands of people showed up. What was the first record they played to kick off the party? 'Paradise' by Change. People made that connection. Look at the lyrics of that song. What a happy, uplifting, bright, energetic track. Yes, it was a harder sound, not as smooth as 'A Lover's Holiday,' but its bass and percussion were more pronounced. If I was on a dance floor, you'd have to get out of my way with that one!"

*[See also: **A Lover's Holiday - Change.**]*

Paradise - Mad Romeo (1989), Mercury (G)
Producer: Reinhold Heil

Smooth, lean electro-pop/rock from a four-man band out of Germany, sung in English. It's got a catchy chorus and strong male lead vocal work, and in its extended "Parachute Mix," the jazzy horns, playful electronic effects and snapping beat give it a hot Saturday afternoon feel. Try it; you'll like it.

Paradise - Sade (1988), Epic (UK)
Producer: Sade

In its June 11, 1988, issue, *Music & Media* described the song as a, "Brooding, percussion-oriented, summery track. Highly swinging through its persistent, up-tempo, although at the same time somehow restrained, groove." Taken from Sade Adu's *Stronger Than Pride* set, it sounds more electronic than tropical, but the groove is undeniably still sensual and has an unexpected spontaneity about it. A departure from the softer, jazzier side of her music, but no less distinctive or sophisticated, and the artist's signature elegance remains intact. Sade would clear the sand from the shore for love. A top 20 *Cash Box* pop single in the US.

Paradise - Timmy T (1990), Pump (UK)
Producer: John Ryan

Despite the inviting tropical beach pictured on the record jacket, this innocuous electro-house jam by the American pop singer ("One More Try") trades more on its beat rather than atmosphere. A "jazz" remix by the UK's Alan Coulthard pumps up the rhythm, but the song falls short of conveying the summer magic for which it may have been aiming.

Paradise In Your Eyes - Jermaine Jackson (1982), Motown (US)
Producer: Jermaine Jackson

After a surprisingly lengthy and languid intro featuring the sounds of ocean waves and exotic birds, this romantic song seems like it doesn't know in what direction to go—a Stevie Wonder-like rhythmic soul track complete with harmonica (played by Jackson) or a dreamy lullaby? While it scores points for an atmospheric set-up, it ultimately feels like paradise lost.

Paradise Mi Amore - Lune De Miel (1984), BMA (F)
Producers: SPARKER (F. Partouche, S. Brugère)
Paradise Mi Amore - Vanilla (1985), Metronome (G)
Producers: Helmut Rulofs, Harry Baierl

Nearly identical, completely interchangeable versions of an electronic '80s disco song about having no job, no guilt, enjoying breakfast by the sea and drinking champagne. If one buys the premise of this song, and who wouldn't, it seems like The Cayman Islands, St Lucia, Antigua or St Kitts and Nevis are the places to be for those seeking a responsibility-free lifestyle. How glorious does that sound—two six month vacations every year? Male vocals on the verses, females on the chorus, and both do a terrific job of spelling out the benefits of getting away from it all. Vanilla appears to have been a German production, Lune de Meil was from France, and the latter had the more popular version, reaching the top 20 of the European Top 100 Singles chart on the *EuroTipSheet* in mid-September of 1985.

People From Ibiza - Balearic Sound Collective (1999), Logic/BMG (G)
Producers: Detlef Hastik, Ralph Fritsch, Flex

In the mostly spoken lyrics of the radio cut for this electrified house club track, the narrator/vocalist (Chris Smith) advises us that summertime is party time, in case we didn't know, and it's time to pack our bags and head to Ibiza. There we'll find drag queens, friends partying on the beach, and DJs spinning butt-shaking music at off-da-hook clubs. That sounds pretty Gucci to me. It turns out to be a very convincing jam that one can use to justify all the expenses we're likely to incur investing in a slammin' holiday such as this song describes. The track is connected to Sandy Marton's 1984 dance classic in name only. Let's check in with him next.

People From Ibiza - Sandy Marton (1984), Ibiza Records (I)
Producer: Claudio Cecchetto

Thanks to this big international hit and #1 song in Italy during the summer of '84, Sandy Marton (Aleksandar Marton) became permanently associated with Ibiza. He was the first to really popularize (in an English language dance/pop song at least) the mystical draw the island off the coast of Spain possesses. Of course, over time, Europeans, especially young partiers, whose appetite for sun, beach and nightlife was insatiable during the summer holiday months, soon swarmed the place, increasing by the thousands every year. "People From Ibiza" perhaps spoke to a simpler time in the island's history and may have inadvertently enticed *too many* people to enjoy its pleasures. Marton scored a few more hits that pulsated with a hot summer beat, including "Camel By Camel," "Exotic And Erotic," "Modern Lovers" and "La Paloma Blanca."

"I had been in Ibiza since 1980," remembers Sandy Marton. "One night, I was in a bar—the only bar in Ibiza at the time. Nina Hagen and her boyfriend were walking around; everyone was looking so beautiful. I thought to myself, these are people from Ibiza! Then a girl came up to me and gave me a bracelet. It was one of those cloth bracelets with three knots in it, and it had the words "Gente de Ibiza" on it. That's where I got the name of the song. I stole a sequencer from somebody, and, with that in mind, I created the track 'People From Ibiza.' [My producer, Claudio Cecchetto] liked it a lot, and we recorded it for real. I had never sung before that record. It just happened! I think people throughout Europe responded so well to it because it was simply a good song. It would be very difficult to make another song like it.

"I was extremely happy when 'People From Ibiza' started climbing the charts," he says. "I was even happier when the money from the song rights arrived! It was in Italian lire, I remember. The first check arrived, and I was so excited that I had thought I made [the equivalent of] 8,000 Euros. But, actually, it was 80,000 Euros. It was great!" *[From the book: Europe's Stars of '80s Dance Pop, Vol. 2, Arena, Bookbaby, 2018.]*

Place In The Sun - Denise Cole Ft. Dr. Weedy (1996), Happy Music (G)
Producers: Christian Kelvin, Nautilus, Oliver Fahrenheit, XL

Yah mahn, it's got that wonderfully tropical Jamaican atmosphere. A very pleasant and positive ragga pop rendition of the Bryan Wells/Ron Miller soul nugget with a smooth dance beat. Ms. Cole and Dr. Weedy make an agreeable duo with contrasting sounds that are satisfyingly in sync. Dr. Weedy ends the song saying, "That's good!" You're likely to agree. Don't overlook the gentle bonus track by Dr. Weedy found on the maxi-single, "Cool Down," a wonderfully soothing and encouraging jam with gentle guitar strumming and a peaceful beat. Just as effective as therapy (and a hell of a lot cheaper).

Place In The Sun, A - Winjama (1988), Creole/PRT (UK)
Producers: Morris Michaels, Bigga

A UK charity single to support aid for Jamaica after ferociously intense Hurricane Gilbert struck the island in September of 1988. The popular Wells/Miller song is given a mid-tempo reggae/pop update, but the real draw is the stellar line-up of artists participating, many of whom were well established in the period's Brit dance/pop scene. They include Andy Bell of Erasure, Sinitta, Leee John of Imagination, Errol Brown of Hot Chocolate, Ruby Turner and Simon Climie of Climie Fisher.

Playa Blanca - Audrey Landers (1983/84), Ariola (G)
White beach.
Producer: Jack White

Never mind who shot JR. Where is this beach? Originally a track on the "Dallas" TV show star's first English-language LP for the German market in 1983 (*Little River*, which also contained the artist's biggest hit, "Manuel Goodbye"). The song was given a fresh remix in 1984 and broadly released as a single across the continent. It had been covered earlier by Linda Susan Bauer, also in English, and in German by schlager singer Andrea Jürgens, both in 1982 and under the production supervision of veteran Deutschland music maestro Jack White. White frequently enlisted a variety of artists to sing the same song, some targeted to a German audience, others, like Ms. Landers, to a more diverse international market. White's release of Audrey's version was successful in Germany, the Netherlands and a few other territories, peaking at #41 on June 4, 1984, on the *EuroTipSheet* pop singles chart.

While there are only marginal differences between each of the afore-mentioned vocalists' take of the song, Audrey's is likely *the* standout version and undeniably a hallmark within the summer niche of the schlager genre. Complete with the musical sensation of shimmering ocean water and an atmospheric, carefree melody, "Playa Blanca" solidified the American actor/singer's standing as a European '80s pop star. And she certainly has a gift for singing pleasant tropical themes. However, the official video shoot for the track has a rather harrowing Gilligan's Island-like backstory, according to Ms. Landers, one far removed from the tranquil mood the song projects. Though we spoke over Skype, I'd prefer to imagine we were chatting over cocktails at the Lido Key Tiki Bar of The Ritz-Carlton, overlooking Sarasota Bay.

Commentary from Audrey Landers:

"The 'Playa Blanca' video story is *unreal!* The song had just been recorded and the record company wanted to do a music video. They wanted to do it quickly, and they wanted white sand beaches. I guess it was winter at the time. I was with my mother *[Ruth Landers, Audrey's manager]* in Germany, and they sent us to the Canary Islands to shoot it—Gran Canaria. It began as a disaster right away. We arrived there so late at night that everything was closed, and the hotel didn't have a means of accepting credit cards or German or American money. They only wanted whatever their currency was. We hadn't eaten all day or night, as I was working TV shows all day, and we were traveling. And on top of that, as exotic as it is, their sand was black—not white! The song is called 'Playa Blanca' (white beach), and the sand is black on their beaches! *[Audrey laughs.]* A videographer and a small crew were with us, and somebody from the promotions department of the label—nobody spoke Spanish.

"The next morning comes and we are supposed to film on this boat. They ended up renting out an 1800s-style schooner that I assume was used for tourism, with a full crew on it. It was an enormous schooner. We get on this vessel at 6 AM, and there's this funny old captain, dressed in full 1800s regalia. We still haven't eaten yet. They start cooking some kind of fish stew in the belly of this ship, in a huge galley, for their crew. So there are these big bubbling pots, boiling away. My mom and I are up on the deck, and we notice the weather is getting nasty. Somehow, we get blown off course. We didn't know what the course was supposed to be in the first place, but we no longer could see the shoreline. So my mom asks the captain (we're trying to communicate), 'Where are we going?' The wind is really kicking up. I thought we were going to a little island to start filming. The captain reassured us, so we went up on deck and attempted to make a pass at filming something up there for 'Playa Blanca.'

"We had two video or film cameras. I'm hanging onto these two guide wires, and I'm singing 'Playa Blanca.' We're rocking side to side, the weather is horrific, and my dress is blowing all over the place. I'm just hanging on for dear life, and suddenly one of the cameras goes *poof*—overboard! It was gone. At this point I felt it wasn't safe to be on the deck and felt we really needed to get ashore—fast. Now by this time, the fish smell from below is beyond belief, and it appeared like the whole crew was seasick. Okay? The captain had these maps (they looked like they were from the 1800s) and a compass of some kind and he seems to be lost.

"Well, we finally see land, and my mom tells the captain to 'pull over!'— but there's no dock. It was more like a cliff with this rope ladder you had to sort of climb up to get to the land. They anchor the schooner and we take the dinghy, and they load the camera equipment up and start passing it up this ladder. My mom and I are the last to go up. By the way, there's no vanity at this point. Whatever you look like, that's it. When we get up the ladder, we are met by seven guys with machine guns pointed at us! They were detaining us because we didn't have the papers for that island for all our camera equipment. So they think we're smuggling camera equipment onto the island. We've been out for six hours, and we still haven't eaten in about 48 hours. My mom approached the armed men, explained she and I have nothing and [aren't responsible for this situation], and they permit us to leave to find coffee. We found a cafe and finally got to eat! (That place took our money!)

"We mosey on back to the others and discover that the mayor of whatever town we were in was a huge fan of mine. He did not want us to leave before he could bring his family over to meet us. So we were actually held at gunpoint until he could gather his wife and children to say hello. That was—unbelievable—and it was really, really frightening because of the whole gun situation. We were running out of light and had no idea what we were going to shoot or how we were going to get around—we had only that one day to get all this done. To get things moving, my mom told the mayor he could be in the video playing a JR type of character (he was a big 'Dallas' fan), someone had a convertible, the mayor wears a cowboy hat, they film me in the car with him and with some little children in front of a church. Done—my mom really put together that whole thing. The costumed captain then gets us back to the island where our hotel is.

"The next morning they want me to film one more scene where I'm at the airport and get into somebody's little private plane and I wave good-bye. And now there's a sandstorm! I said, 'No, I'm *not* doing that.' I gave them my hat and a wig—anybody who wants to wear them can do it. But I was not going up in some little plane on this crazy island. So that's it, we're ready to leave, and I just want to get out of there. Then we find out there are no outbound flights—the airport was shut down, probably because of the sandstorm. I think I had a little breakdown at that point. We finally did get back to Frankfurt. I was never so happy to be in a real hotel! I've never seen the video; I do not know if it ever got made. And *that* is the 'Playa Blanca' video story!"

Despite her troubles in paradise, Audrey still enjoys summer-themed music:
"I love The Beach Boys. 'Kokomo' and all their songs are lots of fun. For a totally different summer feeling, I really love Ricky Martin, especially 'Livin' La Vida Loca.' He's one of my favorites, and his music always has that summery vibe. I just love Latin music."

*[See also: **Sun Of Jamaica - Audrey Landers**.]*

Pleasure Island - Paul Jabara (1978), Casablanca (US)
Producer: Bob Esty

At over 10 minutes long in its extended 12-inch version, Mr. Jabara has plenty of time to explore his idea of paradise, creating a compelling, imaginative sonic experience that's just the right elevation of over-the-top. Bob Esty's (he also was behind Cher's "Take Me Home" and Donna Summer's "Last Dance") stellar production captures the transportive magic of the classic disco era sound (synthesizers, strings and that glorious four-on-the-floor hit-hat rhythm), adding a midway break that oddly turns the dreamy nature of the opus into a trippy electronic stomper. Somehow it all works—must be that island magic.

Portofino - Engelbert (1985), Ariola (G)
Producer: Jack White

Teaming with German music producer Jack White was a well-timed move in the mid-'80s for Britain's Engelbert Humperdinck, as White's romantic pop style was an ideal platform for the crooner in Deutschland. As a result, Engelbert had numerous hit singles and albums (continuing to sing in English) during the period. "Portofino" is one of his most pleasant melodies, a Spanish-accented ode to the charming place where a man falls in love to a swaying beat. So successful were Engelbert's songs in German-speaking territories that producer White remixed and re-released "Portofino" in 1992 as part of the artist's greatest hits album. Give the crooner's later songs such as "Acapulco" and "Tropical Sunshine" a listen too.

Says Mr. Humperdinck, "Jack [White] was a good producer. He always surrounded himself with great musicians, arrangers and engineers. We recorded in a style that I was used to. We would record all the music tracks first, and Jack would use a demo singer to give me a rough idea of how to approach the song. I would 'live' with the songs for a while and then 'Humperdinck' them. Of course, if I didn't want to record a particular song, Jack would replace it. However, I knew he was having great success in certain markets and that he had a good idea, a good ear for knowing how the songs needed to sound to please the audience he was going for. The albums we did together were very much a combined effort." *[From the book: Europe's Stars of '80s Dance Pop, Vol. 2, Arena, Bookbaby, 2018.]*

Puerto Rico - Découpage (1982), R&B Records/MCA (UK)
Producers: Tony Swain, Steve Jolley

A British production helmed by the team who delivered several hits for Bananarama ("Robert De Niro's Waiting," "Cruel Summer") and Imagination ("Body Talk," "Just An Illusion"). The song features strong female lead vocals and a rich, layered disco hustle groove. While other Caribbean destinations get most of the attention in summer holiday songs, it's pleasing to see "The Land of Enchantment," a wonderful island and the homeland of Ricky Martin, getting some love.

Puerto Rico - Vaya Con Dios (1988), Ariola/BMG (B)
Producers: Dani Klein, Dirk Schoufs

In its splendidly produced extended maxi-single form, "Puerto Rico" is filled with drama and emotion as it tells the story of a girl whose lover must vacate the island to try and make it in mainland USA. (It's still a real life social issue on the island today.) There's a theatricality here that works because of singer

Dani Klein's sultry, soulful delivery and her ability to express the complexities of human relationships so fluidly and passionately. The song has a gentle Latin rhythm, with congas and Spanish guitars adding to the atmosphere. It's ironic how so many of us who visit Puerto Rico as tourists and experience its way of life, its sun, beaches, wonderful food, arts and music (where, by the way, the rhythmic bomba genre and dance evolved, becoming a mainstream part of the island's culture) *never* want to leave the place.

Rain In The Summertime - The Alarm (1987), I.R.S. (UK)
Producers: John Porter, The Alarm

It's fair to compare the sound of this synth-rocker to the work of U2 or Simple Minds during this period, as it has that same kind of anthemic, mesmerizing and majestic energy. And just as those bands would be highly unlikely to phone in shallow, generic summer fare, The Alarm also stays at the deep end of the pool. Only it's not such a refreshing dip. By any measure, this is heavy stuff, with sobering lyrics about the sun feeling like an anvil, beds of fire and bodies burnt to dust. This song is a tad hellish, feeling like a well-orchestrated score to a fever dream.

Raving On The Beach - Port-O-Spain (1982), Dureco Benelux/ Salsoul Records (NL)
Producer: Victor Scott

Though its title suggests a trance blast, hands-in-the-air crowd-pleaser, the raving here is far more subdued—more stolid than enthusiastic. An odd, kind of heavy-footed electro-disco stomper with a bit of an urban funk style and some horns thrown in, repetitive in its simple lyrics about having a good time on the beach. I can be sure of only one thing. They were determined to make sure you wouldn't forget the title.

Reach The Beach - The Fixx (1983), MCA (UK)
Producer: Rupert Hine

The title track from the 1983 album by the English rock band (famous for "One Thing Leads To Another") symbolically references being drawn down by the tide and clutching to reach the beach (so strikingly and literally illustrated in the album's cover art), all of which suggests these waters, and the elements of life reflected here, have depth. It's all a bit ambiguous and subject to interpretation, yet it's anything but dull. Cy Curnin's powerful vocals tread within a haunting new wave synth-pop arrangement, and a powerful bass line evokes a sense of struggle and desperation, rather than the usual upbeat feeling found in pop music beach references.

Real Fashion Reggae Style - Carey Johnson (1987), 10 Records/ Virgin (UK)
Producer: Bubbles Cameron

Very cheerful reggae/pop with a swaying retro feel and a crisp '80s beat. Authentic vocal work by a singer whose music dates back to the late '60s. Rest assured, everything's gonna be alright.

Red Red Wine - UB40 (1983), A&M/Virgin (UK)
Producers: UB40, Ray "Pablo" Falconer

In addition to being a song about raising a glass to forget one's troubles, I'd add it's an incentive for being barefoot in the sand. Simplicity was the group's hallmark, and this Birmingham reggae band (whose name was derived from a UK unemployment form, so they clearly had a sense of humor) turned their uncomplicated style into gold with their rendition of "Red Red Wine." The song was written by Neil Diamond, whose own version is far removed from the reggae style found here. Those sometimes caustic critics over at the UK's *Record Mirror* were at it again, reacting to the record on August 13, 1983. "Aargh!" its reviewer growled, "The thought of this blasting over the airwaves for weeks means I'm heading for the fallout shelter in the garden." As you may have noticed, this publication was often proficient at cranky, drag queen level burns back then (though I'll admit they're amusing). But, then again, I've heard they do get a lot of cold, dreary, moody days over there. Few shared their viewpoint, as the song reached #1 on *Billboard*'s Hot 100 pop chart and was a hit throughout Europe. As much as it is so often amusingly classified as a "favorite drinking song," "Red Red Wine" is also indelibly connected to summer. Let the gentle pulse of this song go right to your head.

Reggae Inna Summertime - Big Mountain (1993), Quality (G)
Producer: Bruce Caplin

Again, the theme here is the sweet escape found in summer sunshine after a long, hard winter and how uniquely reggae music can capture that spirit. The California-based band Big Mountain was terrific at delivering accessible reggae/pop, which some might criticize as a diluted form of the original Jamaican genre. Well, beats evolve and take many different paths, and you're free to choose the one that works for you—I can tell you this path leads directly to the beach!

Revelation Sunshine - Cree Summer (1999), Columbia/Work (US)
Producer: Lenny Kravitz

This Californian artist first came into the spotlight with her role as Lisa Bonet's friend on the TV series "A Different World" and doing voiceovers for the animated program "Rugrats." On April 3, 1999, *Billboard* said "Revelation" had a "Bohemian charm," adding that Ms. Summer, "…wraps her notably Alannis-like vocal cords around the song's rambling structure of acoustic guitars, purring organs and subtle drum loops with an almost psychedelic air." *Hmmm*, that all seems a bit lofty. Instead, just let the "Out Of My Mind Extended Version" surround you with its drifting, warm beat, groovy melody and spacey vibe. Good stuff for a late afternoon at the shore, much like the hot summer jam by our next artist.

Revolution In Paradise - Heath Hunter & The Pleasure Company (1996), Metronome (G)
Producers: Double AA (Achim Oppermann, Achim Sobotta)

No sense putting up a fight. This song will win you over. Warm, spirited dance/pop laced with a vibrant reggae flavor, "Revolution In Paradise" debuted at #89 in late September of 1996 on the *Music & Media* European Hot 100 Singles chart and enjoyed the distinction of a top 20 ranking in Germany. This song, like Kate Yanai's "Bacardi Feeling (Summer Dreamin')" a few years earlier, initially fell under Bacardi's rum and music marketing umbrella, virtually ensuring the money would be there to help bolster pop crossover success and a rock solid connection to holiday escape. The song's lyrics, written by Achim Oppermann, actually have a decidedly sobering message (environmental worries, poverty and human suffering), but it was largely obscured (a la Eddy Grant's "Electric Avenue") by the upbeat tone of the track's infectious dance mixes, its pop framing and the tropical visuals of its spirited video clip. Hunter sings with earnest conviction and dances with brilliant summer fluidity, while rapper Mighty V injects the song with its reggae muscle. Hunter was inspired to re-record the song in 2004.

Commentary from Heath Hunter:

How did you come to record "Revolution In Paradise"?

"In the '90s, I was recording music and always trying to get a deal, while working as a professional dancer. I decided, why should I get a job with someone else when I could actually be the artist? I was in Hamburg, and I started making music and taught these dance fitness classes. While I was there, I met Oliver Helwig (who was somehow involved in the signing of Ace Of Base, from what I was told). He didn't like the songs I presented to him, but he liked me and thought I could go far as an artist. Then there was this girl in one of my dance classes, and she happened to be one of the product managers for Bacardi. I got a call from Bacardi, and they wanted to sponsor me—they felt my image matched their promotion concept for launching Bacardi Breezer in Germany.

"I wanted a song that people could connect me with, otherwise it didn't make sense for me to try and represent their brand just through an unknown guy dancing. [Bacardi's promotion people] knew Ollie, spoke with him, and 'Revolution' was one of the demos on his desk. He thought it would be the perfect song for me. Bacardi said if I would do this song, they would sponsor me and pay for everything. The marketing, the video (which we flew to the Bahamas to make) and the launch. I just went into the studio, we had kids in there for the chorus, and all the back-up singers.

"It got delayed, but we launched 'Revolution' in 1996. But it initially wasn't working; it wasn't going that far. There were quite a few contenders ahead of us, like 'Coco Jamboo' by Mr. President. There was a lot of money riding on this because of the money Bacardi was putting into our song. We were set to perform the song at a huge youth fair with DJ Bobo in Germany, which would give it a boost. But there was a tragic helicopter crash (with fatalities, including, I think, DJ Bobo's manager), and this event was cancelled. But, eventually Bacardi ended up tying 'Revolution In Paradise' to SAT 1's 'Ran World' soccer games that the company was involved with. We did all these performances in these big stadiums, and the song just took off. Bacardi really wanted to get into the sports world with its mass audience, and with me performing there, they were able to advertise their Bacardi Breezer [when normally they would not be able to advertise an alcohol beverage]. It was a really good concept.

(L) Heath Hunter today.

"But anyway, my job was also to create a dance that matched the song. I created this 'cocktail shaker' dance, where you go side to side, wearing clothes with colors that represented citrus. That's how it all came together. The plan really was designed to bring out the dance thing, like Zumba is now. The 'Macarena' hit came out around the same time. Everything just fell into place. The pop side took off so fast—overnight. It was unreal."

Did you feel a positive connection with the song?

"It really did fit with my intentions. But it was written by my producer, and it wasn't really my type of song, the style I would have ideally picked for myself. But you ask yourself, do you want a flop or a commercial hit? I had always bought records at this shop, Container Records in Germany, and they knew the stuff I'd buy. I walked into this after-the-club cafe in the Reeperbahn area in Hamburg—everyone turns up there—when I was in the top of the charts one day, and this guy from that record shop recognized me. He [disapprovingly] said, 'Hey Heath, why did you do that song 'Revolution In Paradise?' I know what music you used to buy.' I responded, 'Are you still in that small record shop with your tiny little studio in the back?' He said yes. 'Well, I'm not,' I responded. He was trying to say I sold out. But if something is successful, why does that mean you're selling out? It's a hit—it means everybody likes it. Do you want to produce music for just the few?"

Tell me about the making of that exceptionally lively, colorful "Revolution" video.

"We flew to Grand Bahama (one of the northernmost islands, which has no palm trees, just pine forests) and, with these crazy pilots, had to find a small island that looked more tropical. These guys were drinking and smoking pot in these small propeller planes. But I have to say, it was fun. Then we had to take little boats to get to the small island; I think it might have been called Paradise Cove. Very luxurious looking—but full of mosquitos and sand fleas, and it was hell! The dolphins you see in the video were from the movie *Flipper,* and they lived in the waters by this island and were trained there. They filmed us on a jetty, and while we were dancing, the dolphins would jump in between us. It was all real. I think they were being fed or handled by their trainer, and he had them jump out of the water at just the right time. These dolphins seemed to be very happy there.

"Everything about this song happened by chance—it is all about being in the right place, right time, and the people you are with. You just never know. I get asked about the clothing we wore in the video all the time. The colors were meant to represent citrus. But I will never wear those shorts from the video again! [*Heath laughs.*] Despite the light, fun images we filmed, the message of the song was perfect—it really was much more serious and was about what was happening in the world."

Do you remember any interesting experiences during your live performances?

"I remember we asked for extra security at one performance. People asked us why we wanted so much, and we said it wasn't for us, it was for the audience. We had recently done a show in Berlin. It was a show for Bacardi, and anyone could turn up. These kids—guys—showed up and were hurling stuff at us on stage while we were dancing. My band was predominantly black, they were huge—street-fighters—and they weren't standing for that kind of thing and jumped down and kicked the shit into them. We got arrested, but luckily the audience defended our actions, and it was dropped. Ironically, it was a group from an [ethnic] minority that was throwing the stuff and [shouting the racist rants]. I thought, you guys are in a minority and complain about the Germans' racism towards you, and yet you're calling us something? There's always jealousy in these situations.

"I also remember a funny story. I was in Munich, in the center of the city, and we did a performance. I used to always make jokes with the audience and integrate broken English and German. I said something like, 'Well we're in Munich; where's the energy, you guys? I thought you guys were beer drinkers?' They all started cheering and saying something. Then someone held up what they called a wheat beer. It was a really big stage, and I told security to hand me that beer. I drank the whole thing all at once. I didn't know that you can't do that with wheat beer. My manager was like, 'Don't do that!' It was too late; I'd already finished it. Everyone in the audience was laughing and cheering and going crazy. We started the song, and suddenly I thought—*what the hell is going on*? In my stomach there was an eruption! Do you remember the movie 'The Exorcist?' I ran off the stage—the group carried on—and I opened my mouth and this stuff just projected out. Pure liquid. The whole audience was laughing; the band, my manager, everyone was laughing. I made a joke out of it with the audience, we carried on and did the next song, but everyone kept holding up beers for me to try it again!"

What inspired you to record a remake of "Revolution In Paradise" eight years later?

"In 2004, I decided to redo the song and wanted to add some real authenticity to it. No effects. It's the version of the song that means the most to me. I went to Jamaica and worked with Damian and Stephen Marley, Sly Dunbar and Robbie Shakespeare, and remade the song in Bob Marley's actual home, one of his homes. I felt like a manufactured kind of artist, you know? I was glad for that, if you know what I mean, but I wanted to put my own spin on it this time. I made a second song as well, 'Trench Town,' and recording these songs was all a highpoint in my career."

Rhythm Of The Night Summermix (Compilation CD) - Various (2002), Universal/Polystar (G)
Producers: Various

Better have potholders to pick up this red hot two-CD compilation album, a big, fat super high energy summer music heatwave! One disc plays like a crazy night at a tropical club, with the SWG DJ Team (Andreas Peine [aka DJ Deep] and Uwe Jagusch) sequencing a carefully curated, non-stop assortment of period and vintage pop/dance hits, including Gipsy Kings' "Bamboléo," Vengaboys' "Megamix: Boom, Boom, Boom, Boom!!," DJ Sammy's "Sunlight," Chocolate's "Ritmo De La Noche," "Cuba" by The Gibson Brothers, "No Tengo Dinero" by Righeira, and more. The other disc features individual single versions of party jams that include Sophie Ellis Bextor's "Murder On The Dancefloor" and The Partynator & Sharon Williams' "(I've Had) The Time Of My Life." Summer-themed compilation albums are usually just predictable hits thrown together, and they serve their purpose, but this one was creatively assembled by people who seemed to really want to capture the power of a hot resort holiday. They understood the connection of pop music to the season and created, in audio, a perfect summer getaway world. If this CD happens to be in your collection, it's proof you really *can* have it all.

Rio - Duran Duran (1982), EMI/Capitol (UK)
Producer: Colin Thurston

A girl named Rio danced on the sand a few decades ago, and we never forgot her. The song, taken from the revered UK band's sophomore album, *Rio*, was the type of sleek, accessible new wave sound that was sweeping the US and Britain at the time, and the five-member band (Simon Le Bon, John Taylor, Andy Taylor, Nick Rhodes) was at the forefront of this movement. Much like their previous breakthrough single, "Hungry Like The Wolf," "Rio" is an example of terrific storytelling in a high-energy setting, visually enhanced by a playful video filmed in Antigua and set on a yacht that traverses the

Caribbean. "It's pure bliss, it's pure pleasure, and there's just optimism," Annie Zaleski, author of "Rio" (a book celebrating the Birmingham band's album) said in an interview with David Chiu for *Forbes* online ("Duran Duran's Classic 'Rio' Album Gets The Royal Treatment In New Book," May 10, 2021). "It's one of those songs you hear and you just wanna dance. It's very inspiring if you're kind of in the doldrums. You hear that song and you're like: 'I can do this.'" Amen!

Ritmo De La Noche - Chocolate (1990), Teldec (G)
Rhythm of the night
Producers: Matiz, AC16

The opening piano riff samples the well-trodden notes of Peter Allen's "I Go To Rio," but thereafter we are taken into richly fluid, summery, captivatingly Latin, disco and house music territory. With vocals by Verona, it's a seductive dance track, short on lyrics but big on atmosphere and an infectious Brazilian samba beat. *Music & Media* called Chocolate "the *Fiesta Tropical* of the German dance scene" (March 2, 1991). Several songwriters/composers are credited on track—Bela Lagonda, Jeff Wycombe, Harry Castioni and AC Beat (who was also the co-producer of the track, better known as Alex Christensen of U96's "Das Boot" fame)—and so irresistible was their composition that the song was almost immediately covered by a slew of other artists and groups. While Chocolate went top 30 in Germany (and would issue many remix versions of their hit), the group Lorca reached *Music & Media*'s Eurochart Top 100 Singles survey thanks to success in Belgium. It was also covered by German groups Ibiza Sunrise and Mystic, and, according to *Music & Media*'s Robert Lyng, spotlighting German music talent on October 19, 1990, at least 14 cover versions had been made of "Ritmo De La Noche" at the time. A lot more by now. Don't let that overwhelm you. I'd argue you can play *any* variation of this song into your earbuds (they all sound remarkably alike), and it will wash over you like the swirling waters of a resort hot tub—that's the stuff!

Rock Lobster - The B-52's (1978), Warner (US)
Producer: Chris Blackwell

Some seriously hefty '60s pool party energy, right here! But it isn't all about nostalgia. Keith Strickland, brother and sister Cindy and Ricky Wilson, Fred Schneider and Kate Pierson's debut single is an irresistible slice of off-the-wall electro-punk, pop and new wave vivacity, with a healthy dose of kitschy sci-fi to make it even more fun. Word of mouth was largely responsible for breaking the campy "Rock Lobster" track as the band, originally from Athens, Georgia, became the rage of New York's late '70s club scene. The song quickly became a summer anthem, a quirky and rebellious dance rock alternative to the period's disco music. *Rolling Stone* called it "...a psychedelic beach rocker for the ages" in their 2020 online list of the "Best Summer Songs of All Time" and the publication ranked it 300 in their 2021 list of "500 Greatest Songs of All Time." And it goes great with matching towels.

(L) B-52's circa 1980, Warner Bros. (press still).

Rockaway Beach - Ramones (1977), Sire (US)
Producers: Tony Bongiovi, T. Erdelyi

Said to have been inspired by the actual Rockaway Beach in Rockaway, Queens, a borough of NYC, this frantic head-shaker is cooked like a lobster in a breathless two-minute flash. However, the band's biggest commercial hit ever gets its point across very efficiently. Famous for its hyper-speed rhythm guitar work, it's a punk rock/pop jam that celebrates hot concrete and making a getaway to the city's legendary summer shore line. The band (none of whom looked liked they ever saw a lick of sunlight) first formed in a neighborhood of New York's Forest Hills, where this book was partially written, so summer vibes must still linger in the air here. For sure there is *something* in the air here.

Run To The Sun - Erasure (1994), Mute (UK)
Producer: Martyn Ware

Frantic, spinning electro-dance much in the style of the duo's '80s synth-pop hits, this one's crackling with introspective lyrics about self-awareness that would seem a touch sorrowful were it not for all that relentless energy. On July 30, 1994, the song was *Cash Box*'s Pick of the Week, with the publication saying, "Vince Clark flicks his snappy keyboard strings throughout, while Andy Bell's songbird voice and longing-for-thou lyrics shoot right for the heart." Okay, better freshen your drink and reapply your sunscreen, because the S section is next, and it's got about a week's vacation worth of songs with a "summer" title! But we'll start off with a few sailing lessons first.

S

Sail Away - Juliane Werding (1999), WEA (G)
Producer: Andreas Bärtels

The gentle voice of Ms. Werding, a veteran pop/rock/schlager singer in Germany, encourages us to toss away our cell phones and indulge in the luxury of forgetting our passwords and what day of the week it is as our private vessel sails us to warm southern destinations. Consider it done! Very Enya-like in its beautifully poetic message and smoothly rolling, deliciously escapist musical arrangement. It has much the same effect as Christopher Cross' "Sailing," and even with its intriguing mix of English and

German lyrics, its uncomplicated, take-a-deep-breath tenderness registers easily. Included on the artist's "Alles Kann Passiern" (*Anything can happen*) maxi-single. All day for this track! But don't take off your lifejacket, we've got a few more boat excursions on our schedule.

Sailing - Christopher Cross (1980), Warner (US)
Producer: Michael Omartian

The amazing artistry often at the core of commercial pop music sometimes allows for the creation of melodies and lyrics that can generate sensations in our hearts and minds that feel every bit as vivid and real as anything we experience in life. With "Sailing," is it possible Mr. Cross gave us such an intensely tranquil feeling of drifting on a calm sea that it perhaps surpasses the real thing? Let's say he came mighty close! The song hit #1 on the *Billboard* Hot 100 chart on August 30, 1980, and with that achievement the relatively unknown singer/songwriter quickly became a mega pop star, winning Grammys for "Sailing" as Best Record and Best Song. On June 7, 1980, *Cash Box* described the enchanting tune as, "Riding an easy rhythmic current of bell chimes, woodblock and maracas, coupled with breezy guitar and piano. A pop/adult contemporary dream." Earlier in the year, they called Cross "one of the brightest hopes of 1980." Feeling tense or agitated while stuck in traffic or with your flight to paradise delayed for three hours at the airport? Get this track on your buds and all will be right with the world again.

Sailing On The Seven Seas - OMD (1991), Virgin (UK)
Producers: OMD

Orchestral Manoeuvres In The Dark blend an austere but irresistible dance/pop melody with dark, gothic synthesizers as if they were riding the new wave of the early '80s rather than steering into the eclectic '90s. Still, the group runs a tight ship, and the track's steady as she goes momentum is strong and determined for the duration of this diverting nautical journey. *Music & Media* ranked it a top 20 single across Europe in the early summer, and the LP *Sugar Tax,* from which it was lifted, reached the top 15 on their albums chart. The B-side of the maxi-single offers a trippy/dubby electro-beat variation of the song featuring whispery female vocals called "Floating On The Seven Seas" that takes one into even murkier waters.

Samba De Janeiro - Bellini (1997), Virgin (G)
Producers: Bellini Brothers

Another *Music & Media* top 10 pop hit across Europe during the summer of '97 bursting with a party vibe and a relentless Latin meets house beat. Bellini started out as a five-member group based in Germany with members from a variety of countries, including Brazil, Turkey and Thailand. Developed by Gottfried Engels and Ramon Zenker (Bellini Brothers), the song takes its core from Airto Moreira's Latin jazz composition "Tombo In 7/4" from 1974, and fuses it with a club beat and Brazilian rhythms.

Sandy Beaches - Delbert McClinton (1981), Capitol (US)
Producers: Barry Beckett, Muscle Shoals Rhythm Section

Delbert wants to make love to his special woman, and getting busy on a sandy beach seems as good a spot as any in this soft rock popper. No wonder they invented a "Sex on the Beach" cocktail. Said *Cash Box* in a November 7, 1981 review, "As you might imagine from the title, McClinton's newest conjures up images of dreamy days and nights in an idyllic coastal setting." Heads up, sand doesn't always mix so well with mouths and private parts.

Santa Lucia By Night - George Baker Selection (1985), CNR (NL)
Producer: Hans Bouwens

Nothing this group recorded before or after ever reached the tremendous heights of their worldwide 1975 smash hit "Paloma Blanca," which perfectly blended English pop and a melodic Dutch sing-along sound. However, the group had a number of equally pleasing modest hits, many of which captured a summer and tropical sensibility. Songs such as "Paradise Island," "Que Viva Summer Holiday," and "Santa Lucia By Night" proved especially popular with European audiences. The latter track captures the magical, romantic atmosphere of a place where you can forget your troubles and worries under starlit evening skies.

São Paulo - Chic (1977), Atlantic (US)
Producers: Bernard Edwards, Nile Rodgers, Kenny Lehman

Although its liquid piano work might give it away, few may recognize this as a Chic track. It's an epic instrumental with a wonderfully experimental jazzy tone, bright, uplifting and with a bit of a funk vibe. Somewhat distant from the familiar strings and groove sound Chic delivered so famously with their better known disco classics, "São Paulo" is a magnificent sonic adventure, as if you've taken a detour off an arduous path and you suddenly discover a heavenly, tranquil beach that's waiting there just for you. Another brilliant track from Chic's self-titled debut album, which included the disco anthem "Dance, Dance, Dance (Yowsah, Yowsah, Yowsah)."

Sausalito Summernight - Diesel (1981) Regency (US)
Producer: Pim Koopman

A foot stompin', upbeat, wry pop/rocker about saving the airfare and driving one summer to Frisco in a Rambler, blowing a gasket, and a bunch of other complications that happen along the way. A sizzling guitar solo and clever storytelling make this warm weather road trip an absorbing little excursion. A *Cash Box* US top 30 pop hit. Next time, consider a Triple-A membership.

Sea, The - Morcheeba (1998), Indochina (UK
Producers: Morcheeba, Pete Norris

Morcheeba is an English trio—brothers Paula and Ross Godfrey and Skye Edwards—known for a generally lazy groove and trip-hop sound. The group takes a pop-oriented approach here andthere on their appropriately named album, *Big Calm*, which reportedly sold more than a million copies. An exceptional moment from the LP, "The Sea" is a gentle but powerful down-tempo guitar and electronic swayer, dreamily drifting in a swirl of summer tranquility. You can almost smell the sweet ocean air surrounding it. In an article by Paul Sexton for *Music & Media* (September 2, 2000) regarding a later album release, Paul Godfrey was reported to have said, "However hard you try and be arty and intelligent, you really just want a record out that everyone can hear in the sunshine." You certainly can feel those sunbeams with "The Sea," and it's unquestionably one of the most evocative beach songs discussed in this book.

Sea Sex And Sun - Serge Gainsbourg (1978), Philips (F)
Producer: Phonogram/Philippe Lerichomme

Everything comes in threes. This vintage and highly seductive disco track from the versatile Paris-born singer/songwriter and actor may best be compared to, stylistically, Donna Summer's come-hither "Down Deep Inside (Theme From 'The Deep')." It seems Gainsbourg is whispering to a very young, attractive woman that, as a Frenchman, he finds her very appealing. I can smell the Drakkar Noir in the air. There's no beating around the bush here, so to speak, and that's presumably where the sea, sex and sun theme comes in, since all three tend to get the blood pumping. Location, location, location!

Seaside Week End - Antena (1985), Les Disques Du Crépuscule (F)
Producer: Martin Hayles

With an electronic jazz/dance sound highly reminiscent of both Sade and Swing Out Sister, vocalist Isabelle Powaga takes us on a playful getaway accentuated by a fluttering piano and a light Latin rhythm. You may want to stay an extra day and sea more. Again, location is everything.

Second Summer Of Love, The - Danny Wilson (1989), Virgin (UK)
Producers: Danny Wilson, Fred Defy

I guess the first wasn't worthy of a song. A zippy pop/rocker that's all about *love, love, love*. The track was a top 30 hit in the UK and popular in Italy. The Scottish band had a summer hit in the US with "Mary's Prayer" a few years earlier and toured with Simply Red. Betty Page at *Record Mirror* called it "A jolly romp of a pub rock-folk singalong..." on June 10, 1989.

September - Earth, Wind & Fire (1978), ARC/Columbia/CBS (US)
Producer: Maurice White

Summer usually ends in the Northern Hemisphere around September 22nd or 23rd, and since this song references the date September 21st, it squeaks in just under the wire as a brilliant "Boogie Wonderland"-like farewell to the season. "This track has a bright, optimistic arrangement of funky punctuating rhythm guitars, brassy horns, high flying strings and a pleasant mix of falsetto voices," said *Record World* on November 18, 1978. In 2021, *Rolling Stone* ranked the song 65th among their "500 Greatest Songs of All Time." The remix team of Phats & Small revisited the track in 1999, respectfully reformulating the energy of the original to suit turn-of-the-century styles, returning the song to the European pop charts as a result. It will surely keep autumn at a distance.

Seven Days In Sunny June - Jamiroquai (2005), Sony/BMG (UK)
Producer: Mike Spencer

The London-based Jamiroquai band have been delivering a broad range of upbeat music since the early '90s. Their sound is part soul, disco, acid-jazz, and, really, just about anything that inspires them. Led by the soothing yet commanding voice of Jay Kay, "Seven Days In June" reached the top 20 on the British pop chart, weaving a story of rejection (the old "being friends too long" bomb drop). But ultimately, the song feels rather uplifting, especially when the "Ashley Beedle Heavy Disco Vocal Mix" kicks in on the dance floor.

Sex On The Beach - T-Spoon (1997), Alabianca (NL)
Producers: Serge Ramaekers, Dominic Sas

If Disney produced an R-rated pop song with a PG-13 radio edit, it might sound something like this single. Musically, this Dutch production features predictable female vocalizing in a mid-tempo setting, a kind of "Coco Jamboo" meets "The Sign," with some male ragga-pop rhyming about girls getting frisky. In addition to some helpful dance move suggestions illustrated on the CD jacket to ensure you get lucky, it warns: "Do it safe!" Including a condom might have been more proactive. I guess it's summertime and the livin' is sleazy. Get a room!

Shark Attack - Posh (1996), BMG Eurodisc (UK)
Producer: Richard Evans

Real talk, chum—you're *definitely* gonna need a bigger boat! You don't need to be hammer-headed to bite into this thrilling, punky, danceable synth-pop sharknado with an indie rock edge. The jawsome three-person British group Posh (James Dearlove, Pippa Brooks and Richard Evans) cleverly explore shiny white teeth and bright red water metaphors, and all the warning flags are up. I'm not pulling your leg when I say there's something sinister going on below the surface of this wonderfully murky musical brine, so try not to thrash about too much as this biting number foul hooks you hard. Fin.

Shores Of The Mediterranean Sea- Friends of Carlotta (1994), Hansa (G)
Producers: Lutz Fahrenkrog-Petersen, Peter Wagner

This seven-member German band got their single released through the sponsorship of Paul McCartney and the Liverpool Institute For Performing Arts, which offered opportunities for young talent at the time. Catchy, upbeat rock, highly danceable, very summery—and choosing a Mediterranean focus makes it seasonally ideal.

Singin' In The Rain - Taco (1982), RCA (G)
Producer: David Parker

Spit take! Hold up now, what? While it might seem highly unlikely that an '80s dance mix of a really old Hollywood classic tune about stormy weather would qualify as a noteworthy hot summer jam, it most certainly does. In the opening seconds of Taco's clever, rollicking take on the optimistic song (most famously performed by Gene Kelly in the 1952 film musical of the same name), the singer laments having traveled thousands of miles to a tropical destination on holiday, only to be disappointed by downpours from Mother Nature. Typical tropical, as he says! Remember—a rainy vacation day beats a sunny work day. From the same album, *After Eight*, that included the artist's earlier worldwide smash, "Puttin' On The Ritz."

Commentary from Taco Ockerse:

"When a young singer *dares* to even touch an American classic like 'Singin' In The Rain,' he has to bring his own attitude to it. Everybody knows this song, so if you're going to try your hand at it, you better find a whole new approach. With our version, people didn't have a clue what was coming after that introduction about being on a holiday and stuck with bad weather. I was going for that crooner vibe from the 1930s. That was the whole fun of it. We borrowed that kind of reggae beat at the opening from the intro to Stevie Wonder's 'Master Blaster (Jammin').' You know, speaking of 'Singin' In the Rain,' I did a show tour once on a big cruise ship like 'The Love Boat' in the Caribbean, which was hilarious. I remember we either had intense sunshine, a lot of rain, or a hurricane."

*[See also: **Mageña - Taco**.]*

Sippin' On Bacardi Rum / Sittin' In The Summer Sun - Groove Connection / The Natural Mind (1995), RCA (N/G)
Producer: John Groves

Time flies when you're having rum! The unbranded roots pop version featuring an acoustic guitar, "Sittin' In The Summer Sun," is paired with the reggae/pop/steel drum styled "Sippin' On Bacardi Rum" version, which emphasizes the liquor manufacturer's promotional lyrics. If this sounds familiar, flip back a few pages to "Bacardi Feeling (Summer Dreamin')" by Kate Yanai. The song is offered in two interpretations sung separately by anonymous vocalists, one a very soulful male singer (Groove Connection) the other by a female vocalist (The Natural Mind, sounding a bit like, you guessed it, Kate). Yep, the Bacardi marketing folks, whose rum has been promoted as "a taste of the Caribbean," once again seek to fuse pop music with tropical holiday getaways and getting a buzz on, and they do it quite effectively. The tracks are undeniably catchy and deliciously laid back, and the maxi-single jacket contains recipes for a Bacardi Cola and a Bacardi Orange Daiquiri in case all this summery propaganda makes you thirsty. Hook your friends up.

Slingshot - Michael Henderson (1981), Buddha (US)
Producer: Michael Henderson

If we can have a young lady parading around in an "Itsy Bitsy Teeny Weeny Yellow Polka Dot Bikini," it's only fair we allow youthful and lean bassist/singer Michael Henderson from 1981 to strip down to a thong on a tropical beach for the cover photo of his *Slingshot* LP. John Pinderhughes took the photo, the same photographer who lensed that memorable cover shot for Roberta Flack's *Blue Lights In The Basement* album. But I digress—what about the song "Slingshot?" It's a crazy little funk jam something akin to Little Richard meets Rick James meets Parliament-Funkadelic. In an album that's otherwise relatively tame, middle of the road soul music, there's nothing subtle about this track, which stands out like a banana hammock on a beach filled with board shorts. Don't be shy, try it on and see how it fits you. Then you can really soak up the sun.

Soak Up The Sun - Sheryl Crow (2002), A&M (US)
Producers: Sheryl Crow, Jeff Trott

Girls just wanna have sun! Evocative summer guitar pop/rock with a neat electronics flair, a hint of country twang, a cool pulse and a catchy chorus. It adds up to an appealing summer escape anthem, though not everyone feels that way. At drownedinsound.com, Raziq Rauf rated "Soak Up The Sun" a four out 10, saying, "That sexy voice, the one that initially drew me to her, is still apparent but is lacking the gloom and reality of her earlier work. She's just too goddamn happy!" (April 10, 2002). Well, even the sun can't please everyone. Ms. Crow peaked at #17 on the *Billboard* Hot 100 chart on July 20, 2002, and claimed the #1 spot on its dance chart.

Soca Dance (1989) / Soca City (1990) - Charles D. Lewis, Polydor/Baxter (F/G)
Producer: Gary Gordon

Mr. Lewis tells us that if we're feeling down and out, the spicy rhythm of soca is the remedy. For a time it seems soca-pop hybrids became the opioid of summer hit music across Europe. "Soca Dance" hit the #5 spot in *Music & Media*'s August 25, 1990, Eurochart Hot 100 Singles survey, inspiring Polygram to take out a full page ad in that issue declaring Lewis' single had sold over half a million copies in France alone. Later, on January 12, 1991, the publication described his follow-up "Soca City" single as, "more festive music from Trinidad adapted to Western standards: synthesizers, a fast talking jock in the bridge and the occasional heavy guitar lick." The artist carried the general theme over to a number of other follow-up singles, including "Life Is Beautiful," and "Another Friday Night."

Soca Party Sur La Plage - La Compagnie Créole (1986), Carrere
(F) *Soca party on the beach*
Producer: Daniel Vangarde

A popular quintet from French Guiana and the French West Indies mixes in a bit of the English language as they shell-abrate hitting the beach in Trinidad when their work is done, making noise and dancing to the rhythm of congas. It is classified as zouk music (and it's also a dance style), a musical movement where disco sounds meet Caribbean rhythms. It can be safely conjectured that "zouk" dance bands (forming in the '80s and characterized by their strong, beat-driven rhythms and vibrant horns—such as La Compagnie Créole, Kassav' and Zouk Machine—blending in Caribbean, African and North American music styles) are responsible for some of the most amplified feel-good summer sounds on the planet. Here we have proof of that with music perfectly supporting the act of cutting loose.

Soleil - Kassav' (1988), Epic (F) *Sun*
Producer: Jacob Desvarieux

The zouk sound, a music style pioneered by this French Caribbean group, most often in a recorded pop music setting and especially popular in France, is both highly danceable, theatrical and exotic, and it never sounded better or more accessible than it does here. Striking horn stabs heighten a familiar Latin beat. *Music & Media* was absolutely on point to call the remixed version of the track "utterly contagious" in an August 20, 1988, review. It's like a vaccine for winter blues.

Soleil - Madeleine Lang (1990), RCA (G) *Sun*
Producers: The Feldhahn Brothers

A superior, upbeat electro-pop single with that late '80s feel about the sun and its positive effects on well-being, sung by 25-year-old Lang and released in May of 1990. She was regarded as one of Germany's top back-up singers, and she's worked with a bevy of famous artists, including Kid Creole And The Coconuts, Germany's Westernhagen, Peter Maffay and Roland Kaiser. Though she's blessed with a distinctive and powerful set of pipes, she never had a big hit single of her own, and "Soleil," unfortunately—because it's quite good—ultimately failed to make an impression. Madeleine is also the daughter of Werner Lang, who co-wrote/arranged much of Taco's *After Eight* album and his hit, "Puttin' On The Ritz." Miss Lang was also a back-up singer on that project, as well.

Some Like It Hot And The Heat Is On - The Power Station (1985) Capitol (US)
Producer: Bernard Edwards

It's said that with great power comes great responsibility, and Robert Palmer, John Taylor, Tony Thompson, Andy Taylor and Bernard Edwards were more than up to handling all of it. This debut dance track from the ensemble is the perfect melding of Palmer and Duran Duran's (Andy and John) persuasive pop focus, Thompson's life-giving drum playing and the flexing of Edwards' funk muscles. Caution: Palmer's take charge vocals and that unceasing beat easily take up residence in one's brain and linger there longer than a New Yorker in an Orlando time share. On March 16, 1985, *Cash Box* called it, "A crossover single made in heaven."

Someone Somewhere (In Summertime) - Simple Minds (1982), Virgin (UK)
Producer: Peter Walsh

Though this powerful and melancholy synth-pop/new wave track predates the Scottish group's stupendously evocative hit "Don't You (Forget About Me)" from "The Breakfast Club" 1985 film soundtrack, it has much the same mood and energy. Lead vocalist Jim Kerr would sound thoughtful if he was reading a tax return, let alone singing these introspective lyrics about love searching over the striking notes hit by electric guitarist Charlie Burchill. Soul-stirring.

Sommersonne - Pitt (1997), Frequenz/BMG (G) *Summer sun*
Producer: Peter Prestel

A one-off summer pop song linked to the marketing of Condor, a German charter airline based in Frankfurt. Pitt's gritty rock-style vocals, a crisp, highly danceable beat, and a catchy acoustic guitar-fused melody elevate this higher than one might expect, even at an airport. "Sommersonne" gives you wings!

So Schmeckt Der Sommer! - Edward Reekers (1995), Polydor (G)

The taste of summer

Producer not indicated.

Langnese Ice Cream in Germany turned their summer taste treat into an emotional experience with this touching rock/pop song featured in their television advertising and later released as a single. The joy of being young in the summertime is conveyed with affecting sincerity by Reekers, giving the song a legitimacy it likely would not have otherwise attained. The tune was also reimagined in an Italian dance style ("Gusto d'estate") with gelato in mind by the artist Giacomo in 1997 and Partynator revved up the energy in 2003. Gobble it up!

Souvenirs - Voyage (1978), T.K. Records/Marlin/Sirocco (F/US)
Producer: Roger Tokarz

Voyage is gonna give it to ya—a dance-till-the-sun-comes-up classic! Flourishing, engagingly orchestrated disco music, the song builds to a magnificent crescendo that transports the listener/dancer to a dreamlike place that feels positively otherworldly. Sylvia Mason, lead singer of the France-based group for this project, lends a soulful, multi-cultural, and compelling quality to the track, giving the production even more significant depth. Lyrically, the essence of "Souvenirs" is similar to that of Desireless' multi-national French hit "Voyage Voyage" in its poetic quest to discover destinations far away, and musically it's reminiscent of "Hills Of Katmandu" by Tantra. A #1 *Billboard* disco hit in the US, picked up and promoted by Ray Caviano for T.K. Records at the time, the track remains, without doubt, one of the genre's finest moments. Also noteworthy was the similarly themed single "Let's Fly Away" from the group's *Fly Away* set, the same album that yielded "Souvenirs." If the world was a big glitter ball, "Souvenirs" would be making it spin like a top.

Commentary from Ray Caviano:

"I was working at T.K. Records, a label that was big with the R&B sound in disco. They had T-Connection ('Do What You Wanna Do'), Peter Brown ('Dance With Me'), etc. I was [label president/co-owner] Henry Stone's man in New York at the time. In the clubs, 12 West, Flamingo, and on Fire Island, they were going for that energetic, upbeat peak sound. I had heard about Voyage as an import record. It was made in France and wasn't out in America. I contacted the producer, Roger Tokarz, and told him I was very interested in the record, and we did the deal. I would say that 'Souvenirs' is probably—boy it's hard to say—I would say it's in my top three of those records I signed. I think it was #1 for seven weeks on the club charts. That was a new sound for T.K. I wanted T.K. to be competitive with Casablanca and have that eurodisco sound. People were astounded that funky T.K. Records would put out Voyage."

Spanish Harlem - Mo (1988), EMI/Columbia (A)
Producer: Günter Mokesch

Hear me out. Austrian vocalist Günter "Mo" Mokesch respectfully takes the Jerry Leiber/Phil Spector evergreen (about a rose growing through the concrete of a city street where no sunlight can reach it) and transforms it into an affecting Latin/calypso flavored synth-pop experience, punctuated by dreamy horns and strings. The production has the vibe of the late '80s, gloriously tempered with the warmth of the late afternoon sun, and it's sung with a cool kind of detached romanticism. A pleasure. Is it Miss Aretha or Ben E. King? Of course not, but, come on, give the guy a break. He went to all the trouble of leaving Austria to film portions of the video in Miami and New York.

Stars De La Pub (L'Avion Décolle Sur Les Champs Elysées...) - Movie Music (1982), Philips (F) *Stars of the pub (The plane takes off on the Champs Elysées ...)*
Producer: D. Blanc-Francard

Featured in the French movie drama "Été 85" (*Summer Of '85*, based on the novel "Dance On My Grave" by Aidan Chambers), an official selection from the 2020 Festival De Cannes written and directed by François Ozon. This wonderfully melodic electronic new wave/disco track, a pristine example of vintage (not to mention utterly quirky) French '80s synth-pop, conjures up the excitement and optimism of summer with its Marc Almond-esque vocals and mixed-up lyrics reflecting the unbridled enthusiasm of young love. The effect was already burned into this song's grooves decades ago, but becomes enhanced by its contribution to this film's bittersweet story of friendship and love between two teenage boys at a seaside resort in Normandy. The film has been compared to the 2017 Italian movie "Chiamami col tuo nome" (US title, "Call Me By My Name"). "Stars De La Pub" by Movie Music also proves one can chew gum and dance at the same time.

Scene from the 2020 French film "Été 85" (Summer Of '85), Music Box Films.

Steal My Sunshine - Len (1999), Columbia (US)
Producer: Mumble C

Rolling Stone included the song in their online list of "Best Summer Songs of All Time" (May 20, 2020), saying, "Marc and Sharon Costanzo [Len] were thinking of the Human League's summer-of-'82 smash 'Don't You Want Me' when they wrote this loopy tune about sippin' slurpy treats, fryin' on a bench slide in the park and teenage romance gone weird…" The song is also noteworthy for incorporating the rhythm track of The Andrea True

Connection's summer of '76 disco classic, "More, More, More," composed by Gregg Diamond. It's like a slice of very random and delectable nothingness.

Stir It Up - Haddaway (1993), Arista (US/G)
Producers: Dee Dee Halligan, Junior Torello

By 1993, Trinidad-born Nestor Haddaway was a staple on dance floors and singing distinctively high-energy house music with a European slant. So it was a bit of a surprise when he decided to slow it down and tackle Bob Marley's groovin' reggae evergreen—and he doesn't disappoint. Haddy's voice is strong, and the track's arrangement is oozing with summer appeal. It has a simple island vibe and a dash of steel drums, but enough electronic embellishments to make it '90s hip. Just in case all that didn't catch on, the flip side offered the hot club-ready track "Rock My Heart." *Oh, snap!*

Streets Of Miami, The / Summer Holiday* - First Patrol Ft. Napoleon / *Napoleon And Friends (1987), ZYX (G)
Producers: First Patrol, Walfried Böcker / *H.W. Grossmann, * T. Gesell, *Walfried Böcker

"Streets Of Miami" is a fun, sugary, pop/rap/dance homage to "Miami Vice" and its chief characters, Sonny and Rico, ransacking the pop hits of the day and pinning the vibe of Jan Hammer's "Miami Vice Theme" and the chorus of Falco's "The Sound Of Music" for its appealing hook. There's nothing enigmatic going on here (its catchy tongue-in-cheek top 40 all the way), and the track does emphasize nose candy, beach parties, and girls going crazy—all of which sounds a lot like Miami! Rapper Napoleon Hatten (and friends) had another beach-themed release in 1987 titled "Summer Holiday." Following the same formula as "Streets," the artist performs more dance/pop/rap, this time with a track that is suspiciously similar to Madonna's "Holiday."

Suddenly Last Summer - The Motels (1983), Capitol (N/US)
Producer: Val Garay

The sensual, yearning voice of Martha Davis makes this atmospheric, haunting power rock ballad an unforgettable journey into introspection and melancholia, triggered by that memory of a certain summer where life completely changes. Martha just nails it. The single reached the top 10 of *Cash Box*'s Hot 100 pop singles chart in the fall of '83. Speaking of motels, you may need a Holiday Inn to rest up at before sifting through the following monster traffic jam of songs that kick off their titles with the word "summer."

Summer - War (1976), United Artists (US)
Producers: Jerry Goldstein, Lonnie Jordan, Howard Scott

The funk group from Southern California offers a melodic, groovy street jam that rolls along at just the right easy-going pace for a hot, humid day. It's not taking you to any place glamorous, but Santa Monica's Malibu Beach and Atlantic City will do nicely. The seasonally perfect atmosphere, vaguely reminiscent of "Up On the Roof," is polished and real. A big seller and *Billboard* top 10 pop hit in the summer of '76.

Summer, The - ATB (2000), Kontor (G)
Producer: André Tanneberger

André "ATB" Tanneberger has had more than his share of summer hits. "9 PM (Till I Come)" springs to mind, his smash Spanish guitar-drenched debut single that reportedly sold over 1.5 million copies. But here the artist/producer is more deliberate, making a direct reference to the season and capturing the sensation of it with his electro-expertise. This trippy number glided onto the *Music & Media* Hot 100 Singles chart in July of 2000 and achieved a top 10 ranking on the publication's European Dance Traxx survey. Fueled by smash-level popularity in Scandinavia and a few other countries, it may coast on a catchy melody and simple, whispery vocals, but it delivers a powerful summer punch that sneaks up on you. The track, especially in its "Ibiza Influence Mix," captures the emerging EDM sound of the new century perfectly, and no doubt it had Millennials jumping the night away at all the southern European summer hot spots.

Summer Babe (Winter Version) - Pavement (1992), Matador (US)
Producer: Treble Kicker Music

If the dry sting of piercing, scratching guitars and the grungy yet melancholy sound of this indie meets art rock jam (a variation of an earlier 7-inch single recorded by the band) evokes a summer sensation in you, you've no doubt got a taste for vintage '90s underground California alternative rock at its most primal. From the album *Slanted And Enchanted,* it has an energy that is raw and gritty, pushing its way to the center from somewhere way on the far side of the pop spectrum and throbbing like a sore thumb among most of the songs in this book. It's hot, prickly, gets under your skin, and it somehow feels right. It won't take long to feel its effect.

Summer Breeze - Nicki Richards (1991), Atlantic (US)
Producers: Ronin Inc.

The radiant Ms. Richards throws down with her winning reinvention of the Seals & Crofts classic, giving it such a soulful, heartfelt rendition you're sure to get chills listening to the song on even the hottest of summer days. With a dazzling remix by Frankie Knuckles, the transformation of this normally easy going standard into such a muscular and riveting house experience feels completely natural, totally exciting and quite genuinely magnificent. Talk about breathing new life into an old song. Like a hot dog in summer… just relish it.

Summer Breeze / Tequila - A.L.T. & The Lost Civilization (1992), Atco (US)
Producers: Mike Greene, Geoff Rios

Picture cruisin' with the top down in the city, the warm air blowin' on a hot day in June, honnies on the street lookin' fine, and a super cool soul jam playing on the radio. If that scene turns it up for you, you'll want to jump on "Breeze," a very potent, deep grooved hip-hop boiler. On the party tip, this crew's dope rendition of "Tequila," a top 50 *Billboard* pop hit, is one of the most infectious rap salutes to summer swigging ever—but remember, always enjoy the sauce responsibly! A.L.T. (French-Mexican Alvin Lowell

Trivette) also contributed to the Latin Alliance's crackling remake of the War hit "Low Rider (On The Boulevard)" in 1991.

Summer Dance - The Ritchie Family (1977), Marlin (US)
Producer: Jacques Morali

A rousing disco number that is oddly soothing at the same time, thanks in large part to The Ritchie Family trio's silky vocal work. Taken from their *African Queens* album, it spent three weeks at the #1 spot on *Billboard*'s disco chart in combination with two other cuts from the set, "Quiet Village" and the album's title track. *Cash Box* injected some drama into a review of the LP on July 9, 1977, saying, "Don't expect those root sounds—thick drum talk that trembles the rainforest, striking fear into the hearts of timid missionaries that should have stayed home. This is disco gone African in name only."

Commentary from (original group member)
Cheryl Mason-Dorman:

"'Summer Dance' is one of my favorite songs that we recorded. I love the orchestration, the beat, the verses, our harmonies, and the high energy it exudes. It's happy, bright, and fun, and it celebrates love and one of my favorite seasons. Unfortunately, although I thought it should have been released as a single, [composer, producer and co-writer of the song] Jacques Morali did not agree. When I asked him why not, he responded, 'It is not summer, my darling!' My response to him was, 'Well, it *will* be summer again someday!' Jacques was unmoved by my logic, however, and 'Summer Dance' was never released as a Ritchie Family single."

Cheryl's music choices for that warm weather feeling:

"The Ritchie Family song that feels like a sunny getaway to me (other than 'Summer Dance') is 'Quiet Village.' I love the sultry, lazy summer day feeling in a tropical setting that it evokes. The other song that feels like summer and a holiday getaway to me is 'Happy' by Pharrell Williams. I love this song! Although it wasn't released in the summer, it really does live up to its name and makes me happy when I hear it. It feels like a summer/all-year-round party, and I can't help singing along with it and dancing to it whenever it is played."

Summer Dreaming - Fun Brothers (2004), Andorfine (SW/G)
Producers: Stacccato, Blue Nature, Ray Knox

Energized trance with diverting female vocals and an ethereal sense of urgency. While many tracks in the EDM genre simply slap the word "summer" on their productions, this one actually delivers a connecting seasonal spirit and flavor. Is it a big standout in the very crowded club market? Not especially, but it's clean, portable and gratifyingly uplifting.

Summer Fever - Donna Summer (1976), Casablanca (US)
Producers: Giorgio Moroder, Pete Bellotte

Still singing in the sexy, whispery, high-pitched voice that characterized her spicy "Love To Love You Baby" hit the year before, Ms. Summer turns the season into a hotly sensual affair. One can sense "Last Dance" and "Hot Stuff" germinating in the background of this production, but there was still some distance to go before the artist's personality really got to radiate. Though "Summer Fever" isn't a particularly great showcase of the singer's talent (and usually gets ignored in discussions of her extensive catalog), this vintage disco track is a reasonably diverting highlight from the thematic *Four Seasons Of Love* album.

Summer Fun - Bill Summers And Summers Heat (1981), MCA (US)
Producer: Bill Summers

A lightweight and groovy percussive jam with jazzy horns, a steady funk beat and a '70s soul groove. There's an agreeable "party" break in the mix that's great for cultivating that "get down on it" vibe. Summers, based in New Orleans, was a renown instrumentalist and master of the congas, and he worked closely during his career with Herbie Hancock, Patrice Rushen, Quincy Jones, and other notables.

Summer Girls - LFO (1999), Arista (US)
Producers: Rich Cronin, Brad Young, Dow Brain

No surprise Lyte Funkie Ones, a boy band out of Massachusetts, was considered da bomb after this track reached the top three of *Billboard*'s pop singles chart late in the summer of '98 and sold millions. Its seemingly impromptu rhymes about a summer relationship flow so effortlessly, and, well, randomly, that it has an almost hypnotic effect. Callouts to New Kids On The Block, Larry Bird and, most significantly and memorably, fashionmongers Abercrombie & Fitch place the riff of this time piece firmly in that late '90s, with all the elements somehow tied together by the summer. Two members of LFO have since passed, Devin Lima in 2018 and Rich Cronin in 2010.

Summer In The City - Joe Cocker (1994), 550 Music/Capitol (G)
Producers: Chris Lord-Alge, Roger Davies

In the concrete and steel canyons of the city, summer takes on a spunky and heated new dimension. Cocker's earnest, brawny rendition is a citrusy revisit of The Lovin' Spoonful 1966 rock classic that he makes distinctly his own. Bright horns, stirring strings, fiery guitars, a lively pop arrangement and, in ever so fleeting moments, a barely discernible hint of the Caribbean make this a very memorable track that travels far beyond the boundaries of its familiar roots. Cocker's gritty but elegant version debuted on *Music & Media*'s Eurochart Hot 100 Singles survey in late June of '94 and was top 25 by the end of August. It was supported by a terrifically edited black and white video with a "youth meets experience" vibe that is highly engaging. From his *Have A Little Faith* album, recorded in L.A. and a sizable chart hit in Europe and the UK. Our loss—Joe departed this world in 2014.

Summer In The Street - Carrie Lucas (1984), MCA (US)
Producer: Stephen Shockley

Miss Lucas is certainly responsible for creating one of the earliest forms of "solar energy" when she recorded a handful of hot disco hits for the Los Angeles-based Solar record label during the heyday of the genre. The beats of popular singles such as "Dance With You" and "It's Not What You Got (It's How You Use It)" resonated with dancers, as her voice carefully balanced itself in that tasty zone between pop, disco and California soul. She created possibly her most atmospheric work with "Summer In The Street," a zippy, innocent and cheerfully warm and nostalgic ode to how great those summers (and summer romances) of the past used to be. It's also right on point with the funk dynamic of dance music that was going mainstream in the early '80s.

Summer Is Calling - Aquagen (2002), Dos or Die (G)
Producers: Olaf Dieckmann, Gino Montesano

This eurodance/trance summer anthem from Germany offers compelling female vocals, positive lyrics and a rapid-fire beat mixed with a melody that is utterly soul-pleasing. It moves faster than one of those tic tac UFOs. I can't imagine a dance floor in Ibiza with any room to breathe when this track seared its way through club sound systems. Do I hear some notes from P. Lion's Italo disco classic "Happy Children" twirling around inside this mother-thumper?

Summer Is Crazy, The - Alexia (1996), DWA (I)
Producer: Robyx

No relation to "Summer Madness," though the symptoms are similar. Alexia (Alessia Aquilani) hails from La Spezia on Italy's Ligurian coastline, not far from the headquarters of her label at the time, DWA, noted for its popular house and eurodance material, including Corona's "The Rhythm Of The Night." DWA was founded by writer/producer Robyx (aka Roberto Zanetti), who previously enjoyed great success as an Italo disco star known as Savage with the '80s hit "Don't Cry Tonight." After touring with popular house rapper ICE MC, Alexia grabbed the spotlight herself with the Zanetti-produced hit single, "Me And You."

"Summer Is Crazy" (written and arranged by Roberto) was the energized eurodance smash follow-up, a sophisticated, serious-minded affair, not the palm trees and pool party tune one might expect by its title. With its simple piano melody, powerful, driving beat (which follows a haunting ballad-style intro), and its mature, appealing lyrical hook, the track spent 14 heated weeks on *Music & Media*'s Top 100 European Singles chart, fading out only with the end of summer. The song, which emotes a wistfulness to forget a summer lover, was particularly popular in Spain and reached #1 in Italy.

Commentary from Roberto Zanetti:

How did the "Summer Is Crazy" production come about?

"Summer is the best season for dance music, and at that time in Italy we had a very important TV program named 'Festivalbar.' As a producer, I had many summer hits years before, such as Double You's 'Please Don't Go,' Corona's 'The Rhythm Of The Night,' and ICE MC's "Think About The Way." The boss of 'Festivalbar' was in love with my productions, and every year he used to call me between February and March asking me which song I had to offer to him for the upcoming summer season. To do that I concentrated my production on songs to be released during summer. Alexia already had summer hits, first with ICE MC and then with her first solo single, 'Me And You.' I usually start to write a song from a chorus and a theme—that theme was summer. Usually I write all music plus the lyrics of the chorus, and that was the way I began creating 'Summer Is Crazy.' As usual I recorded a simple musical base where it was possible to record vocals. After that, with the vocals recorded, I added instruments and effects."

In some ways, "Summer Is Crazy" has a melancholy, one might even say gothic, feel. It's not the standard hands in the air summer party song. It reminds me of your own Italo disco masterpiece as Savage, "Don't Cry Tonight."

"I like to do dance music with a sad and melancholic influence inside. This is the way I did many hits in my career. I think people love to dance and sing to that kind of song."

Why do you think the track resonated so strongly with listeners, clubbers and DJs? Are there certain guidelines you follow when creating a summer song?

"You have a hit if you reach the heart of people, if you transmit to them sensations and vibrations. Alexia has a voice that touches the heart of people. Also, the video was unusual because it was so gothic, sad and dark—you do not expect that kind of video from a dance song.

"A summer song has to be easy, you have to be able to sing it when you walk, when you're in the shower, when you are in the gym, and when you dance. You need easy lyrics with words that everybody can understand, especially if English is not your audience's mother tongue."

You mentioned the video. It was a bit darker than the colorful videos one usually associates with summer songs.

"When the video was ready, many TV outlets rejected it because it was too sad, too strange. But when the song became a hit, they all started to show it on all programs. I was really involved in the creation of that video for 'Summer Is Crazy.' I asked Alexia to move her hands like I did when I was singing 'Only You' in my artist days as Savage. It was nice! A lot of Savage is in that song, in that performance!"

When creating "Summer Is Crazy," were you confident it would be a summer hit?

"Yes, it was planned to be out in summer. Summer is the season of dance songs so if you produce that style of music, you have to focus your releases in that period. The usual schedule was first single in summer, second single, end of summer, album in December, in time for Christmas.

"Alexia had her first #1 hit the year before, so I was sure that the new song could be another #1 for her. After that, Alexia was called 'the queen of summer' and for many years she had #1 singles every summer. She had a long run of summer hits for years, like 'Uh La La La,' 'Gimme Love,' 'The Music I Like,' 'Goodbye,' 'Ti Amo Ti Amo'—every summer a new hit!"

Do you recall an exceptional or exciting summer performance with Alexia in a holiday setting where you witnessed the power and connection this song has to the season?

"I remember the song was everywhere—radio, bars, clubs. Alexia was already very popular, but with 'Summer Is Crazy' she became a *star!* I remember people going crazy in Napoli, Italy, at 'Festivalbar' with 25,000 people dancing and singing along with her. You can see it on YouTube."

Do you feel like you've accomplished something special having created "Summer is Crazy" and so many other hits that people will continue to identify with summer for many years to come?

"At that time, everything was so moving so fast, [we were producing] one song, then another one. And every song became a hit. I was amused by that! Only now do I realize how big that success was in the'80s and '90s. I was lucky to find the right artists to promote my music and my artists were lucky to have found me to produce and write their hits."

I would love to include a brief list of songs that you might listen to when you want to get in a summer mood.

"There are many songs that make me think of summer. I remember Righeira's 'Vamos A La Playa,' Kaoma's 'Lambada,' 'Macarena' by Los Del Rio, Aqua's 'Barbie Girl,' Psy's 'Gangnam Style,' and 'Un, Dos, Tres, Maria' by Ricky Martin."

Is there a special location you enjoy visiting in the summer?

"It's difficult to say because I live in a summer place, Forte dei Marmi. I like to spend summer here in my place and doing a summer holiday when it is winter here. I might go to Miami, Maldives or Mexico. It's great to have a break when outside it's cold. Usually I do shows in Russia at the beginning of December when the temperature is -22° F (-30°C) and then go to the Caribbean for a holiday, where it's over 86°F (+30°C)."

Summer Is Magic, The - Playahitty (1994), Wicked & Wild Records/ZYX/Dig It (I)
Producer: Emanuele Asti

The Italian concept-group Playahitty joined an illustrious who's who of '90s pop stars that included La Bouche, C+C Music Factory and Arrested Development when it was ranked #25 on *Music & Media*'s countdown of the year's Top European Dance Radio records (December, 24, 1994). To generate its palpably warm sensation, the smash song "The Summer Is Magic" steers clear of gimmicks, offering a brisk, persistent beat, a strong vocal (uncredited on the release, but actually that of original Corona ["The Rhythm Of The Night"] singer Giovanna Bersola, aka Jenny B) and evocative lyrics that speak to the excitement of one man's summer encounter with a lovely girl. (To be more precise, it's one girl during the day and another one at night!)

The song has an enchanting quality about it, which no doubt helped propel it to #2 on Italy's pop chart in late summer of that year, as Europeans flocked to places like Capri on the Mediterranean. "The Summer Is Magic" peaked at #34 on *Music & Media*'s Eurochart Hot 100 Singles chart on September 24, 1994, after gaining immense popularity in France, Germany, the Netherlands, and other countries. Earlier that month the publication said, "Just at the moment when summer is over, this Euro dance single with the voice of Corona brings back memories of your holiday in Italy better than any photo album could ever do."

(L) Emanuele Asti today.

The track was the brainchild of a young songwriter and producer named Emanuele Asti, who partnered with Italian arranger Stefano Carrara to launch the version that became so popular. A few additional singles were released by Asti under the Playahitty moniker, while his original hit single resurfaced in numerous remixed versions and appeared on literally hundreds of summer compilation albums over the years. "The Summer Is Magic" is widely regarded as one of the all-time champion eurodance songs, and few can match its energized celebration of the season. The song's creator is the first to admit this was no accident.

Commentary from Emanuele Asti:

How did you become a part of the dance music industry?

"I made my first record when I was about 16 thanks to a friend, Alex Orlowski, who was already working in the music field as a professional audio sales representative. He would hang around the best recording studios, knew a lot of people, and had a knowledge of sound engineering. So we soon came to make a record together, which was an acidhouse music dance track. I actually loved pop songs with strong melodies and rich harmonies—the top for me were (and are) the classics performed by The Beatles, ABBA and The Police.

"But the international pop music scene was not easy for an Italian guy singing in English. There was, however, big interest at the time (also in Italy) for this new house music style, which led to new opportunities. Italian producers started to obtain success on the international market. In Milano, all labels and distributors were feverishly looking for new productions within this genre. So I took the chance to release some club-oriented house music records, which attracted me a lot because I danced to these kinds of tracks in the clubs. However, they didn't really fit with the pop-ish chorus style I liked. Then around 1993, I first listened to the newly released hits that were so-called 'eurodance' productions. It was an 'a-ha moment!' I realized that with the arrangements found in this type of dance track I could dress up some easy, sunny pop melodies—and I turned 100 percent to dance music."

Where did you find inspiration for your songs? Can you describe your songwriting process?

"Chorus melodies and the titles of songs usually come to me out of nowhere during the day or night—it's natural and it's fun! Verses, lyrics of verses, arrangements and production are quite the opposite—made of sweat, trials and experience. I had to learn everything, and it's a job! I learned to write the verse lyrics from my grandmother, Maria Hermanseder, who was a teacher and taught me her method to develop a concept after I had the first intuition of the title. Thanks to my grandmother, I did this with school essays, and

I must say it works! Concerning arrangements and music composition, I learned the basics in a music school and a lot on the job, where I'm still learning now."

Before we discuss "The Summer Is Magic," would you tell me where the unusual group name— Playahitty—came from?

"The evening before the record label pressing of the release, I still didn't have the project name yet. I wanted something that would be unequivocally associated with summer, and I wanted it to contain the word 'playa.' Since it *is* a beach song, 'playa-song' came to mind, 'playa-hit'— but 'hit' was maybe too arrogant. So I invented 'hitty'—like a little hit, a little song for the playa (beach). I knew it was absolutely *not* an easy name for people to remember, and many people advised me to change it. But I decided to keep it when I realized, on the other hand, it could be very effective because it contained two subliminal imperatives for the people, DJs and radio programmers: 'play-a-hit!' + 'play-it!'"

Well, now I'm extra intrigued to know how you came to create, produce and compose this remarkable super-hit.

"It was February, 1994. The turning point was that my father Umberto decided to help me financially to rent a little room, where I could open my first recording studio in Parma. He rightly promised me only one year of support. I knew that if nothing worked out, I would have to close the business, so it all was extremely motivating and thrilling for me!

"One night that February, I was driving to the club when this chorus melody came into my mind with the words 'you have to imagine.' In 1994, I had no cell phone, so I stopped my car. I fortunately, thank God, found a phone booth on the side of the road, and I sang the tune into the answering machine of my studio (I still have the original cassette!) This melody was perfect to be arranged in the new eurodance style, so I found the reference records for the arrangement and sound and finished the rough demo 'puzzle,' adding an original lead synth riff and a verse. Then I called my friend, 'maestro' Stefano Carrara from the Conservatory, to utilize his expert skills to put all the puzzle pieces together in a musically 100 percent accurate way, so that the verse, the chorus and the lead synth parts would perfectly combine.

"The working title was still 'you have to imagine,' but some days later I changed the first line of the chorus because I absolutely wanted the song to be a summer song. I put the words 'the summer' but didn't have the substitute rhyming word for 'imagine.' So I took a rhyming book I bought in London, and I found 'magic.' At the beginning, I didn't like the word 'magic' so much, and I looked for other words. But then I thought about the 'Magical Mystery Tour' track by The Beatles, and it was 'magic!' I wrote the lyrics of the verses about summer all in the same day. Some days later I called the singer and finished the demo version.

"Then I started my pilgrimage tour to shop the demo of the song to every record label. The fundamental person who immediately and strongly believed in the song was Fabio Carniel, owner of Disco Inn, which was the best record shop for DJs in Italy, and he also had his own dance label. So I decided to sign with his label, and I will be always thankful to Fabio for his excellent job and great intuition! With him, we planned to give the song a proper mix and vocals in the nice studio of Alex Bagnoli. Then Fabio took the master to the distributor. Also important to the launch of this project was the support of Giuliano Saglia, who took care of some promotional details with Fabio."

So you went into this with the full intention of creating a summer season anthem?

"Yes, I absolutely did! All my childhood friends would make fun of me every summer because I kept on saying how I wished I could write a summer anthem. This song is simply—about a day in the life of someone enjoying the Adriatic sea beaches, Rimini, Riccione, my beloved Lignano Sabbiadoro. Cheap, light-hearted beach playboys and nightlife! The imprint of the song is fully autobiographical; it's simply my summer feeling!

"Every summer since I was a little child, when school in Parma was over, I went back to my grandmother Maria and my best friends in my hometown, and then to the nearby tourist seaside resort, Lignano Sabbiadoro. There I discovered a new world, spreading fantasy, sun, foreign girls, music, freedom—a new life pulsating, and it all was just 50 km away from my hometown! It was the start of the game of summer! All my best adventures and memories that are contained in the song come from that feeling. The club version of the song is titled 'Gambrinus Club Mix,' which is the hotel in Lignano Sabbiadoro where I mainly stayed every summer."

Did the worldwide success of the project come as a surprise? When did you realize something big was happening?

"In June, 1994, one week before the record came out, I went to Milano to accompany DJ [Roberto] Passera, a friend who had to buy some records for the record shop he worked in. We went to the distributor warehouse, a company that was to distribute my Playahitty record, and I heard my song booming over and over again from the office of one of the bosses there—that was the first sign. Then, a week later, something really curious happened!

"I went to Milano again with [Passera], this time to sell the license of a new club track we made together for another record label. When we were in the office of the A&R director, my friend gave him the Digital Audio Tape to play our track. The manager took the tape, pressed the button of his sound system, and 'The Summer Is Magic' came out from the speakers instead of our new club track. So I said to my friend, 'Hey, you gave him the wrong tape!' My friend replied that it was the tape I gave him, so we started discussing it. The A&R director stopped us and said he had mistakenly pressed the radio button, and it was the national radio! He added that this song was proposed to be the 'song of the day,' and everyone was talking about this track, and that it would be *the* summer hit! I could not believe my ears because the song was released only a few days before, and I could never imagine it would be on national radio so quickly. The A&R guy was a bit angry because I didn't give him this song. Instead, he ruefully signed the club track, the one I had brought him that day."

Why do you think the public reacted so strongly to the song?

"I don't know exactly—maybe it has an easy, catchy chorus and a good title—plus that inexplicable little bit of magic!"

Was the goal to then make Playahitty a primarily summer-oriented musical act after the success of "Magic"?

"Yes, all Playahitty records were released every year in June, starting from the summer of 1994.

Also released in June [of 1997] was the only remix I produced as Playahitty (Ciaobella's 'One Nait Stand', the 'Hotel Playa' 101 BPM Mix). Until the last minute, this track was considered to be a Playahitty single."

What music do you personally associate with and enjoy most when you're looking to get that summer holiday feeling?

"'Vamos A La Playa' by Righeira! Then a number of reggae songs, and many Italian classic summer pop songs, arranged by 'maestro' Morricone, such as Edoardo Vianello, then Lucio Battisti, and Loredana Bertè. I also enjoy many tracks from the '90s, from artists such as Ace Of Base and Haddaway. I also like some easy reggaeton tracks here and there from the recent years. I think I naturally associate summer mainly with the classic '70s, '80s and early '90s songs because they have been growing in me year-by-year. They come from my childhood and teenage summer life, but they are still very much played in the summertime today."

**Summer Jam - Quad City DJ's (1997), Atlantic (US)
Producers: "Jayski" McGowan, "Thrill Da Playa"
(aka Bass Mechanics)**

Built around the melody of Sister Sledge's disco classic "We Are Family," this infectious hip-hop pop-spinner revels in beach parties, scorching temps and cute girls wearing Daisy Dukes and (rather quaintly) two-piece bathing suits. A total party with a positive, sun-drenched, hands-in-the-air vibe, though the ground had been covered earlier and with equal enthusiasm by M.C. Miker "G" and Deejay Sven on "Celebration Rap" in 1986, which additionally mixed in the hook of Kool & The Gang's "Celebration." From the album *Get On Up And Dance*, which also featured the huge summer pop hit "C'mon N' Ride It (The Train)."

Summer Jam - The Underdog Project (2000), Loop Dance Constructions (G)
Producer: Toni Cottura

The Underdog Project was originally a dance music concept developed by DJs Steve Browarczyk, Toni Cottura and Sahin Moshirian who planned to combine eurodance, reggaeton, R&B and freestyle influences. They hit it big with "Summer Jam" at a time when dance music artists delivering this kind of electric melody-driven techno hook (and house vibe) were in full swing (think Benny Benassi, Gigi D'Agostino). It's all about partying till dawn in the heat of the summer, with a groove that's just as casually fluid as its beats are determined to declare, "We're going to enjoy the *shell* out of this season!" A plethora of remixes are out there, including the notable reinvention, "Summer Jam 2003" (DJ F.R.A.N.K.'s Summermix) by The Underdog Project Vs. The Sunclub, which made sure that this track's reign as top dog lasted a very long time.

Summer Jammin' - Inner Circle (1994), WEA (SW)
Producers: Ian Lewis, Touter Harvey

Featured on the Jamaican group's *Reggae Dancer* LP, released in the heart of summer and produced under the Swedish arm of Warner. It's a track that, like the album, can "fortify the summer feeling" boasted Mattias Wachtmeister, Warner Sweden's A&R Product Director (*Music & Media*, July 23, 1994). This breezy, pop radio-friendly track is bursting with pure summer beats, which the group was now synonymous with, especially in its "Miami Box Mix." Reggae purists may dismiss the track, but "Summer Jammin'" is unpretentious, easy-going, pop groovin' fun for a summer afternoon. The original track was featured on the soundtrack to the film "Beverly Hills Cop III."

Summer Lady - Narada Michael Walden (1982), Atlantic (US)
Producer: Narada Michael Walden

Hard, crisp, Gap Band-like jam from Walden, who was busy producing notables like Sister Sledge, Stacy Lattisaw and Angela Bofill during this period. Plenty of cute banter between Walden and the gal on his radar suggests a man in full-on summer pick-up mode. On July 31, 1982, *Cash Box* said the artist, "opted for a large ribald funk sound (emulating Rick James, specifically)…"

Summer Lady - Santana (1979), Columbia (US)
Producers: Keith Olsen, Santana, David DeVore

A vibrant pop/rock tune sung by Alex Ligertwood, with Santana's signature Latin and jazz flair. It's a reflection of youthful male longing for a lady love, very poetic in its own way. Carlos Santana's superb guitar playing is from the heart, as always. While disco music was stealing all the thunder at the time, this is an example of very sunny rock music (from the album *Marathon*) that was, unfortunately, a bit eclipsed by the competition of the day. It's said to have marked the beginning of a commercial slide for Santana, but I don't hear the problem.

Summer Love - Sherbet (1975), EMI (AU)
Producer: Sherbet

No surprise such a powerful warm weather classic rock anthem would come from a country with the #1 best beach in the world (according to *GQ*'s Brad Nash, online, February 24, 2021). That would be Whitehaven Beach on Whitsunday Island, with what a friend of mine describes as "crystal clear waters and sand that is pristine white." This Australian band out of Sydney was also known as Highway (in the US) and The Sherbs in a later incarnation. With sort of a Manfred Mann meets the Eagles vibe, the band was hugely successful in their native country and reached the top of their pop charts with "Summer Love," a bouncy pop/rocker boosted by the rousing vocals of Daryl Braithwaite. Sherbet correctly identifies summer love as being like no other. Consider also the band's 1977 single, "Midsummer Madness." From the land down under we head to our next port of call, the Hellenic Republic.

Summer Lovers - Michael Sembello (1982), Warner (US)
Producer: George Duke

"Summer Lovers," starring Daryl Hannah, Valerie Quennessen and Peter Gallagher, is perhaps one of the most enjoyable and atmospheric modern "beach beat" movies ever made, a not-too-silly romcom (with lots of youthful nudity) taking place on a stunningly picturesque Greek island. There, a young couple on holiday experiencing a state of romantic flux invite another woman into their relationship and complications ensue. You'll want to get a buzz on for this 3-way. The on-screen soundtrack is a masterpiece of early '80s dance/pop, with supercharged, hot-blooded songs by the Pointer Sisters ("I'm So Excited"), Lime ("Your Love") and Depeche Mode ("Just Can't Get Enough"), among others. The US soundtrack LP featured a more limited musical sampling from the film, including Elton John's "Take Me Down To The Ocean." Singer, songwriter and guitarist Michael Sembello was a seasoned musician at this time, and though he wasn't a big pop star yet (still a year or so away from the movie "Flashdance" and his #1 hit "Maniac"), he hints at what was to come with "Summer Lovers." A jittery electro-pop synth jam about warm lips, wet skin and making love on the beach (with a fitting injection of Greek bouzouki), the song was effectively played during the film's opening title sequence. A goofy 1980 German sex comedy flick, "Beautiful and Wild On Ibiza" ("Die Schönen Wilden Von Ibiza"), directed by Sigi Rothemund, has gorgeous holiday locations and a plot strikingly similar to "Summer Lovers," in case you're looking for more island holiday movie escapades.

Scene from the film "Summer Lovers" (1982), photo by David James, Filmways Pictures (press still).

Summer Madness - KC Flightt (1989), RCA (US)
Producer: KC Flightt

A vintage hip-house, electro-dance street jam from Flightt (Frank Toson, Jr.) serviced in both a staid "Love Is In The Air Mix" and a raunchy "Sex For Days Mix." But you can be sure both roads lead to a hot, horny summer. In the latter, you'll find all kinds of discussion about how there's more to summer heat than air temperatures and dialogue which would normally be reserved for present day sexting. The madness reaches a climax midway through the jam when a, shall we say, a slippery young female expresses her desire to provocatively stretch out on the beach as guys walk by, their looks getting her all—well, you get the picture. Warning: this song takes you to a very trashy beach.

Summer Megamix - Boney M. (1989), Hansa (G)
Producer: Frank Farian

Sequenced by Michael Newman and Charles Key B and remixed by Pete Hammond for PWL, the Boney M. fair weather hits "Sunny," "Ma Baker," "Hooray! Hooray! It's A Holi-Holiday," "Gotta Go Home," "Kalimba De Luna," and "Summer A Go-Go" are blended together for a lively warm weather rundown that shows why the venerable group, musically speaking, has always kept one foot in the sand.

Summer Mix - Various Artists (1987), Solar France (F)
Producers: Various

Commissioned by Solar Records for the French market and mixed non-stop by Mario Aldini, this three-medley maxi-single features a wide range of funk jams by some of the biggest R&B/dance acts from the American branch of the label, including Shalamar ("Second Time Around"), The Whispers ("And The Beat Goes On") and Lakeside ("Fantastic Voyage"). The first rate mix/editing by Aldini is handled with much the same finesse as he displays on his "Italo Boot Mix" series for ZYX Records in Germany, which he was whipping up around the same time.

Summer Mixes (Hits Medley) - Gipsy Kings (1994), Columbia (G)
Producer: Columbia Records

The brothers and cousins collective known as Gipsy Kings hail from the French region of the Camargue (Montpellier and Arles), close to the Spanish border, and they officially formed their group in 1979. Complementing their nomadic gipsy nature, they enjoyed a global triumph nearly a decade later with their feverish 1988 hit "Bamboléo," whose sensual and passionate lead vocal was handled by Nicholas Reyes. Here, they take some of their signature songs and meld them into a stirring high-energy mash-up that fits the season magnificently. This quick-fire, guitar-fused flamenco megamix has a style and warmth custom-made for club play during the summer months, and it offers a captivating look at the group's unique catalog. The single, released in France and Germany, includes the aforementioned smash plus the hits "Volare," "Djobi Djoba," "Pida Me La" and "Baila Me." Announcing a worldwide licensing deal with Sony in 1991 in *Music & Media*, Claude Martinez (a French producer and manager of the group at the time) had hopes of making the Gipsy Kings "one of the top five bands in the world." This medley may have been a marketing tool to help achieve that goal and to support the release of their 1994 *Greatest Hits* album.

Gipsy Kings circa 1989 (L-R Paco Baliardo, Diego Baliardo, Tonino Baliardo, Andre Reyes and Chico Bouchikhi), photo by Gilles Larrain, Elektra/Elektra Musician (press still).

The band managed to be much more than a novelty act on the pop charts, enjoying success in the US and especially Europe long after "Bamboléo." Their mainstream-friendly blend of Spanish and Hungarian flamenco became something of a summer standard. In his article for *Music & Media,* "The Pop 'Fiesta' Of Gipsy Kings" by Machgiel Bakker (May 28, 1988), the author quotes manager Martinez, who began overseeing the Gipsy Kings in August of 1986. "I was never satisfied with what I heard," Martinez said. "Although I was impressed with their rich melodies, something was missing. We worked in the studios for almost a year to find a new sound." The new sound, according to *Music & Media's* Bakker, was the result of the band deciding to mix modern technology (the subtle use of synthesizers and electric bass) with their fluid gipsy melodies. Gipsy Kings singer, guitarist, and main spokesman of the band, Chico Bouchikhi, added, "I think pop music needed this sort of inspiration." Agreed!

Summer Moved On - a-ha (2000), WEA (G)
Producers: Boogieman, Roland Spremberg

Shuffling synth-popper makes the connection between relationships changing and the seasons passing. A warm, sophisticated and mature production made nearly two decades after the Norwegian group had introduced us to the video age with their immortal '80s synth-gem "Take On Me."

Summer Night City - ABBA (1978), Polar (SW)
Producers: Benny Andersson, Björn Ulvaeus

A single release recorded during the group's *Voulez-Vous* album sessions, but not included on the actual LP. ABBA was reportedly rather ambivalent about the track, as am I, perhaps because the production sounds a bit too experimental, blurring its effect. "Summer Night City" is a bit of a hodge-podge blending the disco/rock elements of, say, "Does Your Mother Know" and the gothic vibe of "The Visitors" with harmonies that evoke the Bee Gees. It doesn't quite hit the mark as either a summer song or a perspicacious reflection of city night life, but even a slightly confused ABBA is something worthy of appreciation. A more memorable summer night is on tap next from the movie "supercouple" I like to call Jolivia.

Summer Nights - John Travolta, Olivia Newton-John (1978), RSO (US)
Producer: Louis St. Louis

John Travolta and Olivia Newton-John, possibly the quintessential movie musical power duo of the twentieth century's second half, sing what may be the most American ever of US summer songs, as written by Jim Jacobs and Warren Casey and featured in the 1978 film version of "Grease" (and also the stage show). Though its vintage '50s set-up seems delightfully antiquated today, prehistoric by other standards, the song's simple he said/she said story-telling and its infectious sing-along melody helped make "Summer Nights" one of the most popular songs to ever celebrate the season—and the "teen" romance/sex drive that comes with those warm weather months. On August 5, 1978, *Cash Box* casually said, "This fourth single [from the *Grease* soundtrack album] has a bright, enthusiastic sound suited to summer Top 40 action. Fine singing by Travolta and Newton-John and cast." It's amusing how casual first listen reviews like this often seem unable to recognize the potential impact some pop music will have, especially over the span of a few decades.

A sliver of controversy has arisen in recent years in light of the Me Too (#metoo) movement involving the suggestion that "Summer Nights" is sexist in tone and makes light of unwanted advances. Ms. Newton-John pushed back on that notion, according to a report by Laura Fox for Mail Online, published by Dailymail.com on October 26, 2020. The article quoted the singer (from an interview with *The Guardian*) making the point that "Grease" is fiction, saying, "It's a movie. It's a story from the 50s where things were different." Others have also observed that Ms. Newton-John's character, Sandy, was actually empowered in the story and made her own lifestyle decision at the movie's end. Whatever filters we may view the film through today, you can be certain in the late '70s, precious few among the public were considering all those angles while listening to the tight hooks of "Summer Nights" and soaking up the infectious charisma of its star performers. John and Olivia's duet was ranked #41 on *Cash Box*'s December 30, 1978 listing of the US Top 100 Singles of the year. (The pair's other hit duet from the movie, "You're The One That I Want," came in at #9.) The publication ranked the *Grease* soundtrack as the year's third biggest album.

Twenty years later, the "Martian Remix" of "Summer Nights" (the engineer who created it was known as Martian) found its way into record shops, designed to promote a 1998 re-release and 20th anniversary celebration of the *Grease* film in the UK. At the same time, a repackaged version of the movie's soundtrack was also issued there. At the height of the record label's music campaign, Polygram UK product manager Matthew Tilley said he hoped the reimagined track would be "this summer's thing" on radio, according to *Music & Media* (June 13, 1998). Purists need not fear. The retro-spirit of the top five US pop original is faithfully preserved in this understated remix, and the track is only gently touched with some feather-light Afro-Cuban bongo percussion and a Spanish guitar that inch the temperature up a few degrees. Though I'm not sure how effective the "Martian Remix" was in hyping the success of the anniversary edition of the "Grease" soundtrack, by August of '98 *Music & Media* was reporting that the album was the top sales breaker on their European Top 100 albums chart. A still lively but very lean Martian remix of Olivia and John's "You're The One That I Want," coupled with "The Grease Megamix" (mixed by Harding & Curnow for PWL), was also issued by the label.

(L) Olivia Newton-John and John Travolta in the 1978 film "Grease,"
Paramount (press still).

Speaking of the *Grease* soundtrack and summer, I'm pretty sure it was among the most popular double LPs of its time to wrap in tin foil and use as a suntan reflector in the backyard.

Summer Nights - Hi-Skool (2003), Kontor (G)
Arjan "DJ Acesone" van Midden, Joris van Dijk, Michel Clerx

Remakes of popular songs often beg the question—why? However, this update lets its energy speak for itself. The "Grease" evergreen is given a very potent injection of pulsating eurodance power while the decidedly competent production remains completely faithful to the song's original structure and tone. It's sort of like seeing an off-Broadway production of the show staged in a techno club. You'll want to get friendly with this pumper, down in the sand!

Summer Nights - Stevie B. (1997), Dance 2000 (US)
Producers: Brian Wayy, Stevie B, David Allen Jones

One of the Miami-based artist's most accessible freestyle jams, generating its solid groove from the singer's reliably smooth vocals and a minimal electro beat. There's some welcome suggestions of Man Parrish's '82 classic "Hip Hop, Be Bop (Don't Stop)" in the "South Beach" and "Turtle Beach" mixes, too. If that Latin-seasoned syncopated-beat was your groove back in the day, you know Stevie B. is just the man to heat up your summer nights.

Summer Of '42 - Biddu Orchestra (1975), Epic (US)
Producer: Biddu

"The Summer Knows," the dreamy Grammy-winning theme from the 1971 film "Summer Of '42," composed by Michel Legrand, serves as the foundation of this British-Indian artist's vintage disco instrumental piece. Artistic in design, the track's signature strings and nuanced production flairs are lavish, detailed and richly textured. Biddu is best known for his pop collaboration with Carl Douglas, the hit "Kung Fu Fighting" from 1974.

Summer Of '69 - Bryan Adams (1985), A&M (C)
Producers: Bryan Adams, Bob Clearmountain

Canadian rocker Adams was making a solid impression in the US at the time with his top 10 album, *Reckless*, and a #1 single, "Heaven." Though reportedly the artist was initially uncertain about the viability of "Summer" (co-written by Adams and Jim Vallance) as an album track and single, the uptempo song, with its forceful power chords, was strong enough to return the singer to the top five of *Billboard*'s Hot 100. But the song may not have been the emotional deep dish pizza we thought it was. The singer appeared on the September 8, 2008, edition of the CBS-TV program "The Early Show," as posted online by cbsnews.com, divulging that the song was about making love in the summertime, with 69 referring to the sex act, rather than a year. Well, research has proven that sex occurs more frequently during summer (or at least it did in teenage beach party movies), so I don't think anyone will argue with Adams' inspiration. On June 29, 1985, *Cash Box* said "Summer Of '69," "...recalls the sound and arrangement of Springsteen with Adams' own streamlined sheen…" Germany act Topmodelz covered the song with a jumping hi-tech electronic dance version in 2007. You get what you give!

Summer Of Love - David Hasselhoff (1994), Ariola (UK/G)
Producers: Phil Harding, Ian Curnow, Mark Holden

Though his career in entertainment seems to rarely get serious attention, it can be argued that David Hasselhoff enjoyed a formidable run as a successful pop singer in Europe, especially Germany, but at this point his music popularity even in Deutschland was waning. Best known for his starring role in the iconic '90s surf side TV series "Baywatch," this song seems tailor-made for the series and its beachy themes. As a lightly danceable, mid-tempo synth-ballad, this inconspicuous track treads water effectively. Plenty of whispering and female background vocals give it a romantic late summer feel. Music and mixes for the track were created by Britain's Phil Harding and Ian Curnow.

Commentary from Dr. Phil Harding:

"This was 1994, so Ian [Curnow] and I would have been working with East 17 and bands like that at the time. We were looking for a few different things to get involved with. Beginning in 1992, we had a publishing deal with BMG Music, and we were quite focused on hooking up with their affiliates in other countries. One of the people we clicked with was a guy in the BMG Publishing office in New York, who had Mark Holden, the co-writer of this song, signed. He hooked us up with Mark, who was working with David Hasselhoff out in California and trying to get some new tracks going for him. He obviously had come up with the title 'Summer Of Love,' and we were thinking of the 'Baywatch' TV program, something summery and a bit cool in our discussions of the project. 'Summer Of Love' ended up being dreamy, floaty, and quite down-tempo.

"In some ways it's a good example of the type of collaborating we're all doing today, where you are collaborating with people all over the world. Back then, we were swapping tapes and CDs as opposed to files now. So we got into a routine of talking to Mark, and he would have suggested this kind of groove—sending him tracks and seeing what clicked. I think we did three or four tracks with him, maybe more (we did two with David), and once he had the song fully written, he would send it to us with his vocals (Mark was also a singer) on it. He thought David would go for it, and the 'Baywatch' people seemed to like it. Off we went from there."

Did you have any reservations about working with a TV personality?

"We were uncertain about David's vocal abilities. But we were assured by Holden that he'd be fine. We had worked with TV personalities before, so we were well geared-up to surround David with backing vocals. We sent out our 24 multi-track to New York. There wasn't enough money in the budget to fly us out there, but Mark said not to worry, he would record David. We trusted him, but we also did manage to have an engineer friend of ours in New York named Dave Dale to engineer the sessions. We knew he would do a great job on our behalf. Listening to the track now [*Dr. Harding plays a portion of the extended version*], it sounds to me like Holden is singing with him. It takes like a minute to get to the verse—that's a really long intro—and we hear David's character coming across, but I'm not sure he was entirely alone.

"It's a great example of a summer song, with the reference to everybody loving the sunshine. We gave him a good platform to just go for it. Most of his other work was much more uptempo, and this was a slower track for him to tackle. The closest we ever got to David Hasselhoff was a phone call while they were recording the vocals. As the song was part of the television series soundtrack, we still get performance royalties to this day for it, and it did quite well in Germany."

I can picture this song being played at a bar, beachside, somewhere in southern Europe.

"Oh, yes. The European summer culture very much involves a DJ set up on the beach. Almost at every average beach bar, in Spain in particular, and if it's quite a commercial area, there will be a DJ set up in the corner where the bar looks out over the beach, and they will turn up in late afternoon and play right through the night. It's not radio, it's not TV, you're in an open space. 'Summer Of Love' would have worked, definitely. However, I was thinking, there are a lot of tracks you *wouldn't* guess would work in this scenario, but they do. One that sticks out in my mind was when a DJ played 'Have You

Ever Seen The Rain?' by Creedence Clearwater Revival—an old west coast rock track that he played around dance tracks. It just came across great in that setting. I guess there's a big sort of European demand for old classic tracks, no matter what genre in that environment. It will still go over well with a beach crowd. Not that anyone was dancing to it, but they did enjoy it."

Dr. Harding's must-have music for that summer mood:

"The first song I always want to put on at the beach, or if I want to feel like I'm back there, is Anita Baker's 'Sweet Love' and the *Rapture* album. If you were to ask [singer] Rick Astley, he'd go for the same album as well. Another my wife and I do love is the Gipsy Kings' 'Bamboléo.' That one may be obvious, but they both take me right back to summertime and the beaches."

Summer Of Love - Lonyo (2000), Riverhorse Records/Epic (UK)
Producer: Paul "Sweet P" Watson

A bare-bones production on the surface doesn't make this lean fusion of UK soul grooves and Latin heat any less full-bodied. It's a bangin' Spanglish house/rap/Brit garage beats jam (containing a sample of "Cruel Desilusión" by Oscar D'Leon/La Critica) that had more than enough propellant to reach the top 10 of the UK's pop singles charts. The track, recorded in London, feels sonically complex and bursting with inviting, dreamy undercurrents, and the infectious D'Leon hook is subtle and irresistible. The overall hot summer vibe is absolutely undeniable, especially in its original extended version. Check it out. In addition to his music, Lonyo Engele also pursued an acting career.

Summer Of Love - Ondina (1997), Remixed Records/Interhit (SW)
Producer: Jonas Ekfeldt

A Swedish singer, Ondina has a powerful voice, and she neatly steers this energized eurodance club jam like the little red Corvette it is. "Summer Of Love" rocks with a catchy melody, infectious keyboards, and a supporting ragga rap by MC Milton on its "Balearic Extended Mix." Wait for the cool "splash" at the end, a simple but rather brilliant conclusion to the party! The artist had an even more popular house-fused eurodance hit single the year before with "Into The Night." Both tracks were produced by Jonas Ekfeldt (using his John Oakfield alias for "Into The Night"), the man behind the Robin Cook moniker and hit remake of "I Won't Let The Sun Go Down On Me."

Commentary from Dr. Jonas Ekfeldt:

"These were my summer projects. The Ondina project was born at the same time and in the same studio in Sweden that I recorded 'I Won't Let The Sun Go Down On Me.' I managed to get 'Night' licensed to a small record label in Sweden, but nothing happened with it there. I was very saddened by this because I knew the song would have potential in France or Italy. I was very inspired by the hits of Corona, Playahitty, La Bouche, that were getting all the attention at that time. When my Robin Cook project catapulted, I started getting requests from labels, especially in Italy, asking if I had anything else in my catalog. [Jonas laughs.] I only had two tracks—one was already licensed, and the other was happening right then, Robin Cook. So I had to convince my small Swedish label to send a license agreement to Milan, to this Italian label that picked up 'Into The Night,' immediately. It was June, so if it was going to happen, it was going to have to happen quickly. August would be the official summer season in Italy, France and Spain. So, Ondina suddenly took off, a top summer hit in those countries, and a much bigger track there than my Robin Cook single ever was, I must say.

"'Summer Of Love' was the follow-up. I wrote it in the autumn. It was very gray—a feeling all over—like a great cloud over everything for days and days. I wrote it when I was longing for summer, to go to Spain or Italy. I believe the composers of the famous song 'O Sole Mio' had the same issue when they wrote their song. 'Summer Of Love' managed to find itself in strange places. It was picked up in the US—it didn't do that well, but at least it was released there. However, it did well in Canada and all over Latin America."

*[See also: **I Won't Let The Sun Go Down - Robin Cook**.]*

Summer Of Love - The B-52's (1986), Warner Bros. (US)
Producer: Tony Mansfield

Featured in the movie "Earth Girls Are Easy," it's only fitting that the females of the group, Cindy Wilson and Kate Pierson, take the vocal leads, belting over a clanking Flying Lizards' "Money" styled beat. The single, taking us from away from their private Idaho and not as kitschy as some of the group's earlier hits, was lifted from the *Bouncing Off The Satellites* album. It arrived at a challenging time for the band following the 1985 AIDS-related death of guitarist Ricky Wilson, Cindy's brother. As a result, The B-52's did not tour for this project, and the album failed to garner much media or record buyer attention. Though the background story is somber, "Summer Of Love" is decidedly *not*, especially in its bright, magnificently extended "Summer Party Mix" by Shep Pettibone, which reached #3 on the *Billboard* dance chart.

Summer On A Solitary Beach - Alice (1985), EMI (I)
Producer: Angelo Carrara

So who needs crowds? The yearning, passionate voice of Alice (also known as Alice Visconti), an Italian artist and San Remo festival winner (in 1981, with the hit "Per Elisa") projects a melancholy vision laced with wandering and poetic musings about a sun-drenched summer. With a remarkable arrangement and creative synthesizer and drum machine work, the complex track brilliantly envelops the listener in the sensation that one is within reach of the shimmering sunbathed sea. Songwriter Franco Battiato recorded the tune himself in 1981.

Summer Son - Texas (1999), Mercury (UK)
Producer: Johnny Mac

Proud and confident electronic rock with a gritty, infectious quality that stems from a sharply determined rhythm and the wonderfully unforced vocals of Texas' ("I Don't Want A Lover") Sharleen Spiteri. With yearning lyrics that equate a broken heart to, poetically speaking, a sun burn, the track was a monster hit in the UK during the summer of '99, reaching #1 on *Music & Media*'s European Radio Top 50 late in August. Be warned—there's a jarring Giorgio Moroder commercial remix out there that turns the track upside down with a saccharin '70s disco groove. Moroder's retro-production utterly ignores the edgy original spirit of "Summer Son," and, polished and competent though it may technically be, the mix comes off sounding like a dusty ol' 12-inch from the Studio 54 vaults, at least by 1999 measures. *Why?*

Summer Summer - Loft (1993), RCA (G)
Producer: Cyborg DMP GmbH

Co-written by Nosie Katzmann, who penned Culture Beat's smash "Mr. Vain," released the same year. Popular across the continent that summer, the song is a rap/euro-dance hybrid (although the act claims it's genre to be roots rock reggae at the track's opening) with a female lead vocalist who dreamily assures us that summer has the power to take any cares away. Real talk!

Summer Vacation - The Party (1990), Hollywood (US)
Producer: Ricky "The Rocket" Ross

A squeaky clean five-teen Florida-based Xennial group raps about what every high school kid back then craved desperately—*no*, not that. Get your mind out of the gutter (well, yes, maybe *that*, too). The group members were all graduates of "The Mickey Mouse Club" TV show a few years before, so this must be their version of cutting loose. It's completely catchy, they look like they're having a blast in the video, and it got them all the way up to #21 on the *Billboard* dance chart. You're likely to feel a bit nostalgic for your lost youth after hearing this one.

Summerfire - B-U (2000), Stereophonic/BMG (G)
Producers: Boris Blenn, Luca Krumm

A relentless, exuberant, and dramatic electro-pumper 'n' house-crasher from the "Queer As Folk" series soundtrack, highlighted by slamming keyboards and some well-placed advice that you *really* need to let yourself be free. Can I get an amen? Callouts to London, New York and Ibiza.

Summerfling - k.d. lang (2000), Warner (US)
Producer: Damian LeGassick

Charmingly sung and insightfully written (by k.d. Lang and David Piltch), this song expresses the joy of a summer love, enhanced by the honeyed burn of the sun. The track has a polished retro feel and a simplicity and honesty that is incredibly refreshing. Positive, uplifting, and as welcome as a cool breeze on a hot summer day, but not nearly as cliched as that descriptor. Lots of charged remixes (most notably, Victor Calderone's) made "Summerfling" a noticeably club-friendly track, resulting in a top 25 position on *Billboard*'s dance chart. The world needs more of this!

Summerfun & Oceanwaves - Barry Levy (1994), Deshima (G)
Producer: Gunther Illi

An obscure German production with a surprisingly very, very California meets Caribbean beach vibe, it captures the easy living groove of having fun in the sun and splashing around at the shore. Mixing in a Caribic rap, it's pure electronic beach beat dance/pop and very likable in its innocence and good spirit.

Summertime - Aaron Carter Ft. Baha Men (2002), Jive (US)
Producers: Martin Bushell, Nicky Cook, Tony Momrelle

Born in Tampa, Florida, youthful white rapper, singer and songwriter Carter no doubt already had a built-in appreciation for the joys of warm weather. It's palpable in the likable Disney-esque track "Summertime," from the *Another Earthquake!* album, a jam aimed squarely at turn of the century teens. The injection of Baha Men ("Who Let The Dogs Out") might have been a stab at earning some urban credibility for the artist, but the combination feels a bit forced and slightly awkward, which is really the only cloud on this otherwise sunny day.

Summertime- DJ Jazzy Jeff & The Fresh Prince (1991), Jive (US)
Producers: Hula, K. Fingers

Will Smith and Jeff Townes unwind in a nostalgic, laid back, heavy-grooved, hip-hop/dance jam that is as seemingly clean, uncomplicated and happy as the family and friends we see partying in the sunny outdoors in the song's appealing video. There's nothing here but fresh air, the smell of barbecue, and the good energy of friends and loved ones—a perfect "family" portrait of everything we'd like summer to include. The track, which made the top 15 of *Cash Box*'s US pop singles chart on August 15, 1991, samples Kool & The Gang's 1975 soul hit "Summer Madness." Tired of the family drama? Here's your ticket to a hassle-free feel-good afternoon.

Summertime - Jazzini (1992), Dino (NL)
Producers: Martin Boer, Jay Z Jazzy

Pleasant and ambitious instrumental work places the Gershwin song in a jazzy house setting. The B-side, "Desert Cry," is also quite evocative. Both are from the album *Almost Incognito,* which is filled with famous jazz themes dipped in house and hip-hop beats. It's especially interesting that the producer of this calm, soulful jam, Martin Boer, is the same man who gave us the feverish '90s stomper "Can't Help Myself" by 2 Brothers On The 4th Floor!

Summertime- Morcheeba Ft. Hubert Laws (1998), China Records (UK)
Producers: Morcheeba, Pete Norris

The Gershwin jazz evergreen is given a rhythmic, intensely sensual, spaced out interpretation in the sonic processing of Carlos Bess' "C12 Remix," rolling across the warm night sky with its deep groove, the stunning vocals of Skye Edwards, and the spiritual flute work of Hubert Laws. It doesn't get any more regenerative than this. The original version is featured on the *Red Hot + Rhapsody* AIDS benefit album.

Summertime And I'm Feelin' Mellow - MFSB (1976), Philadelphia International (US)
Producers: J. Whitehead, G. McFadden, V. Carstarphen

Smooth as the ocean surface on a still, windless summer day, the track has that clean, early disco/soul instrumental sound (vibrant strings and horns, syncopated bass lines) with choral vocals cheering the listener to get out and dance (no matter how mellow one might be feeling). A vintage beach hang.

Summertime Fun - Vicki Sue Robinson (1982), Promise (US)
Producer: Warren Schatz

A marked departure from Vicki's club-friendly dance music, this doo-wop throwback is an odd but diverting bopper and a pleasant, summery showcase of the singer's talents—though DJs might not have known what to do with it. Produced, arranged and engineered by Warren Schatz (who helmed Ms. Robinson's mega-smash "Turn The Beat Around," as well as hits for Evelyn "Champagne" King and Viola Wills).

Commentary from Warren Schatz:

"I had heard a shuffle record that I loved, I can't remember what it was, and I thought, let me mess around with this kind of time signature. I just started making it and the idea came to me to have a bass voice singing about summertime fun, that old doo-wop, style—I come from the doo-wop school. So I kind of made it with a more modernized '80s pop style. Really, it was just for fun—I liked it, but I knew it wasn't gonna do anything. Vicki liked it because it wasn't the same old disco, disco, disco. And she could really sing anything. And she wrote a lot of the lyrics and riffs with me. At this time, I was trying to just have fun and not be so serious anymore. And certainly not to chase 'Turn The Beat Around' for the rest of my life."

*[See also: **Hot Summer Night - Vicki Sue Robinson**.]*

Summertime / Summer Of '82 - The Fun Boy Three (1982), Chrysalis (UK)
Producers: The Fun Boy Three

The Gershwin reliable is given a compelling, even a bit theatrical, ska-meets-new wave-meets-jazz reinvention by the English trio. The track has a hint of tribal undercurrent, but retains the original composition's lazy warm weather feel. On July 24, 1982, Daniela Soave of *Record Mirror* said of the evocative single, "Shut your eyes and you're sitting on a fire escape in New York on a humid day." The B-side features the entrancing synth-beat jam "Summer of '82," whose story focuses on a summer of discontent with jazzy horns and a feeling of being very deep inside one's own head. After all that, you'll probably be ready for a lighter and more festive beach vibe from the fellas. Try giving the Bananarama hit "Really Saying Something (He Was Really Sayin' Somethin')" featuring Fun Boy Three, a remake of The Velvelettes '64 single, a spin. *Cash Box* called that one a "percussion and piano dominated party" on October 23, 1982. That should snap you out of it!

Summertime Of Our Lives - a1 (1998), Sony (UK)
Producer: Metro

Yep, another boy band singing about summer romance—and guess what? They crush it! A driving pulse supports terrific high energy, hook-laden harmonies, instead of the other way around, in this squeaky clean production that pleasantly coats your brain with a summer-fresh harvest of honey. This is late '90s floor-filling europop at its best. The group did a splendid job reinventing a-ha's "Take On Me" a few years later. Good energy like this is positively contagious!

Summertime, Summertime - Nocera (1986), Sleeping Bag (US)
Producer: Floyd M. Fisher

Freestyle never sounded better than it does in this rocking electronic debut jam by Italian vocalist Lulu Maria Nocera. Reminiscent of The Cover Girls' freestyle hits of the period, this highly melodic and lushly produced classic, mixed by Mantronik, is irresistibly danceable and hopelessly feel-good. It reached #2 on *Billboard*'s dance chart.

Summertime, The - BZN (1985), Phonogram (NL)
Producer: Roy Beltman

BZN (short for Band zonder Naam or "Band Without a Name"), sometimes affectionately called "The Mantovanis Of Pop," was a Dutch ensemble founded in 1966. "The Summertime" is a spry, spirited track with a poppy new wave flavor, very accessible to the general population, and (ironically, way ahead of season) it reached the *Music & Media* Top 50 European Airplay chart in the cold of January, 1985. It also reached the #1 spot on the *Stichting Nederlandse Top 40* radio survey. From the Netherlands we take flight to a region of South Africa, where things are heating up.

Sun City - Artists United Against Apartheid (1985), Manhattan Records (US)
Producers: Little Steven (Steve Van Zandt), Arthur Baker

A "We Are The World" styled effort (though it received far less media support) to protest apartheid in South Africa that featured a constellation of talent, all of whom reportedly agreed not to play the popular Sun City resort/casino complex due to the region's racial segregation policies. The stellar line-up included artists from a wide range of music genres, from rap to rock, country, jazz and R&B, such as Afrika Bambaataa, Pat Benatar, Bono, Nona Hendryx, Jimmy Cliff, Herbie Hancock, Lou Reed, Kashif, Miles Davis, Bonnie Raitt and many other notables. According to music industry publication advertisements, artist royalties from the project were given to The Africa Fund, a charitable trust registered with the United Nations to benefit political prisoners and their families in South Africa, and other related support efforts.

It took quite some time for the "Sun City" single to catch on, and there were concerns the track and album were too controversial to easily lend themselves to radio and MTV programming. However, the effort ultimately proved reasonably successful in the US, UK and across much of Europe. It's a wildly funky, upbeat, rousing, and infectiously danceable record with a message. And check out the video, with its carefully sequenced footage of fist-pumping protestors, brilliantly timed to match the track's determined, stomping groove, thereby making the issue it was highlighting indelible. "Sun City" may have done something unusual for a (musically speaking) "summer suggestive" production. It may have persuaded holiday travelers *not* to go to a luxury resort. Unfortunately, the injustices addressed in this track still remain headline material over two decades into the twenty-first century.

Sun Goddess - Ramsey Lewis/Earth, Wind & Fire (1975), Columbia (US)
Producer: Maurice White

Wayo-wonderfully rhythmic and largely instrumental track from the Chicago-born jazz pianist, with the hip influence of Earth, Wind & Fire brilliantly evoking a sunny mood. It reached #14 on the *Billboard* disco chart, and marked the first time Earth, Wind & Fire appeared on that publication's dance music survey. A funky but overall relaxing jam. An updated "Sun Goddess 2000" version was released in 1996 on the Verve label.

Sun Goes Down (Living It Up), The - Level 42 (1983), Polydor (UK)
Producers: Larry Dunn, Verdine White

Brilliantly catchy jazz/funk/synth-pop with a stirring bass line, unusual syncopation and so many hooks it's almost overwhelming. Vocally and stylistically, one may be reminded of Men At Work, but this UK band had a bright spark and sense of originality that's all their own. Level 42 earned top 10 pop positions in the UK and US with "Lessons In Love" and "Something About You" a few years after this release. "Sun Goes Down" was given both a reggae flavored and nearly unrecognizable techno remix in 1998, which did the song and the group no favors. Stick with the original extended version, a mix whose nearly seven-minute running time prioritizes your summer pleasure.

Sun Is Shining - Bob Marley Vs. Funkstar De Luxe (1999), Edel (G)
Producers: Lee Perry & The Wailers

The summer of 1999 is around the corner, and the Ibiza crowd is going to have a monster appetite for sun, surf and dancing. Okay then, why not mix the gritty vocals of Bob Marley's tropical flavored reggae classic with a pulsating house beat and give the people something mind-bending to inhale? That's exactly what Danish DJ Martin Ottesen, aka Funkstar De Luxe, supplied to those eager clubbers, and it earned him a #1 *Billboard* dance/disco chart hit, a top 10 ranking on *Music & Media*'s pop singles chart, and the #31 spot for the entire year on the publication's countdown of 1999's biggest European singles (published January 1, 2000). The energized reinvention of the song, originally recorded by Bob Marley And The Wailers in 1971, features a trippy trance feel that Marley's ethereal vocals glide over effortlessly, ideally suited for revelers on the party island or virtually any beach and club setting anywhere. *Music & Media* (September 11, 1999) reported that about 100 white label copies of the remix had been floating around Ibiza since June, securing a significant amount of radio and club play throughout that summer and for the rest of the year as well. And what a year it was for Marley fans, with remastered CD sets released, a virtual duets album on store shelves (*Chant Down Babylon*, produced by Marley's son Stephen and featuring A-listers such as Lauryn Hill and Erykah Badu), and a tribute concert for the legendary artist held on Oracabessa Beach in Jamaica.

Sun of Jamaica - Audrey Landers (1990), WEA (G)
Producers: Christian de Walden, Steve Singer

For this pleasant, whispery and beachy production, the male perspective found in the original lyrics of the 1979 hit version by Goombay Dance Band was altered in a romantic fashion befitting Ms. Landers, but the dreamy essence and warm melody remain intact. Co-produced by Modern Talking's Luis Rodriguez. The track was given a "Lambada Remix '90" by Geoff Peacey, which may have been an attempt to get in on the massive record sales that Kaoma's "Lambada" was enjoying around the same time. Admittedly, "Sun Of Jamaica" seems out of place on Audrey's otherwise synth-pop focused album, *Meine Träume Für Dich/Love Me Tender* (1990), which, along with her previous LP, *Secrets* (1988), was designed to move the singer away from this type of summery, romantic schlager music and toward a hipper rock, pop, and dance sound. With that in mind, the artist reveals the reason the tropical track *isn't* one of her favorite recordings.

Commentary from Audrey Landers:

"I hope this doesn't spoil the image, but I was so disappointed at the time that I would have to sing 'Sun Of Jamaica.' I wasn't familiar with the song's illustrious past, I did not know the awesome producer of that track, and, most importantly, I was not given a choice. That probably was the main reason for my disappointment. My producer, Christian de Walden, and I had decided that this album would have a more American sound. He came up with this song that, at the time, made me feel as if I was going backwards, creatively.

Of course it was a great track, and it had a very tropical vibe, but—I felt like I was going back to 'Honeymoon In Trinidad.'

"From a commercial standpoint, deep down, I knew that was relevant, and it may have been successful, I don't know. (I never knew how successful my music was. I would record the songs, many self-composed, and I'd fly to Europe, popping in and out to do promotion and concerts at a whirlwind pace, and immediately fly back to the US for filming of 'Dallas.') But I thought, come on Christian, I thought we weren't doing schlager music for this album. I was promised that we would create an album that could potentially appeal to American ears, not just the European market. I went into the studio, I read the lyrics—I didn't learn it—I just thought let's get this over with as fast as possible. Then I think they did an extended version of it—I was like, what is happening here? I hadn't heard of 'Lambada' (the extended version was called 'The Lambada Remix') and I had no creative control, no input. I was trying to go in a different direction with this album, with a musical style that was more organic, and I was hoping that Christian would facilitate that. In my mind, this was a digression, creatively, and I wanted to focus on the art."

Sun Of Jamaica - Goombay Dance Band (1979), CBS (G)
Producers: J. Petersen, E. Clinton

An exotic, sentimental dance song about a young man finding love on the famous island, performed by a German band that bears a look and sound much like that of Boney M. It's a simple, warm and endearing tune with universal appeal. The track, written by Wolff-Ekkehardt and Wolfgang Jass and covered by countless other artists over the years, was a huge success in Europe and the UK, earning its writers mad coin, but Goombay's subsequent releases didn't fare as well. The group recorded many versions of this song in varying styles during the '80s and '90s and, inevitably, it shows up on nearly every European summer compilation album or playlist in one form or another. Fun fact: one of the background singers on the track is Taco Ockerse, who a few years later had a monster hit with "Puttin' On The Ritz."

Sun Of Mallorca - DJ Costa (1998), Coil (G)
Producers: Manuel Rodriguez, Carlos Cojones

An off-the-rack eurodisco variation on Goombay Dance Band's "Sun Of Jamaica." The deliciously sexy cartoon cover painting on the CD jacket by artist "Jaikai's noitpanic," featuring a titillating beach party scene with sexy revelers, is the most alluring part of this production.

Sun Struck Lovers - Voggue (1983), Matra (C)
Producers: Michel Daigle, Francois L'Herbier

This dreamy tale of romance under the sun, complete with ocean wave sound effects, is a mid-tempo old skool disco vehicle designed for a female Canadian duo that sounded a bit dated, even by 1983 standards. Voggue was reportedly created by Denyse Lepage of Lime ("Your Love"), but was fronted by other singers, as was eventually the case with Lime. It's believed Denyse was no longer involved with the Voggue group project by the time of this release. Voggue had scored a big club hit in the US with "Dancin' The Night Away" in 1981.

Sun...Sun...Sun - Jǎkki (1976), Pyramid (US)
Producer: Johnny Melfi

An eight-member group with a female lead delivers a complex, rather soaring and literal celebration of the sun artistically combining soul, R&B and disco styles with a funky vibe and intermittent jungle beat. There's so much going on here, one realizes how much sweat and effort was put into many of these early disco creations. It feels a little like Broadway meets The Salsoul Orchestra. A top five hit on the *Billboard* disco chart in the summer of '76. One sun is not enough!

Sun Sun Sun Sun Sun - Marti Jones (1987), Columbia (US)
Producer: David Kahne

Say it again, please! Marti Jones does a stellar job wrapping up the 1987 movie "Back To The Beach" with this feel good, highly catchy 'n' funky '80s synth-pop jam—kind of a Toni Basil meets GoGo's meets Bananarama sound. The title redundancy is a nothing short of a rallying cry. Let's go!

Sunchyme - Dario G (1997), Eternal/Warner (UK)
Producer: Dario G

A haunting trance/pop fusion with a well-placed chant chorus lifted from elements of The Dream Academy's "Life In A Northern Town." The track reached #1 on the *Billboard* dance chart and #40 for the year on the 1997 *Music & Media* Eurochart Hot 100 Singles chart. The song conjures up exotic locales (as did its African-themed video) and a rich summery atmosphere that is actually quite stirring as it swells with emotion, a trademark creative touch of Dario G. founder Paul Spencer.

"*I hated it!*" said Spencer, referring to the video for "Sunchyme." "I had envisioned people on a beach having a good time, like in Ibiza. I didn't picture people being painted and jumping into rivers and dressed as lions. It wasn't really my idea of what would best represent the music. I suspect if that video had been used on a different piece of music that wasn't as popular, I don't think it would have taken hold. It was kind of silly and experimental. But because the music had caught on so well, the video got airplay and took on its own life." *[From the book: Stars of '90s Dance Pop, Arena, 2016, McFarland.]*

Sunglasses - Tracey Ullman (1984), Stiff (UK)
Producer: Peter Collins

The brilliantly offbeat UK comedian/actor, born in Buckinghamshire, had a noteworthy singing career as part of her early entertainment journey, hitting it big with the pop single "They Don't Know" in 1983. The following year she debuted at #93 on the *EuroTipSheet* European Top 100 Singles chart with this cute, very radio-friendly, '60s style bop track and and spent eight weeks of the summer on the publication's European Airplay Top 50 survey. Ms. Ullman's relatable checklist of beach necessities and use of summery castanets is charmingly amusing. The light-hearted video for the song, filled with surf-side antics and played out on an ordinary public beach with all of the artist's terrific sense of humor on full display, is smile-inducing. In a review of Tracey's *You Caught Me Out* LP, from which the single was lifted, *EuroTipSheet* described the artist as "a good singer with a good nose for the right type of material." Incidentally, Ms. Ullman claims to never have had plastic surgery. Turns out her cute, pliant face was a natural for television comedy, so you don't fix what ain't broke.

Sunglasses At Night- Corey Hart (1983), EMI (C/US)
Producers: J. Astley, P. Chapman

After handing host Dick Clark a complimentary pair of sunglasses on an installment of ABC-TV's *American Bandstand* as his catchy synth-pop hit was playing all over US radio, the Canadian singer admitted the track was an afterthought conceived post-completion of his new album. The song (which he wrote) was so powerful, he confidently concluded, they just *had* to record it. Reminiscent of "Sweet Dreams (Are Made Of This)" by Eurythmics, Hart's slightly paranoia-seasoned yarn has a sweaty undercurrent that runs somewhat parallel to Rockwell's "Somebody's Watching Me," both from the same year. In a June 27, 2012, online posting, Songfacts.com quotes the singer saying, "I think I first knew I had a hit on my hands when I landed in the Detroit airport en route to my first US tour as opening act for Rick Springfield in June, 1984. I was mobbed at the airport by frenzied fans. We needed security to get me through the terminal to catch the connecting flight. It was a surreal experience." The track reached #62 on *Billboard*'s dance chart.

Sunmachine - Dario G (1998), Eternal/Warner (UK)
Producer: Peter Oxendale

A remarkably appealing and uplifting hand-clapper, expertly orchestrated and guaranteed to make one feel a sense of jubilation. The track reinterprets and samples portions of David Bowie's "Memory Of A Free Festival." From the LP *Sunmachine*, which also contains the hit single "Carnaval De Paris." *Music & Media* described the set on June 6, 1998, as a "sunny, easy-going pop/house album which will keep holiday memories fresh for a little longer."

Sunny - Boney M. (1976), Hansa (G)
Producer: Frank Farian

An early international hit for the revered quartet, sort of a soulful, tropical incarnation of ABBA, Boney M.'s "Sunny" has a contagious sense of unbreakable optimism as it hails wonderful love conquering windswept sand and speeding the retreat of rain. The writer of the track, Bobby Hebb, originally recorded it as a soul single in 1966 and released it again in 1976 with more of a dance flavor. But it was Boney M. that gave "Sunny" the rich glitter ball texture the song was crying out for and lifted it to new heights with their distinctive vocal unison and the production polish of Frank Farian. Both Mr. Hebb and the original male lead of Boney M., Aruban Bobby Farrell, passed in 2010. "Sunny" is one of the most widely recorded pop songs of all time.

Sunny - Boogie Pimps (2003), Superstar Entertainment/ EastWest (G)
Producers: Boogie Pimps (Mark J Klak, Mirko Jacob)

If rollerskating was more of a thing in 2003, this big, bright electro-house/ disco trick would be one of the leisure activity's slickest anthems. This version even missed the rollerblading peak of 1998. The Hebb composed evergreen rolls effortlessly over a contemporary mix that has a touch of that Chic sound and vocals that evoke an island feel, a la Boney M. Tastes like a Capri Sun.

Sunny - Maxim Rad (1999), WEA (G)
Producer: Christoph M. Kaiser

A smoldering, attention-getting, wonderfully hip European take on the Bobby Hebb standard, preserving the '60s musical vibe of the original and stirring in rock-style vocals and a Motown-like beat. Despite being over 20 years old, Maxim's (André Rademacher) version sounds as if it was recorded yesterday. The intricate production has an edgy sense of confidence and coolness and might have been ideal as a James Bond film theme. Can you imagine the 007 theme opening guitar licks playing and this smoldering track kicking right in just as the film credits begin? Play the two together and you'll see what I mean. From Germany, with love.

Sunny - Yambu (1975), Montuno Records (US)
Producer: Al Santiago

Yambu described themselves on their self-titled debut album as "The unabashed sound of Latin New York. This distinctive sound is the result of exposing Caribbean music…to the larger culture of the 'melting pot.'" Despite its age, there's way too much bouncy energy bottled up in this vintage disco version of the Hebb evergreen for any cobwebs to gather. Stellar musicianship (bongos, congas, trumpets, drums and electric guitars abound) and a brisk, exciting tempo make this groovy hustle joint an irresistible piece of nostalgia. It will send you right back to summer nights in those glorious, smokey NYC clubs of the mid-'70s, when the mercury was high and so was everyone in the place.

Sunny Aruba - George McCrae (1991), Magnif (G)
Producer: Manfred Holz

Florida's original disco godfather, George "Rock Your Baby" McCrae, takes a very logical and overdue trip to the tropics with this swingbeat, Caribbean-flavored dance/pop tune. A sunny, mid-tempo disco thump recalls his 1974 signature classic with some steel drums adding atmosphere to the track, lifted off the artist's *With All My Heart* album. McCrae, known for effortlessly hitting those high notes, doesn't have to work too hard in this breezy German production, and that's how it should be when you're jammin' about an island that has perfect beaches and mostly clear, sunny skies all year round.

Sunset Now - Heaven 17 (1984), Virgin (UK)
Producers: B.E.F. (British Electric Foundation), Greg Walsh

Man, did the '80s give us great music or what? It's got that vocal coolness of Duran Duran, the softer rhythmic charm of Level 42 and some romantic and dreamily ambiguous lyrics about watching the sun go down. It fits summer like a Tommy Bahama T-shirt. On September 22, 1984, *Billboard* said, "British synth masters present a new and characteristically complicated story-song to dance to or wonder about; backing vocals by Afrodiziak." A taste of the good life.

Sunshine - Jaÿ-Z Featuring Babyface & Foxy Brown (1997), Roc-A-Fella/BMG (US)
Producer: Prestige

There's something compellingly hypnotic and irresistible about the way Jay-Z turned the core of Kraftwerk's icy 1978 synth-pop hit "Die Mensch" into a smoldering, soulful hip-hop jam. This track may not have anything to do with summer, but it sure has the season's vibe—hot and lusty. If a song that ponders whether a lover should be willing to give up a kidney is too much to process, just kick back with the instrumental mix.

Sunshine Hotel (Just Walk On In) - Richard T. Bear (1978), RCA (US)
Producer: Jack Richardson

Disco mix by Warren Schatz. Well, it's not the Four Seasons in Bali, but it is a cool, under-appreciated vintage funk/disco banger with a chug-chug-chug groove and a bluesy vibe. It features some infectious piano-playing that vibrates the air with lively chords, terrifically fun lyrics about a carefree place to get down, and Bear's (Richard Gerstein) gritty New York rock vocal style. It's a jumble of musical elements that seem like oil and vinegar, but mix quite well together. Have no reservations about this place. They'll leave the light on for ya.

Sunshine In The Music / Reggae Night* - Jimmy Cliff (1983), CBS (US/Europe)
Producers: Jimmy Cliff / *Amir Bayyan, *Jim Bonnefond, *Ronald Bell

Positive energy abounds in Jamaican Jimmy ("The Harder They Come") Cliff's brand of soulful crossover reggae/pop, and these selections from his mainstream '83 *The Power And The Glory* LP are prime examples. Francois Kevorkian's remix of "Night" channels the vibe of Deniece Willams' "Let's Hear It For The Boy," giving the track a commercial pop slant aimed at Top 40 audiences (which proved successful). Meanwhile, "Sunshine" has a touch more of that choice Cliff calypso flavor. Lyrically, "Night" reminds us of the power of summer music to help distance one's self from politics, ambition, and, yes, even nuclear weapons. I feel like we still have to do that. And, really, who wants to drag that kind of baggage along on a holiday getaway?

(R) Jimmy Cliff, circa mid-80s, Columbia Records (press still).

Sunshine Reggae - Laid Back (1983), Sire (D/US)
Producers: Laid Back, The Seven Dwarfs

Tim Stahl and John Guldberg helped make Denmark the unlikely source of infectious island spirit when they released the remarkably peaceful "Sunshine Reggae" across Europe, a sort of synth-pop homage to reggae. It's an odd-sounding electronic song with a kind of "underwater" sonic quality, uniquely disarming and as comforting as a loved one's arm around your shoulder. Though it asks us to put away the frown (it's from an album actually called *Keep Smiling*), there's a touch of sadness, or at least sentimentality, in the tone of this track. The fact that it can stir such a variety of emotions is a testament to the sun-baked serenity that is the song's foundation. That brings us to the flip side of the 12-inch single—these laid back Danes are best known for their #1 *Billboard* US dance chart hit, "White Horse," which, on the other side of the spectrum, was often interpreted to be a reference to blowing rails. "Sunshine Reggae" received an Ibiza-ready remix by Funkstar De Luxe in 2000, but the song is nearly unrecognizable in that souped-up reinvention. The act scored a few hits over the years in the wake of their original "Sunshine" success.

Sunstroke (1997) / Offshore* (1996) - Chicane (1997), Xtravaganza (UK)
Producer: Chicane / *Leo Elsttob, *Chicane

What makes many trance tracks so fascinating is that they are musically able to paint wonderful summer landscapes without the use of a single lyric. They often achieve the same getaway sense of euphoria as songs that directly and vocally reference beach, palm trees or partying. Chicane's (Nicholas Bracegirdle) "Sunstroke" has a timbre that's a bit dark, but its melody is electrifying and dripping with mood, and it's got a looping energy that never seems to dissipate. A distinctly artsy black and white (rather than vibrant color) video with evocative summer holiday images supports the track, and the "Disco Citizens On The Train" remix gives it an even stronger house-fused beat. His earlier hit, "Offshore," soars in its ambient mix with a fresh, flowing melody that evokes a tropical feeling and visions of sunsets. There's a reason the 1997 album, from which the tracks were lifted, is called *Far From the Maddening Crowd*. That's just where Chicane's music takes you, and I guarantee you'll want to stay there.

Sun Will Be Shining, The (1998) / Can't Help Myself (1990) - 2 Brothers On The 4th Floor (1998), Bounce Records/Arcade/ Lowland (NL)
Producers: 2 Brothers On The 4th Floor (Bobby Boer, Martin Boer)

On stage, rapper D-Rock and singer Des'Ray have most recently represented the group, but the masterminds behind the project are the Boer Brothers, Bobby and Martin, Dutch producer/DJs with a knack for creating hip, exciting and captivating eurodance hits. Their fiery signature hit, "Can't Help Myself," was a blockbuster across Europe and caught on in the US during the summer of 1991, reaching the top 10 of *Billboard*'s dance chart with its sly lyrical admission to one being branded as a "freak" because of a her, his or their dance floor moves. Following the duo's numerous other hits, "The Sun Will Be Shining" uses that warm weather energy as fuel in a more dreamy musical setting.

Commentary from Martin Boer:

What is it about Dutch artists and music personalities that have made them so skilled, so on-point, when it comes to creating wonderful dance music hits? What makes the Netherlands such a good place to create dance music?

"This is very hard to say, maybe because Dutch DJs/producers are perfectionists. Maybe we have a very critical audience. Maybe it's because Holland is the port to Europe, or maybe it is because dance music is mainstream music on Dutch radio. But what I do know is that it was very normal for me as a teenager to buy import music at the local record store. Listening to good music and studying how it was made. What synthesizers and drum computers are used. That's how we produced our first 2 Static and 2 Brothers On The 4th Floor music."

In those early '90s days, how did you plan to stand out in a crowded dance music market with 2 Brothers On The 4th Floor?

"We just did what we liked, no commercial starting point. Just having fun in the studio, and it worked!"

Why do you think "Can't Help Myself" made such a huge impression on the masses worldwide?

"The song was a feel good dance record and it had 'over the top' raps, a little bit like MC Miker G. & Deejay Sven's 'Holiday Rap.' Everybody could sing and rap along with it. It sounded great on the radio. It was the right track at the right moment."

When you have such a tremendous hit like "Can't Help Myself," how does your creative process change? How do you still stay inventive and excited by creating music when everyone expects another hit of the same magnitude (and possibly in the same style)?

"It wasn't easy because acid house and rave music became popular in the early '90s, and we didn't like that kind of music. But suddenly there was a commercial move going on. Music became more melodic with a good chorus and happy synth sounds. Acts like Snap!, Culture Beat and Haddaway made a new sound called eurodance. This was the sound we understood! We went back into the studio with new creativity to create new songs like 'Never Alone' and 'Dreams (Will Come Alive).' Happy songs with actual feel good lyrics."

With the track "The Sun Will Be Shining," was it your intention to create a summer anthem?

"Yes, we wanted to create a summer hit, something like Gala's 'Freed From Desire' or Corona's 'Rhythm of the Night'—a song that could be played at bars and clubs in your favorite summer vacation location in the south of Europe (Spain, France, Italy, Greece, etc.)"

When creating and fashioning a song for a potential summer audience, do you believe a track needs to have a certain type of sound, certain elements that signal this is a summer anthem?

"It should be a sing-along song with a happy sound. A song that you want to buy when you come back home after your summer vacation. A song that gives you happy vacation memories about dancing in the clubs, holiday love, drinking cocktails at the beach, etc. Dance music is always developing, but in [its foundation] is the same formula based on the prevailing style at that moment."

What songs personally give you that summer vibe?

"For sure the '80s summer hits, the years of my youth! Like Righeira - 'Vamos A La Playa,' Twenty 4 Seven - 'I Can't Stand It,' Baltimora - 'Tarzan Boy,' Den Harrow - 'Future Brain.' A lot of Italo music with the song formulas we discussed earlier: catchy sing-along songs with that happy vibe! Also, the '90s were very impressive with the music of Snap! - 'Rhythm Is A Dancer,'

Haddaway - 'What Is Love.' And more recently, Avicii - 'Wake Me Up' and Gigi D'Agostino - 'L'Amour Toujours.'"

*[See also: **Mega Hit Mix - Fun Fun**.]*

Surf Or Die - Surf MC's (1987), Profile (US)
Producer: Norman Kerner

The song title implies options are few heading into the soup. Limitations proved to be the band's tombstoning as well. "In short," wrote Troy Croom in the "New Faces To Watch" column of the September 19, 1987, edition of *Cash Box*, "the Surf MC's are dead serious about having fun, but they don't take themselves too seriously." Their debut single (and album of the same name) was tagged as "surf rap" by the media, though the multi-racial quartet "sound here more street than beach," according to *Billboard* (August 29, 1987). It's bitchin' alright, it's got some juice, and most definitely has a pumping beach vibe, but with the novelty quickly exhausted after the swell of just this one track, the crew soon found themselves in the middle of a wipeout and ended up as hodads.

Sweat (A La La La Long) - Inner Circle (1992), WEA (G/US)
Producers: Ian Lewis, Touter Harvey, Roger Lewis

Moisture is the goal here. The veteran Jamaican group (their remake of Marley's "I Shot The Sheriff" was a significant hit in 1975) often called themselves the "Bad Boys of reggae," a title earned after the widespread popularity they achieved with the single "Bad Boys" in 1990, the theme from the popular TV series, "Cops." As a follow-up, "Sweat" offers a much happier mood and a super sticky, very commercial, lightly sexual sound that is quite in sync with the summer season. The song, from the LP *Bad To The Bone*, had no problem reaching the #1 spot on *Music & Media*'s Eurochart Hot 100 and stayed on the survey for 56 weeks. In its "Sweatbox Construction" version, Inner Circle offers a hard to resist remix with plenty of funk-fused grind. As if that weren't enough, in their July 23, 1994 issue, the publication ranked the track as fourth on its list of "10 Most Successful Eurochart Hot 100 Singles" (from 1984 to 1994). If you're wondering what was #1, pull out your copy of Ace Of Base's "All That She Wants" from 1992.

Sweet, Soft, N' Lazy - Viktor Lazlo (1985), Polydor (F)
Producer: J.P. Hawks

Model, singer and songwriter Viktor Lazlo (Sonia Dronier) serves up the glamour with a capital G! The artist, born in France, may remind one of Sade in the way she creates a sophisticated, intimate, romantic atmosphere with her music. With its smoky horns, gentle, swaying bossa nova rhythm, and Ms. Viktor's sweet, sensual, velvety vocals, this jazzy track simmers. The Latin-tinged extended maxi version should have "Beach Ready!" stamped on every pressing. "Look out! Viktor Lazlo is a lady!" proclaimed *Music & Media* on May 9, 1987. Hold your applause till the end.

Sweet Summer Day - Chris Rea (1998), EastWest (G)
Producer not indicated, though likely Chris Rea.

The voice of "Fool (If You Think It's Over)" from 1978 offers a sort of soft rock ballad wrapped in a disco-glazed arrangement and sung in the raspy style for which the English singer/songwriter is well known. Clearly, Rea gets the lure of the season and how a sweet summer day can make your troubles drift away. As a single, the track is offered in equally compelling "Remix" and "Ibiza Remix" versions. Originally from the album *The Blue Cafe*.

Sweets For My Sweet - Chriss (1986), Transparent (G)
Producers: Reinhard Windmann

Robotic, '80s style pop/disco remake of The Searchers' hit from a female vocalist out of Hamburg, Germany, that has a cold, mechanical edge despite the warm palm tree artwork on the single jacket. The track isn't bad; the icy arrangement just feels disconnected from the song's lyrics.

Sweets For My Sweet - CJ Lewis (1994), Black Market (G)
Producers: CJ Lewis, Philip Leo

Quite the opposite of the previous selection, The Searchers' 1963 standard is delivered in a pure summer, irresistibly danceable, ragga-pop style that instantly invades your senses and commands your feet to start moving. Recorded in London, nearly everything about it is bright and fun. The single jacket features a ribald photo of a young girl lifting the front of her skirt for a leering Lewis, who apparently gets an intimate view, but the track itself plays much more innocently. But that's not to say there isn't some spice in all that sweetness. It was a sizable hit across Europe in the summer of '94.

Sweets For My Sweet - Tony Orlando (1979), Casablanca (US)
Producers: Hank Medress, Dave Appell

If one agrees the song "Sweets For My Sweet" has that summer vibe, Tony Orlando's version can't be ignored. It has a Captain and Tennille meets "Montego Bay" feel, deliciously pop with just a hint of the Caribbean. It's not quite as kitschy as one might expect, though it's certifiably in the campy camp. That said, Orlando is in fine vocal form surrounded by a solid production with a funky beat and a satisfying use of strings and soulful backups (who presumably aren't Dawn).

Sweet Summer Music - Altitudes (1976), Dark Horse Records (US)
Producer: Jay Lewis, Altitudes

Soulful pop with a Stevie Wonder meets The Spinners vibe. Somewhat mature looking Paul Stallworth and Danny Kootch handle lead vocals, oddly singing about (high) school being out in June, layin' in the park and wanting that sweet summer music—maybe they were just having flashbacks. This single from the *Good News* album ironically hit the *Billboard* pop chart as the summer was fading and school was back in session, right around the time Captain & Tennille's "Muskrat Love" was debuting.

Swept Away - Diana Ross (1984), RCA (US)
Producer: Daryl Hall, Arthur Baker

Here's the chain—La Ross, off it! The supreme diva dove right into the summer season by whispering about lying on the beach, the sensuality of the sun, heat and waves, and the hot touch of her man. As if that wasn't torrid enough, a determined, driving beat, like that of a heart pumping fiercely with lusty excitement, pulls us into the swirling waters of her sensual, steamy paradise. You'll need a cigarette after hearing it. (Just kidding, those things 'll kill ya.) It was the type of hard-edged, razor-sharp dance track that you always wanted from the singer—and, damn, if she didn't deliver. *Cash Box* accurately described the single's qualities on September 1, 1984, insisting, "This power rocker...combines the best of Ross' amazing voice with the chords of hard rock and the downbeat of the best funk...shows this classic lead vocalist at her romantic and gritty best as she tells the story of being swept away by the man in her life." The song reached #1 on the *Billboard* dance chart that month and dented the top 20 on the pop side. Miss Ross' look? Fierce. The sound? Your head goes bang. The mood? Feverish. She's got you covered!

Swimming - Figures On A Beach (1983), Metro-America (US)
Producer: Ben Grosse

A Detroit-based quartet with a sound that recalls the best of UK electro-new wave, going a bit darker and deeper than some of their Brit counterparts. Brisk beats tread water in a sea of synthesizers and guitars in the "Wet Mix" by Ivan Ivan. Dance music columnist Brian Chin, working for *Billboard* at the time, said the song "wins this week's freaky-but-accessible award with its 'Maniac' tempo and strange subject matter" (October 1, 1983), no doubt a reference to the track's odd theme of disorientation.

T - U

Tahiti, Tahiti - Voyage (1978), Marlin (F/US)
Producer: Roger Tokarz

Really colorful '70s-style disco, drenched in that Pacific island feel. A highlight from the French group's second and most popular album, *Fly Away*, which happens to play like an exotic, uplifting travel brochure. Recorded in London, Sylvia Mason's vocals and a lush, soulful production give this track a Boney M.-ish feel, which was probably quite intentional.

Tar Beach - Limahl (1984), EMI (G)
Producers: De Harris, Tim Palmer

Christopher Hamill, the former lead singer of Kajagoogoo ("Too Shy"), hit it big solo-style performing under the moniker Limahl with the single "The NeverEnding Story." The Moroder-Forsey penned synth-pop theme was featured in the movie soundtrack of the same name. With "The City Blues

Mix" of "Tar Beach," the artist attempted to keep that momentum going via an affectionate electronic homage to catching rays on the metropolitan alternative to sand and surf—the top of an apartment building. The roof and the song proved to be a bit too sticky, and it was only just a modest hit in Europe.

Tequila - No Way José (1985), Fourth & Broadway/Island (UK)
Producers: Mark Reilly, Phil Harding

It's easy to imagine Kid Creole And The Coconuts throwing down a shot of this irresistible hand-clapping mambo jambo, a chaser pulsating with electronic summer party energy. Its foundation was based on Chuck Rio's (Daniel Flores, who passed in 2006) classic song "Tequila" and the No Way José duo was Venezuelan vocalist Vik Hugo and percussionist Robin Jones. Phil Harding at PWL and Mark Reilly (of Matt Bianco fame) brought the track to life, and the record was released in Spanish and English versions.

Commentary from Mark Reilly:

"It was an idea by London DJ Nicky Holloway who got Island Records to contact me to make a new version of 'Tequila.' It was going to be for the clubs and for a comedy drama by The Comic Strip team called 'A Fistful Of Travellers' Cheques.' I brought in with me Robin Jones and a singer called [Vic] Hugo, who were both well known in the London Latin scene, and Phil Harding on the production. It was great fun!"

Commentary from Dr. Phil Harding:

"We used to go to Ibiza, and the whole Ibiza club thing back in the '80s was massive. The DJs would come back from there and play all the tracks [that had been hot down there] in the UK clubs. That would get us [the producers and remixers] thinking, okay, what can we do for next summer in Ibiza? 'Tequila' was one of those songs. I specifically co-produced that single with Matt Bianco's Mark Reilly for Ibiza, or what we called at the time 'the new type of summer dance sound, an Ibiza sound.' But it was requested by Island Records. They wanted the Matt Bianco sound, they put a few people together to be the act, and it was all specifically designed for summer and those DJs in Ibiza. This was an excellent example of something we definitely *did* make specifically for summer."

This Summer - Squeeze (1995), A&M/I.R.S. (UK)
Producers: Peter Smith, Glenn Tilbrook

The upbeat, yearning sentiment (cloudless skies, being in love) found in this pop-glazed rocker from the UK band, lifted from their *Ridiculous* album, is further enhanced by Mark Stent's stealthy remix, released in '96. The original and the remix versions were separately modest hits in the UK about a year apart, but the engagingly simple poeticism of this production should have been enough to garner the track a lot more attention. The song has an agreeable, youthful power-pop finesse with its feel-good melody and Tilbrook's craggy voiced ardor. And now for something you can *really* squeeze into.

Thong Song, The - Sisqó (2000), Def Soul (US)
Producers: Bob Robinson, Sisqo the Golden Child, Tim Kelley

(L) Sisqó circa 2000, photo by Robert M. Ascroft II, Island Def Jam (press still).

Just to clarify, East Baltimore's Mark Andrews, better known as Sisqó (and a one time member of Dru Hill), connects livin' la vida loca with hot girls wearing those spandex neon booty thongs, *not* rubber flip flops for the feet. It should have been nothing more than a kitschy "less is more" hip-hop throw down, but between Sisqó's earnest vocal passion and the slick, airtight production of this electronic/R&B/garage hybrid, it manages to defy its own boundaries. It makes "indecent" tangas seem, well, *pretty decent*! A summer pop classic that strings you along with its unstoppable g-force that rides up on you in a good way. And what about that showy (and truly awesome) beach party video? Still as fresh 'n' as the day it was filmed. Nominated for Best R&B Song at the 2001 Grammys, "Thong Song" was voted Best Hip-Hop Video at the 2000 MTV Video Music Awards.

Ticket To The Tropics - Cristina (1984), Mercury (US)
Producer: Don Was

Cristina Monet Palaci's tangy new wave/avant-pop jammer is a slightly altered (and a tad more bitter-minded) version of The Coconuts' recording made the year before. Cristina's take has songwriting attributed to herself and Doug Fieger, while The Coconuts' goes to Kid Creole's August Darnell and, again, Cristina Monet, so clearly some kind of arrangement was made for both acts to release the song. (Kid Creole And The Coconuts also recorded it in 2011, incorporating the composition into his "I Wake Up Screaming (In The Tropics)" track.) So this song has racked up some milage. In this version, Miss Monet's incredulous attitude gives the track a fun, feisty edge. Described in her label bio as "a rich brat," Cristina had a brief but spectacular moment with this song, lifted from the LP *Sleep It Off* and produced by Don Was (Don Fagenson), the man who gave us "Walk The Dinosaur" and "Out Come The Freaks." The singer also offered us much to love with her unconventional remake of Lennon-McCartney's "Drive My Car," found on the popular 1981 Island/Ze Records compilation, *Seize The Beat (Dance Ze Dance),* and the single "Things Fall Apart." For sure, things fell apart when we lost Cristina in 2020.

Ticket To The Tropics - The Coconuts (1983), EMI (US)
Producer: August Darnell

Life is better with coconuts! Kid Creole's famous reinforcements are fully in focus with this sticky weather single. "Ticket" bears a striking sonic resemblance to the Kid's "Annie, I'm Not Your Daddy" (released the year before) but lyrically shifts the attention from paternity to devilry. There's a touch of camp and levity in there, too, with the clever "tropics" double-entendre (subject to interpretation) and the 1940s vibe that Kid Creole forged early on. Here, a woman on a Latin holiday with a male companion discovers his *true* agenda. It's a single designed to place a momentary but highly entertaining spotlight on the so-much-more-than backup ladies who worked tirelessly to help make the Kid Creole experience a dazzling one.

The original Coconuts line-up included Cheryl Poirier, Adriana Kaegi and Taryn Hagey, with other cast members jumping in and heading out over time. The trio's distinctively smooth but sassy harmonies and inventive dance moves conveyed both a stylized brand of female power and a kind of brash, edgy, tongue-in-cheek sexiness that is in perfect sync with the clever musical productions they supported. The Coconuts had a take charge quality that was very unusual at the time, and they were worth the price of admission all by themselves.

With the "Ticket" single and their 1983 debut album, *Don't Take My Coconuts,* this trio showed just how supremely capable they were when placed front and center. On June 25, 1983, *Cash Box* reviewed the album saying, "New music stations that liked Bananarama will go wild over [The Coconuts'] nutty vocal antics…" *Billboard* reviewed the album on the same day, calling it "well done" and saying, "Prince has his Vanity and Rick James his Mary Jane Girls, so why shouldn't the crown prince of international dance rhythms [Darnell/Kid Creole] break out his own backing trio?" Cheryl Poirier can answer that question and then some.

Commentary from Cheryl Poirier:

Miss Cheryl, how does one become a Coconut? And would you mind sharing a bit of the history behind The Coconuts' original line-up?

"I was an athlete in high school here in Maryland, not a singer or dancer, but I had music in my blood. My father played piano and sang like Frank Sinatra. He was my idol—I would sit beside him on the piano bench and listen to him my whole life. But I was pretty good at track and field, so I got a scholarship to college running the 100-meter hurdles. I was training for the Olympics. I made a mistake and switched coaches in '75 and didn't make the '76 Olympics. I ran for another two years, but I lost my drive—I just didn't want to do it anymore. I had been running since I was seven and I asked my father what else I should do. He thought I should try going into drama, and I said okay, even though I had never done it in my life. I quit college, three years, no degree. I went to New York City by myself. I moved into the Village on Perry Street. The best—I should have never left, right on the corner of 4th and Perry! I needed a job so I went into this restaurant that was kind of a lesbian hangout. I met a girl there that was kind of a punk rocker named Lori Eastside. We became friends, and the owner of the restaurant wanted to form a punk band and got Lori and me to be her background singers. We did a couple of weird gigs, super unorganized. After those few gigs I told Lori I was going back to acting because it wasn't for me. I got a job at a place called Blazing Salads, auditioned for some soap operas and off-Broadway shows, and I got a few parts.

"Six months later, Lori called and said she was in another band and that they needed another blonde singer. She thought I fit the bill. It was early in 1980. I went to this rehearsal studio and the band was Kid Creole And The Coconuts. I thought, 'This is really good!' I auditioned, but the young woman who was organizing the auditions and was a Coconut herself, Adriana Kaegi, told August Darnell (Kid Creole) I couldn't be a Coconut because I wasn't sexy enough. I was in jeans, street clothes, whatever. Lori coached me and bought me some purple spandex pants. I went back in with this outfit on for my second interview—I got the part.

"So, there were two women who had relatively short stints as Coconuts before the band started touring and selling records. They were Anna Ratafia and Roni Griffith. Anna was at the rehearsal space, The Daily Planet, when I auditioned in January or February of 1980. I was hired two days after my audition and replaced Anna before any more gigs were scheduled. Adriana Kaegi, Roni Griffith and I were the line-up of Coconuts for the next nine months when we filmed 'Saturday Night Live' [as musical guests] on November 15, 1980. We also did a few local gigs with Roni during those months. I believe Roni was modeling and working on other musical endeavors at that time and she decided to pursue those opportunities. [*Author note* - Roni Griffith went on to have a significant pop and disco hit with "(The Best Part Of) Breakin' Up" in 1982.] She was replaced by Taryn soon after the 'Saturday Night Live' gig. Roni was beautiful and talented and we had a great time working together! Again, her tenure as a Coconut lasted about nine months after I joined. Adriana, Taryn Hagey and I were the line-up when we recorded *Fresh Fruit In Foreign Places* and *Tropical Gangsters*. Taryn was a life-long dancer and was showcased with solo dances on several tours and videos. Taryn also recorded albums and toured during our 'heyday' for several years. Taryn and I were BFFs during those crazy, exciting, wonderful times! She and her husband decided to move to California so she was replaced by Janique Svedberg. For all intents and purposes, I'd say that Adriana Kaegi, Taryn Hagey and I were the original Coconuts. Then the lineup was Adriana, me and Janique for many more years of recording and touring.

"[Early on], we weren't popular. We did gigs on Long Island, and places like that. They had already made the album *Off The Coast Of Me*, and I was with them promoting it. Some great songs on that album, like 'Yolanda.' Oh my God, loved it! Anyway, we were on Ze Records with a lot of great artists like The Waitresses, Was (Not Was), a whole bunch of them. They set us up to open for the Talking Heads, and we traveled up and down the east coast in vans (the early days). And then we opened for the B-52's. So fun! However August managed to arrange it, Island Records became our distributor and that was it! Then the records *Fresh Fruit In Foreign Places* and *Tropical Gangsters* were next and we went to Paris. Then it went bananas—huge!"

It's clear Mr. Darnell wanted to create something more than just a trio of back-up singers with The Coconuts. From your perspective, what goal do you think he had in mind?

"August is steeped, I do mean steeped, in '40s and '50s movie musicals. I think he wanted us to be like these untouchable bombshells who were like 'Jane of the Jungle.' So our first costumes were like ripped loin cloths, leopard skins. If you ever saw us on 'Saturday Night Live,' which was my first TV show, we had our hair wild as if we were stuck in the jungle for six months, with hairy armpits. I think August may have also seen us as kind of like The Andrews Sisters, and each one of us would have been like a '40s star—Marlene Dietrich, Rita Hayworth, you know. It was all movie-influenced. He was like a Cab Calloway type of character, with the zoot suit. That's the way I would describe the band."

Your live shows were remarkable experiences from all reports.

"I, to this day, think it was one of the best live shows—*ever*! That's because it was really a Ringling Bros. and Barnum & Bailey circus! All other artists—well, let's take Madonna. It's you and a bunch of dancers and lighting and effects—but it's you. [Kid Creole And The Coconuts] wasn't like that. It was August as a Cab Calloway, mixed with James Brown, mixed with calypso, salsa and reggae. And he had Coati Mundi, who was the comic relief. And then he had us, The Andrews Sisters. And the band themselves all played characters. It was really a three-ring circus. There was never a dull moment. The Coconuts weren't just background singers. There was so much movement, and we were characters in his movie. And we never smiled. We were untouchable—you could look, but you couldn't touch us. It was the attitude. You might want to meet us, but you never will."

In 1983, The Coconuts got their own album, Don't Take My Coconuts, and released a very catchy single, "Ticket To The Tropics." Why the decision to do this spin-off?

"Great song, right? We're starting to sell lots of records by 1982. But we (The Coconuts) were not royalty members, we were sidemen. But we weren't dumb. Full arenas—people were not all there just to see Kid Creole. A lot of people came to see us. We were working just as hard. We had started pushing August to give us a piece of the action. He's a smart businessman, though, and he agreed we were a big part of the whole thing. So he said he would produce a record for us. He was the songwriter and producer, so [*Cheryl starts laughing*] we will get some puny royalties.

"We got signed to EMI with August as producer and we were happy, but we didn't really get to choose the songs for the album. We were The Coconuts and played our parts. But I did love that album anyway. I think 'Ticket To The Tropics' was beautiful. August produced it for us in a super tropical style. Adriana, I think she probably designed the feather costumes we wore for that song. 'Ticket To The Tropics' did pretty well and a few of the other songs got airplay. We basically toured from spring till fall, and that was a blast.

"But we needed to start making some royalties, because in the United States, you don't have any other income. In Europe, artists get [a form of unemployment] when they aren't touring, which we don't have in the US. That's why we wanted to do the solo thing, but it didn't continue. I remember another thing—there was a backlash. In England, the paparazzi, *Melody Maker*, press like that, were very powerful in the music industry. So Kid Creole was a big hit, then Coati Mundi did a solo release. Then The Coconuts did a solo album. There was a lot of, 'What's this? Everybody's trying to make some money off of [*Tropical Gangsters*]?

"The thing is, we recorded a second EMI album, but it wasn't released. I can't remember why. I don't even have a copy of it. We worked hard on it."

It's the 1980s, and The Coconuts are three young and attractive women. This was a male dominated industry in an era well known for sexism and a lack of guard rails. Was that a challenge for you?

"Wow, yeah. We did this gig in Manhattan, and Sylvester Stallone came to the show with our manager. Mr. Stallone said something like he had admired me ever since he saw me on 'Saturday Night Live.' Cool, okay. I get dressed to go home and am going out the back door, and our manager says, 'Yo, where you going?' I told him I was heading out. He said, 'Are you fucking crazy? Look, he's Sly! You go out with him, you fuck him good, and your career is made.' Now this is the music business, and I was no angel, but, I thought, that's my manager. That's his best advice? There were other things like that, record executives, and 'you'll get more promotion, *if*—'"

Shifting to more pleasant memories, I imagine there must have been some very funny moments being a Coconut.

"There were too many funny things, but here's one. Kid Creole knew that some of our steps were harder than others. We had one where you had to throw [your upper body] down, up, down, up. It was only supposed to be for about six bars, and then he'd make a call and we'd switch to another step. Well, just to mess with us, he shouted to us on that move, 'Keep it up! Keep it up!' I think it was the song 'In the Jungle' or 'Turkey Trot.' He wouldn't stop, just to torture us. He thought it was hysterical. [*She laughs.*] After the show, we were like, 'We're going to get you back for that!' The next night, we're on a two-level stage, the higher one behind him for the song 'Off The Coast Of Me.' Normally he'd come on singing, all suave and gesture upward to us. We normally entered wearing coconuts cut in half, tied together [the top] and grass skirts. This time we came out with no tops on! We had to! He literally almost fell off the stage. It was only for a minute, and nobody cared in the south of France anyway. That's the kind of thing we did."

Tell me a bit about your departure from the group and why it was the right time.

"Going back to our solo project, we didn't just show up for that *Don't Take My Coconuts* album, we worked on it. You think you're going to get ahead and make royalties. Then we worked hard on the second [album], and it didn't get released. And there were times we thought we should have been paid better. So, I think it was about 1986. When I quit something, I quit. The girls [newcomer and Billy Idol girlfriend Perri Lister and Coconut Adriana Kaegi] and I got a [new] record deal with Atlantic Records. We were now going to be a girl group called Boomerang. When Kid Creole went back on tour in South America, Adriana went back with him, but I did not. It was just before Kid Creole's *I Too Have Seen The Woods* album I think.

"I stayed in New York to help promote the Boomerang record we made and the single, 'These Boots Are Made For Walkin.' It was a cute album. We spent a year and a half working on this project, but it never got promoted. We had David Kershenbaum, who produced Tracy Chapman, and a great synthesizer musician, Jeff Lorber. It was just fun, but a lot of work. I knew that Atlantic had big artists, Genesis, Stevie Nicks, and nobody would pay attention [to an unknown new act] except your A&R guy. Swear to God, two weeks before the release date, I go to see [our A&R man] at the record company offices. The receptionist tells me, 'Oh, you didn't hear? He had to go to rehab. He won't be back for three to six months.'

"That was literally the most disillusioning moment in my music career. I mean, I had quit Kid Creole. I thought we (Boomerang) were better than Bananarama! But one guy, and it all just fell apart. [The man] who signed us and loved us wasn't there now. You figure you work hard, you're disciplined, and you win—no, not there. I did a couple of things after that, and I ended up briefly going back with Kid Creole in the early '90s. I still adore him, though. We still email each other all the time. But I had my son, and as a mother it wasn't enough. You need more income and stability, and eventually I became a real estate agent."

Looking back at all of it now, how do you feel?

"I feel like the luckiest person alive! Think about fate. I'm from Maryland, an actress. I would never have gotten near any of these musicians if I hadn't moved to Perry Street in New York City, met Lori, and so on. It was the universe bumping me into that group of people. How lucky am I to have been paid and to have traveled from Norway to Algeria, Hong Kong to Japan, in my 20s, carefree. My goal was to be a great performer, yes, but I had nothing but fun over those 16 years in the music business!"

(R) Cheryl Poirier today.

Your songs have often touched on tropical themes and destinations. Where would you go for a warm weather holiday?

"I haven't been to these places yet, but I want to go! Hawaii, Bali, Tahiti. I'd like to spend a couple of weeks in Jamaica because I love reggae music. When you're raising a kid, it wasn't like you could [drop everything] and say, 'I think I'll go on a holiday!'"

And musically, what gives you that summer feeling?

"I guess because we were touring every summer, I remember we put in a cassette at that time in the tour van—Bob Marley, *Legend*. You just put that on and you might as well have a sarong on and a cocktail in your hand. I also listen to the young Marleys, sit back and have a daiquiri. It's not winter music! I married an Argentinian, so I heard a lot of salsa music and that puts me in a summer mood. And of course, just dance music in general— Madonna, Prince, even Britney Spears was bad ass!"

Well, I can tell you that I listen to Kid Creole And The Coconuts!

"You know what? Let's say I want to do a workout routine today. Do you think I listen to these aerobic girls? No! I started putting our concerts that are on YouTube on my TV. We were known as the hardest working band in show biz after James Brown because everything was choreographed and our shows were an hour and a half, two hours long. And then they'd call for an encore—[August] would do an encore for another hour! I still know the steps, so let me get back into it and do my thing! Honestly, I still do listen and dance to our music and, really, there is nothing better!"

*[See also: **Annie, I'm Not Your Daddy - Kid Creole And The Coconuts**.]*

Ticket Toulouse - Thomas Barquée (1991), Columbia (G)
Producer: Peter Hauke

France's popular holiday destination near the Spanish border gets the spotlight in this addictive and sparkly rock/synth-pop/dance jam from the German-born singer. It tells a romantic story that one suspects most definitely took place in the summer. "The Bondvision Mix" extends the journey with fun electronic quirks and zippy piano breaks, and the inviting melody and lyrics are quite likely to spin around your brain in a happy loop for some time. Get on board!

Tide Is High, The - Blondie (1980), Chrysalis (US)
Producer: Mike Chapman

Written by Jamaica's John Holt, the late icon of the island's ska and reggae music scene, "The Tide Is High" was recorded in 1967 by The Paragons, of which Holt was a member, and by Gregory Isaacs around 1978. Blondie took their shot with it and scored a four-week #1 hit with the song on the *Billboard* dance chart (in combination with "Rapture") and climbed to the top spot on the publication's pop singles chart. On April 17, 2020, Tom Breihan of stereogum.com reflected on the track in an article that was part of a series focusing on number one records. The writer observed, "Nobody would confuse Blondie's record with an actual Jamaican reggae track, but it's still a cool attempt to engage with the genre on its own terms. And considering the American pop records that had attempted the sound earlier, 'The Tide Is High' counts as some kind of miracle." The UK's hugely popular group Atomic Kitten covered "The Tide Is High (Get The Feeling)" incorporating a hip-hop beat and lush harmonies with great success in 2002.

Tirati Su - Cavaliere (1991), Crownhill/Keepon Musik (I/G)
Cheer up
Producer: Ruggero Penazzo

A young, good-looking Italian, Tiziano Cavaliere sought to create innovative pop music that would cross genre borders. The handclap-fused "Beach Mix" of "Tirati Su" evokes that feeling of fuzzy awareness. You know, when you're buzzed and find yourself barefoot at an oceanside clam bake. Wish I had a dime for every time that happened. On July 4, 1992, *Music & Media* noted, "The upcoming summer season is asking for songs that feel like sunbeams. What better place than the Mediterranean to look for the sound of summer? Cavaliere should be any programmer's choice." The publication also likened "Tirati Su" to George Michael's "Faith," which, er, good as Tiziano's song may be, feels like a stretch.

Touch My Bikini - Bikini Girl (2005), Toptrax/ZYX (G)
Producer not indicated.

Bikini Girl encourages you to do it like you mean it, though it's all less provocative than it sounds. A high energy electro-dance no-brainer with an infectious beat, frantic piano riffs, and some "I Feel Love" rhythmical throbbing thrown in to let you know it's bubble gum party time on the beach. Woot! Woot! A word to the wise...look, but maybe *don't* touch that bikini.

Unconditional Love - Donna Summer (1983), Mercury (US)
Producer: Michael Omartian

Though the high-energy hit "She Works For Hard The Money" got most of the attention at the time, "Unconditional Love," a follow-up single featuring support vocals by the UK's Musical Youth ("Pass The Dutchie"), was also something really special. With its warm Caribbean atmosphere, gentle buoyancy, and wholesome vibe, this track was a very pleasing and unexpected surprise from Ms. Summer after the electronic vigor of "Money," arriving just in time for the last weeks of summer in 1983. On October 22, 1983, *Cash Box* commentator Harry Weinger had little to say about the track and seemed ignorant of who La Donna was, passively saying, "another artist with a seasonal surname...hot on the radio with an island flavored track."

Under The Boardwalk - Carl Carlton (1982), RCA (US)
Producer: Narada Michael Walden

From the R&B singer's *The Bad C.C.* album, which featured his blistering hot dance reinvention of Bobby Blue's and The Four Tops' evergreen recordings of "Baby, I Need Your Loving." With "Boardwalk," the artist takes a more traditional and soulful approach than on his scorching hit club hit, mixing in some feather-light reggae touches and a hint of Spanish guitars.

Under The Boardwalk (1982) / Sunshine And Ecstasy* (Feel My Heartbeat) (1992) - Tom Tom Club, Island/Sire (US)
Producers: Steve Stanley, Tina Weymouth, Chris Frantz / *Chris Frantz, *Tina Weymouth, *Mark Roule, *Bruce Martin

The influential group (husband and wife Chris Frantz and Tina Weymouth, Talking Heads alumni, and others throughout the years, including David Byrne) no doubt were affected by the surroundings of Compass Point Studios in the Bahamas where they recorded their version of The Drifters' 1964 hit. The track is smile-inducing, light computerized pop with a new wave edge (though not as robotic as their hit "Wordy Rappinghood"), punctuated by the occasional steel drum. Love the festive summer single jacket artwork on the UK release. *Record Mirror*'s Daniela Soave was uninspired by it, however, saying on July 24, 1982, "This is a prime example of how to murder a bloody good song…this version sends me lurching for the original." Oh, well. Ten years later, the group's club ready "Sunshine And Ecstasy," top 10 on *Billboard*'s dance chart, recreates some of those same "Boardwalk" sensations with a kind of Tom Tom Club meets Kid Creole thing going on, reggae-inspired vocals and a driving beat.

(R) Tom Tom Club's Chris Frantz and Tina Weymouth circa early '80s,
Fontana Records (press still).

Under The Mango Tree - Tim Tim (1998), EMI (A)
Producers: Jerry Rosso, Rene Rosso

Not a bad place to be. It's a hip version of the traditional Jamaican calypso song ("Underneath The Mango Tree"), originally placed in the spotlight thanks to Diana Coupland's rendition in the Sean Connery/James Bond film *Dr. No* (1962). You know the scene—"Mango" was playing in the background as fetching Honey Ryder (the striking and statuesque Ursula Andress) emerges from the limpid aqua blue waters of Crab Key. Tim Tim's (vocalist Beverley Lamothe and ragga rapping by Jerry) version provides a very accessible pop/dance interpretation with a calypso glazing. The song's video, which, with a wink, plays as a homage to 007, was filmed in Nassau/Bahamas. The cd maxi-single offers a recipe for a "Tim Tim Mango Drink," mixing mango syrup, orange juice, an egg yolk, vanilla flavored sugar, and soda water. I feel like it's missing something very important. What could it be? Don't sit under the mango tree and drink it with anyone else but me!

Unemployed In Summertime - Emiliana Torrini (2000),
One Little Indian Ltd. (UK)
Producers: Roland Orzabal, Alan Griffiths

Emiliana, you had me at "Unemployed." It was a dark day when "summer" made that awful evolution into "summer job." How does Ms. Torrini describe the emotions of youth during this period? Let's say—it's complicated. Okay, most summer songs don't make our brains work too much, which is usually a good thing. But Miss Emiliana, who co-wrote this track with Eg White, takes seasonal simplicity and turns it into a slightly tangled, sexually sketchy 'n' flighty (yet decidedly poetic) expression of the season from the viewpoint of a 21 year-old female. No need for money if you're young and your mission is a wet-lipped kiss, she sings—this isn't the usual dancing on the beach ditty. Miss Torrini, from Iceland no less, has a gentle voice with sort of a dazed edge that rides the song's haunting melody like dandelion seeds traveling on a hot breeze. The effect creates a blithe spirit, and the brain impulses expressed here are potently fanciful. The electronic rock charm of the original version is nearly annihilated in the bizarre hip-hop "Dreemhouse Unemployed Club Mix." However, the Tore Johansson edit does a little rearranging and keeps the deep groove experience of the original version intact, packing a melodic wallop if you're able to think and get down with it at the same time. You have to ask yourself, did the summer inspire this music, or did this music inspire the summer? "Unemployed In Summertime"'s co-producer Griffiths collaborated with Orzabal on his earlier Tears For Fears projects.

Un'Estate Italiana - Edoardo Bennato & Gianna Nannini (1989), Virgin (I) *Being Italian (or alternately, Italian summer)*
Producer: Giorgio Moroder

What would summer be without a trip to Italy? Or a soccer game? Two of the country's titans of pop/rock join forces to create a powerful theme for the 1990 FIFA World Cup, itself one of the most popular international sporting events of all time, held every four years in the summer and attracting billions of TV viewers. Very much designed to elicit a sing-along, whether in a massive stadium or at a local pub, this track celebrates the international appeal of the games, the thrill of summer sportsmanship, the excitement of the colors, the desire to win, and, in this case, the unique appeal of a season that is synonymous with Italy. This time around, West Germany triumphed against Argentina at the World Cup, and Italy came in third. Bennato & Nannini's song ranked at #21 in *Music & Media*'s Eurochart Hot 100 Singles wrap-up of 1990.

Up On The Roof - Viola Wills (1980), Hansa/Ariola America (G)
Producer: Jerry McCabe

Trouble-proof paradise is found up on the roof in Viola's wonderful disco remake of The Drifters' R&B hit from 1962. The singer's soulful voice is so distinctive and totally satisfying that you'll want to savor every single minute you're up there with her. Arranged with the same type of balmy dance sensibility as her rendition of "If You Could Read My Mind," a solid hit on the US dance charts also produced by Jerry McCabe. Ms. Wills had a gift for breathing new life into timeless songs (don't overlook her amazing cover of "Stormy Weather"), and with "Up On The Roof" we have what sounds like one of the late singer's most personal and heartfelt performances. In 2009, Miss Viola bid us farewell.

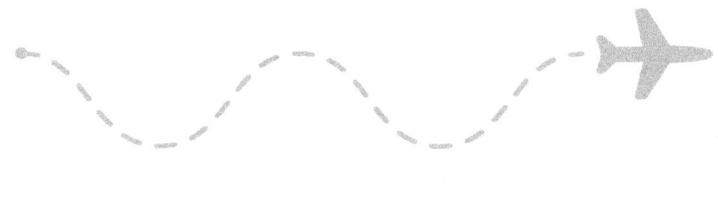

Vacation - Go-Go's (1982), IRS (US)
Producer: Richard Gottehrer

It's hard to believe the Go-Go's (initially consisting of Belinda Carlisle, Charlotte Caffey and Jane Wiedlin, with Gina Schock and Kathy Valentine coming on board in '79), who sold millions singing about jubilant summer escapism, started out performing in a dark, stale-smelling, spray-painted Hollywood punk club called The Masque. From this dank dive joint sprang— *tadah*—a big, bright, sunny, broad daylight sound. Though the lyrics to "Vacation" have the girls mooning over their absent love interests, the song is upbeat, danceable, sassy pop all the way through. In their online list of the "Best Summer Songs of All Time" (May 20, 2020), *Rolling Stone* said, "With a radiant keyboard melody and swirls of surf guitar, the Go-Go's nailed the feeling of trying to use summer vacation to try to get over a crush." On July 3, 1982, *Cash Box* reviewed the single proclaiming, "The girls still have the beat, and it's as buoyant as ever..." They added, "The initial radio reception indicates it could be a summer fave." Over in the UK, Mark Cooper of *Record Mirror* was a smidge less enthusiastic in his August 7, 1982, review of the girls' *Vacation* album. Said the critic, "The Go-Go's are a dance band, as friendly and comfortable as the girl-next-door. They manage this without irony, an unreal achievement in Reagan's America. [The *Vacation* album] is snappy and cheerful, but half way through the second side you wish someone would stop them smiling." The *Record Mirror*'s Robin Smith was also unimpressed reviewing the single on July 31, 1982, saying, "Smarty pants song in their too cute style. They've also been listening to too much Blondie, so there." Guys, lighten up and take a beach day!

Meanwhile, the "Vacation" track was also a kind of "tech" groundbreaker at time—one of the first of the short-lived "cassette singles" on the market in the US, with a retail price of $2.98. A July 3, 1982, article in *Cash Box* by Michael Glynn quoted a label marketing vp, who said, "It just made sense to us since so many kids use personal cassette players [Walkmans] at the beach, the Go-Go's have a very large teenage audience, and the songs are about vacation and the beach."

The good times with the Go-Go's didn't last forever, but the song "Vacation" will be enthusiastically played throughout each and every summer season for as long as our planet still supports human life (so, another 10 or 20 years, if we're lucky). In his March 13, 2003, online interview with former Go-Go Belinda Carlisle for *Good Times,* Greg Archer gave the singer a choice: "We Got The Beat" or "Vacation?" Ms. Carlisle chose "Vacation." (What's my choice? *Hmmm*...my lips are sealed.) The GoGo's were inducted into the Rock & Roll Hall of Fame in 2021.

Vamos A La Playa - Righeira (1983), CGD (I) *Let's go to the beach*
Producers: La Bionda

Arguably one of the most famous summer season dance songs of all-time (except, perhaps, in the US, where it is virtually unknown). During the summer months in the '80s, flocks of Northern Europeans set their sights on the Mediterranean sun. They'd hit the region's beaches during the day and dance to music produced in Italy at night, and a few of these songs would then hit it big on the sales and airplay charts, as the tourists returned to their homelands looking to buy the records they heard. "Vamos A La Playa" is one of the biggest of these summer success stories. This infectious slice of early Italo disco was the brainchild of a production brother act called La Bionda (Angelo and Carmelo La Bionda) and fronted by two young Italian men who went under the names Michael Righeira and Johnson Righeira (real names Stefano Rota and Stefano Righi). If all that sounds confusing, wait, there's more. The song itself isn't quite the uplifting beach party it appears to be.

"'Vamos A La Playa' had a real summer feeling in its title, but hidden in its lyrics was the true meaning of the song," said Carmelo La Bionda. "The theme of the song was a call to go to the beach, a nuclear bomb has exploded and the radiation will tan us. It took six months to have a finished and convincing final master. We couldn't believe that 'Vamos A La Playa' was becoming such a huge international hit. In Italy it is considered the most popular summer song (with a social statement). The Spanish language sounded nice because it was an unusual combination with electronic pop." *[From the book Europe's Stars of '80s Dance Pop, Arena, McFarland, 2017.]*

Vaya Vamos A La Fiesta - Andrea Jürgens (2002), White Records (G) *Let's go to the party*
(Executive) Producer: Jack White

With a danceable Latin meets Eurodisco-pop vibe, this is an enjoy-the-moment song about a night where love is in the air and there's a party on the beach. Andrea assures us the drinks are cold and the kisses are hot. A single very much in tune with the singer's previous schlager styled hits, designed to promote her *Dankeschön • Zum 25. Bühnenjubiläum (Thank you for the 25th stage anniversary)* collection, celebrating a quarter century of her pop friendly German language music. Ms. Jürgens passed far too young at age 50 in 2017.

Voyage, Voyage - Desireless (1986), CBS (F)
Producer: Jean-Michel Rivat

"Voyage Voyage" definitely goes the distance. This exotic, enchanting song by one of France's biggest vocalist discoveries of the '80s was ranked as the sixth most successful single of the year (1987) by *Music & Media* (Madonna's "La Isla Bonita" was #1). In a review of the song that year, the publication summarized this hook-laden, border-crossing track as, "High-pitched, dramatic vocals over a contagious electro-beat, in an Alphaville-type of setting." "Voyage Voyage," which takes the listener on a poetic globetrotting journey from Spain to Ecuador, the Ganges to the Amazon, also topped the UK charts, a rarity for a Francophone release. Desireless (real name, Claudie Fritsch) possessed an unconventional gender-bending image, reminiscent of Boy George. No surprise, since the artist was originally from (and quite successful in) the fashion world. Regarded by some as a one-hit wonder, the artist's limited follow-up singles, notably "John" and "Qui Sommes Nous," failed to gain the broad attention of "Voyage" but were absolutely just as artistically accomplished and diverting.

Walk On The Ocean -Toad The Wet Sprocket (1991), Columbia (US)
Producer: Gavin MacKillop

Summer simplicity abounds as the band from Santa Barbara, California, retreats into nostalgia, seeking to find a place where everything is better and safe. It's a beach filled with memories, as depicted in the song's video. The emotion is thick here, and you're likely to feel some salty tears well up as you become enveloped in equally salty ocean spray. This tracks evokes sentimental memories more vividly than any photograph ever could. Shake it off, slip into your lightest loafers, beach sandals, or mesh water shoes, cuz baby the sun is out and ya better gets ta steppin'! Here come the sunshine walkers.

Walking Into Sunshine - Central Line (1981), Mercury (UK)
Producer: Roy Carter

A cool slice of hot, sophisticated, vintage '80s Brit-funk/R&B that lovingly embraces its '70s soul vibe roots. "Walking Into Sunshine" was the band's biggest US hit, making just a minor dent on the Hot 100 pop side, but going top 20 on the *Billboard* Hot Soul Singles chart. On August 22, 1981, *Record World's* Brian Chin said, "'Sunshine' is a perfect summer sound that manages a notably fresh, unobtrusive use of synthesizer in the rhythm section, and a light, Doobie-ish pop/rock vocal sound." On October 24, 1981, *Cash Box* was equally enthusiastic, saying, "A confident backbeat, along with bright, sunny keyboards and horn parts, instrumentally underscores the joyous lyrics and high stepping vocals." One can hear the influence of island rhythms in this jam's warm backbeat, and combined with its exuberant lyrics and vocals, it conveys the pleasure of getting away for a holiday with a soulful earnestness. "Walking Into Sunshine" is the musical equivalent of a *really* good time.

Walking On Sunshine - Chris Jobe (1995), Gazell (SW)
Producers: Woodgrove-Ofwerman

An electro-reggae and surprisingly imaginative version of the Katrina And The Waves hit from Sweden that works extremely well with its slower, shuffling arrangement. Ms. Jobe's vocals are quite inviting and the shout out loud chorus gives the production some additional punch. On October 7, 1995, *Music & Media* said, "The new Swedish vocal talent has all the qualities required to make this tune genuinely her own." She accomplished that, despite some ill-placed belch-like sound effects at the song's midway point. Pardon me, must be the mangos!

Walking On Sunshine - Eddy Grant (1978), ICE (UK)
Producer: Eddy Grant

Mr. Grant's single and album of the same name weren't originally big commercial successes, but the artist coveys a soulfulness and authenticity in this track that is both shimmering with sunlight and ruggedly uplifting. From the "do it, do it" undercurrent, to the bright horns and pulsating Caribbean groove, this track is a lean, mean funk machine. The song itself reached its zenith when Rockers Revenge turned it into a full-on club blaster in 1982. Grant's version has been given a face lift a few times, including the punchy "Zulu Mix" by Tim Simenon in 1989 and an electro-house mix by Joey Negro in 2001.

Walking On Sunshine '82 - Rockers Revenge Ft. Donnie Calvin (1982), Streetwise (UK/US)
Producer: Arthur Baker

What we have here is an unforgettable summer house jam, a cover of the Eddy Grant-penned song. It's arresting "hey/do it" chants, rolling beat, funk-soul vibe, and feverish vocals by Mr. Calvin, a reggae singer, all contributed to making this groundbreaking dip into the rapidly intensifying house/freestyle music genre a mighty call to *move your body*! And during the hot summer of '82, this garage anthem packed club dance floors in the US (a sweaty staple on Fire Island and in downtown NYC gay clubs for sure), the UK and throughout Europe. A studio creation by producer Arthur Baker (the man behind a huge summer hit, "Planet Rock" by Africa Bambaataa & Soul Sonic Force), the track easily reached the #1 spot on the *Billboard* dance chart and kept the heat up throughout the entire summer and fall. Mixed by John "Jellybean" Benitez and Baker, "Sunshine" has been sampled in dozens of dance tracks throughout the years since. A follow-up 12-inch single, "Sunshine, Partytime" extended the life of this singular dance music event by adding a rap. Rocker's Revenge, as a music act, was unable to keep the momentum going and disbanded just two years later, but Arthur Baker continued his prolific career, remixing dance/pop classics for Bruce Springsteen ("Dancing In The Dark") and Cyndi Lauper ("Girls Just Want To Have Fun"), among many other notables.

Walking On Sunshine - Jennifer Lopez (2002), Epic (US)
Producer: Sean "P. Diddy" Combs, Cory Rooney, Mario Winans

The Bronx-born singer's airy vocals and pristine productions almost never disappoint. Almost. The British "Metro Remix" transforms the rather spare original version of this song into a fairly pumping house jam with a Spanish flair. Not bad I suppose for a summer club night, but it's not a knock-out like "Let's Get Loud." The track only cracked the top 40 on the *Billboard* dance chart, so not among Jenny from the block's most popular spins.

Walking On Sunshine - Krush (1992), Network (UK)
Producers: Dem Two Guyz

The British dance trio who hit it big with "House Arrest" in '87 remake the Eddie Grant/Rockers Revenge jam, giving it a pop/house vibe with bright, zippy piano flourishes.

Walking On Sunshine - Reddbone Ft. Rhonda (1994), WEA/ Eternal (UK)
Producer: The Solution for Small World Productions

Woah yeah! The Katrina And The Waves song composed by Kimberley Rew is given a high-energy '90s dance/pop treatment with a dash of reggaeton/pop/ rap from Peter Lee. Lead vocalist Rhonda Marshall has an uplifting charm that's the perfect sweetener for its caffeine-jolted club-ready arrangement, and it's all quite irresistible. The "Pressed For Time" mix kicks the beats-per-minute up a few more notches. The track has a vibe similar to CJ Lewis' "Sweets For My Sweet" from the same year.

Walking On Sunshine (1985) / Sun Street* (1986) - Katrina And The Waves, Capitol (C/UK/US)
Producers: Katrina And The Waves, Pat Collier / *Katrina And The Waves, *Pat Collier, *Scott Litt

I assure you, you won't be walking when this song comes on. The original, and (approaching four decades later) it's sunbeams still haven't dimmed a bit. This is not a single about feeling good—*it's a song that makes YOU feel good*—the on your feet cheering kind of good! The backstory of perhaps the most upbeat and popular of summer-themed pop/rock song of the century (and maybe all time) begins with a band called simply The Waves, formed by Cambridge college student Alex Cooper and "Walking On Sunshine" composer and guitarist Kimberley Rew. The line-up eventually expanded to include Kansas-born vocalist and guitarist Katrina Leskanich, who became its unmistakable voice, and her then-boyfriend, singer and guitarist Vince de la Cruz. After signing with Capitol/EMI in 1985, the band released their newly re-recorded LP *Katrina And The Waves* and the dynamic single "Walking On Sunshine" (this was material the group had originally recorded two years earlier while signed to a Canadian label, now refreshed by engineer Scott Litt). Capitol took out an ad in *Billboard* on March 23, 1985, that proudly stated the band's self-titled debut album, "showcases the bold, original vocal talents of Katrina Leskanich whose powerful presence and blistering guitar savvy have prompted critical acclaim since the group's inception in 1981. If you're already a Waves fan, you'll know what to expect when the LP pops. If you're not, after you hear their first single, 'Walking On Sunshine,' we think you will be." Right on!

Anyone attempting to gather essentials for a summer music playlist will be happily obliged to include this deliriously energetic song, a stunningly catchy, unstoppably danceable piece of hyper-upbeat energy. "Walking On Sunshine" is as much a landmark of irresistible '80s pop culture history as it is a timeless summer anthem. Literally, every note has the lift-off of a champagne cork escaping the bottle, and after the song reached #9 in the US and #8 in the UK, there was plenty of reason to pop the bubbly. The extended 12-inch remix by Scott Litt (who later went on to produce REM and Nirvana) is five and a half minutes of brilliantly edited bliss that doesn't feel the slightest bit overextended.

"Walking On Sunshine" was featured in the hit films "Secret Of My Success" (1987), "Look Who's Talking" (1989), and "American Psycho" (2000), among others, and was covered by Dolly Parton in 1996, the cast of "Glee" in 2010, and numerous other artists over the decades. Katrina And The Waves toured as an opening act for the Kinks, The Beach Boys, Squeeze, and many other top rock acts.

In many ways, the band's predictably upbeat 1986 single "Sun Street," from their second Capitol album, *Waves,* is just as inviting and upbeat as the band's "Walking On Sunshine" smash—perhaps just a bit more sedate in its enthusiasm. It's a bright, fair weather, hand-clapping sing-along, mixed by Bert Bevans, with the emphasis on a happy piano in the extended dance version. Miss Katrina doesn't need to give the track the exuberance that "Sunshine" demanded, but she still infuses it with an engaging sense of optimism in a more localized fashion. *Cash Box* rightly called it "a cute and fizzy feel-good song" on June 7, 1986, and the song was a hit in the UK, but received a luke warm reception elsewhere.

While "Sunshine" was a colossal achievement, "Sun Street" and the band's subsequent releases, by comparison, did not keep the momentum sufficiently going commercially, and Katrina And The Waves eventually disbanded as a recording group, though not until the late '90s. However, Ms. Leskanich has been performing the eternal "Sunshine" song around the world ever since it first heated up the airwaves. In more recent years, she has expanded her creative horizons to include two published books, *Peggy Lee Loves London* and *Metropoodle: My Cornwall Guide* (Metropoodle Press). She's also released a number of solo albums, including *Turn The Tide* in 2004 (and its digital version in 2010) and *Hearts, Loves & Babys* in 2020.

Commentary from Katrina Leskanich:

At this point in your life, Ms. Leskanich, you've had a chance to view "Walking On Sunshine" as a life experience from every possible angle. How do you feel about this enduring song today?

"'Walking On Sunshine' has a life of its own. I am surplus to requirement, and the song survives with little help from me. If it was a child then I could be perceived as the proud parent of an offspring that did very well in life and managed to make a mark simply by being positive and uplifting, effervescent and timeless."

When you originally recorded this song back in 1983 with a bit more of a punky edge, I wonder if you, the band, and songwriter Kimberley Rew sensed there was something special about it, even though its full potential would not be realized for another two years or so.

"It was different from all our other songs because it was out and out optimistic and bouncy. We were uncomfortable with it at first but I felt like it had something unmistakably irresistible, if not slightly annoying about it, but we all liked the energy of the song. When we played it live in sulky early '80s clubs, the punters rejected it as it went against the grain of cold angsty songs of the time in the UK."

Are you able to identify the emotions or energy in this song that, let's say, the mainstream pop-loving public responded to so enthusiastically?

"The song has a quick tempo and a long established Motown chord progression (think 'You Can't Hurry Love'). The message of requited love and the joy it brings resonated with people feeling giddy and euphorically in love. It is unashamedly exuberant, and that's a little infectious."

Do you recall your mindset when you entered the studio to record "Sunshine?"

"When I sang 'Walking On Sunshine' in the studio, as with most of my vocal recordings from The Waves days, I sang the song three times and we kept the second take. Vince de la Cruz (the bass player) was mooning me through the control room picture window, which is why I am smiling through the line about not being able to wait for that knock on my door. There wasn't the feeling, 'oh here goes, I'm about to record the vocal for this song that is going to go down in history....blah, blah, blah.' I just did what I did and gave it the usual. I tried to get kinda soulful through the outro bit but didn't really have a plan for what I was going to improvise."

Would you share some thoughts about Scott Litt, the American engineer and producer who created the masterful extended versions of "Walking" (and "Sun Street")?

"'Walking On Sunshine' was one of Scott Litt's first big hits. We were mixing in The Power Station in NYC. We had the midnight shift so the idea was to sleep all day in the Milford Plaza Hotel, which was rough as hell in 1984, and go into the studio at midnight. It was January and bitterly cold, and I remember entering the studio and Diana Ross was walking out in a beautiful fur coat and gloves and I was in a flimsy jean jacket and covered in snow. Scott kept the studio in arctic temperatures and bit his nails down to the bone. He got Alex Cooper to re-record the drums in the famous Power Station live room, and it was Scott's idea to start the track with drums saying the DJs would love it. The song had always started with my little 'Ow' but now it was magnificent."

Is there one particular performance of "Walking On Sunshine" that stands out for you? One where you really had that "ah-ha" moment and realized the powerful connection this song has to summer?

"When we first got signed by Capitol, they sent out a demo of four tracks of ours to introduce the band to key radio stations and DJs. The demo kicked off with what we thought would be our first single, 'Do You Want Crying,' followed by 'Red Wine and Whiskey,' 'Que Te Quiero' and ending with 'Walking On Sunshine.' Every single DJ came back and said, 'we love the sunshine song,' and then it was determined 'Walking On Sunshine' would be the first single. This was spring of 1985, and I think the DJs saw the potential of kicking off their shows with a high energy feel-good number. They especially loved the drum intro and exuberant 'Ow!' Scott was right."

With "Walking On Sunshine," we have a pop song that is immediately identifiable and hugely popular. That's a great thing as a career accomplishment, but I get the impression it may also have been a stumbling block in terms of the band's evolution.

"Bring on the stumbling blocks. When we started out in the early '80s and were eventually (after being together five years) signed by Capitol Records for a six album deal, we thought we would go on to be a super group playing Madison Square Gardens, jumping up on stage with Tina Turner, massively successful, because 'Walking On Sunshine' did so well straight out of the gate. It was a phenomenon for one song to become so popular and to be used in so many movies and played whenever the sun shone or at countless joyful events. So in that sense it *was* a novelty song. Although we thought we were a cool edgy little pop/rock band, 'Walking On Sunshine' cemented the image of us as lightweight and disposable."

Would share your thoughts on the song "Sun Street," which was the much anticipated first single from the band's second Capitol LP, **Waves?**

"It seemed obvious after the success of 'Walking On Sunshine' that another song about the summer would hit the mark. 'Sun Street' has a dark subtext and was written about an actual pub in Newmarket (UK) where I used to live that was very rough and off the beaten track. It was on a road called Sun Lane, but 'Sun Street' sounded better."

You've recorded some other songs on your own that have a strong connection to that summer feeling. "Sun Coming Upper" from your 2014 solo album **Blisland** *and, most recently, the exciting single "Drive" from your 2020* **Hearts, Loves & Babys** *album, which has a Blondie-vibe swirling in there, come to mind immediately. Is the summer season—that feeling of escape, sun, fun and freedom—often a part of your creative inspiration?*

"My heart is always pining for summer, and I live for the season. I love writing songs that reflect that."

Knowing what you know now and if given the opportunity to visit your younger self, what music industry advice would you share with Katrina from 1985?

"Just remember you are Cornflakes and the label is Kelloggs. If you have the support of a label who gets behind you, and by that I mean plow a lot of resources into distribution and marketing, and you have a decent product and are willing to work hard, especially at promotion, you can go very far. When Capitol dropped us after our second album as they were struggling with their payola scandal claims, we were adrift and started signing with European labels, losing our grip on the all-important and lucrative American market."

In 2020, with the COVID shutdowns, virtually everyone largely missed that year's summer season. Did you happen to come to appreciate summer a bit more as a result of your experience with the pandemic?

"I had been working extremely hard for several years saying yes to every opportunity, and I welcomed a rest. I'm rested, let's get back to work!"

"Walking On Sunshine" is a song so many people identify with summer and would likely pick as a favorite. Are you able to identify your seasonal favorite song?

"Favorite song of all time is 'It's Getting Better' by Mama Cass. This song, more than any other, influenced the sound of my style and the soul of my singing."

(L) Kimberley Rew (Mr. Rew's photo by Alan Gamble) and
(R) Katrina Leskanich today.

In addition to penning Katrina And the Waves' stellar "Walking On Sunshine" hit, Kimberley Rew, born in Bristol, England, also wrote and composed the band's last major hit, "Love Shine A Light," which was the winning entry in the 1997 Eurovision song contest. Today, he continues to write, record and gig locally in the UK. In 2016, Rew received a BMI (American rights agency) award for three million US plays of "Walking On Sunshine."

Commentary from Kimberley Rew:

Mr. Rew, do you recall how the idea for the song "Walking On Sunshine" first took shape in your mind? Would you tell me what your songwriting process was like back then?

"You have to remember that, at least back then, writing songs was my full time job, so it's hard to pick out the day I wrote 'Walking on Sunshine,' which at the time was just another song, from the 14,000 odd days I've lived since. [For] too much of humanity that song, of course, stands out, simply because they know it, whereas they don't know any of my other songs. But how the song got from being just a song in our repertoire to an evergreen hit was mostly decided by the arcane workings of the music world.

"In regards to my songwriting process—I try to get into an open state of mind, into which ideas can jump. Sometimes they don't for months on end, which makes me a terrible co-writer! Then, hopefully, I'll get the punch line and the music to go with it in one package, and can fill in the verses later.

"I like simple ideas where, for example, you can go 'pom pom pom, pom pom de pom' on the guitar, and it'll be obvious to the bass player and drummer where the groove needs to land. I was lucky to belong to a great band—if you listen to the record you can hear Katrina, and Alex [Cooper] on the drums, both giving the performance of a lifetime."

It's interesting that the feelings expressed in the song actually reflect the joy of reunion with a loved one, but I'm guessing because it was so upbeat and had the word "sunshine" in the title, it became a massive summer-themed anthem instead. Was that a lucky accident?

"I think you're right about the effect of the word 'sunshine,' and including it certainly wasn't a strategic decision, but I do try to be generally upbeat with my songs, if only because I'm terrible at writing 'serious' songs!"

Do you recall a performance or incident where you were first able to appreciate that "Walking On Sunshine" had that summer escapism sound?

"The band was together for another 14 years after 1985. Needless to say, we never came up with a more popular song. We would always finish the show with 'Walking On Sunshine'—the audience, however little attention they'd been paying until then, would go nuts, then we'd come back with an encore like 'Mony Mony' or 'Wipe Out.' We were a surprisingly effective live band! Concurrently, the song became a summer radio staple, so people either knew it from 1985, or from it never having subsequently gone away, or both."

When you are the writer of such a significant pop hit, what pressure falls on you specifically to do it again?

"Of course we wanted to repeat and build on the success of 'Walking On Sunshine,' and we were all writers. You've got to remember that whatever you do it's always in the present, so in 1986 it was the present, 1987 the present, and so on, and we were just trying to get on with our career as circumstances would allow. We were conscious of our relative previous success in 1985, but it wasn't like a haunting, overpowering dead weight. To everyone else in the universe, the band had one fact, which was the song, but to us it was one fact among many."

Would you share with me some key ways in which your life changed as a result of the resounding success of "Sunshine?" If you were to able to go back and advise a younger Kimberley Rew how to handle this newfound fame, what would you say to him?

"I've been fortunate to have done what I wanted to do (music) and been paid for it, which not every musician can claim. There's no way the old me could advise the young me—only the young me (as opposed to the old me) could have gone through what we went through (typical of what so many bands went through, if they were lucky enough to get the chance). The old me would never have tolerated it, and I'd have hated it if he advised the young me to abandon the music and get a 'proper' job."

In your view, is there a special connection between the summer and pop music?

"I am a huge admirer of The Beach Boys, and they'd never have got 'off the blocks' without the inspiration of the summer. There's the Summer of Love too, and people still look back to that as a central moment of the golden age—nothing has come along since to knock it off its pedestal."

Why do you believe "Walking On Sunshine" has endured for so long and resonated with so many as a summer rock staple?

"'Walking on Sunshine' is not a typical song of the 1980s—it harkens back more to the optimistic spirit of the 1960s, which I'm lucky enough to be old enough to remember. And as I was saying, I think Katrina and Alex are underrated—they are genuinely exciting rock 'n' roll performers."

You're also the songwriter of "Love Shine A Light" with which Katrina And The Waves won the Eurovision prize in 1997. How do you view that success? It seems like Eurovision, being a competition, might have been a different experience compared to creating a song as part of an album or to give further scope and identity to the band.

"We never did consistently well enough to follow a 'career plan.' 'Love Shine A Light' was a spare song which found its way into the list of hopeful qualifiers for the British entry to the competition. It was just me trying to write the right thing as usual, without thinking in terms of album, single or special occasion. Then, of course, it won, and was a hit in Europe, which makes it our second most famous song (in a list of two). There are things in the creative arts like awards and competitions, where winners and losers are judged, perhaps more now than in the last century, and they get a lot of attention, because people like to see winners and losers, as in a sports match. But I don't think being judged better or worse than someone else's effort is really what creativity is about."

Looking back on your accomplished life as a musician and songwriter, I'd love to know if you are pleased with the journey so far, and where "Sunshine" fits into it. What would you still like to accomplish?

"Without 'Walking On Sunshine' I'd have no idea what the big world of music is about, as opposed to the smaller local world of music where I've spent most of my life before and since, and I'm grateful for that first hand knowledge. Presently, I'm still searching for my place in the world in whatever time I have left. And, of course, with the benefit of the success of 'Walking On Sunshine' I can do that in relative comfort."

I noticed in your background that you completed a project to walk or navigate all of the navigable coasts and waterways of England and Wales, which seems to suggest an appreciation for our environment. I would love to get your take on climate change and the direction in which our planet seems to be moving.

"I'm lucky that if I get spare time I like to explore the world around, particularly my native country, particularly how the man-made can harmonize with the natural. I'm lucky too to be fairly active for my age. We have given our finite natural resources a huge bashing in my lifetime. I hope we can come to our senses in time."

Walkin' On The Sun - Smash Mouth (1997), Interscope (US)
Producer: Eric Valentine

It's like they threw punk and ska into a shaker and poured out this very cool, groovy, kind of retro-rock summer cocktail. Extremely infectious, the track just feels like you're on vacation and wearing an oversized Hawaiian shirt. The terrific video features a goofy '60s-style beach party sequence—they knew exactly what they were doing. *Sic!*

Warm Summer Daze - Vybe (1995), Island (US)
Producers: Angela Slates, Doug Rasheed

"Daze" is a song about layin' low and havin' fun out in the sun, and it puts you in the tropic zone. Slick, steamy, longing lead vocals turn the temperature up in its hard-groovin' En Vogue-like original version that incorporates the Booker T. Jones penned and produced song "Private Number," originally sung by Judy Clay and William Bell. The "Coolio Mix" helmed by Brian G musically offers a lighter pop tempo with the "Gangsta's Paradise" rapper injecting a solid and spicier '90s west coast party vibe into the jam, giving the single some extra bump.

Welcome To The Sunshine - Carrara (1985), Keepon Music (I)
Producer: Roger Penazzo

Alberto Carrara had a great deal of success in the early to mid-'80s with a melodic and likable brand of Italo disco that was able to infiltrate a number of European territories. "Welcome To The Sunshine" mixed distinctive electronic effects with a player-piano and nostalgic string sounds for a kind of funky/clunky synthesizer dance experience, a bit in the same vein as his fellow hitmakers in Italy, Sandy Marton and Silver Pozzoli. With its inviting title and upbeat vibe, it was a natural for the summer of '85. Don't be afraid to check out his other hits, "Shine On Dance," "Disco King," and "S.O.S. Bandido," all cut from the same cloth.

We're Flying To Ibiza - Logo Vs. Rob D (2004), Toka Beatz (G)
Producers: Raig M, Chris B

No relation to "We're Going To Ibiza!," outside of dipping into the same thematic well, this is a cutting EDM/hardcore rave jam designed to get you jumping with your hands in the air. It never takes its foot off the gas, so the less flexible among us should strap themselves in or sit this one out. Oh, to be this young again!

We're Going To Ibiza! - Vengaboys (1999), Breakin' Records/ Violent Music BV (NL)
Producers: DJ Danski (Dennis van den Driesschen) & DJ Delmundo (Wessel van Diepen)

Take me with you! A hot, sunny (but not too sweaty) and inventive remake of Typically Tropical's 1975 smash "Barbados," this track trades the Caribbean for the Mediterranean and spent nearly six months on *Music & Media*'s European Top Singles chart. Early in its days on the European survey during the summer of '99, *Music & Media* called the track "an unusual record for radio" (July 10, 1999). It was indeed unusual. This stout fusion of dance, pop, and tropical vibes broke from the the the trippy, frantic beats-per-minute crowd so popular at the time, taking amore laid back approach. And, of course, a melody foundation that's already a bit familiar never hurts. A solid arrangement faithful to the original song and a reworking of its lyrics (with a trace of Dutch dialect) that cleverly identified the compelling lure of the club and beach party island quickly caught the ears of young people, summer vacationers, DJs and eventually radio stations. The song was a tremendous success, peaking at #5 across Europe on *Music & Media*'s sales chart in late September of 1999, and reaching #1 in the UK and the Netherlands, the home base of the group.

No one-shot wonders, Vengaboys spent the mid-to-late '90s and well into the twenty-first century performing live and delivering multiple summer hits, including the #1 *Billboard* US dance chart hit "Up & Down (1998), plus "We Like To Party! (The Vengabus)" (1999), "Kiss (When The Sun Don't Shine)" (1999), "Paradise (1999), and "Uncle John From Jamaica" (2000), among others. You can count on this crew.

Commentary from Wessel van Diepen:

How did you become a part of the dance music industry? What drew you to the dance genre?

"I have alway been, and still am, into all kinds of music. But as a young kid I was lucky to witness the explosion of disco. That whole feeling of nightlife, dancing, escapism, amazing bass lines—it really got me hooked. I became a DJ and started an illegal pirate radio station playing mostly dance music.

Years later, I co-founded another station that ended up becoming the #1 radio station in the Netherlands, [a country] where dance music has always been an important part of the top 40 mix. During the explosion of house music I started producing as well. Which led to a bunch of underground tracks of which "James Brown is Dead" (by L.A. Style) was my first international hit."

(L) Wessel van Diepen today, photo by William Rutten, and (R) the Vengaboys crew, photo by Ruud van der Peijl.

Tell me about the vision you had for Vengaboys.

"My friend [DJ] Danski and I started Vengaboys back in 1997. Danski is probably the most talented and funniest person I know. He was still living with his parents when I heard one of his demos. I offered him a deal on the spot. 'Quit your job, and let's conquer the world together.' After releasing [Vengaboys'] 'To Brazil!' and 'Parada de Tettas' our manager, J.P., came on board. We formed our own record label, and the international success took off.

"The happiness you hear in our music is very real. The way our music sounds is a reflection of the fun we are having in the studio. Nothing cynical about our happy sounds. First we looked at what was happening and then decided to go for what was *not* happening at the moment. We were out to sabotage seriousness."

Was Vengaboys always intended to be about summer and the holidays?

"Yes,100 percent! We had a mental vision board where summer parties and holidays were an important part. Our inspiration came from a lot of places, especially Italian disco from mainly the mid 80's."

Please tell me how you came to create "We're Going To Ibiza!"

"After 'Up & Down,' 'We Like to Party! (The Vengabus)' and 'Boom, Boom, Boom Boom!!,' we knew it would be a good move to slow down the tempo. [Typically Tropical's] 'Barbados' has always been one of my favorite summertime feel good songs. Danski came up with the brilliant idea to change the location to Ibiza. So in that way we also made it more our own. We also added a few more hooks to this song, which was already a force of nature. It worked out very well.

"When you are planning to release your own version of an existing song, of course you have to get permission from the original writers. They said yes, and I heard they're happy they did because 'We're Going To Ibiza!' became a #1 record in the UK, their home country.

Did the worldwide success of the project come as a surprise? When did you first realize you had something big here?

"This has been my dream since I was a young kid—starting an act and having hit records with super happy dance music. So, in that way, it wasn't a surprise. Everything sort of went according to plan. The moment we realized we had something BIG happening was the way 'Up & Down' took off internationally. It hit #1 on the *Billboard* dance chart, and we still knew we had much stronger tracks (and tricks) up our sleeve."

Why do you think audiences reacted so strongly to the song?

"Music is emotion. It's not so much what you hear, it's the feeling it gives you. And some tracks just have that magic sauce. It's not something you can force. The circumstances have to be right and your aim true. Prince used to call this a 'visual record,' something that transports you to the world the song is about."

In its original form, "Ibiza" was paced a bit more slowly than most eurodance tracks of the time. It reminds me of "Coco Jamboo," the way it pumps along at a mid-tempo pace. Was that a strategic creative decision?

"'Coco Jamboo' was definitely an inspiration, and also the Ace Of Base classic, 'All That She Wants.' It was strategic in a way that we also wanted to broaden our audience, so slowing down the tempo is one way to do that. Style wise, it was kind of a slow evolution from 'Up & Down' to 'We're Going to Ibiza!,' but still you can hear it's the same band playing. I think what connects it all is basically the sound of a bunch of people not taking life or themselves too seriously."

What elements do you feel a summer hit song needs in order to have a shot at success? Or is it all luck?

"Rather than chase a style, where you inevitably end up sounding second best, it's easier to do something new. And way more fun. Although I've learned some things, there is no magic formula I've distilled from it all. Sometimes it goes well, and sometimes it doesn't. It doesn't mean that cause and effect are connected. The most important lesson is probably: Don't think too much ahead. Just take the first step and get working. The famous designer Raymond Loewy, who redesigned the Coca Cola bottle and made the most amazing futuristic looking planes, trains, cars and vacuum cleaners, invented this concept called MAYA, which stands for Most Advanced, Yet Acceptable. I think this is the key to a lot of great music. People like hearing stuff they have already internalized, but you present it to them in a new way."

What songs do you personally enjoy and associate with summer, holidays and travel?

"Okay. Two extremes. One is Otis Redding, 'Sitting On The Dock Of The Bay.' Also a visual record. And the other is an amazing Italian dance gem from the late '80's. You should definitely check the video for this one. Sabrina, 'Boys (Summertime Love).' It's the complete package!"

We're Goin' To Live In Jamaica - Lucas (1987), Jupiter (G)
Producer: Mel Jersey-Team

I can't blame them. An odd little pop/reggae/dance jam that features a young man with an affable Chico DeBarge-like persona and voice who says he's heading to the island to hang with a rasta-man. The track is catchy, with quirky sound effect stabs that sonically resemble scratching.

Wetsuit - The Sunclub (1999), Sony Dance Pool (NL)
Producers: Jaydee, Typar, Atbe

This Dutch act's briskly paced, mostly instrumental trance/dance/pop piece has a brilliant, plucky melody hook that's completely exhilarating. There's a video featuring an off the hinges indoor pool rave that looks just as fun as the track itself sounds. Flaming hot, and yet oh so refreshing!

When The Feeling Comes Around- Jennifer Warnes (1988), Arista (G/US)
Producers: C. Roscoe Beck, Jennifer Warnes, Rob Fraboni

Originally a single off the artist's 1978 *Shot Through The Heart* album, this wine spritzer winner was reimagined and updated by Frank Wolf and Steven Strassman for inclusion on the soundtrack to the German motion picture "Zartliche Chaoten II" (*Tender chaos II*). The results are pleasing—a warm-hearted, rhythmic, lightly danceable confection with evocative storytelling. Ms. Warnes' calming, folk-rock vocal delivery, and an arrangement that effectively conveys a gently rolling sea are hard to resist. The song paints a summertime landscape that elicits a sensation of pure contentment.

Wipeout - Fat Boys And The Beach Boys (1987), Tin Pan Apple/Polydor (US)
Producers: Albert Cabrera, Tony Moran (Latin Rascals)

The hugely popular plus-size rap trio serves up big, bangin' electronic hip-hop beats that collide with the melody of The Safaris' instrumental hit from 1963 and the unmistakable backing harmonies of The Beach Boys. The results are truly off the wall, and it's a loud, wild, incredibly fun ride in the back seat of a convertible. And they never pump the brakes! The song fell just shy of the US top 10, but was a #2 hit in the UK. The track was supported by a terrifically off-the-wall video featuring Times Square mayhem and a beach party blast. As hard to resist as the smell of burgers and fries at the beach pavilion, and just as tasty.

Ye Ke Ye Ke - Mory Kanté (1987), Barclay (F)
Producer: Nick Patrick

It's easy to understand why this world music smash by Guinean Mory Kanté, with its frantic, hi-tech feel, had been such a potent summer song at the time, not just in France, where the song first broke, but across the continent. One need not necessarily appreciate the single's spirited lyrics about loving a pretty girl. The track is sung with such an authentic kind of energy (undeniably Westernized for crossover palatability) that it's easy to appreciate its sunny enthusiasm and the beauty of its inventive mix of African, jazz and funk styles. Included on Kanté's *Akwaba Beach* album, the track reached #1 on the *Music & Media* Top 100 Singles chart early in the summer of '88. In a June 11, 1988, article about the artist, the publication acknowledged Kanté as, "the latest in a series of ethnic artists recording in France and crossing over. The Gipsy Kings' flamenco, Johnny Clegg's Afro-pop and Kassav's tropical disco (zouk) have forced their way into the French music melting pot and turned Paris into the main A&R scene in Europe." Forced? That writer sounds a tiny bit vexed by it all, no? But don't get bent, the record-buying public back then welcomed such an influx of talent and creativity. The singer departed our world in 2020.

Zouk Megamix - Kassav' (1993), Sony (F)
Producers: Jacob F. Desvarieux, Didier Lozahic

The lifeguards are climbing down from their perches and the sun is setting, so that means we've reached our last hot summer jam. We end our journey just where we should—on a tropic high note. This group, who date back to 1979 and first came together in Guadeloupe, takes their influences from the music of the West Indies, adding a bit of salsa, disco, merengue and a little reggae into the pot. Kassav' found popularity across Europe, but most especially in France in the '80s and early '90s. This lively, sun-drenched mix of their singles "Wép Wép," "Mwen Ale," "Sye Bwa," "'Se Dam' Bonjou" (and others on the extended mix) have one thing in common: the deliciously exotic, immensely upbeat sound of tropical joy.

SUMMER POSTCARDS - HAVING A WONDERFUL TIME, WISH YOU WERE HERE

International music artists share their memories of summer-powered experiences.

Terri B! (aka Terri Bjerre)
Vocalist
"Oh La La La" (1997) - 2 Eivissa

"I was performing with [DJ and house music producer] Jerry Ropero (of Avante Garde's 'Get Down,' for which I sang vocals) in about 1998 in Spain with over 300,000 people there. Just the one song, and it was massive—my largest crowd! You couldn't see hands or faces after a certain point—crazy times!"

Bart&Baker (Bart Sampson, Jo Baker)
Producers
"Allez Viens (Via Con Me)" (2012) - Ft. Pierre Santini & Lada Redstar

"We have played many places and festivals over the summer, but one particularly remains vibrant in our memories. It's Calvin On The Rocks – the french Coachella. We performed there in 2007 and 2014. Located in the french citadel of Calvi in the north of Corsica, it blends big stage performances (Andrew Weatherall, Body & Soul, 2 Many DJ's) with impromptu sets on the beach and late night underground parties all around the city."

Claudja Barry
Vocalist
"Down And Counting" (1986)

"I remember performing in front of 100,000 people at Festivalbar in Italy, one of the biggest summer music festivals in the world, in one of the area's oldest arenas. They had these big screens outside the place [so that people near the venue] could see what was going on inside. I opened the show with a song called 'It Takes Two' with Ronnie Jones, and I never experienced anything like that in my life. To have done that kind of performance in a setting that was so historical and that had so much story to go with it, I was overwhelmed. That was something I'll never forget for sure. It was definitely an incredible summer event. So many artists—Adam Ant, Andy Gibb, all kinds of amazing artists were a part of the production. The audience was so loud I could barely hear."

Judy Cheeks
Vocalist
"Reach" (1994)

"A story from the '70s, comes to mind. My friend Tina Turner rang and asked me to join she and Ike on a tour of Europe, just to hang out. It was fortunate for them I accepted the offer, as I ended up standing in for one of the Ikettes, Yolanda (Goodwin), who was rushed to the hospital where she remained for several days, leaving me to do multiple dates of the tour. The Turners were contractually required to have three Ikettes, so to avoid the tour being halted or further complicated, I stood in—without rehearsing or any formal prepping. Tina said, 'Judy, put on Yolanda's wig, shoes and costume and get out there!' And I did.

"Unfortunately, while performing in Paris, my top came down! Lejeune (Richardson), another Ikette, pointed at my boobs, and I nearly fainted on stage with embarrassment! But I pulled my top up and kept on performing. After the show, they all teased me a bit knowing how modest I was—I didn't even like dressing in front of the girls in the dressing rooms. They assured me it was fine because it was quite normal in Paris. Well, since all this led to me living in Germany and recording my first hit 'Mellow Lovin', I think it was worth it!"

Inaya Day
Vocalist
"Horny '98" (1998) - Mousse T vs Hot' N' Juicy

"One particular memory of a summer performance that stands out for me where I really felt and enjoyed that positive summer energy and vibe was the Full Moon event in Cairns, Australia. People from all walks of life attend and it's massive. I sang 'I Am Tha 1' [mrTimothy Ft. Inaya Day], which hit the top of the ARIA chart over there, and the *Billboard* chart in America. The entire crowd heaved with excitement as they sang that song and 'Horny '98' [Mousse T vs Hot'N'Juicy] with me. When the show was over and they had their fill of singing, everyone ran through the sand and jumped right into the ocean; clothes and all! What an amazing event! What an incredible night! I'll never forget it!"

D.O.N.S. (aka Karl "Ollie" Goedicke)
DJ, producer
Warp Brothers - "Phatt Bass" (2000)

"Perhaps the most unforgettable performance was New Year's Eve 2005/2006 at the Harbour Bridge in Sydney. It was the European winter but high summer there. We had the gig time shortly after midnight at a NYE festival and played our legal Warp Brothers version of 'Smells Like Teen Spirit' as the first song. What happened next remains unrivaled to this day, and I have never seen or experienced anything like it again. At the moment when the legendary guitar riff by Nirvana kicked in, the crowd of probably 10,000 party maniacs screamed so much during the entire guitar break that the music could no longer be heard. We were completely overwhelmed. T-shirts, bras and more were thrown onto the stage, and I was so touched that I was close to tears."

Joy Dorris representing Lime
Vocalist
"Babe We're Gonna Love Tonite" (1982)

"Lime songs are all summer fun time songs. Over the past few decades, we have performed indoors and outdoors from Japan to Chile. If I had to choose an outdoor summer performance that was the highlight of them all for me,

I would say Riptide. That was a two-day music festival right on the beach in Ft. Lauderdale, Florida. Ocean spray in our faces, beach balls bouncing overhead! The best part for me was that also performing that evening was Earth, Wind & Fire, and I got to sing along with 'September' at the top of my lungs, dancing barefoot in the sand, with sun-kissed cheeks. Best day ever!"

Nicki French
Vocalist
"Total Eclipse Of The Heart" (1993)

"My first promotional tour of the USA in 1995 during the summer stands out for me, simply because I had not done anything so huge, so full-on and tiring—and yet so enjoyable—before. We arrived in Boston just as the summer months were beginning, and the tour was for six weeks. The shows were always big summer events, laid on by the big radio stations in each state or town, with loads of other artists on the bill as well (who were also gracing the charts at the time), many of whom I traveled with from one show to another. Even they were getting excited about my song still moving upwards, and they were so supportive! I would turn up at baseball stadiums and huge park venues, and although everyone knew my song from the radio, nobody really knew who Nicki French was. So I would arrive backstage totally anonymous. Yet after each performance, there would be loads of people wanting autographs and photos! I will remember it forever!"

Lane McCray of La Bouche
Vocalist, rapper
"Be My Lover" (1995)

"There are so many memories that stand over the 25 years I have been touring. I would have to say Festivalbar in Marostica, Italy. The festival itself was a celebration of the top 20 radio hits for the year and included Bon Jovi, Joe Cocker and Eros Ramazzotti to name a few. It was the first open air concert for us, and we were virtually unknown, save for 'Sweet Dreams.' Melanie [Thornton] and I, both from the southeast part of the country (USA)—and I do mean *country*—[*Lane laughs*] were exposed to 60,000 screaming Italian fans. What was remarkable was that the entire place knew every single word. When it came time for me to drop the rhyme the crowd went ballistic. Young girls were crying and falling out, and for a moment I felt like the biggest rockstar on the planet! I will always cherish and never forget that event."

Wardell Piper

Vocalist

"Super Sweet" (1979)

"My favorite summer music memory was when I performed in July or August of 1979 for the opening celebration of Six Flags Great Adventure theme park on "Soap Factory," the disco dance television show, for the 50th Anniversary of Palisades Park in New Jersey. Sarah Dash, Deniece Williams, Ronnie Dyson, and I did our thing for that celebration. What was most memorable to me about it was my performance of my hits 'Captain Boogie' and 'Super Sweet' in front of the audience and a cage full of tigers [nearby]. I had on my cowboy hat, tight straight jeans, blouse, my high heels, and I went for it! My performance was well received, and there even was a newspaper clipping of it in a local paper."

Rozalla
Vocalist
"Everybody's Free (To Feel Good)" (1991)

"When I first went to Ibiza, the land of clubs, to perform—the first time ever—it was in the early '90s with a massive DJ at the time from MTV. It was my first time ever being invited by MTV to perform at a club there. The DJ's name was Alex P, and it was his party. The show was out in the open on a dance floor with some roofing to keep people cool. They put this podium in the center of the stage, just enough room for me to stand on and sing. The people went berserk! Alex was so happy, and I sang 'Everybody's Free'—that's the experience that comes to my mind first when it comes to the summer. I did the gig, and they were to fly me out the next day, in the evening. So that gave me the whole next day to check Ibiza out.

"I saw the beaches and was amazed—it blew my mind! I was born in Zambia and raised in Zimbabwe; these countries are landlocked. All we had were lakes. So when I tell you about Ibiza, that was also my first time ever seeing a beach! That's why I will never forget, for the life of me, walking on the beach there—the water and sand, it was surreal. To this day, when I go to the beach, it's just a wonderful experience!"

Amii Stewart
Vocalist
"Knock On Wood" (1978)

"Earth, Wind & Fire in an open air concert in D.C. with my brothers and sisters! We sang and danced for two straight hours. We should have bought 'standing only' tickets because we never sat down! I have never felt such joy. Another wonderful summer memory—[artist, songwriter and producer] Van McCoy was a D.C. native like me and one summer's day he threw a huge barbecue at his 16th Street mansion to celebrate 'The Hustle' becoming a massive hit. Baby, we danced up a storm! Everybody who was anybody was there, and it was glorious!"

Harriette Weels of MaiTai
Vocalist
"History" (1985)

"I had a wonderful personal experience with my group MaiTai when we went to Surinam in the summer of 1985. This experience had nothing to do directly with pop music, but it had a lot to do with the music of Surinam called kawina/kaseko/bigi poku. It's a genre that is punctuated by big African drums (the skratji drum), mixed with African/Latin sounds, and it's a very happy kind of music, very exciting. All three of us from MaiTai, myself, Mildred Douglas and Caroline de Windt, grew up in Europe and had spent most of our time there, but Mildred and I were originally from Surinam. It's a very beautiful country, destroyed in course by bad leadership and such, but still a very beautiful place. We did a tour there, and this was the first time I had been back to the country in many, many years. We were really breaking through [in pop music] at that time with the song 'History.'

"When we stepped out of the plane, there was this kaseko (stylistically, like zouk and soca) band and some children standing there, singing to greet us. This was one of the—well, I still have goosebumps when I talk about it. All three of us felt the same about it. It wasn't even so much that the welcome was so big and so nice, it was that we had come home to the place where Mildred and I, where our mothers had given birth to us. The children and the band were in traditional Surinam dress and playing this music—*bubba-deebuh-buh-bam*—and we were coming down the plane steps, dancing and just enjoying every moment. It was one of the most beautiful experiences we ever had. What impressed us the most that day was the music. We had missed hearing it—it certainly wasn't on the radio all the time back in Europe. This experience stayed with us, this feeling we had. We still talk about it now and then, when we are reminiscing about the '80s and all that we've done."

HIGH TIDE

Before we check out and catch an Uber to the airport, I'd like to offer just one more thought to close this sun soaked musical adventure. Unfortunately, it's a bit like the "in the event of an emergency" notice we tend to zone out through at the beginning of airline flights, but perhaps you'll indulge me.

Most of the pop songs discussed in these pages took a carefree approach to summer and holiday getaways, as they should. That was the past. We now must look to the future. At the start of this book I suggested that even a global pandemic appeared to be effective at only temporarily sidelining our quest to find coveted holiday escape destinations. I fear there is something that has the power to actually put an end to it.

Oh, hell yeah, I admit I like the weather hot, but I don't much care for the idea of our planet heating up so much that poles melt, oceans start rising, millions of acres of forests and homes start burning, fresh water becomes scarce, food insecurity rises, and air becomes unbreathable. Our present-day planet is undergoing some sobering changes, even if we don't fully understand all the causes that are bringing them about. We certainly know the big man-made ones. What does this portend for the future? As climate change, global heating and extreme weather go, so goes our favorite time of year. And the environments we love to visit (especially lowland, coastal and island regions)—the homelands and habitats of the people who are kind enough to host us. I'd love to delude myself into thinking it's a distant crisis. The climate emergency feels quite present and real to me—and there's enough scientists around the world with degrees and such who have universally confirmed this observation. I believe in science, and I believe what I see happening with my own eyes. And it's not like we weren't warned about this decades ago.

I hope you'll support the professionals, organizations, companies, legislators, and innovators who work hard to protect our planet's health and natural environments. I'm complicit in our planet's predicament, and I am certain my own carbon footprint is the size of the Chicxulub crater. I need to do *a lot* better. Though I realize the personal efforts we can make (all easily researchable online) aren't going to make much of a dent in emissions or improve the health of the planet, if we collectively take them in big enough numbers and make our shared will known, we may actually do some good. I hope that's not a fantasy. It won't be a terrible inconvenience for me to be more conscious of my actions, and maybe you will feel inspired to make some lifestyle changes too. We *can* take steps in the right direction—only maybe we need to be running, *really* fast, not stepping.

There's no other celestial body in our little solar system to head to if we continue to wage war on this island Earth. Have you seen the tragic surface shots of Mars and Venus lately?

We celebrated lots of fun music in this book. Wouldn't a healthier, cleaner globe *really* be something to sing about?

THE HEAT INDEX - WHERE TO FIND EVERYTHING ON HOLIDAY

THE SONGS:

THE ARTISTS AND PROFESSIONALS:

NOW TELL ME...
WHAT'S IN YOUR BEACH BAG?